Politics Past

Dwight Macdonald

Politics Past

ESSAYS IN POLITICAL CRITICISM

Formerly published as
Memoirs of a Revolutionist

NEW YORK THE VIKING PRESS

The article on Dorothy Day, in the section entitled "Saints," originally appeared in *The New Yorker* in more extensive form.

Reissued in 1970 by The Viking Press, Inc.
625 Madison Avenue, New York, N.Y. 10022

Published simultaneously in Canada by
The Macmillan Company of Canada Limited

SBN 670-00306-9

Library of Congress catalog card number: 72-104161

Printed in U.S.A.

The third section of the article "The Neo-Non-Conservatism" first appeared in *Commentary*. "Politics Past" and "The Great Thaw" first appeared in *Encounter*. "The Unconscious War," "Kulturbolshewismus & Mr. Van Wyck Brooks," "The Eisenstein Tragedy," "The Question of God," "Liberal Soap Opera," and the second section of "The Neo-Non-Conservatism" first appeared in *Partisan Review*. The first section of "The Neo-Non-Conservatism" first appeared in the *Reporter*. Date of publication is given at the end of each article.

CONTENTS

Articles whose source is not identified at the end of the piece appeared first in the magazine *Politics.*

Politics Past

Introduction

LONDON, 1957

Over here, wrote Emerson to Carlyle apropos the America of the 1830's, everyone you meet has a project for universal reform in his pocket. So did everyone that someone like Emerson might have met in the America of a century later (but our scripts were all Marxian). An interest in *avant-garde* politics was expected of every proper intellectual. Those few who were "unpolitical" were *déclassé,* accused of Escapism, Living in an Ivory Tower, etc. Even so unpolitical a type as Edmund Wilson signed *Culture and the Crisis,* a celebrated pamphlet-manifesto, in support of the Communist candidates in the 1932 presidential election. (Other signers included Sherwood Anderson, Newton Arvin, Erskine Caldwell, Malcolm Cowley, John Dos Passos, Theodore Dreiser, Sidney Hook, Sidney Howard, and Lincoln Steffens.) Later he wrote reportage for *The New Republic* on unemployed riots in Detroit, a trip to the Soviet Union, etc., joined the "Trotsky Committee," and spent several years learning Russian and German in order to read Marx and Lenin in preparation for *To the Finland Station.* Of later years he has gone back—in the thirties I would have written "retreated"—to the literary interests he pursued in the unpolitical twenties. This parabola seems to me now quite natural, if only because I have described a similar arc myself, and I now think no one has a duty to interest himself in politics except a politician. Even in the thirties, we on *Partisan Review* defended the autonomy of art and opposed the Stalinist efforts to politicalize literature (also the Trotskyist efforts to integrate *P.R.* into their movement—we had a long, solemn, and, as of 1957, slightly comic debate by mail with Trotsky in Mexico on the subject). But this came from our head, and perhaps also from an instinct of self-preservation; in our hearts we felt, as did the Auden-Spender-Strachey-Orwell London of the thirties, that political interest, nay commitment, was an essential part of the equipment of The Compleat Thinker.

Things have changed. We are less interested today in radical politics—that is, parties, programs, ideologies that assume a radical (in the sense of going to the roots) reconstruction of the old order. Indeed, one might almost say we aren't interested at all, and that this kind of politics no longer attracts intellectuals (who, since the time of Babeuf and Saint-Just, have normally been the most energetic propounders of radical ideas as well as the most faithful audience for them). The apathy and, not to put too fine a point on it, ignorance of the present younger generation about these matters is striking, and a little depressing, to one who like myself was young in the thirties.

1.

The difference then and now in the New York intellectual atmosphere—in this context, New York is America, as Paris is France—is that then we believed in revolution and now we don't.* 1930–45 was filled with dramatic and terrible

---

* Though I remember once walking in the street and suddenly really *seeing* the big heavy buildings in their obstinate actuality and realizing I simply couldn't imagine all this recalcitrant matter transformed by socialism. How would the street *look* when the workers took it over, how would, how could revolution transfigure the miles

events: the depression, the rise of Nazism, the Spanish Civil War, the Moscow Trials, the Nazi-Soviet Pact, the war itself, Hitler's extermination of six million Jews, Stalin's murderous forced-labor camps, Truman's atomic bombings. These events aroused our sympathy and indignation, and we felt we ought to respond politically. And they were of such a drastic, unheard-of nature that we thought only an equally drastic solution would do.

In America, where even the most optimistic of us couldn't see revolution around the corner, or around several corners, the coming war was our trump card. We expected, or at least hoped, it would create "revolutionary situations" abroad as the First World War had, and that from these socialist influences might cross the Atlantic. ("Socialism in one country" was as historically inconceivable in advanced America as in backward Russia.) The situations did occur, but they never got beyond the embryonic stage; there was nothing like the 1917 Russian revolution, nothing like even the timid 1918 German revolution. Moscow was, of course, as frightened of revolutions as the West, and between them the two great imperial powers, USA and USSR, were able to control the postwar world. The "Third Camp" of the oppressed masses never got beyond the stage of a slogan and today is not even that. Therefore, most of us have made a "lesser evil" choice—the pages and pages of argumentation I have written exposing the illogic and immorality of this position! And since the imperfect democracy of the West is clearly a lesser evil than the perfected tyranny of the Communists, we have chosen the West.

While necessary, this choice is not very stimulating. (The

---

and miles of stubborn stone? I couldn't conceive of a flame hot enough to melt into new forms this vast solid Is.

A few years later, the bombing fleets did melt great sections of the world's cities and the political structure of many nations was also pulverized. But there was no energy to build Utopia on the ruins. Either the rickety old building was patched up, with a tarpaulin slung overhead to keep out the rain, as in France, or else the Communists imposed a new order much worse than the old. Such a mountain of destruction, such a political mouse!

prodigal son must have found home life, once the fatted calf was eaten, as boring as ever.) So intellectuals are less interested in politics than they were, feeling that their special qualities of idealism and rationality, useful in times of radical change, are not much needed merely to keep things going. We have also become leery of revolution even if it were possible. If tradition, privilege, custom, and legality restrict, they also preserve, and after the Russian experience, it is hard to respond with the old enthusiasm to Bakunin's "Creative Destruction" or Marx's "Change the World!" One inclines to endure familiar evils rather than risk unknown and possibly greater ones. Even private property, detested by every right-thinking, that is left-thinking, intellectual in the thirties—the ordinary people had a more sensible view on this as on other matters—even this *bête-noire* of Marxism now presents a democratic aspect. A citizen with property has that much firmer a base of resistance to the encroachments of the State, as Jefferson and Madison knew, or Stalin when he forced the peasants into collective farms. Of course, Burke, Tocqueville, and other conservative thinkers have been telling us this for two hundred years, but nobody listened. The revival of a true, principled conservatism—not the bully-boy adventurism of McCarthy or the Suez Group—would be of the greatest value today. It is a task that would employ the special talents of intellectuals, and if it wouldn't give them the kick that revolutionism did, the hangover wouldn't be as bad either.

2.

I came late to the revolutionary movement (or what we then took to be such) partly because I went to Yale instead of, for example, "City College" (the College of the City of New York). Many of my Trotskyist comrades had begun handing out antiwar leaflets and marching in May Day parades while they were in short pants, and by the time they had started to shave were able to distinguish between social-revolution, social-democracy and social-fascism. At thirty, when I first read Marx, they were scarred veterans of several left-wing parties and numberless "faction fights." If they were the Chattertons of revolution, I was its William De Morgan.

It wasn't that I wasn't by temperament as logical and combative as they were; just that for a long time my dissidence took nonpolitical forms. Thus at Phillips Exeter Academy (1920-24) I was a founder of an exclusive club—there were only two other members—called The Hedonists. Our writing paper bore the motto, *"Pour Épater les Bourgeois,"* and, boldly marching down the margin: "CYNICISM, ESTHETICISM, CRITICISM, PESSIMISM"; our culture-heroes were Oscar Wilde and H. L. Mencken; we wore monocles and purple batik club-ties at meetings, carried canes as much as we dared, and mimeographed two numbers of *Masquerade,* a magazine of extreme preciosity. At Yale I looked with bored amusement on the earnest handful who struggled to keep alive the Liberal Club—there were no campus Marxists in those pre-depression days, at least I never heard of any—but managed to get into trouble with the dean by writing an editorial asking the venerable Professor William Lyon Phelps, who had undertaken a new course in Shakespeare, if he honestly thought he was competent to give it; with the president by writing him a man-to-man letter about the unreasonableness of compulsory chapel (he felt, among other things, that it was disrespectful to have used both sides of the paper); and with my fellow students by trying to organize a "Hats Off!" campaign, a revolt of the lower classes—freshmen, sophomores and juniors—against the exclusive privilege of the seniors not to wear a hat on the campus. When I graduated in 1928, I became a member, at $30 a week, of the Executive Training Squad at Macy's department store. My plan was to make a lot of money rapidly and retire to write literary criticism. But I was appalled by the ferocity of interexecutive competition, I disliked the few big-shots I met (and doubtless *vice versa*) and I soon realized not only that I was without business talent but also that even a modest degree of success was possible only if one took merchandising far more seriously than I was able to.* After six months I was graduated from the Training Squad and offered a job at the necktie counter, salary $30 a week. I resigned and after a depressing hiatus of a month or two, for I had no income, I got a writing job, through a Yale classmate, on Henry Luce's embryonic *Fortune*.

The first issue of *Fortune*, a lushly illustrated dollar-a-copy monthly dreamed up by Luce to celebrate the "saga" of American business, appeared shortly after the stock-market collapse in the fall of 1929 that inaugurated the Great Depression. Many entrepreneurs would have given up, but Luce had the Stalingrad spirit and persisted—the magazine still appears, in a more sober and sophisticated mode—and I with him. There was a difference, however, in our evolution. I became increasingly skeptical about American capitalism, which I saw at close quarters. My undergraduate suspicions were confirmed—the men running our capitalist system were narrow, uncultivated and commonplace; they had a knack for business as unrelated to other qualities as a talent for chess, and they could have been replaced as our ruling class without any damage to our culture by an equal number of citizens picked at random from the phone book; their social and economic theories, or rather prejudices, were childish; their Republican Party was as unable to cope with the depression as they were. The New Deal was inspiriting to me, as to my fellow writers on *Fortune*. To Luce's dismay, we became increasingly liberal; we wanted to write about Roosevelt's farm program, about the NRA (National Recovery Administration), the CIO, the Wagner Act, unemployment, social security, anything but business. Luce was divided between his pro-business convictions and his journalistic instinct, which told him the CIO was news and that the wonders of American Cyanamid Co. weren't; his typically American pragmatic fascination with Power and Success told him the same

* Cf. the dream every American little-magazine writer has had, at some time, of financing his serious work by writing pot-boilers. I have never heard of this working out. It seems one must be whole-hearted even to be a successful hack.

thing. He compromised (as did we) and for a few years *Fortune* was a pastiche of mildly liberal articles on "social" themes and reluctantly written "corporation pieces" dealing with enterprises that had somehow managed to make a profit. The conflict was resolved, in my case, by a series of articles on the U.S. Steel Corporation which I wrote in the winter and spring of 1936. The more research I gathered, the more it became evident that the biggest steel company in the world benefited neither its workers (wages were low and trade unionism forcibly discouraged), its customers (prices were kept high by monopolistic practices) nor its "owners," the stockholders, who got slim dividends because the Steel Corporation was antiquated and inefficient. The series became more and more critical, and the fourth and final instalment, which I headed with a cheerful quotation from Lenin's *Imperialism* to the effect that monopoly was the last stage of capitalism and led "inevitably" to socialism, was so bowdlerized by Luce's editors * that I resigned in protest. The protest was the easier to make in that (a) I had grown tired of writing for *Fortune*, which was stimulating when I was learning the craft of journalism but whose mental horizon now seemed restrictive, and (b) I had accumulated some savings and my wife had an income from a trust fund.

3.

For much of the year after I left *Fortune* I gathered material for a history of the American steel industry which never got written, partly because I seem unable to sit down and write a book in cold blood, so to speak—the three I have published, *Henry Wallace, the Man and the Myth* (1948), *The Root Is Man* (1953), and *The Ford Foundation* (1956), were written as serial magazine articles—and partly because

* Notably by Ralph McAllister Ingersoll, then managing editor, who two or three years later founded the left-liberal daily, *P.M.*, with capital supplied by Marshall Field III and a staff supplied largely from the Stalinist ambience. Such whirligig changes, such conjunctions, were typical of the period.

my belated interest in politics now grew so rapidly as to make economic history seem academic. Toward the end of my time on *Fortune,* I had begun to read Marx, Lenin and Trotsky (at last!). As much of a pragmatist as the next American—fellow by the name of Luce—I leaned toward the Communists because they alone on the American Left seemed to be "doing something." I became a mild fellow traveler, giving pay-parties for Class-War Martyrs like Angelo Herndon, attending Stalinist-sponsored meetings to help Southern sharecroppers, support the Theatre Union, free Tom Mooney, etc., and accepting as a matter of course their guidance in founding the *Time-Fortune* unit of the Newspaper Guild. Then, in the late winter of 1937, I read *The Case of the Anti-Soviet Center,* a thick volume printed in Moscow and sold for a pittance in the Party's bookstores, which gave the verbatim transcript of the second Moscow Trial. It was fascinating reading, and, I must admit, persuaded me, for a time, that *some* kind of conspiracy was going on; later I began to notice contradictions, lack of motivation, and absence of supporting evidence. But even a first reading, with a pro-Soviet bias, convinced me of the absurdity of the trial's main political thesis: that Trotsky had conspired with representatives of Hitler, Mussolini, the Mikado and most of the surviving Bolshevik leaders to kill Stalin and restore capitalism in Russia.* A lead review of the book by Malcolm Cowley in *The New Republic* took the hypocritical line both American liberal weeklies (*The Nation* was the other) followed on the Trials—"suspending judgment until more conclusive evidence is produced" while actually endorsing the essentials of the prosecution's case and smearing Trotsky and the de-

* "For nothing at all, just for the sake of Trotsky's beautiful eyes," testifies Radek (p. 543) apropos an alleged letter from Trotsky "which, unfortunately, I burned" as he, unfortunately, burned all the others, "the country was to return to capitalism. When I read this, I felt as if I were in a madhouse." I agreed, but wondered if the head keeper's name was Trotsky or Stalin. It shows, by the way, how far the Stalinists had already lost contact with reality that they took such pains to circulate a document that could only arouse grave doubts in most non-Party readers.

fendants. This stimulated me to write a five-page letter-to-the-editor, of which, after considerable haggling, they printed a third. Instantly I received an invitation, and accepted it, to join the Committee for the Defense of Leon Trotsky, headed by John Dewey, which had been formed to find a refuge for Trotsky, to look into the charges against him, and to give him a hearing. The "Trotsky Committee" attracted an extraordinary roster of intellectuals—the Stalinist cultural front was never the same again—and achieved its aims; Trotsky was admitted to Mexico, the Trials were thoroughly investigated and he testified at length before a commission headed by Dr. Dewey.

That spring (1937) I made my début as a liberal journalist with a three-part, now-it-can-be-told serial on the Luce magazines in *The Nation.* Extrapolating the rightward trend of *Time* (it admired Franco and Mussolini and contemned Blum, the CIO and the New Deal) and of Luce himself, I talked about "protofascism" and predicted that, as the class war hotted up, the Luce papers would drop the "proto." I was wrong—extrapolation is a dangerous toy for a Marxist, like giving a Sten gun to a baby. The class war cooled down as the CIO solidified itself in the mass industries and Roosevelt, with his 1938 "Quarantine the Aggressor" speech in Chicago, began to develop an interventionist foreign policy that at last brought back prosperity and also pleased a large section of the Right. Henry Luce soon kicked upstairs the pro-Franco foreign news editor and reoriented his magazines in a more liberal direction. Similarly, U.S. Steel, within a year after my articles appeared, had peacefully signed a contract with the CIO, and was gently modernizing itself. The credit for these improvements should probably go to the *zeitgeist,* and the coming war, rather than to the power of my pen.

My début on *The Nation* was also a farewell tour, for I soon became politically *non grata* with the liberal weeklies. The speed with which I evolved from a liberal into a radical and from a tepid Communist sympathizer into an ardent anti-Stalinist still amazes me. It was much the quickest of my political transformations—which some have seen as indicating an open mind, others as evidence of levity—probably because the Soviet myth is least able to bear close inspection. Presently, along with two Yale friends, F. W. Dupee and George L. K. Morris, I was treating with Philip Rahv and William Phillips, the disaffected editors of the leading Communist literary magazine, *Partisan Review.* Rahv and Phillips had founded *P.R.* in 1934—twenty-three years later, they still edit it, an unprecedented run in the little-magazine world—as the "organ" of the John Reed Clubs, then the Party's literary front. They had suspended *P.R.* in 1936 for several good reasons: the Party's heavy-handed "proletarian-literature" line; the Moscow Trials and other Soviet scandals, which had shaken their political faith; and the new turn away from ultra-revolution to a "popular front" with the New Deal, which had caused the Party to lose interest in *avant-garde* efforts like *P.R.* By the end of 1937 the five of us had revived *P.R.* on a new basis. We announced our political independence, though confessing a bias for revolutionary socialism and against Stalinism; we also defended the Autonomy of Culture, which meant we selected our poems, stories and articles according to intrinsic merit rather than ideology. The Communist press accused us of social-fascism, Trotskyism, infantile ultra-leftism, White Guardism, dilettantism, hypocrisy, venality and grand larceny (this last in reference to the rape of *P.R.*). In the *Daily Worker,* V. J. Jerome, the Party's Matthew Arnold, drew a lurid and, alas, false picture of us being incessantly "wined and dined by the *haute bourgeoisie.*" (It was an interesting case of Freudian projection—he had himself just returned from a missionary tour in Hollywood, where they really know how to wine and dine a comrade.) The usual efforts were made to get writers to boycott us, but the Moscow Trials had done their work and, if Howard Fast and Albert Maltz were adamant in refusing to write for us, we were able to rub along with Dos Passos, Farrell, Gide, Silone, Orwell, Mary McCarthy, Delmore Schwartz, Meyer Schapiro, Edmund Wilson, and T. S. Eliot.

A good part of the next five years I spent helping edit *P.R.*

and writing for it. Other activities, typical of the period, were:

—organizing committees. Ex.: The League for Cultural Freedom and Socialism, whose initial Statement (1938) was addressed to "all artists and writers who are concerned about the present drift of the United States to reaction and war."

—writing protests and getting Names to sign them. Ex.: a cable in the fall of 1939 to President Daladier denouncing the imprisonment of thirty French intellectuals because they signed an antiwar pamphlet. Ex.: a press release, signed by some Names, pointing out the falsifications in the film Warner Brothers had made, *circa* 1943, as their private lend-lease offering, out of ex-Ambassador Davies' *Mission to Moscow.*

—writing letters-to-the-editor. Ex.: one to *The Nation* pointing out its correspondent's failure to report the Communists' control of the 1937 American Writers Congress, whose sessions I had attended as a delegate. (I remember praising Trotsky's prose style amid a murmurous hush.)

—writing letters to editors. Ex.: a tense correspondence at the end of 1937 with Freda Kirchwey, editor of *The Nation,* an ironical antistrophe to the memorandum I had written my employer, Henry Luce, the year before, demonstrating with examples *Time*'s right-wing bias ("In times like these, a truly objective and impartial magazine wd. perform a unique and extremely valuable service."). "I've long had the idea that *The Nation* exists to tell the truth about social issues," I wrote Miss Kirchwey. "But it now appears that *The Nation,* like *Fortune,* has its commitments. A journalistic investment in Soviet Russia seems to me no more admirable than one in Big Business. . . . I'm genuinely disturbed. . . ." (I wasn't at all disturbed—just angry.)

—reading and answering letters from Marxist thinkers, both ends of the correspondence tending to length. Ex.: a communication from a German refugee in Havana in 1942 (". . . If you want, I would send you a copy of my manuscript. . . . To give you an idea about the whole: First Part: historical—the antecedents of fascism in Germany; general backwardness plus absolutism plus protestantism.

Liberty, egality as sloogans of the national foe. . . . A small general chapter about imperialism. . . . Part II: The fascist revolution as social revolution. . . . E. Conclusion about: what is totalitarism? with quotations of most important definitions of Marx. . . . Bukharin's conceptions; contradictions inside the system. . . . Now you see. Unhappily I hadn't at my disposition the major part of material and books—there isn't not even The Statistical Abstract of the U.S. in Havana (!). . . . Perhaps you could find out if an american editor would take it, eventually. People here are criminally unreliable, criminally unserius.")

—reading the N.Y. *Times* closely every day (one hour), looking for signs and portents of social change; also clipping it lavishly; between 1937 and 1947 I accumulated bales of carefully filed clippings, almost all of which had finally to be thrown away, unused, in self-defense. (The N.Y. *Times* was to us what Aristotle was to the medieval scholastics—a revered authority, even though Pagan, and a mine of useful information about the actual world.)

—reading (and underlining) long, heavy works in economics, politics and sociology: Marx, Engels, Trotsky, Lenin and Luxemburg; Mosca, Michels and Pareto; Hobson, Hilferding and Sombart; even a little Kautsky and Plekhanov; contemporary works like John Strachey's *The Coming Struggle for Power* and R. Palme Dutt's *Fascism* (these two were the bibles of my pre-Trotskyist days), Berle & Means's *The Modern Corporation and Private Property,* Ferdinand Lundberg's *America's Sixty Families,* the Lynds' *Middletown,* and James Burnham's *The Managerial Revolution* (which I reviewed unfavorably at length in *P.R.*—the others I admired, then); also an incredible quantity of "data" books on Nazism and on Soviet Communism plus the multivolumed reports of the period's Congressional investigations. For some reason, I don't seem to get around to reading this sort of thing any more.

4.

In the summer of 1938 I began to contribute to *The New International,* the Trotskyists' theoretical monthly. This was partly due to the urging of James Burnham, then one of the

Trotskyist leaders, whom I had known since I had written for *The Symposium*, an ultra-highbrow quarterly he and Philip Wheelwright had put out for a time around 1932. (About then, I had also been an editor—with Dupee and Morris—of a similar, though less elegant, venture, *The Miscellany*; it was an era of "little" magazines; typically, neither *Symposium* nor *Miscellany* showed much interest in politics.) Not that I needed urging. The Trotskyist movement was at that period attractive to people like me because it was the most revolutionary of the sizable left-wing groups (by "sizable" I mean over 200), because of the moral shock of the Moscow Trials, because of its high level and above all because it was led by Trotsky, whose career showed that intellectuals, too, could make history.

In the late thirties the *avant-garde* political spectrum looked like this, reading from right to left: *Communists* (who had moved overnight, on orders from Moscow, from the far left to the extreme right, becoming "critical supporters" of the New Deal and later not-at-all-critical supporters of the war), *Social Democrats* (a small but well-heeled group of aging right-wing Socialists centering around the Rand School and the weekly *New Leader*), *Socialists* (led by Eugene Debs in World War One and now by Norman Thomas), "*Lovestoneites*" (called after their leader, Jay Lovestone, whom Stalin had deposed from the leadership of the American Communist Party in 1929 because Lovestone was an adherent of Bukharin; all groups to the left of the Lovestoneites sneered at them as "centrists," a fighting word, because they tried to steer a middle course between reform and revolution), *Socialist Workers Party* (Trotskyites, led by James P. Cannon and Max Shachtman, former Communists who had founded the party when Trotsky was exiled by Stalin in 1929 and who still lead it—or rather each leads one of the halves into which it split in 1940), *Socialist Labor Party* (followers—or, as we called them, "epigones," another fighting word—of Daniel De Leon, a turn-of-the-century theoretician whom Lenin had called the only American to have made a contribution to Marxian theory, an accolade about equal to a K.C.B.; the De Leonites were so pure they opposed trade unions as "reformist sops to the toiling masses"; one never ran into them or read their press; they were not intellectuals but real lower-middle-class workers, like the Jehovah's Witnesses, and like the Witnesses they continue stubbornly to exist, putting out primitive-Marxist tracts whose typography and diction are so antiquated as to raise a suspicion they have been using up an overstock from De Leon's time; they run a presidential candidate every four years, an activity which, not being intellectuals, they conduct with remarkable energy and method—in 1952 they got more votes than the much better-known Socialist Party), and a whole brigade of "ites," tiny groups that were in a constant fever of birth or dissolution, splitting or merging—the Fieldites, the Stammites, the Ohlerites, the Marlenites (literally a family party, the majority faction of which was alleged to consist of Mr. and Mrs. George Marlen and their parents, children and collateral relations), and the Weisbordites (an intransigent little band led by Albert Weisbord, whose one big moment came, unfortunately, at the very beginning of his career, in the late twenties, when, just out of Harvard, he led to victory the great Passaic textile strike).

The evolution of the Weisbordites was typical, if a bit extreme, of these "splinter groups" (chips off the old Marxist block) as was their leader, brilliant and able but devoured by the worm of sectarianism which dieth not. The "ites" dropped off one by one until the Revolutionary League of America or whatever it was called—the title generally made up in scope for any restriction of numbers—consisted of the leader and his wife. Then there was a divorce, and the advance-guard of the revolution was concentrated, like a bouillon cube, in the small person of Albert Weisbord, who sat for years at his secondhand desk behind the dusty glass door proudly emblazoned REVOLUTIONARY LEAGUE OF AMERICA—HEADQUARTERS writing his party organ and cranking it out on the mimeograph machine.* This contrivance played the same part in the American revolutionary movement that

* Weisbord is now a trade-union official. *Sic transit* . . .

machine guns did in the Russian. The mimeographs were the instruments of production, which, as any Marxist schoolboy knows, are the base of power of every ruling class, and many a faction-fight was decided by who seized control of them first.

The splinter groups looked on us Trotskyists as we looked on the Communists, as opportunists who had sacrificed principle for popularity. Nor could it be denied that, compared to theirs, our party membership was vulgarly large. We had about 800 members.

5.

From the fall of 1939 to the spring of 1941 I was a member of the Trotskyist party. My decision to join was, perhaps typically, moral rather than intellectual. I remember reading Marx and Engels intensively in the summer of 1939 in an effort to find out whether I was a Marxist or not. I could never really make up my mind: the critical side attracted me, and also the protest against capitalist injustice, but the dogmatism and the insistence on explaining everything by one system of thought repelled me (as did a certain moral callousness). When the war began, however, I felt I should stand with the party. James P. Cannon tried to convince me I was more valuable, and would be happier, as a sympathizer than as a member; perhaps he felt a fatherly concern at my political innocence; perhaps he suspected I would be a troublesome recruit; perhaps both. And in fact I was always a "new boy" in the party, looked on by my comrades as a bit of a political dilettante; they centered their lives in "the movement," finding their friends and even their wives or husbands within it, but my friends and work (*P.R.*) were mostly outside; nor were they reassured by my criticisms of the dogmatic and undemocratic elements in Leninism.

A few months after I joined the party the Red Army invaded Finland and a faction-fight broke out which by the spring had broken up the party into two parties. (Like divorce in a family, a "split" in a Marxist party was dreaded even by those who longed for it, and each side tried to maneuver the other into taking the guilt.) On one side was Cannon, backed (alas) by Trotsky, insisting we must support the Russians because theirs was a "workers' state" ("degenerated") and therefore the Red Army was bringing socialism (degenerated) to the Finns. The minority faction, to which I enthusiastically adhered, was led by Shachtman and Burnham; we held that the invasion was imperialist aggression and therefore opposed it. "Support" and "oppose" had no practical meaning, of course; the Cannonites didn't volunteer for the Red Army (which would have shot them); nor did any Shachtmanites go to Finland to fight under Baron Mannerheim. The controversy expressed itself not in action or even in proposals for action but in interminable and (to me) exciting party meetings and tall stacks of mimeographed articles in the "Internal Bulletin" that was circulated only among party members.

I found the struggle educational—I learned a good deal about Marxist theory, the Soviet Union, methods of argument, and party organization—but frustrating. I couldn't get into the fight. I wrote three long articles for the "Internal Bulletin" but, although I had had no trouble getting printed in *Fortune, Harper's, The Nation, The New Yorker*—or, for that matter, the *N.I.*—my manuscripts were monotonously rejected. The eight hundred members of the party, steeped in Marxicology, aged in the Bolshevik-Leninist wood, were a highly esoteric audience, while I was a highly exoteric writer. They were professionals, I was an amateur. Finally I managed to break into print, or rather mimeograph, with a modest little piece titled "Shamefaced Defensism." This was an analysis of a current article by Trotsky in *Liberty*: I demonstrated that The Old Man was much tougher on Stalin's Russia (and the Red Army) in the bourgeois press than in the Internal Bulletin, and I gave some disrespectful reasons therefor. The article roused the majority faction to fury, not because of its arguments, which they paid no attention to, but simply because a new boy had talked back to the principal. (Besides the Russian Question, there was another important point of disagreement between the factions—the minority wanted a more democratic party, while the majority thought there was too much democracy running around already.) "These *parvenus* who have hardly wet their feet in the water of the class struggle and who presume to polemize with Trotsky on political questions!" thundered Cannon, fatherly no more, at a meeting of the Downtown Branch (mine), while The Old Man himself wrote a waspish message from Coayacan under the headline, "BACK TO THE PARTY!":

> Dear Comrades,
>
> . . . The opposition leaders seem to have passed over into guerilla warfare. It is the fate of many other defeated armies. One of the most curious examples is the more valiant than sensible attack of comrade Macdonald on my *Liberty* article. He didn't find, you see, in this article an analysis of the contradictory character of the Soviet state and of the "progressive" rôle of the Red Army. With the same logic which he shows in the editing of *Partisan Review* as in his analysis of the Kronstadt uprising,* he discovers that I am "in reality" a minorityite, a Shachtmanite, or a Macdonaldist. . . . If we should express Macdonald's discovery in a more articulate manner, it would signify: when Trotsky wishes to adapt himself to the readers of *Liberty*, he writes like Shachtman and almost like Macdonald, but when he speaks to the party, he becomes terribly antiminority. *Partisan Review* is very interested in psychoanalysis and I permit myself to say that the editor of this review, if he analyzes himself a bit, would recognize that he has uncovered his own subconscious.

6.

In the spring of 1940 the Trotskyists split, Cannon retaining the Socialist Workers Party, while Shachtman founded the Workers Party (originality in nomenclature was not a strong

---

* I had written a letter to the *N.I.*, criticizing Trotsky's defense of the suppression of the Kronstadt mutiny; it appeared in the same issue (July 1938) that contained my first article for the paper; I was always a little schizoid about Trotskyism, as about Marxism. . . . Apropos the sneer at *P.R.*, it was interesting that, while the Stalinists were sure the magazine was secretly affiliated to the Trotskyists, the latter were constantly attacking it.

point of the American Left). I went into the WP, but Burnham, although he had been co-leader of our group right up to the split, didn't.* Burnham's sudden evaporation was a special blow to me because he had stood for a more democratic and less orthodox party than Shachtman who, understandably, given his political background, wanted to get the new party back on the Leninist rails rather than press on to fresh triumphs of freethinking. The shock of the German breakthrough in Europe that June created another difficulty. It stimulated me to make a study of Nazi society, especially the post-Schacht economy, which in turn led me to conclude that Nazism was neither socialism nor capitalism but something for which Marxian theory had no place, namely, "bureaucratic collectivism"—Burnham had argued much the same thesis about Russia while he was in the party, which didn't help—and this in turn led me to write a 30,000-word article about my discoveries for the *New International*. The editors were not enthusiastic; they were, frankly, rather disappointed in the article, which struck them as half-baked, superficial, trivial, boring and badly written. They finally agreed, under prodding, to print 4,000 words. Since everything else I'd submitted since 1938 had been gladly printed—professional journalists don't grow on trees, not on Trotskyist trees—I concluded they might also have some objections to the heterodox nature of my thesis. Several other sore points developed, and finally, on March 22nd, 1941, I wrote an 8,000-word letter to my comrades, beginning, "For some time, as is well known, there has been increasingly sharp

---

* A year or so later he published *The Managerial Revolution*, whose thesis was as dramatic as it was flimsy. Burnham treated Marx as Marx had treated Hegel; he "stood him on his head," replacing the proletariat with the industrial managers as the new ruling class, while at the same time keeping the worst faults of Marx's method: the ethical indifference, even cynicism, the romantic belief in a science of History, the grandiose predictions that didn't work out. The difference, aside from the fact that Marx was a genius, was that it took several generations for it to become clear that the proletariat was not the new ruling class, while Burnham's "managerialism" was forgotten, even by the author, in a few years.

conflict between the undersigned and your representatives, the Political Committee, on questions of both theory and organization"; rehearsing my grievances and generalizing on the stuffy intellectual atmosphere in the party; and ending with some "minimum demands" (to restore me to the board of the *N.I.* and publish an additional 4,000 words of my Nazi-economics article) followed by a dignified, to say the least, peroration:

> If these rectifications are made by the Political Committee, as the result of pressure from the National Committee and from the party membership, I will conclude that it will be possible to have a fruitful discussion of the more general issues raised in Section Two—"Should Party Discipline be Applied to Matters of Theory?" And above all, it will be possible to hope that there is some possibility of arresting the present rapid degeneration of the Workers Party into the kind of undesirable bureaucratic-conservative régime we rejected last year in the Socialist Workers Party.

The rectifications were not made, the degeneration was not arrested and a few weeks later I resigned from the party. The massive "document" just quoted is an impressive performance, demonstrating an energetic logic, a fertility in subtle distinctions and a power to isolate the essentials of a complex situation and present them with forceful clarity that astonishes even so critical a rereader as myself. On the other hand, when one considers the discrepancy between the effort invested and (a) the occasion (very minor) and (b) the chances of success (zero—after all, I was trying to persuade Bolsheviks to tolerate free thought so that I could remain in the party, *their* party), then it seems hard to believe that I was practically middle-aged when I wrote it. The whole business was an excellent example of the "as if" political behavior we went in for in those days; we behaved as if our tiny sects (even the Communists were insignificant in national politics) were making History, as if great issues hinged on what we did, or rather what we said and wrote. And so we devoted enormous energies and even some intellectual ability to "documents" like the above. It was all rather like engraving the Lord's Prayer on the head of a pin. But it was excellent training in political thinking. Marxism, like Latin, is a good discipline for the mind.

7.

What strikes me most, looking back, is the contrast between the scope of our thought and the modesty of our actions. The problems we were concerned with were so vast that, until History came to our rescue, we couldn't *do* much about them. We were really engaged not in politics but in metapolitics, which the Oxford Dictionary defines as "theoretical political science," adding "often derog." When it was a matter of discussing the Soviet system (was it a "degenerated workers' state" or a "bureaucratic collectivism"? What was its class structure? Were there, indeed, classes at all or merely social groups?), we handled it masterfully in erudite, closely reasoned articles, in formal debates in cheap meeting-rooms off Third Avenue, in arguments around the cafeteria tables of Fourteenth Street. I have not before or since lived in such an atmosphere of passionate, if somewhat scholastic, intellection. But when we had to act, when the problem was, for example, a Congressional campaign, we—or in this case I—wrote leaflets like a 1941 exhibit that began "FOR A SOCIALIST DEFENSE AGAINST HITLERISM! People of the Bronx! Take the First Step! Elect Shachtman to Congress!" and then gave the Ten Point Platform of the Workers Party, of which point 3 was "Hands off Latin America!" and point 9 "Nationalize All Defense Industries!" Shachtman was not elected. Nor did an earlier Ten Point Platform in an election for mayor prove more successful—point 7 was "Modernize the Subway System!"; point 10: "For a Socialist Society!"

Inept we were, but had we been each of us a compound of Robespierre and Northcliffe, Lenin and Luce, we should still have found it hard going. The discouraging response of the masses to our street meetings, picket lines, leaflets and publications was due to deeper causes than our faulty technique. The last time in American history that radical ideas have had any mass appeal was just before the First World War, when the Socialists published half a dozen *daily* papers, elected Congressmen and almost defeated Gompers with their candidate for the presidency of the American Federation of Labor, and when that strange and unique contribution of America to anarcho-syndicalism, the "Wobblies" (officially the Industrial Workers of the World, or IWW, also called I Won't Work), organized great masses of unskilled workers and led strikes in the New England textile mills, the Minnesota iron mines and the Pennsylvania steel industry that were as much social rebellions as economic conflicts. During and immediately after the war the Government, by the use of quasi-legal force and violence, permanently destroyed the Wobblies and the more militant section of the Socialist Party.

The radical tradition never came back, except among the intelligentsia. Not even at the lowest point of the depression, in 1932–33, were the Communists or the Socialists a serious political force. The CIO in a few years subsided from youthful rebellion into bureaucratic conservatism, a devolution that had taken generations in the German and British labor movements. (It was an ironical illustration of Trotsky's "Law of Combined Development," according to which backward nations don't develop gradually as their more advanced predecessors did, but use the existing high level of technique as the springboard for a "dialectical leap" into modernity.) Between 1935 and 1939 the CIO organized the workers in steel, auto, rubber and other mass industries, but all that happened was that those particular workers greatly improved their position inside capitalism, a Good Thing but hardly revolutionary. We didn't even get a Labor Party out of it.

The failure of socialism to attract the American masses was all the more discouraging because the depression was far worse in the United States than anywhere else except Germany. By the summer of 1932 the "soundest" common stocks were selling at fantastic prices: U.S. Steel was $22 a share, down from $262 in September 1929; American Telephone & Telegraph had dropped from $304 to $72, General

Motors from $73 to $8. By 1933 there were thirteen millions unemployed, a fifth of the working population, and national production was one-third less than it had been in 1929. The usual explanation of the inability of the Left to exploit this breakdown is that the New Deal offered a solution. And so it did, politically; the great reforms of Roosevelt's first six years—Wagner Act, Wages & Hours Law, Social Security, etc.—brought American capitalism instantly (as historical time goes) up to the British level, another illustration of the Law of Combined Development. But the New Dealers were unable to cope with the economic crisis. It took the war to do that. Unemployment stuck at eight million or more up to the end of 1940, except for a brief improvement in 1937, which was quickly erased by the sharp recession that began that autumn and was finally overcome not by New Deal measures but by war orders.

Thus all through the thirties there seemed to us radicals no reason to believe in the "viability" of American capitalism. And yet the masses remained apathetic about socialism. We were right, but they wouldn't listen. Nothing is more frustrating for an intellectual than to work out a logical solution to a problem and then find that nobody is interested.*

In our isolation and impotence we metapoliticians were kept going by the illusion that we had in our pocket a skeleton key to History. We were the Marxian *illuminati*, whose esoteric knowledge enabled us to divine the real,

* It's even worse now. In the thirties we foresaw that American capitalism might find a basis for survival in what we called "a permanent war economy," but we saw this in terms of Goering's alternative—"guns or butter"—and we predicted a decline in living standards and a consequent growth of mass discontent. The war economy has come and is relatively "permanent"—that is, one can see no end to it as long as the USA and the USSR are life-or-death rivals—but American capitalism has shown an extraordinary and unexpected capacity to produce; living standards—especially of the low-income groups—are at levels that would have been considered fantastic in the thirties; and, in short, the economy is producing both guns *and* butter.

hidden nature of events and, when the time came, to Take Advantage of Revolutionary Situations. We were the "cadres of leadership" ("*cadre*: permanent establishment of a regiment forming nucleus for expansion at need") and the masses would fall in behind us as they had followed the Bolsheviks in October. The smallness of Lenin's pre-1917 party was a great comfort—if he could take over Russia with a mere handful of disciplined comrades, why not . . . ?

Viewed from 1957, much of our behavior appears absurd and even mildly insane ("*metapolitics*: . . . often derog."). But if our actions compared grotesquely to our aspirations, if we were intellectually arrogant and morally more than a little smug, we did believe in a great cause and we did make real sacrifices for it.

8.

In the summer of 1943 I resigned from the editorial board of *Partisan Review,* thus graduating, after six years, from the third and last of the educational institutions that have been important in my life—the other two were Phillips Exeter Academy and the Trotskyist movement. After Pearl Harbor Rahv and Phillips had come to feel it was their war and their country, while I had remained disaffected. They wanted to reduce the magazine's political content and concentrate on literary criticism, while I wanted to continue the mixture as before. (Political writing those days meant Left-wing writing; those who supported the war felt no impulse to rush into print; patriotism was still morally suspect and intellectually unfashionable—and besides, they hadn't any conservative vocabulary.) We had some first-class rows, and finally I resigned, writing a sharp letter-to-the-editors which appeared in *P.R.* with an answer in kind.

At once I began to project a magazine of my own which materialized in February 1944 as a monthly called *Politics.* I was the editor, publisher, owner, proofreader, layout man and chief contributor; my then wife, Nancy, was the business manager, as she had been before that of *P.R.* (The business manager is the Unknown Soldier of the little-magazine world.) *Politics* ran for five years, the first three as a monthly, the last two, when I had become somewhat jaded, as a quarterly. The vintage year was probably 1945; I had got some experience by then and yet was still fresh; coincidentally or not, the deficit was smallest that year, about $953; other years it ran from $2,000 to $6,000. The chief contributors (five or more articles) were Andrea Caffi ("European"), Nicola Chiaromonte, Lewis Coser ("Louis Clair"), Paul Goodman, Peter Gutman ("Peter Meyer"), Victor Serge, Niccolo Tucci and George Woodcock. Perhaps significantly, Goodman was the only American; Caffi was Italian-Russian, Coser was German, Gutman was Czech, Tucci and Chiaromonte were Italians, Serge was Belgian-Russian and Woodcock was English.

Politics began with a circulation of about 2,000, which went up to something over 5,000, where it stuck fast. Its readers were mostly male (81 per cent), college graduates (90 per cent), urban (66 per cent lived in cities of over 100,000 population), without party ties (52 per cent—of those belonging to a party the Socialists, with 24 per cent of the total readers, were far in the lead; the Democrats had 12 per cent, the Republicans 4 per cent and the Trotskyists 3 per cent), and young (67 per cent were under thirty-five; 22 per cent were students and another 22 per cent were in the armed forces.) * The class alignment was about what one might expect: 78 per cent of the readers were middle-class professionals (as against 10 per cent in the population at large) and 13 per cent were wage-workers (as against 71 per cent nationally). The only surprise was that businessmen were repre-

* Cf. "The Fascinated Readers," a report by Ruth Harper Mills on a questionnaire drawn up by C. Wright Mills and sent to our subscribers. This is in the Winter, 1948, issue, which also contains a four-year index. About the same time *The New Republic,* the liberal weekly, surveyed *its* readers. They turned out to be older, more conservative and prosperous and religious and female, less urban and well-educated.

sented just about as heavily as in the general population: 7 per cent v. 9 per cent. It was a responsive, irritable readership, who wrote many letters-to-the-editor, most of which I printed, especially the more unfavorable ones.

While I was editing *Politics* I often felt isolated, comparing my few thousand readers with the millions and millions of nonreaders—such is the power of the modern obsession with quantity, also of Marxism with its sentimentalization of "the masses." But in the last eight years I have run across so many nostalgic old readers in so many unexpected quarters that I have the impression I'm better known for *Politics* than for my articles in *The New Yorker*, whose circulation is roughly seventy times greater. This is curious but should not be surprising. A "little magazine" is often more intensively read (and circulated) than the big commercial magazines, being a more individual expression and so appealing with special force to other individuals of like minds. Being a one-man magazine, *Politics* was especially, some thought excessively, personal; it expressed my own temperament quite well, and any true mirror of an individual is in itself interesting. This freely personal note—which, as an editor, I welcomed in the contributions of others, my "formula" being to have none—this note, I think, is one reason there is still life and bite in the forty-two back numbers. The other is the period (1944–49), which was one when American intellectuals were beginning to feel uneasy about Marxism and yet retained enough interest in it to write about it; disillusion had not reached the stage of apathy; whence a tension that produced some good arguments. It was also a time of troubles: the terrible last years of the war, with the Nazi death-camps and the atomic bombings and the gray dawn of "peace," when the reality behind the illusions of the antifascist crusade began to emerge, with Stalin's Russia smoothly taking over the rôle of Hitler's Germany. All of this demanded attention, reporting, exposure, analysis, satire, indignation, lamentation.

The magazine, after the first two years, forsook the true Marxist faith to whore after the strange gods of anarchism and pacifism.* This was partly a matter of my own evolution: now that I was out of the Marxian atmosphere of the Workers Party (also of *Partisan Review*, where my colleagues' mind-set, like Burnham's, retained its Marxist form though now filled with how different a content) my thinking took its natural bent toward individualism, empiricism, moralism, estheticism—all cardinal sins, that is deviations, in the Marxian canon. It was also partly a reaction to Hiroshima and Nagasaki, two scientific experiments which gave the final push to my already tottering faith. Writing in 1944 I had defined the magazine's "values in general" as "scientific, materialistic, this-worldly, democratic, humanist—in the tradition of Rousseau, Jefferson, Darwin, Marx, Freud and Dewey." But from 1946 on only Freud and Jefferson remained of the culture heroes (like two ill-assorted creatures cast up as sole

---

* It was odd that anarchism took no root in the thirties, considering (1) the American temperament, lawless and individualistic, (2) the American anarchist tradition, from Benjamin Tucker to the Wobblies, and (3) that anarchism gave a better answer to the real modern problem, the encroachment of the State, than did Marxism, which was revolutionary only about bourgeois private property (not a real issue any more) and was thoroughly reactionary on the question of the State. But (3) also explains Marxism's popularity (though it doesn't justify it): while the centralized State is the chief danger now to freedom, it is also necessary to the operation of a mass society based on large-scale industry. Thus Marxism is "practical," since it fits into the *status quo*—as in Soviet Russia—while anarchism is "impractical" because it threatens it. The revolutionary alternative to the *status quo* today is not collectivized property administered by a "workers' state" whatever *that* means, but some kind of anarchist decentralization that will break up mass society into small communities where individuals can live together as variegated human beings instead of as impersonal units in the mass sum. The shallowness of the New Deal and the British Labour Party's postwar régime is shown by their failure to improve any of the important things in people's lives—the actual relationships on the job, the way they spend their leisure, and child-rearing and sex and art. It is mass living that vitiates all these today and the State that holds together the *status quo*. Marxism glorifies "the masses" and endorses the State. Anarchism leads back to the individual and the community, which is "impractical" but necessary—that is to say, it is revolutionary.

survivors of a flood), while "scientific" and "democratic" came under increasing suspicion because of their abuse by the industrialized mass society that had produced the atomic bomb.

In the spring of 1946 I published a two-part article, "The Root Is Man," whose title came from an early (1844) statement of Marx's: *"To be radical is to grasp the matter by its roots. Now the root for mankind is man."* This was partly a demonstration that Marxism is no longer a reliable guide to either action or understanding, partly a discussion of the problem of values in politics and the limitations of the scientific method, partly some rather desperate suggestions for a new kind of radical approach—individualistic, decentralized, essentially anarchist. The crucial distinction was between "Progressive" and "Radical":

> The Progressive makes history the center of his ideology. The Radical puts man there. The Progressive's attitude is optimistic both about human nature (which he thinks is basically good, hence all that is needed is to change institutions so as to give this goodness a chance to work) and about the possibility of understanding history through scientific method. The Radical is more aware of the dual nature of man; he sees evil as well as good at the base of human nature; he is skeptical about the ability of science to explain things beyond a certain point; he is aware of the tragic element in man's fate not only today but in any conceivable kind of society. The Progressive thinks in collective terms (the interests of society or of the working class); the Radical stresses individual conscience. The Progressive starts off from what is actually happening, the Radical from what he wants to happen. The former must have the feeling that history is on his side. The latter is pleased if history is also going his way, but he is stubborn about following his own road, that of "ought" rather than "is."
>
> The Radical admits the validity of science in its own sphere, but thinks there also exists another sphere that is outside the reach of scientific investigation, one in which value-judgments cannot be *proved,* though they can be *demonstrated* in the traditional terms of art and ethical

teaching. The Radical sees any movement like socialism which aspires toward a better society as rooted in this second, non-scientific sphere, however its growth may be shaped by historical process. . . .

The Marxists still hold fast to the classic Left faith in human liberation through scientific progress, while admitting—some of them—that revisions of doctrine and refinements of method are necessary. This was my opinion until I began to edit *Politics* and consequently to follow in some detail the events of the last two years. The difficulties lie much deeper, I now think, than is assumed by the Progressives, and the crisis is much more serious.

It was, oddly enough, the emphasis on morality that caused the most scandal. "Macdonald's notions about politics are advanced under the banner of morality; actually they are neither political nor moral, being rather a peculiar hodgepodge of both," my former colleagues on *Partisan Review* observed in an editorial that reproached *Politics* for allegedly substituting "moral uplift" for "political realism." Yet some of the best things that appeared in *Politics* were "peculiar hodgepodges," such as Bruno Bettelheim's "Behavior in Extreme Situations"; Andrea Caffi's "Violence and Sociability"; Albert Camus' "Neither Victims nor Executioners"; Niccolo Tucci's regular column, "Commonsense"; and four articles by Simone Weil, especially "The Iliad, or the Poem of Force," written during the German occupation of France. What worried many of my old comrades was that an undue concern about morality might be a symptom of what Sidney Hook had called "the new failure of nerve," leading to idealism, obscurantism, and, horror of horrors, like the drunkard's grave, the church! *Time* also filed "morals" under "religion": two of the "hodgepodge" articles were reported on in the "Religion" department simply because the 20th-century mind seems unable to conceive of any other pigeon-hole for ethics. In actual fact, *Politics* showed slight interest in religion. My own record is impeccable: I am not now and have never been a member of any church. Nor have I ever, not even in late adolescence, believed in God or an afterlife or a power or consciousness beyond this world that is interested in this world. Nor have I ever felt the need for such a belief, or even any interest in the whole question. Religion, in short, bores me even more than Marxism.

In the fall of 1947 I wrote a letter to the subscribers apologizing for not having got out an issue since the summer and promising to start up again—on a quarterly basis—early in 1948. "This has been a one-man magazine," I explained, "and the man has of late been feeling stale, tired, disheartened and—if you like—demoralized. . . . This mood seems to be due to three factors: (a) the ever blacker and bleaker political outlook; (b) my own growing sense of ignorance, which requires more time to investigate and reflect before sounding off in print; (c) the psychological demands of a one-man magazine which, at first stimulating, have latterly become simply—demands." The magazine did revive as a quarterly, but it was the beginning of the end. A year later the psychological factors had improved only slightly, and the money question had become acute, between an impressive rise in the cost of printing (in the first three years of *Politics* the printer's bill doubled—this by the way is one big reason there aren't more "little magazines" nowadays in the United States) and an equally impressive decline in my own bank account. So I gave up the magazine and went back to writing for my living (and my children's) after the thirteen-year sabbatical that had followed my resignation from *Fortune* in 1936. In recent years I have devoted most of my time to *The New Yorker*, where I have been able to write the kind of social-cultural reportage and analysis that now interests me more than political writing. This is an anticlimactic end to these memoirs of a revolutionist, but there it is, and there I am.

Encounter,
March and April, 1957

THE RESPONSIBILITY OF PEOPLES

The Responsibility of Peoples

We talk of the Turks and abhor the cannibals; but may not some of them go to heaven before some of us? We may have civilized bodies and yet barbarous souls. We are blind to the real sights of this world; deaf to its voice; and dead to its death.

HERMAN MELVILLE

Germans have thought in politics what other peoples have done. . . .

Although Germany has only accompanied the development of nations with the abstract activity of thought, without taking an active part in the real struggles incident to this development, she has, on the other hand, shared in the suffering caused by national development without sharing in its enjoyments, or their partial satisfaction. Abstract activity on the one side corresponds to abstract suffering on the other side.

Consequently, one fine day Germany will find herself at the level of European decay before she has ever stood at the level of European emancipation. The phenomenon might be likened to a fetish-worshiper who succumbs to the diseases of Christianity. . . .

The only liberation of Germany that is practical or possible is a liberation motivated by the theory that declares man to be the Supreme Being of mankind. . . . In Germany, no brand of serfdom can be extirpated without extirpating every kind of serfdom. . . . The emancipation of Germans is the emancipation of mankind.

KARL MARX (1844)

Now I must say goodbye. Tomorrow mother goes into the gas chamber, and I will be thrown into the well.

FROM A LETTER WRITTEN BY A CHILD
IN A POLISH "DEATH CAMP"

WE WERE a little nervous when she was taken," the girl's mother said afterwards. "You never know what will happen when they start to use the electric needle. But we should not have worried. She never gave the Germans a single name or address and no one was arrested."

The girl was a member of the French underground; she was caught by the Gestapo; she was tortured, while her mother was held in a nearby cell so she could hear her daughter's screams; and she died. This was Europe under the Nazis: the matter-of-fact reference to torture; the technological modernity of the instrument; the mother's politicalized attitude—"we should not have worried," since "she never gave a single name." Something has happened to the Germans—to some of them, at least; something has happened to Europe—to some of it, at least. What is it? Who or what is responsible? What does it mean about our civilization, our whole system of values? This is the great moral question of our times, and on what our hearts as well as our heads answer to it depends largely our answer to the great practical questions.

In this article, I want to consider this question as an aspect of the general problem of what my friend, Nicola Chiaromonte, calls "the responsibility of peoples."

In the last war, we believed many "atrocity stories" which later turned out to have been propaganda. Compared to the German atrocities which are reported by the press in this war, those of 1917, however revolting in detail, were (1) quantitatively negligible (rarely involving more than a score or so of alleged victims), and (2) deeds done in hot blood by individual soldiers using bayonets or guns rather than the systematic tortures and massacres with specially designed instruments that are now reported. So tender was the civilian mood of those days that the British were able to arouse great indignation over the execution of Edith Cavell, who, as a spy, by all the rules of warfare "deserved" her fate. Today we are more tough-minded—we have to be, or go crazy, so severe are the shocks administered to our moral sensibilities, indeed to our very nervous systems, by each morning's newspaper. Yet even so, one's heart fails at some of the reports.

The French War Crimes Commission recently estimated that between 200,000 and 250,000 French civilians had been killed by the Germans during their occupation of France. The Commission has also assembled a museum of torture devices: branding irons, pincers for pulling out fingernails, an "electrical shoe," a steel helmet studded with screws that can slowly be tightened. . . . Not since the Spanish Inquisition has such an array been seen. Who would have dared predict, in the 19th century, that one of the most advanced nations in Europe would employ such instruments? Marx himself might well have shrunk from the supposition. His epigram of 1844 must now be reversed: the Germans have *done* in politics what other peoples have up to now dared only to *think*.

In the last war, all this could have been dismissed as propaganda. But the great difference between the "atrocity stories" of World War I and those of World War II is that the latter are as convincingly authenticated as the former were not. To disbelieve the accounts of today, one would have to assume that almost every war correspondent is a liar on a Munchausen scale, that various neutral observers are liars, that certain internationally known religious and charitable institutions have fabricated detailed reports. We know, also, from the Nazis' own theories and from what they did in Germany itself that such horrors are not improbable.

Let us not only accept these horrors; let us insist on them. Let us not turn aside even from the greatest of all: the execution of half the Jewish population of Europe, some four million men, women, and children, in Silesian and Polish "death factories." * In the last war, the farthest our propagandists ventured was to fabricate the tale of the German "corpse factories," in which the bodies of dead soldiers were alleged to have been boiled down for their fat and chemicals. Not only was this untrue, but it would never have occurred to any one in 1917 even to *invent* a story about abattoirs in which human beings took the place of cattle. And yet we know, from irrefutable evidence, that *these things have been done*. They are part of our world and we must try to come to some kind of terms with them.

Detailed reports about the "death camps" have only come out within the past year. The chief ones I have seen are the descriptions of the camps at Auschwitz and Birkenau in Upper Silesia which appeared in the N. Y. *Times* of July 2 and 5, 1944, sent in from Switzerland; the stories in the *Times* (Aug. 27) and *Time* (Sept. 11) based on a Russian-

* *This essay appears here as published in* Politics, *March, 1945. The following footnote was added in 1953:* Later estimates put it at six million. By an ironical twist of history, the victims have now become oppressors in their turn. Since 1948, some 800,000 Arab refugees, who fled from Palestine during the fighting, have been living wretchedly in camps around the country's borders maintained by UN charity. The Israeli government—opposed by no important Jewish group that I know of—refuses to let them back and has given their homes, farms, and villages to new Jewish settlers. This is rationalized by the usual "collective responsibility" nonsense. This expropriation cannot, of course, be put on the same plane as the infinitely greater crime of the Nazis. But neither should it be passed over in silence.

conducted tour of the former death camp at Maidanek; and the report, based on stories by three eyewitnesses who were able to escape, of the Auschwitz and Birkenau camps that was released by the War Refugees Board, a Government agency, on Nov. 26, 1944. The first report is the most impressive, because it was put out by the well-known Swiss relief organization, the Fluchtlingshilfe of Zurich, whose head is the Rev. Paul Voght. It is also sponsored by the Ecumenical Refugee Committee of the World Council of Churches. But in all the reports, the atmosphere is the same: rationality and system gone mad; the discoveries of science, the refinements of modern mass organization applied to the murder of noncombatants on a scale unknown since Genghis Khan.

These camps, which the Nazis called "model extermination camps" and which were operated by specially trained *Judenvernichtung* (Jew-killing) experts, were literally "death factories," often with railroad sidings running into them for the transport of their raw materials. These "materials" were processed in an orderly fashion: shaved, bathed, deloused, each given a slip of paper with his or her number typed on it, then routed into another room where this number was tattooed on the body—on the breasts of the women. (So in Kafka's "The Penal Colony," the mechanism executes the criminal by tattooing the record of his crime on his body—one of too many modern instances in which reality has now caught up with Kafka's imagination.) The cooperation of the victims was necessary to save time (and make production records possible). By experiment, it was found that death came quicker when the body was warm, washed and wet. The execution buildings were therefore sometimes given the appearance of bathing establishments, the illusion being methodically carried out by having two attendants in white jackets give each victim a towel and a piece of soap. There were even simulated shower-entries in the death chamber itself: a concrete room into which as many naked persons were packed as possible. "When everybody is inside, the heavy doors are closed. Then there is a short pause, presumably to allow the room temperature to rise to a certain level, after which SS men with gas masks climb the roof, open the traps in the ceiling, and shake down a preparation in powder form labeled 'Cyklon,' for use against vermin, which is manufactured by a Hamburg concern. It is presumed that this is a cyanide mixture of some sort which turns into a gas at a certain temperature. After three minutes, every one in the chamber is dead." The bodies were then taken into the crematorium (which at Maidanek looked like "a big bake shop or a very small blast furnace") where they were cut up by butchers, loaded onto iron stretchers and slid on rollers into the coke-fed ovens. With such methods, death was produced on a mass scale: at Birkenau alone, over a million and a half persons are estimated to have perished from April, 1942, to April, 1944.

As in the Chicago stockyards, no by-products were wasted. The clothes and shoes were shipped into Germany to relieve the shortage of consumption goods: "We came to a large warehouse. It was full of shoes. A sea of shoes. . . . They were piled like coal in a bin halfway up the walls. Boots. Rubbers. Leggings. Slippers. Children's shoes, soldiers' shoes, old shoes, new shoes. . . . In one corner, there was a stock of artificial limbs." Also: "Near the ovens were the remains of a room with a big stone table. Here gold fillings were extracted from the teeth. No corpse could be burned without a stamp on the chest: 'INSPECTED FOR GOLD FILLINGS.'" The ashes and bones of the burned bodies were used to fertilize cabbage fields around the camps. Nor did the Germans, devotees of science, lose the chance to advance human knowledge. All identical twins that passed through Birkenau were removed for "biological examination" at a German scientific institute. In the Vosges section of France, a "laboratory camp" was recently discovered, where thousands of persons were experimented on, always with fatal results. Some were vivisected, some were given leprosy and plague, some were blinded (to see if their sight could be restored), many were put to death by gas while observers watched their reactions through a window. Perhaps the most humanly appalling details of all were certain juxtapositions which one would be tempted to say showed a typical Germanic tastelessness, were it not for our own "war-theme" advertisements. Thus at a Dutch camp, there were found certain cells so constructed as to cause death by slow suffocation—and a nursery for prisoners' children whose walls were decorated with scenes from fairy tales. And at Maidanek, the camp loudspeaker blared out all day over the countryside . . . Viennese waltzes.

But enough! We may say that those who planned and carried out such things were insane. This may have often been true, in a medical sense. But once granted the ends, the means were rational enough—all too rational. The Nazis learned much from mass production, from modern business organization. It all reads like a sinister parody of Victorian illusions about scientific method and the desirability *in itself* of man's learning to control his environment. The environment was controlled at Maidanek. It was the human beings who ran amok.

1. The German War Crimes Are Unique

A considerable portion of the atrocious acts of the Germans in this war are chargeable rather to war in general than to any special inhumanity of the Germans.

There was much moral indignation, for example, about the robot bombs. But the effects of "saturation bombing," which the British and American air forces have brought to a high degree of perfection, are just as indiscriminate and much more murderous. "The Allied air chiefs," states this morning's paper, "have made the long-awaited decision to adopt deliberate terror bombing of German population centers. . . . The Allied view is that bombardment of large German cities creates immediate need for relief. This is moved into the bombed areas both by rail and road, and not only creates a traffic problem but draws transport away from the battle front. Evacuation of the homeless has the same result." The only mistake in the above is to say the decision has just been adopted; actually, the Allies have used "terror bombing" for several years. We might also recall the indignation we felt, in

1940, at the strafing of refugees by the Luftwaffe. "How typically Nazi!" we exclaimed—but we were more tender-minded in those days. The first contracts have already been let for the manufacture of our own robot bombs, and no one at all conversant with modern warfare doubts that the robot bomb will be a key weapon in World War III.*

The ruthless economic exploitation, accompanied by mass starvation, to which the Nazis subjected Europe when they held it was deplorable. But our own press for many months now has carried articles about the failure of the Allies to provide any more food to the "liberated" (and hungry) Europeans than the Germans did (and often, as in Italy and Belgium, not as much). "Military necessity" apparently rules "us" as absolutely as it ruled "them," and with the same terrible results for the peoples of Europe.

Some of the most horrible brutalities chargeable to the Nazis have been committed in their attempts to deal with the maquis. Throughout military history, franc-tireurs have always been dealt with severely; the Hague rules of warfare even authorize the shooting of civilian hostages in reprisal for franc-tireur attacks on the invading soldiery. One should not forget that the Germans occupied almost all of Europe for four years, and that our own armies are only just beginning to occupy enemy territory. If a German resistance movement materializes that is anything like as determined as the one the Nazis had to deal with, we shall probably see our own armies climbing down a bit from their present pinnacle of moral superiority.†

---

* Six months after this was written, "we" humane and democratic Americans dropped atomic bombs on Hiroshima and Nagasaki, destroying in the twinkling of an eye some 90,000 civilians—men, women and children. This was the climax of the Anglo-American policy of massacring civilian populations from the air, a policy which later evidence shows to have been morally indefensible, politically disastrous, and militarily of dubious value. See Appendix A. (*Footnote added in 1953*)

† The resistance did not materialize, and, on the whole, the conduct of the American and British armies in Germany was no worse than that of most conquerors—a modest enough standard. The Red

Even the extermination of large numbers of helpless people is not so unknown in modern times as our own propagandists would have us think. Great numbers of the colored races have been wiped out since 1800 by the whites: the "rubber atrocities" of the Amazon and the Belgian Congo (cf. Conrad's *Heart of Darkness*); the large scale executions that followed the Boxer Rebellion in China; the slaughter of the bulk of the Australian Black-fellows and the American Indians; not to mention dozens of lesser "episodes" throughout Asia and Africa. In England itself, furthermore, in the first half of the last century, millions of men, women and children of the working class were starved and worked to death in conditions which were often almost as brutal and degrading as those of Maidanek and which had the disadvantage of prolonging the victims' suffering much longer (cf. the Parliamentary "Blue Books" of the period, Engels' *Condition of the English Working Class* in 1844, or J. L. and Barbara Hammond's *Lord Shaftesbury*). And in Soviet Russia in the last fifteen years, millions of peasants and political prisoners have been starved to death in State-created famines or worked to death on forced-labor projects.

After the acids of sophisticated inquiry have done their worst, however, a considerable residue remains. It is this residue which makes the German atrocities in this war a phenomenon unique at least in modern history.

It is partly a question of the intimate individual cruelty shown in much of the Germans' behavior. That the Allied forces will execute hostages and burn down towns if "necessary" I have no doubt; but I should be surprised if they do it on the scale the Germans did (50 lives for one was the lowest "rate of exchange") or with the brutality and sadism

Army, however, sunk far below even this standard. The first few weeks of the Russian occupation of Eastern Germany, Austria, and Hungary were an orgy of unrestrained and wholesale raping and killing on a scale unknown in the West for many centuries. See the four terrible first-hand reports by survivors I printed in *Politics* (January 1946, pp. 4-8; October 1946, pp. 315-319). (*1953*)

shown in the extermination of whole villages and the common use of the most revolting tortures.

But it is mostly what might be called the "gratuitous" character of the worst atrocities. What has been done by other peoples as an unpleasant by-product of the attainment of certain ends has been done by the Germans at Maidanek and Auschwitz as an end in itself. What has been done elsewhere in violation of the doer's code of ethics, and hence in a shamefaced way draped over with hypocritical apologies, has been done here in conformance with the avowed Nazi moral code, and thus done as publicly and proclaimed as exultantly as the winning of a great battle.* The Allied

* Untrue, indeed the reverse of the truth. "Why I wrote so false a statement, I don't know," I wrote later. "There was no evidence for it: the intoxication of rhetoric must be my only feeble excuse." Another excuse was that I failed to make a crucial distinction (that others also often fail to make) between the *death* camps (as: Maidanek, Auschwitz, Oswiecim) and the *concentration camps* (as: Buchenwald, Dachau, Sachsenhausen). The latter existed through the Hitler regime; the death rate in them was very high, but their aim was to terrorize, torture, and demoralize the prisoners, and also, during the war, to exploit their labor, rather than just to kill them. Their existence was no secret—the Nazis indeed took care to let the Germans know about them—in general, not in revolting detail—as a means of intimidating opposition. They could not have been kept secret anyway, since they were all in Germany itself and since, up to 1940, their prisoners were all Germans. But the death camps were mostly in Poland, and they "processed" only Jews, most of them Polish, and other non-Germans. So they could be kept secret, and they were. Only Germans with very good connections with the high army staff ever learned of their existence. For their aim was simply to kill all the Jews, male and female, adults and children, for no alleged political or criminal offenses, but just because they were Jews. And this aim would have disgusted and shocked everybody, in Germany or out of it, except fanatical Nazis.

The blueprints for "mobile gas chambers" (closed trucks specially equipped to asphyxiate people) were approved by Hitler in the fall of 1941, and the first units began operating in occupied Russian territory in the spring of 1942. The first death camps were opened in the fall of 1942 and operated to the fall of 1944, when Himmler closed them down, without telling Hitler, as part of his preparations to open negotiations with the Anglo-Americans, be-

bombing of German cities killed many innocent civilians (though not as many as a single one of the German death camps), but there was at least this much humane rationality about it: that it was thought necessary to the winning of the war, which in turn was thought necessary to the self-preservation of the Allied nations. Furthermore, some kind of an argument could be made that it *was* necessary. But the extermination of the Jews of Europe was not a means to any end one can accept as even plausibly rational. The Jews constituted no threat to their executioners; no military purpose was served by their extermination; the "racial theory" behind it is scientifically groundless and humanly abhorrent and can only be termed, in the strictest sense of the term, neurotic. The Jews of Europe were murdered to gratify a paranoiac hatred (as the robot bomb was christened "V" for "Vengeance") but for no reason of policy or advantage that I can see.*

Or consider the Stalin regime's massacres, the only other ones of our day which have been on the Nazi scale. In Russia today there is much less respect for human life and

---

hind Hitler's back, for a truce. Rumors began circulating about the mobile gas chambers and later the death camps in 1942, and the British Foreign Office almost certainly was informed by Moscow about the camps early in 1943. *The Black Book of Polish Jewry* appeared that year, with sensational reports of the camps. But precisely because the whole thing *was* so sensational, so beyond all Western experience—indeed beyond good and evil, as the acts of an insane person are juridically recognized to be—these reports for some time were simply not believed. There are even many stories of Jews who were warned but refused to believe it, and dutifully reported for shipment to Maidanek. It was not till the summer of 1944 that the non-German world began to believe it, and if some Germans then heard about the death camps from Allied broadcasts, what wonder if they discounted it as enemy "atrocity stuff"? But most were not even that much informed. (Best source on the death camps is Leon Poliakov's *Breviare de la Haine*, Paris, 1951.) (*1953*)

* This statement provoked much dissent at the time, but I have become more and more convinced of its truth, especially after reading Hannah Arendt's brilliant and profound *The Origins of Totalitarianism* (Harcourt, Brace, 1951). (*1953*)

less ideological resistance to acts of violence on a mass scale than there is in the bourgeois democracies. Yet even here, there is at least the justification for, say, the State-induced famine of 1932 that it represented the carrying out, by brutal and abhorrent means (which of course corrupted the ends—but that is another story) an agricultural policy whose aim was to increase productivity. This may not be a good end in itself, but it is certainly not a bad one. It is, in any case, rational. And the kulaks were starved incident to this aim, not because there was any desire to exterminate them in themselves. It may be said, justly, that it makes little difference to the dead kulak or to the dead Jew what the motives of his executioners were. But it makes a great deal of difference to the executioners, and to our evaluation of their act.*

To put it briefly: the English mill-owners in the last century and the Russian bureaucrats in this one showed a disregard for human life which was shocking enough. But the Nazis have not *disregarded* human life. They have, on the contrary, paid close attention to it. They have taken it for the pure, disinterested pleasure of taking it. There was no ulterior motive behind Maidanek, no possible advantage to its creators beyond the gratification of neurotic racial hatreds. What has previously been done only by individual psychopathic killers has now been done by the rulers and servants of a great modern State. This *is* something new.

We now come to the question: who is responsible for these horrors?

2. German Anti-Semitism Is Not a "People's Action"

If we can conceive of a modern people as collectively responsible in a moral sense at all, then it must be held account-

* I now think I overestimated the rationality of Stalin's policy. At first it was more rational than Hitler's but the dynamic of totalitarianism seems to lead towards irrationality, and by 1945 there was less to choose between the two horrors, in this respect, than I then thought. (*1953*)

able only for actions which it takes spontaneously and as a whole, actions which are approved by the popular *mores*. It cannot be indicted for things done by sharply differentiated sub-groups.

How does this apply to the Germans and the Jews? It is true there was and is widespread anti-Semitism in Germany, as in this country. But anti-Semitism is one thing and violent persecution of Jews is another. If the German people as a whole had approved of the Nazis' Jewish policy, one would expect that between 1933 and the present, a period in which the Nazis used the State power to place the Jews outside the pale of legality and indeed of humanity itself, there would have been many mob attacks on Jewish institutions and individuals. Actually, as far as I can recall, the American press reported none. And I remember distinctly that in 1938 when the Nazis took advantage of the assassination, by a Jew, of their Parisian diplomatic agent, Vom Rath, to intensify the anti-Jewish terror in Germany, the press reports stressed that there was very little hostility shown by the street crowds against the Jews. The controlled German press was filled with incitements to anti-Jewish violence. Storm troopers and SS men arrested thousands of Jews with great publicity, wrecked Jewish stores, burned synagogues; but the crowds that watched these organized atrocities were silent and withdrawn when they did not venture to express their disapproval. There were many more cases reported of Germans who dared to help Jews than of those who helped the Nazi pogromists—and this, too, in papers like the N. Y. *Times* which were not at all friendly to Nazi Germany.

In contrast, the constant and widespread acts of violence against Negroes throughout the South, culminating in lynching, may be considered real "people's actions," for which the Southern whites bear collective responsibility. As Dollard showed in *Caste and Class in a Southern Town*, the brutality with which Negroes are treated is not the work of a differentiated minority or of individual sadists but is participated in, actively or with passive sympathy, by the entire white community. "White aggression against Negroes and the social patterns which permit it are forms of social control. They are instrumentalities for keeping the Negro in his place and maintaining the supraordinate position of the white caste. . . . It must not be supposed that the major or perhaps even the most significant part of white aggression against Negroes consists of the few dramatic acts of lynching featured in the newspapers. *Massive and continuous pressures of other types are far more important in achieving social stability.*" (My italics.)

So too with the 1943 Detroit race riot, in which hundreds of Negroes were killed or horribly beaten up by large mobs of whites, in the very heart of the city. This kind of behavior has the general support of the Southern white people, and has enough popular support even in a Northern city like Detroit to allow it to be carried out without interference from the police. This latter point suggests that whereas anti-Negro violence in America is a real "folk" activity, carried on *against* the State and its police (which, of course, wink at it), in Germany it is the reverse: pogroms are carried out by the State and the forces of "law and order" *against* the folkways.*

* This is, I think, one of my shrewdest points. But I must add that the Negroes have made remarkable gains since 1945: Jim Crow segregation in the armed forces has been largely abolished; the Supreme Court for the first time has begun to enforce the 14th and 15th Amendments and even the Civil Rights Acts of 1866, 1870, and 1875, so that the whole structure of "white supremacy" in the South is cracking, and Negroes are *beginning* to vote in large numbers, to be admitted to hitherto all-white Southern universities, and to travel unsegregated on interstate trains. Lynchings have become very rare (sometimes a whole year goes by without one, as against the old days when several hundred Negroes died annually "*pour encourager les autres*"), and several cases have arisen in which white men have actually been punished for murdering Negroes. These post-1945 advances toward racial equality have come about because a more determined assertion of their rights by Negroes has coincided with a less determined denial of those rights by the whites, who now show a (belated) bad conscience that may be somewhat connected with the necessity for a united nation to face the Nazi and now the Soviet threat. There is still plenty of "folk activity" against Negroes, as the recent episode in Cicero, Ill., showed, but on the governmental level there has been a notable improvement since 1945. (*1953*)

But *someone* killed the Jews of Europe? And those who did were Germans. True. But a particular kind of Germans, specialists in torture and murder, whom it would be as erroneous to confuse with the general run of Germans as it would be to confuse the brutality-specialists who form so conspicuous a part of our own local police forces (and who occasionally burst out in such sensational horrors as the Chicago Memorial Day massacre) with the average run of Americans. It is of capital significance that the death camps for Jews and the mass killings of Russian prisoners of war have apparently not been entrusted to regular German Army units but rather to specially selected and trained SS squads. The Swedish journalist, Avid Fredborg, for example, has this interesting description in his book, *Behind the Steel Wall:*

> SS soldiers forming the execution squads in the East are carefully chosen. They are recruited from the most brutal elements and are gradually trained to become harder and more ruthless. At first they may only have to take Jews out for street cleaning and snow shoveling. After a time they are assigned to perform single executions. Only after this training is completed are they ordered to do mass executions.
>
> Many have refused to take part in these and have been shot. . . . Others have had nervous breakdowns and have been sent to asylums. Even the most hardened have at times caved in. Time and again, physicians have been called to attend soldiers on leave who have had severe attacks of hysteria or prolonged insomnia or delirium tremens (soldiers in the firing squads often get intoxicated before executions, and many stay so continually). . . .
>
> The chief instrument for these ghastly practices is the SS. Sometimes it seems that the SS is driving the policy beyond the intention of the Party leaders. In any case, it is certain the German public has little real knowledge of what is going on.

Bruno Bettelheim's article on Nazi concentration camp life in the August, 1944, issue shows in detail how *given complete control over the individual,* it is possible to condition even anti-Nazis to accept Nazi values. Major Applegate's little treatise, *Kill—or Be Killed,* indicates that it is not only the Nazis who are consciously trying to break down the civilized individual's inhibitions against taking life.

But if the Nazis can thus condition their SS men and their concentration camp prisoners, cannot they—and have they not in fact—so conditioned the German people as a whole? To some extent, of course they can and have, especially in the case of the youth. Hitler said in 1937:

"We still have among us old-fashioned people who are not fit for anything. They get in our way like cats and dogs. But this does not worry us. *We will take away their children.* We will not permit them to lapse into the old way of thinking. We will take them away when they are ten years old and bring them up in the spirit of nationalism until they are eighteen. They shall not escape us. They will join the Party, the SA, the SS and other formations. Later on they will do two years of military service. Who shall dare say that such a training will not produce a nation?"

But we must remember that the great majority of present-day Germans were adults when Hitler came to power, and that even what the Nazis called their "conquest of youth" (a revealing phrase, by the way) is not complete, judging from reports of executions of university students. More important, it would seem probable that the kind of extreme *behavior* required of mass-executioners and torturers can only be psychologically conditioned by extreme *situations,* as Bettelheim calls them, involving either complete physical control of the individual in a prison camp or else his willing cooperation in a lengthy and rigorous training process. Neither of these conditions is possible in the case of the average German: eighty million people or even ten or five million can neither be subjected to concentration-camp control nor can they be put through any elaborate training course (even if they consented to be). Propaganda and force are not adequate substitutes for the more intimate types of conditioning; their effect is weakened and even negated constantly by the family and working life of the individual, which goes on still along the traditional lines of Western civilization.*

Nazi Germany is often called "one big concentration camp," but one should not forget that this is a metaphor and not a literal description. Misled by the metaphor, some *Politics* readers have drawn from Bettelheim's article, for instance, the unwarranted conclusion that the whole German population—and even that of the occupied Europe of 1940–1943, which journalists also have called "one big concentration camp"—was being conditioned by the Nazis as effectively as the prisoners Bettelheim writes about. The fallacy in the case of Europe is apparent at a glance: as "Gallicus" showed in the January, 1945, issue, the Nazis failed to make much impression even on the youth, and soon found themselves confronted by an overwhelmingly hostile population—and, worse, corrupted by it. In Germany itself, the Nazis obviously could make more progress, since the German people were offered superior material rewards and since national hatred of a foreign conqueror was not involved. But even there it seems unlikely that propaganda and terrorism applied to a population still working and living in comparative (by concentration-camp standards) freedom have been sufficient to effectively Nazify a people the majority of whom were definitely anti-Nazi when Hitler assumed power in 1933. The very fact that concentration camps have continued to exist on a large scale is one proof of a continued popular opposition to Nazism, as are the scores of executions for "treason" which are still announced daily.†

---

* Stalin's regime has gone much further toward subjecting the whole population to "extreme situations" by "concentration-camp control" and "the more intimate types of conditioning" than Hitler's did. Morally, this makes the Russian people no more "responsible" than the German people were, but practically it does present a problem that, however painful, must be faced up to by pacifists and other men of good will. (*1953*)

† A wrong inference, I now believe. Perplexing though it is, the fact seems to be that, as Hannah Arendt writes in *The Origins of Totalitarianism* (p. 379): "Terror increased both in Soviet Russia and Nazi Germany in inverse ratio to the existence of internal polit-

3. Things Happen *to* People

All this is not to deny that Nazism has had a great effect on the German people. It is simply to deny that this effect has as yet changed the average German's attitudes enough to cause him to commit pogroms or to approve of them when his Nazi rulers commit them; and to indicate the limitations on Nazi indoctrination outside the concentration camp and the special training schools. The Germans have been changed by Nazism, but it has been a slower process and has gone less far than concentration-camp analogies would suggest, and certainly less far than our town Teutonophobes claim.*

---

ical opposition, so that it looks as though political opposition had not been the pretext of terror (as liberal accusers of the regimes were wont to assert) but rather the last impediment to its full fury." Viz.: the Nazis killed six million Jews not when they were fighting to consolidate their power in 1933–36 but in 1942–44, when they had long since destroyed effective opposition, when the Jews offered no threat to them at all, and when the German people were forced to back them in the war as a matter of national survival. And viz.: Lenin's "Red Terror" of 1918–20, when internal opposition was still strong and the Red Army was fighting defensively on Russian soil against a half dozen invading armies, was minuscule compared to the terror Stalin unleashed in 1937–39, years after forced-collectivization had crushed the peasants into shape, the first Five Year Plan the workers, and Stalin's intra-party tactics the Old Bolsheviks (the Moscow Trials were merely the juridical ratification of a *fait* long ago *accompli*). In more normal or at least familiar kinds of societies, even dictatorships like Perón's or Mussolini's, repression is used to overcome resistance. In the irrational world of totalitarianism, it is sometimes so used (executions soared after the 1944 attempt on Hitler's life), but in general it increases as the opposition weakens, since the rulers are chiefly concerned not with just keeping their power but with a laboratory experiment in changing men into bundles of conditioned reflexes. (*1953*)

* The more virulent of them, like Vansittart and Rex Stout, have concocted a theory of German "responsibility" which is just the reverse of the one discussed here: that the German people, far from having been conditioned to Nazi attitudes by external pressure (which of course implies they were decent people *before* Hitler) have been warlike barbarians throughout European history. This is such an obvious inversion of Nazi racial theory, and is so wide open to the same scientific refutations that it does not

It is a process, furthermore, which is also going on in our own society, in England, and in Russia—in the last-named perhaps * even faster and farther than in Germany itself. Modern society has become so tightly organized, so rationalized and routinized that it has the character of a mechanism which grinds on without human consciousness or control. The individual, be he "leader" or mass-man, is reduced to powerlessness vis-à-vis the mechanism. More and more, things happen TO people.

Some examples, mostly drawn from the "democratic" side in this war, may suggest what I mean:

A. The *New Yorker* of Aug. 12, 1944 ran a profile of a 22-year-old lieutenant in the Army Air Force who had just completed thirty bombing missions in the European theater. He seemed to be of superior intelligence, not politically radical; his main personal interest was in jazz music. "Whatever I tell you," he said to the interviewer, "boils down to this: I'm a cog in one hell of a big machine. The more I think about it, and I've thought about it a lot lately, the more it looks as if I'd been a cog in one thing after another since the day I was born. Whenever I get set to do what I want to do, something a whole lot bigger than me comes along and shoves me back into place. It's not especially pleasant, but there it is." The lieutenant's personal aspirations would seem modest and attainable enough: to live with his wife, to have a home, to play and hear good jazz. Our society has been unable to give him these satisfactions. Instead, it puts him in the plexiglass nose of a bomber and sends him out to kill his fellow men and destroy their homes, at the most terrible psychological cost to himself, as the profile makes clear. Society is not ungrateful, however: the lieutenant wears

seem worth wasting any more space on here. Combating it is a task for the propagandist, not for the analyst: like the Nazis' ideas on the Jewish people, it is as easy to refute on the scientific plane as it is difficult to combat on the psychological level. It seems more fruitful here to discuss a more sophisticated and tenable theory of German collective responsibility.

* I would now delete this word. (*1953*)

the Purple Heart, the Distinguished Flying Cross, and the Air Medal with three oak-leaf clusters.

B. At the Mare Island, California, naval base last summer two munitions ships blew up while they were being loaded. In a twinkling, the blast leveled everything for miles around and killed some three hundred sailors. The next day, the admiral in charge issued an Order of the Day in which he paid tribute to the "heroism" and "self-sacrifice" of the dead.

Now obviously the men who were killed were killed because they happened to be around when the explosives went off, and not because of any decision or action of their own. (So, too, civilians die in air raids; and so, too, nine out of ten soldiers die in a modern battle because they happen to be around when a bomb or shell lands.) The dead had no choice but to be "heroic," in the admiral's concept of heroism: TNT offers no surrender terms. These particular sailors had not even a choice about being around so dangerous a neighborhood: they were mostly Negroes, and they were assigned to this dirty and dangerous work because of their race (about which they had had no choice either). Indeed, they most definitely did not want the job. The fifty Negro sailors who were recently convicted and sentenced to long prison terms for mutiny were all employed at Mare Island unloading munitions and most of them were survivors of last summer's blast. They felt so strong a disinclination, after the tragedy, towards sharing their dead comrades' "heroic" fate that they risked a possible death penalty for mutiny.

The admiral's Order of the Day was thus a fantastic distortion of reality. Yet the administrative reflex which prompted him to issue it was sound. Instinctively, he felt it necessary to give to something which was non-purposive and impersonal a *human* meaning, to maintain the fiction that men who die in modern war do so not as chance victims but as active "patriots," who heroically *choose* to sacrifice their lives for their countries. It was his misfortune that the Mare Island explosion did not even superficially lend itself to this purpose. It is the good fortune of our war correspondents that battle deaths can be given at least a superficial plausibility along these lines.

C. The people of London are constantly being applauded for their "heroism" by war propagandists, and doubtless many individual Londoners did show heroic qualities during the bombing raids. But others doubtless also showed mean and cowardly traits. Insofar as the concept of heroism can be applied, it must be used on an individual not a collective basis. But when journalists salute the "heroism" of the Londoners or of the Russian people—they really mean a kind of collective heroism which can never exist actually, since as a collectivity the people of London had no alternative except to endure the bombings. As a Cockney retorted to a war correspondent: "Everyone's sticking it? And just what the bloody hell do you think anyone can do? You'd think we had some bloody choice in the matter!"

D. Perhaps the most heavily bombed community in this war is the strategic British-held island of Malta, which in a 28-month period had 2,315 air-raid alerts, or an average of three a day. One in 200 of the civilian population died during these raids. Some time ago the British Government awarded a collective Victoria Cross to the people of Malta for their "heroism"—which, once more, consisted in simply enduring what they had to endure, since their British masters would not have allowed them to leave the island anyway. And only the other day the same Government issued a booklet on the "siege of Malta" full of the usual nonsense, on which the N. Y. *Times* commented with the usual idiocy: "The island remained unconquered, a light and a symbol."

An incident reported in *Time* of Aug. 7, 1944, illuminates the myth of Malta. It seems that on July 14, 1943, a British army captain caught a Maltese citizen looting his parked car. He took him to the Maltese police, who promptly freed the thief and put the captain in jail—for false arrest. When it appeared that the Maltese authorities planned to keep the captain in jail indefinitely, his commanding officer appealed to the British Governor (without result) and finally direct to

London. The British Government replied that "in view of the present tense relations with the Maltese population and urgent military necessities, it is impossible to intervene." The captain remained in solitary confinement for nine months, until April, 1944, when his case came up in a Maltese civil court. He was then sentenced to thirteen *additional* months imprisonment at hard labor. Lord Gort, the British Military Governor, ventured to reduce the sentence, on appeal, to three months.

"We walk on tiptoe in Malta," explained an English officer. "We dare not cross a Maltese citizen in any way. Military experience demands appeasement of the pro-Fascist population." Whether the Maltese are pro-Fascist or anti-British or both is not the present point. The thing is that the collectively decorated people of "heroic Malta" detest their British "allies." We may be sure that the British don't allow their army officers to be treated this way by "natives" unless there are compelling reasons.

E. With their customary thoroughness, the Germans have carried what might be called "collective irresponsibility" to its logical extreme. To cope with the Anglo-American armies poured into France after D-Day, they impressed great numbers of Poles, Russians, Frenchmen, Italians, Czechs, Georgians, Mongolians—most of them war prisoners given a choice between starvation and service in the Reichswehr. In some German regiments, the colonel needed an interpreter to make his commands understood. Even crack SS divisions were filled out with these foreign conscripts, all of whom, even the Mongolians, were officially listed as "Volksdeutsche." The Allies in France found themselves confronted by a veritable International in Reichswehr uniforms. Many of these "Volksdeutsche" shot their officers and came over to the Allied side at the first chance, giving our High Command a typical modern problem. Were they allies? (But they wore the German uniform.) Or were they prisoners? (But they hated the uniform they wore.) All that could be said with certainty is that they were fought on the German side. The passive verb is intentional: the modern soldier does not "fight"; he "is fought," like a battleship or other inanimate mechanism.*

The following story was related by George Orwell in his column in the Oct. 13, 1944 London *Tribune:*

> Among the German prisoners captured in France there are a certain number of Russians. Some time back two were captured who did not speak Russian or any other language that was known either to their captors or their fellow-prisoners. They could, in fact, only converse with one another. A professor of Slavonic languages, brought down from Oxford, could make nothing of what they were saying. Then it happened that a sergeant who had served on the frontiers of India overheard them talking and recognized their language, which he was able to speak a little. It was Tibetan! After some questioning he managed to get their story out of them.
>
> Some years earlier they had strayed over the frontier into the Soviet Union and been conscripted into a labour battalion, afterwards being sent to western Russia when the war with Germany broke out. They were taken prisoner by the Germans and sent to North Africa; later they were sent to France, then exchanged into a fighting unit when the Second Front opened, and taken prisoner by the British. All this time they had been able to speak to nobody

---

* The Communist soldier also "is fought." At this writing, the Korean truce negotiations have been hung up for a year on the issue of whether prisoners shall be forcibly repatriated. The Communists insist they shall be; the UN that they be allowed to choose whether to go back or not. The firmness of the UN position may be partly due to memories of the shameful forced repatriation of Russian prisoners by the West in 1945–46. This was one of the dirty deals at Yalta between Stalin and Roosevelt, and it was dishonorably honored by the West until the political break with Russia in the fall of 1946. British and American MP's (who "were fought" also by their commanders) performed the noble work of herding and dragging Russian prisoners—some of whom cut their throats rather than return—into trains to be shipped back to the land of socialism, where they were punished because (a) they had been taken prisoner, and (b) they were assumed to be "unreliable elements," since they had lived beyond the Iron Curtain and so had a standard of comparison with conditions in Soviet Russia. (*1953*)

but one another, and had no notion of what was happening or who was fighting whom.

It would round the story off neatly if they were now conscripted into the British Army and sent to fight the Japanese, ending up somewhere in Central Asia, quite close to their native village, but still very much puzzled as to what it is all about.

4. Political Animism—the Theory of the "Organic State"

The above instances suggest that the difference between "civilized" and "primitive" social organization is growing less. The great circle is slowly closing, and a contemporary Soviet or German citizen would feel more in common with an Australian bushman in many ways than with, let us say, a French *philosophe* of 1780 or a Jeffersonian democrat of 1810. In place of the rigid, unexamined customs which determine the individual's behavior in primitive communities, there is substituted today a complex politico-economic organization which is equally "given" and not-to-be-criticized in its ultimate aims and assumptions, and which overrides with equal finality the individual's power of choice.

The parallel goes farther. As primitive man endowed natural forces with human animus, so modern man attributes to a nation or a people qualities of will and choice that belong in reality only to individuals. The reasons are the same in both cases: to reduce mysterious and uncontrollable forces to a level where they may be dealt with. The cave dweller feels much more comfortable about a thunderstorm if he can explain it as the rage of someone like himself only bigger, and the urban cave dwellers of our time feel much better about war if they can think of the enemy nation as a person like themselves only bigger, which can be collectively punched in the nose for the evil actions it collectively chooses to do. If the German people are not "responsible" for "their" nation's war crimes, the world becomes a complicated and terrifying place, in which un-understood social forces move men puppetlike to perform terrible acts, and in which guilt is at once universal and meaningless. Unhappily, the world is in fact such a place.

One of the reasons anthropology is so interesting to the politically-minded today is because its method of observation, already used successfully on primitive societies, can be applied very usefully to contemporary society, and is already being so applied by Dollard, Benedict, the Lynds and others. May we not, indeed, expect some future historian to write of us as one scholar has written of the ancient Hebrews:

"They explained nearly all phenomena by the direct action of superhuman and invisible persons and powers, resembling the human spirit. Like the 'primitives,' they recognized no essential difference between the spiritual and the material. Like them, too, they conceived of a solidarity, or more accurately, a practical identity, between many beings, events and things which we regard as absolutely distinct."

This animistic confusion marks the common man's thinking (with plenty of help from his political rulers) not only on relations between nations but also on the relation between the State and the individual citizen. Precisely because in this sphere the individual is most powerless in reality, do his rulers make their greatest efforts to present the State not only as an instrument for *his* purposes but as an extension of *his* personality. They have to try to do this because of the emphasis on the free individual which the bourgeois revolution has made part of our political assumptions (for how long?).

Hegel, who developed an anti-individualist theory of Statism while the cannons of the Napoleonic wars were still echoing, saw the problem clearly and tried to meet it in such terms as these:

> In the State, everything depends upon the unity of the universal and the particular. In the ancient States, the subjective purpose was absolutely one with the will of the State. In modern times, on the contrary, we demand an individual opinion, an individual will and conscience. The ancients had none of these in the modern sense; the final

thing for them was the will of the State.* While in Asiatic despotisms, the individual had no inner self and no self-justification, in the modern world man demands to be honored for the sake of his subjective individuality.

The union of duty and right has the twofold aspect that what the State demands as duty should directly be the right of the individual, since the State is nothing but the organization of the concept of freedom. The determinations of the individual will are given by the State objectivity, and it is through the State alone that they attain truth and realization. . . .

To the complete State belongs, essentially, consciousness and thought. The State knows thus what it wills, and it knows it under the form of thought. . . . The State must be regarded as a great architectonic edifice, a hieroglyph of reason, manifesting itself in reality. . . . That the State is the self-determining and the completely sovereign will, the final decision being necessarily referred to it—that is easy to comprehend. (Hegel: *The Philosophy of Law.*)

We may be sure, at any rate, that Stalin—or Roosevelt—would find these animistic formulations of the great philosopher of modern reaction "easy to comprehend." Nor would they be at all fazed by another passage in the same essay:

The people without its monarch and without that whole organization necessarily and directly connected with him is a formless mass, which is no longer a State. In a people, not conceived in a lawless and unorganized condition, but as a self-developed and truly organic totality—in such a people, sovereignty is the personality of the whole, and this is represented in reality by the person of the monarch.

* Hegel fails to mention the great and shining exception: the Greeks, who, to Plato's disgust, were individualistic and democratic to what today would be considered an insane degree. They found the State sometimes boring, sometimes absurd, and sometimes hateful, but never worthy of a man's respect. For an informative, learned, witty, and fascinating account of these curious folk, to whom we are still indebted for most of the few decent and agreeable aspects our culture still retains, see H. D. F. Kitto's *The Greeks* (Penguin Books). There were only a few hundred thousand of them, and their society lasted only a century or so, but never in history have so many owed so much to so few. (*1953*)

Will, consciousness, conscience, thought, personality—these are the attributes of the Hegelian State, the whole theory culminating in the "person of the monarch" as the symbol and expression of the "organic totality." The "responsibility of peoples" is direct and all-embracing, according to such a theory.

"Lives of nations," said Roosevelt in his 1940 Inaugural Address, "are determined not by the count of years, but by the lifetime of the human spirit. The life of a man is three-score years and ten. . . . The life of a nation is the fulness of the measure of its will to live. . . . A nation, like a person, has a body. A nation, like a person, has a mind. . . . A nation, like a person, has something deeper, something more permanent. . . . It is that something which matters most to its future, which calls for the most sacred guarding of its present."

5. If Everyone Is Guilty, No One Is Guilty

From the "Organic State" conception, it follows that no individual citizen or group of citizens may think or act otherwise than in accordance with the policies laid down by those in control of the State apparatus. When cells in a biological organism cut loose from their organic function, the result is cancer. Similar behavior by the citizen-cells of the Organic State is political cancer. The old Roman fable of the belly and the members by which the patricians defended their position against the plebs, this is still the basic argument of the "organicists."

In an organism, obviously no line can be drawn between the whole (the nation, or the people) and the parts (the individual citizens, the specific classes and interest-groups). The hands that strangle are no more guilty than the belly which nourishes them; the specialized "Jew-killing experts" are no more guilty than the peasants who raise the food they eat or the metalworkers who forge their instruments.

Thus the theory is convenient for those in power on two scores: internally, it preserves the ladder of hierarchy, making rebellious behavior treason not only to those in authority but also to the alleged common interests of everybody, to what is reverently termed "national unity" these days; in time of war, it makes it possible to treat the enemy population as a homogeneous single block, all of them equally wicked and detestable. This second use is what concerns us here: it is the theoretical underpinning of the concept that the German people are responsible for the horrors of Nazism.

But if everyone is guilty, then no one is guilty. The dialectics of this are wonderfully illustrated in an anecdote quoted by Hannah Arendt ("Organized Guilt and Universal Responsibility," *Jewish Frontier*, January, 1945) from *PM* of Nov. 12, 1944. An American correspondent interviews an official of a "death camp" who had fallen into the hands of the Russians:

Q. Did you kill people in the camp? A. Yes.

Q. Did you poison them with gas? A. Yes.

Q. Did you bury them alive? A. It sometimes happened.

Q. Did you personally help to kill people? A. Absolutely not. I was only paymaster in the camp.

Q. What did you think of what was going on? A. It was bad at first, but we got used to it.

Q. Do you know the Russians will hang you? A. (bursting into tears) Why should they? What have I done?

What have I done? These words ring true. One feels that the worthy paymaster—imagine the civilization that has produced the job of paymaster in a death camp!—is sincerely outraged by the proposal to hang him for his part in killing several million human beings. What had he done indeed? Simply obeyed orders and kept his mouth shut. It was what he had *not* done that shocks our moral sensibilities. But from the standpoint of the Organic State he is no more and no less guilty than every other person in Germany and deserves hanging no more and no less. Soldiers must obey their officers, just as citizens must obey the law. Stalin and Roosevelt would certainly not permit their own soldiers to discriminate, on the frivolous grounds of personal conscience, between one military order and another. Harold Denny in the N. Y. *Times* of Feb. 17, 1945, tells about a captured noncom who had witnessed the execution of forty Jewish men, women and children in Brest-Litovsk. "The only thoughts I had about it," he said, "were that it was ordered from above and that those who ordered it must have had their important reasons. By now we have been educated in such a manner that we no longer discuss given orders but agree to them without question." Asked whether he himself would be capable of carrying out such an order, he replied, after reflection, that he thought he would be, adding: "I cannot say I would have had fun doing it—not the least little bit. It could only be under the compulsion of an order. To volunteer for it, that I could not do."

It is not the law-breaker we must fear today so much as he who obeys the law. The Germans have long been noted for their deep respect for law and order. This foible, which one could smile at as an amiable weakness in the past, has assumed a sinister aspect under the Nazis. One of the most hopeful auguries for the future of this country, with the Permanent War Economy taking shape, is that we Americans have a long and honorable tradition of lawlessness and disrespect for authority.

Only those who are willing to resist authority themselves when it conflicts too intolerably with their personal moral code, only they have the right to condemn the death-camp paymaster. Certainly those who preach, or practice, the Organic State have no such right. (For all that, the Russian authorities, untroubled by such nice points, have probably long since hung the fellow—while we agonize over the rights and wrongs of the case.) Yet can even *we* really condemn the paymaster? For the Organic State is by no means only an ideological slogan devised by those in authority; it also corresponds to the real arrangement of things in the modern world. The principles on which our mass-industry economy is built—centralization of authority, division of labor (or specialization of function), rigid organization from the top down into which each worker fits at his appointed hierarchical level

—these have been carried over into the political sphere. The result is that, as we have seen above, the individual has little choice about his behavior, and can be made to function, by the pressure and terror wielded by the masters of the Organic State, in ways quite opposed to any he would voluntarily choose. I have been told that the Nazis created a Jewish section of the Gestapo and that these creatures were much more feared by their fellow Jews than were the regular Gestapo men, since they would never dare take a bribe or show the slightest good nature. There were also Jewish policemen in the Warsaw ghetto, working loyally with the Nazis. We may imagine the pressure against these individuals, and their families, which produced this behavior. And doubtless some Jews refused to play the role, and took the consequences. But probably not very many, for such Jews were heroes, and there are not many heroes among the Jews or among any other peoples today (except primitive folk like the Greeks and the Poles). Our paymaster was not a hero, and the Russians hung him for not being one—as they would have hung him for being one in *their* State.*

With their usual unerring cynicism, the Nazis exploit this moral weakness in the German people—that they are not heroes. The official SS organ recently editorialized:

> There are no innocents in Germany. We have not yet met a single German who for political reasons had refused marriage, children, family support, reductions of taxes or paid vacations only because National Socialism had made them possible. On the contrary, they grew fat and stout under the prosperity of National Socialism. They felt no pangs of conscience at the "Aryanization" of Jewish businesses. They had their full share in the prosperity. And they shouted "Hurrah" to our victories. . . . There were,

* Since the war ended, we have had much experience, most of it depressing, in trying to assess criminal responsibility for political crimes. The de-Nazification program and the Nuremberg Trials got all snarled up in the Responsibility of Peoples. That bewildering concept also transmuted the whole population of Berlin in three years from Nazi beasts to democratic heroes. See "The Germans—Three Years Later." (*1953*)

> it is true, lamblike innocents who did not want to declare war upon any country and who did for the German war effort only as much as they had to. But even these did not object to making money from the war or from National Socialism. They liked to ride in their new cars on our new highways and to travel on our "Strength through Joy" excursions. Nobody, after all, has preferred a democratic death to a National Socialist life.
>
> (Editorial in *Das Schwarze Korps*, quoted in the *Neue Volkszeitung*, New York City, for Feb. 10, 1945.)

The *Schwarze Korps*, of course, exaggerates: as we shall presently see, scores of Germans every day "prefer" (at least get—which I admit is not necessarily quite the same thing) a "democratic death" to a "National Socialist life." But, from the Organic standpoint, it is quite true that "no one is innocent." With their customary political logic, the Nazis of late have deliberately tried to involve the whole German people in the moral responsibility for their crimes. In her brilliant article in the *Jewish Frontier*, Hannah Arendt describes this process and its political consequences.

> The terror-organizations, which were at first strictly separated from the mass of the people, admitting only persons who could show a criminal past or prove their preparedness to become criminals, have since been continually expanded. . . . Whereas those crimes which have always been a part of the daily routine of concentration camps since the beginning of the Nazi regime were at first a jealously guarded monopoly of the SS and Gestapo, today members of the Wehrmacht are assigned at will to the duties of mass murder. These crimes were at first kept secret by every possible means and any publication of such reports was made punishable as atrocity propaganda. Later, however, such reports were spread by Nazi-organized whispering campaigns and today these crimes are openly proclaimed under the title of "measures of liquidation" in order to force "Volksgenossen" whom difficulties of organization made it impossible to induct into the "Volksgemeinschaft" of crime at least to bear the onus of complicity and awareness of what was going on. These tactics resulted in a victory for the Nazis, and the Allies

> abandoned the distinction between Germans and Nazis. . . .
> National Socialism's chances of organizing an underground movement in the future depends on there being no visible signs of distinction any longer, and above all on the victorious powers' being convinced that there really are no differences between Germans.

6. We, Too, Are Guilty

If "they," the German people, are responsible for the atrocious policies and actions of "their" (in the possessive and possessing sense, again) government, then "we," the peoples of Russia, England and America, must also take on a big load of responsibility.

We forced defeated Germany, after World War I, into a blind alley from which the only escape was another blind alley, Nazism; this we did by throwing our weight against socialist revolution. After Hitler took power, more or less with our blessing as a lesser evil to revolution, we allowed him to rearm Germany in the hopes we could turn him against Russia, and we used "non-intervention" to aid him and Mussolini to overthrow the Spanish Republic in the "dress rehearsal" for World War II.

In the present war, we have carried the saturation bombing of German cities to a point where "military objectives" are secondary to the incineration or suffocation of great numbers of civilians; we have betrayed the Polish underground fighters in Warsaw into the hands of the Nazis, have deported hundreds of thousands of Poles to slow-death camps in Siberia, and have taken by force a third of Poland's territory; we have conducted a civil war against another ally, Greece, in order to restore a reactionary and unpopular monarch; we have starved those parts of Europe our armies have "liberated" almost as badly as the Nazis did, and if we explain that the shipping was needed for our armies, they can retort that the food was needed for *their* armies; we have followed Nazi racist theories in segregating Negro soldiers in our military forces and in deporting from their homes on the West

Coast to concentration camps in the interior tens of thousands of citizens who happened to be of Japanese ancestry; we have made ourselves the accomplice of the Maidanek butchers by refusing to permit more than a tiny trickle of the Jews of Europe to take refuge inside our borders; we have ruled India brutally, imprisoning the people's leaders, denying the most elementary civil liberties, causing a famine last year in which hundreds of thousands perished; we have—

But this is monstrous, you say? We, the people, didn't do these things. They were done by a few political leaders, and the majority of Americans, Englishmen and (perhaps—who knows?) Russians deplore them and favor quite different policies. Or if they don't, then it is because they have not had a chance to become aware of the real issues and to act on them. In any case, *I* can accept no responsibility for such horrors. I and most of the people I know are vigorously opposed to such policies and have made our disapproval constantly felt in the pages of the *Nation* and on the speaker's platforms of the Union for Democratic Action.

Precisely. And the Germans could say the same thing. And if you say, but why didn't you get rid of Hitler if you didn't like his policies, they can say: But you people (in America and England, at least) merely had to vote against your Government to overthrow it, while we risked our necks if we even talked against ours. Yet you Britishers have tolerated Churchill for five years, and you Americans have thrice re-elected Roosevelt by huge majorities.

It is a terrible fact, but it is a fact, that few people have the imagination or the moral sensitivity to get very excited about actions which they don't participate in themselves (and hence about which they feel no personal responsibility). The scale and complexity of modern Governmental organization, and the concentration of political power at the top, are such that the vast majority of people are excluded from this participation. How many votes did Roosevelt's refugee policy cost him? What political damage was done the Churchill-Labor government by its treatment of India, or by last year's Bombay famine? What percentage of the American electorate is deeply concerned about the mass starvation of the Italians under the Allied occupation? As the French say, to ask such questions is to answer them.

7. The Political Meaning of Collective War Guilt

The theory of the German people's collective responsibility for Nazi policies not only (1) ignores the deep cleavages between the Nazis and the people, but also (2) cements these cracks up again.

(1) If the theory were correct, one would expect to find the German people following the Nazis' war leadership with docility if not with enthusiasm. Actually, according to official German figures (N. Y. *Times,* Dec. 20, 1944), "People's Courts" executions (mostly involving treason and other offenses against the State) rose 5,000% in the first four years of the war: from 99 in 1939 to 1,292 in 1941 to 5,336 in 1943. These figures don't include the death sentences passed in the regular courts, nor the thousands of Germans executed annually without trial by the Gestapo, the Elite Guard, etc. The 1944 figures are unavailable but are probably much higher than 1943: estimates of the executions after last summer's attempt on Hitler's life run into the tens of thousands. "After the proclamation of total mobilization as a link in 'the holy war of the entire people,'" writes a neutral correspondent just back from Germany (N. Y. *Times Magazine,* Sept. 24, 1944), "Nazi leaders ordered all Nazis to report immediately to the Gestapo any defeatist utterances. . . . Well above a hundred of my worker friends and their acquaintances have recently disappeared, 'spurlos versenkt.'" Facts like these, even if we grant there is little organized opposition to the Nazis inside Germany, suggests the fuel is ready from which might spring the flames of an anti-Nazi revolution, if the right spark were provided. But it would be difficult to say which dreads such a spark the most, the Nazis or the Big Three.

(2) It is likely that not since 1934 have the Nazis commanded the popular support they have today. Goebbels and

Roosevelt are agreed on one thing at least: that the German people's destiny is identical with that of the Nazis. On the one hand, we have the Nazis organizing a popular *maquis* to carry on the struggle against the Allies for years after the war, pointing to the Morgenthau Plan as conclusive evidence of the Jewish plot against Germany, and telling the German people—with the novel advantage that the propaganda is true—that there is no alternative except a fight to the bitter end under Hitler's leadership. On the other hand, we have the Big Three insisting on "unconditional surrender" (a formula, let us note, which was evolved not by the totalitarian Stalin nor the Tory Churchill but by the common man's friend, Roosevelt), proposing to enslave millions of German males, to reduce Germany to a semi-agricultural status, etc. Thus from both sides of the battle-lines, the German people are told that the Nazis' survival is their only hope of survival, that the Nazis *are Germany* (a claim the Nazis have long made but up to now have been unable to get generally accepted).

For one curious result of the "all-are-guilty" line, which is put forward by those who profess the utmost detestation of Nazism, is that it makes Nazism (or its equivalent called by some other name) the logical *postwar* form of regime for defeated Germany. This comes out nakedly if one considers the most fully developed "organic" theory on Germany—that, fittingly enough, propounded by the Nazis' fellow totalitarian regime in Russia. One finds Moscow promoting hatred of Germans as Germans (not only as Nazis) and proposing the most Draconic treatment of Germany after the war, and at the same time encouraging German military nationalism through the Von Seidlitz officers' committee. A contradiction? Only superficially. The "organic" theory leads precisely to the retention of the Nazis and *junkers* as the German people's rulers. The logic: all are guilty; therefore no one is more guilty than another; therefore, the Nazis and the *junkers* are no more guilty than their opponents; therefore, if it is convenient—and it *is* convenient—it is permissible to keep the Nazis and *junkers* (except a few that are hung for demonstration purposes) in power. Thus we have Stalin using the generals and Eisenhower using the SS and the Nazi police. "In Germany there will be no fraternization," proclaimed Eisenhower's Order of the Day of Oct. 12, 1944. "We go in as conquerors." * The logical result of this Order was reported in the London *Tribune* of Nov. 24, 1944: "Front-line correspondents report that posters have been put up everywhere in the British and American zones announcing that 52 different Nazi organizations are to be disbanded. This figure does not, however, include all Nazi organizations. Some

---

* Eisenhower's Order of the Day resulted in such edifying scenes as the following, reported by a private in the occupation forces in the Sept. 1945 *Politics:* "We had finished eating and there was a large amount left over. Children of between six and ten were standing around hoping to catch a morsel. We then proceeded to dig a hole and bury the food." For, according to the purest form of the Responsibility of Peoples doctrine, no moral distinction is made between children and grown-ups. "Would not the punishment of all Germans inflict needless hardship on millions of German children who can in no way be held responsible for the crimes of their elders?" a man in the audience asked Major Erwin Lessner during a 1945 Town-Meeting-of-the-Air debate between the major and Dorothy Thompson. "Of course it would," admitted, or rather insisted, the major. "These innocent German children are the potential soldiers of World War III, just as the innocent German children who had been fed after 1918 later served in Hitler's army and did remarkably well." Today, General Eisenhower (and doubtless the major too) thinks highly of the German people, since he needs them desperately in his NATO army, and it is a plus and not a minus for German kids that they are "potential soldiers of World War III." In seven years, the German people have risen from beasts to defenders of democracy, and the Russian people have changed as radically in the reverse direction.

Personally, I find the attitude of Louis XIV more congenial. France was at war with England when the second Eddystone Lighthouse was being built, early in the eighteenth century. A French privateer carried off the builders to France, where they were imprisoned. Louis XIV learned of this action when the French captain applied to him for a reward. *Le Roi Soleil* was indignant. "I am at war with England, not with mankind," he declared, in the grand manner. And he sent the Eddystone builders back to England with rich presents, thoughtfully filling their prison cells with the French captain and crew. (*1953*)

of these have been ordered to their stations and barracks, to await further orders. Among them are the Hitler Youth, the Nazi Police, and the SS." Some all-are-guilty enthusiasts even insist that the German people are so despicable that they *deserve* to be ruled forever by the Nazis! Thus the most extreme anti-Nazism turns into its dialectical opposite.

So much for the effect on the German people of the collective responsibility theory. It is equally disastrous for the Allied peoples. Last summer everyone thought the war in Europe would be over by the fall. The Anglo-Americans had broken out of Normandy and were racing across France in pursuit of the disorganized German armies; the Russians were advancing on all their fronts; an attempt on Hitler's life was almost successful; the popular mood inside Germany was one of panic and loss of confidence in Hitler's leadership. At that moment, it would not have taken much political pressure to pry loose the people from the Nazis and to bring the whole structure down. Instead of applying this pressure, the Allies reiterated the "unconditional surrender" line, embellished with such grace notes as the Morgenthau Plan. They succeeded in convincing the German people, as Hitler's most frenetic orations could not have convinced them, that their only hope was to stand firm behind the Nazis. To make sure the Germans didn't miss the point, the American High Command staged a special demonstration at Aachen, the first sizable German city our troops reached. Aachen was defended by a single second-rate division, reinforced by one SS unit and a few fortress troops. The defenders cooperated splendidly with the attackers: for one week, the city, ringed with American divisions and artillery units, was bombed and shelled. It was finally taken "the hard way," by an all-out infantry assault backed up by tanks and God knows what else. Militarily, not exactly brilliant. But politically sound enough, for the city was reduced to rubble, thousands of its inhabitants were killed (and a good many American soldiers, too), and notice was served on all Germany (and on the Americans) of what was in store for it (and them).

It is not worth wasting printer's ink to prove that, militarily, the "Aachen policy" is inferior to a policy which would split the German people from the Nazis, and that such a policy would save an enormous number of American, British and Russian lives. But when have military considerations been allowed to interfere with the more serious business of politics (except, of course, when bestarred generals urge strikers not to interfere with the "war effort")? The Big Three want things to be done in an orderly way, with the masses' properly constituted rulers remaining on top; they don't want any unauthorized popular movements behind their own lines and they don't want them behind the enemy lines either. Only a liberal editor would seriously point out to them that military victory could be had more rapidly by encouraging the internal break-up of Germany. They are well aware of that fact, but, as responsible ruling-class leaders, they are unwilling to abandon their principles for the sake of military expediency.*

"Modern war," wrote Simone Weil, "appears as a struggle led by all the State apparatuses and their general staffs against all men old enough to bear arms. . . . The great error of nearly all studies of war . . . has been to consider war as an episode in foreign policies, when it is especially an act of

* No! No! Marxistical baby-talk! Not a question of "the masses' properly constituted rulers remaining on top" at all; goes much deeper than these antiquated class-war concepts, profound a century ago but now superficial and misleading. The only serious threat to Nazi rule from within Germany during the war came not from the masses, but from the upper class: the conspiracy of generals and Junker aristocrats, plus a couple of liberal politicians, which culminated in the near-assassination of Hitler in August, 1944. The conspirators wanted to overthrow the Nazis and make peace simply because they were (correctly) convinced that Hitler was leading Germany to ruin. They envisaged a capitalist democracy not very different from our own (or from the present Bonn Government, for that matter), and certainly no revolutionary upheaval. Yet the concept of the Responsibility of Peoples, as expressed in Roosevelt's "unconditional surrender" line, was so strong that they got no encouragement or support from the Allies in their effort to destroy Hitler's rule from within. (*1953*)

interior politics, and the most atrocious act of all." (*Politics,* February, 1945.)

The common peoples of the world are coming to have less and less control over the policies of "their" governments, while at the same time they are being more and more closely identified with those governments. Or to state it in slightly different terms: as the common man's *moral* responsibility diminishes (assuming agreement that the degree of moral responsibility is in direct proportion to the degree of freedom of choice), his *practical* responsibility increases. Not for many centuries have individuals been at once so powerless to influence what is done by the national collectivities to which they belong, and at the same time so generally held responsible for what is done by those collectivities.

Where can the common peoples look for relief from this intolerable agonizing contradiction? Not to their traditional defender, the labor movement. This no longer exists in Russia, and in the two great bourgeois democracies, it has quite lost touch with the humane and democratic ideals it once believed in. Last fall, the British Trade Union Congress endorsed, 5 to 1, a statement that the German people are responsible for the crimes of Nazism; and a few weeks later the CIO convention over here resolved: "The German people must . . . atone for the crimes and horrors which they have visited on the earth." Such international working-class solidarity as once existed has vanished, and the workers of the world, including and especially those of the Soviet Union, are as brutally and rabidly nationalistic—*in their capacity as organized workers*—as their own ruling classes are.

We must look both more widely and more deeply for relief from the dilemma of increasing political impotence accompanied by increasing political responsibility. To our essential humanity and to a more sensitive and passionate respect for our own and other people's humanity.

Harold Denny in the N. Y. *Times* of Feb. 18, 1945, tells the story of a captured SS private. He was a young Ukrainian farmer who was impressed into the SS when the Germans retreated from Russia last summer. Fed up, apathetic, without interest even in tracing his family, he "appears to have no hatreds, no likes and little resentment. . . . To all questions he replies, 'I cannot know anything about that. Everything's so mixed up.' He looks and acts like a man in a profound state of shock." But the Ukrainian-farmer-SS-man had learned one thing, and he gave it as his only value-judgment:

"We are all human beings. If we had peace, if people would work together, they'd perhaps be comrades. But now—."

Massacre from the Air

"Aerial bombardment for the purpose of terrorizing the civilian population, of destroying or damaging civilian property not of a military character, or of injuring non-combatants is prohibited." Thus, Article 28, Part II of the Rules of Warfare adopted by the great powers, including the US (or us), at the 1922 Washington Conference on the Limitation of Armaments. By the time World War II was over, some 500,000 European civilians had died under American and British bombs. (Since only about 300,000 of them were Germans, it is evident that the Responsibility of Peoples, or at least the Punishment of Peoples, had a much wider scope than can be explained by virtuous indignation over the crimes of Hitler. For the 200,000 non-German civilians killed by Anglo-American bombs belonged to the peoples who had been conquered by Hitler's armies and whom we were "liberating"—in this case, from life itself.)

The Allies' decision to rely so heavily on strategic bombing (i.e., bombing directed against cities, industrial plants, seaports, and workers' housing—some 3,600,000 German homes were destroyed—as distinguished from tactical bombing, which is used in direct support of military operations on the battlefield) was doubtless due not to wickedness but to a belief in the military effectiveness of such bombing as a means of destroying the enemy's industry and breaking the morale of his population. How effective it actually was against industry is problematical. It is doubtful if it broke down morale; on the contrary, most evidence suggests the Germans reacted as the people of London did to the great Nazi air-raids: they hated the enemy all the more and felt all the more that their only hope lay in supporting their own leaders. Even if it did damage morale, there was little the Germans could have done about it. As General Montgomery bluntly put it: "Destruction is now going on wholesale. Every single big and little town is being blown up. . . . German public opinion cannot say they are sick of it. So it's got to go on. If there were any public opinion left, it would rise up and say, 'Finish!' But if any one does rise up, he gets bumped off." (N. Y. *Times*, April 14, 1945.) So it's got to go on, and, according to the theory of the Responsibility of Peoples, the Germans deserved what they got. But we Americans, according to the same theory, have some slight Responsibility ourselves for massacring a half million European civilians.

It is interesting to note that, just as the democracies and not the totalitarian powers developed and used the atomic bomb, so too the British and American air forces relied mostly on strategic bombing, directed against civilians, while the Nazis and the Russians went in more for the relatively more civilized tactical bombing, directed against troops and military installations. This was, of course, not for humanitarian reasons, but partly because the democracies had the industrial production to sustain the vast operations of strategic bombing (the US alone spent some $43 billions on bombing Germany and occupied Europe), and partly because—at least according to General J. F. C. Fuller in his brilliant and provocative military history of World War II—the totalitarian powers thought in military terms and realized that from the purely military point of view strategic bombing is not worth while. If this be true, and the general makes a *prima facie* case that it is, then our murderous bombing policy must be set alongside Roosevelt's Unconditional Surrender policy, which prolonged the war by many months since it offered no inducement to any group of Germans to try to overthrow Hitler and come to terms with the Allies. The theory behind both policies was that the whole German people, without exception, must be punished as the guilty accomplices of Hitler. In short, to Roosevelt-Churchill as much as to Hitler, the war was a crusade, a Day of Judgment with heavy bombers in the role of archangels with flaming swords. "The worst thing about crusades," writes General Fuller, "is that their ideological aims justify the use of all means, however abominable and atrocious. Thus though in 1139 the Lateran Council, under penalty of anathema, forbade the use of the cross-bow 'as a weapon hateful to God and unfit for Christians,' it sanctioned its use against infidels." But, of course, the general is a political reactionary and an old-fashioned militarist who thinks that "the object of war is not slaughter and devastation but to persuade the enemy to change his mind."

Apropos this last point, cf. an editorial paragraph I wrote in *Politics* for May, 1944:

> Roosevelt's reply to the protest of the American clergymen against saturation bombing of Germany is a curious exercise in logic. "Obviously," writes Presidential Secretary Steve Early, "Obviously the President is just as disturbed and horrified by the destruction of life in this war as any members of the committee. Thousands of people not in uniform have been killed. The easiest way to prevent many others from being killed is to use every effort to compel the Germans and Japanese to change their philosophy. As long as their philosophy lasts, we shall have more deaths, more destruction and more wars. That philosophy has nothing of Christianity in it." Thus we have this interesting syllogism: The Germans' philosophy is not Christian because it is based on death and destruction. Our philosophy *is* (by implication) Christian. Therefore, the only way to get the Germans to accept our philosophy is to inflict unlimited death and destruction on them. Q. E. D.

From "The Root Is Man," 1953

The Germans—Three Years Later

Note: The Russian blockade of Berlin in the winter of 1948-49 produced a dramatic reversal of the wartime roles of two aggregations of people, the US Air Force and the population of Berlin. The former changed from executioners into relief workers delivering coal and food instead of bombs to the latter, who in turn were transmuted, in our press, from cowardly accomplices of one kind of totalitarianism into heroic resisters against another kind. Since these reversals had very little to do with any free-will choice or action by the human beings who made up the two groups, the episode struck me as an ironic verification of my objections to the concept of collective responsibility, and I wrote for the Winter, 1949, issue of Student Partisan, *a mimeographed undergraduate publication at the University of Chicago, the following article:*

Man lives in history but is not at all comfortable there. Even at best—by which I mean in a smallish, integrated community like the ancient Greek city state—there is always a desperate struggle between what the individual wants and what happens to him as a result of living in society. (The process of hauling the individual about like a bale, or a corpse, and cramming him into some badly fitting context of ideology or action—this is what is euphemistically called "history.") And at worst—by which I mean the big-scale, industrial-bureaucratic societies in which the peoples of USA, USSR, and most of Europe toss and twist—there is not even a struggle: the individual "citizen" (what a mockery!) has about the same chance of determining his own fate as a hog dangling by one foot from the conveyor belt of a Chicago packing plant.

Not since the completion of the River Rouge plant have we seen so dramatic an expression of American industrial genius as the Berlin airlift. For months now, a city of over two million inhabitants has received all its essential supplies by air. The ingenuity, technical precision, and materialistic mastery shown in this operation are the high point of post-Renaissance man's long successful struggle to master nature. What vistas of progress the Victorians, if they could have imagined such a triumph, would have seen stretching away into the future!

Yet we have already seen, only three years ago, another airlift, perhaps not quite so amazing technically but still impressive enough, manned by the same kind of skilful young Americans and aimed at the same city and the same people, but whose cargo was not food and coal but rather blockbusters. Certainly we live in a world of shifting, flickering shadows, of protean shapes that suddenly change from horror to benevolence, from death to life. What is reality and what is illusion here? Were the bombs real, or is the food real? Were the young Americans who so masterfully bombed Berlin evil men? And are their similars who are with equal mastery keeping the city alive good men?

Clearly, such concepts cannot be used here. In the last month of the war, the American air force destroyed in two nights the city of Dresden: one of the loveliest collections of architecture in Europe, a city of no military significance and with no war industry to speak of, a city that at the time was crammed with civilian refugees from the East, hundreds of thousands of whom died under the American firebombs. Yet I venture to say that very few of the Americans who planned and executed this atrocity felt any special hatred of the churches and refugees they destroyed. Nor do the airlift personnel today feel any special love for the Berliners they are feeding. There is indeed a logic to both actions, but it is not a human, not a rational or ethical logic. It is rather the logic of a social mechanism which has grown so powerful that human beings have become simply its instruments.

Such a viewpoint is chill and uncomfortable. Hence the importance of political mythologists who "humanize" these vast impersonal processes by injecting good and evil concepts into them. So in the last war it was possible to convince many Americans—especially those who had been to college and there had acquired the dangerous knack of thinking in general terms—that the German people were the accomplices rather than the first victims of Hitler; that they were collectively responsible for the Nazi horrors. To construct this myth required much rewriting and re-interpretation of history, in the style of the Soviet Politburo, to show that the Germans have been militaristic since Tacitus. It was also necessary to ignore such facts as that the concentration camps up to 1939 were filled with Germans, and only with Germans, that the majority of Germans in 1933 voted against Hitler, and that the existence of the great death camps of 1942–44 was carefully concealed from the German people. It was also necessary to ignore the fact, above all, that there is only one kind of person who can be expected to resist the policy of a totalitarian state like Nazi Germany or Stalinist Russia, namely, the hero.

Heroism, like artistic talent, has always been a rare quality. To expect the average German—or American—to be a hero is about as reasonable as to demand that he be a poet. The absurdity of this whole approach appears in the fact that today the same Berliners who were denounced three years ago as cowards and sadists because they didn't "stop Hitler," are now presented as a race of heroes because they are resisting Russian pressure. The only Germans who can be called heroes are those in the Soviet zone who are actively fighting against the Russians. There aren't many of them, just as there weren't many Frenchmen who took part in the Resistance, and just as there would not be many Americans who would resist a native fascism once it got its repressive apparatus functioning. Heroes just aren't very common, that's all. And nothing is more vulgar than the type of liblab journalist or scholar—like Thomas Mann, for example, or the late editors of *PM*—who demand of others a heroism which it is doubtful, putting it charitably, that they themselves possess.

This does not mean that the Berliners have not showed courage in siding with the West. Nor does it mean that it makes no difference, practically or ethically, which side they choose. I think it makes a great deal of difference, and I am very glad they have chosen the West. The point, rather, is the obvious one—obvious, that is, to everyone except a well-educated liblab—that almost everybody acts politically according to the relationship of two factors: (a) his own values, (b) the risk of expressing those values. In Hitler's Berlin, as in Stalin's Moscow, the risk—assuming one's values, as I believe was the case with the great majority of Berliners and is similarly the case in Moscow, run counter to the policy of the regime—the risk, I say, was so terrifying as to deter all but the tiny minority of heroes. In Berlin today, however, since the Western armies are still in occupation, the only risk is the possible future exit of those armies. (I lack space here to go into the political dilemma posed for socialists and pacifists by the fact that the American army, a most reactionary organization whose purpose is mass slaughter, is the only bulwark protecting the trade unions and popularly elected government of Berlin against liquidation by the Russians. Such feeble civil liberties as the Berliners now have, and the possibility of winning more later on, depend on the US Army staying there. This is a real dilemma for all us Utopians, one not to be charmed away by *our* mythologists.) Since the future exit of those armies is always a possibility, it takes some courage to side now openly with the West. Courage—not heroism; most people *do* have courage, in moderate, reasonable amounts.

The really significant thing about the Berliners' support of the West against the Russians is not the courage it shows—which, as just noted, is what any one but a mythmaker would expect of the Germans, or of any other people—but rather the fact that given the chance to express, without too much risk, their preference, they have so overwhelmingly chosen bourgeois democracy over totalitarianism. This is part of a worldwide phenomenon since the war.

In almost every situation where there have been reasonably

free elections, the Communists have lost out. And this, too, despite the fact that all the West offers is a continuance of a most imperfect status quo. The slogans are all on the Communists' side; even the historical tradition of social revolution is more on their side than on capitalist America's. Yet most people seem to still possess enough primitive sense of their own materialistic interests, enough distaste for the police state even when bedecked with red banners, to prefer Western "decadence" and "stagnation" to the dynamism of the terrible Utopia offered by the East.

This is a modest enough triumph. There is very little that we can honestly say in praise of the institutions and culture of Western capitalism beyond the statement that, now that we have seen thirty years of Communist development, the comparison is greatly in favor of capitalism. But it is something in these dark times that the population of Berlin, after fifteen years of Nazism, saturation bombing, and postwar starvation, still has enough human feeling and vitality left to offer some resistance to totalitarianism. Perhaps human nature is less malleable than the modern dictators assume. Perhaps we may even draw some optimistic conclusions about the "national character" of the *Russian* people from the case of Berlin.

Student Partisan, Univ. of Chicago, Winter 1949

Notes on the Psychology of Killing

ONE OF THE THINGS which make it possible for a modern civilian to participate in war without more psychological resistance than he has is the fact that the murderous aspect of war is depersonalized. Most of the killing is done at such long range that the killers have no sense of the physical effects of their attack. It is true that they themselves are often on the receiving end of such attacks, and might be expected to realize what happens to the enemy by analogy with their own experiences, but the ordinary man, perhaps mercifully, is not especially imaginative that way. And anyway, it is one thing to know that one may be responsible for the death and mutilation of invisible people ten miles away or five miles down, and another to cut a man's throat with one's own hands.

Thinking along these lines, one finds three levels of warfare.

Level No. 1: aerial and artillery bombardment, whether of troops or cities; robot bombs, where the principle of indiscriminate blind destruction becomes dramatically clear, although actually robot bombing is no more indiscriminate than the saturation bombing with which the British night raiders obliterate German cities; mines and booby traps, where time as well as space draws a curtain between killer and victim; naval warfare, in which the opposing fleets often cannot see each other. On both the giving and the receiving end, all these types of warfare seem to be as impersonal as a thunderstorm. This kind of killing by remote control makes up the great bulk of modern warfare.*

---

* "The majority of casualties are now inflicted by artillery fire," writes Col. Lanza, "and may amount to 80% or more of the total." (See his comment on Napoleon's "Maxims" in "Napoleon and Modern War," Military Service Publishing Co., $1.)

A recent dispatch from France gives an idea of the terrible impersonality of this kind of fighting:

"My vantage point was an observation post for saturation artillery that had been pounding Jerry all night and the previous day. The valley stretched away to both flanks like a huge football stadium. An area of about 20 square miles was visible. . . . Spasmodically, like torches, flares would burst on the horizon as the shells found targets.

"At intervals of 20 or 30 minutes, the observation spotters would halt the fire from batteries located four or five miles to the rear. Then in the distance, out from the small forests and hedgerows, would appear a minute figure with a white flag. He would be followed by other small figures almost indistinguishable through the glasses. Another white flag would pop up from the green and soon the column of figures would grow large—20, 30, maybe 60 or 70

Level No. 2 is combat in which soldiers fight against individual and visible antagonists, but separated by distance, which they bridge by firearms. Aerial dogfights, sniping, rifle combat come under this head.* As in No. 1, the killing is done mechanically at long distance, without physical contact. The psychological effects probably resemble those of hunting, which is what it is, with the roles of hunter and hunted being constantly reversed.

On Level No. 3, one kills or cripples another human being by one's own personal efforts, in close physical contact, aided only by a knife, string, club or other simple tool. Here the essence of war cannot be concealed, and comes out nakedly in a way shocking to the normal Western individual. To perform successfully this kind of killing requires a brutalization far beyond that called for by No. 1 and No. 2. Even within level No. 3 itself, the rule holds: if one has no tool at all but just bare hands, the business of killing reaches its peak of horror so far as the killer is concerned. Thus the psychological and the statistical aspects of modern war move in opposite directions: the more powerful the weapons the greater the slaughter and the less the killer's consciousness of it. (This is possibly a factor of some importance in the survival of modern warfare as a social institution.)

---

marching men carrying 10 to 12 white squares of cloth. They would make the long trek to the American lines with upraised hands.

"When the catch was bagged, the merciless pounding would commence anew. The prisoners protested: 'It's nothing but butchery.'"

—*N. Y. World-Telegram,* Aug. 23, 1944

* Although the popular idea of warfare is still soldiers shooting at each other with rifles, fighting at Level No. 2 is today unimportant, at least from the standpoint of bloodshed. "In 1918," writes Col. Lanza, "only 11% of the casualties occurred from infantry fire; and in 1942 Russian statistics indicated that only 10% were due to this cause. . . . Some infantry soldiers in 1918 belonging to regiments which suffered heavy casualties in the six weeks' campaign in the Argonne, never fired their rifles, for they never saw any enemy to fire at."

The above generalizations were suggested by a little book titled *Kill—or Get Killed; a Manual of Hand-to-Hand Fighting* by Major Rex Applegate (Military Service Publishing Co., Harrisburg, Pa.; $2). This is a quasi-official manual, for the use of officers in training troops. After reading it, I'm not sure I should not, if pressed, choose the second alternative; there are limits even to self-preservation. The field is covered systematically, with chapters on such topics as "Strangulations" (by stick—"very efficient"; and by cord—"the thinner the diameter, the more instant the effectiveness") and "The Fighting Knife," with a discussion of the more efficient types —"efficient" is a favorite term of the author—and of the relative advantages various parts of the body offer for cutting, stabbing, hacking and ripping.

But much the stiffest chapter, in line with the rule noted above, is the one with the mild title, "Unarmed Offense." Here we learn the most "efficient" methods of eye-gouging ("best accomplished by placing a thumb on the inside of the eye socket next to the nose and flicking the eyeball out toward the edge of the cheek"), lip-tearing ("hook your thumb in the corner of the mouth and tear towards the hinge of the jaw"), sitting-neck-break (best undescribed), ear concussion blow ("approaching your opponent from the rear, you can rupture his eardrums by cupping both hands and simultaneously striking them against his ears"), kicks-to-kill ("After your opponent has been downed, the kill can be made with a kick. . . . It is best to be wearing heavy boots."), and, above all, the proper exploitation of the testicles. The author becomes positively lyrical about these "most vulnerable and sensitive parts of a man's body. . . . Any strong foot or hand blow delivered in the crotch will enable the weakest man to knock the strongest senseless or to disable him to the point where he is easily finished off by some other means. The strongest holds can be broken at any time by grasping an opponent's testicles and pulling and twisting them."

There is an anatomy of mayhem as well as of healing.

Major Applegate's general rule is simple enough: study the Marquis of Queensberry rules carefully, and then do the opposite. Hit below the belt and always kick a man when he is down (with "heavy boots," if possible). "Ruthlessness is what we seek to achieve. It is best defined in two words: speed and brutality. . . . Forget the rules and use the so-called 'foul' methods." The author recognizes that draftees from civilian life usually have strong prejudices against this sort of thing, prejudices which must be overcome by careful psychological conditioning. "The average American doughboy when shown a fighting knife for the first time, will have an aversion to its use as a killing implement. This same feeling is apparent in preliminary stages of bayonet training." The situation is by no means hopeless, however. Proper training methods can recondition the soldier until "the killing instinct becomes aroused to the point where he has confidence in the weapon and is not averse to using it."

The chapter describing one of these methods—the operation of a "practical indoor course" for hand-to-hand fighting—reads like the account of a Pavlovian experiment in conditioned reflexes, combined with elements of a parlor game and an Eden Musée. The course is laid out in a basement and consists of a series of rooms, pits, tunnels, and corridors in which dummies and targets, in enemy uniforms, are arranged to appear and disappear, to the accompaniment of various colored lights and sound effects, as the "student," armed to the teeth, makes his way over the course.

By a combination of shock, fright and induced rage the subject's civilized inhibitions are broken down and he is conditioned to stab and shoot by reflex action. "There is no limit to the possibilities of this range," writes the author proudly. "The only limitation is the ingenuity of the builder." This is an exaggeration: the British used similar courses in training their commandos several years ago, with additional improvements such as booby traps, collapsible stairs and showers of animal blood, but they had to be toned down, apparently because the effect on the students was too severe. Perhaps by World War III, mankind will have progressed far enough to permit the use of these more realistic devices.

By World War IV, it may be possible to substitute live prisoners for the dummies.

There is one rather interesting problem in operating the course. Although the writer never states so directly, it would seem there is danger that the student's inhibitions will be broken down so thoroughly that he will shoot or stab the coach who accompanies him. ("Your guide and confessor," as the instruction-sheet issued to the students terms him—a kind of Virgil leading his charge through a sordid Inferno.) The coach is advised to keep himself in a position to grab the student's gun arm "at any instant"; after the three dummies along the course have been stabbed, "the knife is taken away from student to prevent accident"; and finally: "There is no place on course where total darkness prevails while instructor is near student."

The author gets into an ironical conflict between ideology and practicality when he has to admit that the Japanese soldier is in many ways the ideal hand-to-hand fighter. As a patriot, he is inclined to see this as one more proof of Japanese barbarism, but as a technician, he views it in quite a different light. The whole chapter on "unarmed offense" takes off from the Japanese technique of jiu-jitsu. The Japanese soldier is perhaps the world's most skillful bayonet fighter; he spends almost half his training time at bayonet practice, and practice of a more effective kind than the American soldier usually gets: "Japanese bayonet training is most interesting because the personal element is injected into everything the Japanese soldier does. Three-fourths of the bayonet drill is given over to personal combat between men." As for using the knife, the Japanese soldier generally has his own personal fighting knife, which is handed down from father to son and "revered with all traditional Japanese rites." Finally, to crown his virtues, "The Jap is extremely testicle conscious." The inhibitions about physical cruelty which have been built up in the Western psyche through centuries of Christian morality and bourgeois humanitarianism are one of the real points of superiority of Western over Eastern culture. (Need it be said that there are equally real points of inferiority?) From the military viewpoint, however, and this is the viewpoint that has come to dominance in our age, this is an element of Japanese superiority, whatever the ideologues say about "Jap barbarism."

BUT this is making a good deal out of a little book on what is, by my own account, a very limited aspect of modern warfare? Listen, then, to the late General McNair, who was until lately in charge of the training of all American troops. Speaking on November 11, 1942, over a nation-wide hook-up, General McNair outlined his philosophy:

> Our soldiers must have the fighting spirit. If you call that hating our enemies, then we must hate with every fiber of our being. We must lust for battle; our object in life must be to kill; we must scheme and plan night and day to kill. There need be no pangs of conscience, for our enemies have lighted the way to faster, surer and crueler killing; they are past masters. We must hurry to catch up with them if we are to survive.

Such sentiments are not to be regarded as indicating any personal bloodthirstiness in General McNair, any more than Major Applegate's competent discussion of the best method of gouging out an eye necessarily convicts him of any lack of humane feeling. Quite the contrary, indeed. The more decent human beings one assumes the General and the Major are, the more strongly the point comes out that war is murder on a big scale, and if one's war aims are simply to defeat the enemy, as is the case on both sides in this war, then it is unreasonable (or hypocritical) to boggle over moral issues. There is still a certain apologetic note in statements like General McNair's: our enemies started it; we have to adopt such methods in self-defense; once the enemy is crushed, we can go back to decency. A decade or two of armed "peace," however, with new enemies materializing, new wars taking shape —already Roosevelt has said we can "never" relax our vigilance against future Japanese attacks—will change all this, and we shall come to accept war and its logical consequences with the same ease with which we now accept the carnage wrought daily in the Chicago stockyards.

The Army Air Force Medical Corps has developed a new technique for psychiatric treatment called "narcosynthesis," in which the patient is thrown into a "synthetic dream state" by the use of drugs. He then talks freely about the anxieties he represses in a conscious state. (The Freudian theory, by the way, that neuroses are the result of repression has been remarkably confirmed by psychiatric experience during this war. The chief technique in treating battle neuroses is getting the victim to talk about his experience—and to realize that every soldier is horribly afraid in battle, so that there is no reason to suppress the expression of fear.)

"One of the most amazing revelations derived by our uncovering technique," states a paper read before the American Psychiatric Association on May 16 last by Lt. Col. R. R. Grinker and Major J. P. Spiegel, "has been the universality of guilt reactions, not only in men who have been removed from combat because of anxiety states but also in those who have successfully and honorably completed their tour of duty." It is immensely significant that these guilt-feelings are apparently connected not, as the civilian would expect, with the slaughter of enemy soldiers and civilians, but rather with the soldier's own comrades. The report continues:

"These guilt reactions are related to the most varied, irrational and illogical experiences. A comrade was killed during a mission which he took instead of the patient. . . . We hear often the guilty cry, 'I should have got it instead of him.' . . . At first, the soldier's love is for his country, but soon he comes to love his outfit, his commanding officer and his friends. . . . He transforms a considerable share of his personal self-love to affection and pride in his outfit by the process of identification, and thus is enabled to overcome many obstacles to the performance of his military duties."

Thus to the process of conditioning described above in considering Major Applegate's treatise, we may add another psychological explanation of how men can endure modern warfare: the identification of the individual soldier with his "outfit" and the loyalty, pride, self-sacrifice, cooperation, and comradeship which this identification brings into play. In some wars, the soldier identifies himself with a great principle: the Rights of Man, revolutionary socialism, the liberation or defense of a nation. These great impersonal political convictions aroused the common soldiers of the French Revolutionary armies and of Trotsky's Red Army to a pitch of fanaticism which swept all before it. In this war, as we shall see below, the complete absence of any such emotion in the ranks of the American armies is the first thing that impresses most observers. Simple group loyalty thus becomes the most important factor in morale. "I've been around war long enough to know that nine-tenths of morale is pride in your outfit and confidence in your leaders and fellow-fighters," writes Ernie Pyle. A *Time* correspondent is even more explicit: "I think men fight for two reasons: (1) ideals; (2) *esprit de corps*. Since we in the United States have done such an abominable job of educating a generation, few of our men fight for things they believe in—they don't know what to believe in. The Marine Corps, which must be the finest organization of fighting men the world has ever seen, does not know what to believe in either—except the Marine Corps. The marines fight solely on *esprit de corps*." (Robert Sherrod in *Time*, Dec. 27, 1943.) The reason there are not more nervous breakdowns among bomber crews, who are "living beyond their psychological means" much of the time, is partly *esprit de corps* and partly "the strong common love of the plane itself." (Lt.-Col. J. W. Murray, of the Air Surgeon's Office, quoted in *PM,* May 15, 1944.) The airman's fatherland is his plane.

There are thus important psychological offsets to the boredom, horror and futility which war means to those forced to engage in it. Lt.-Col. Murray, noting that it is impossible to tell in advance what type of soldier will crack under strain, adds that some draftees who in their civilian life had suffered severe neurotic symptoms get along very well in a military environment. "Army life and combat seem to fulfill important emotional needs and thereby to stabilize these individuals." One of the psychological advantages of army life over the competitive dog-eat-dog environment of capitalist society must be the sense of comradeship and of cooperative effort. Just as war releases the productive energy of industry from the bonds of property and profit, so it also allows expression to some very fine traits of human nature which have little outlet in peacetime society. An army psychiatrist who went along as an observer on a bombing mission, for example, gives a really inspiring picture of men working together:

> During the violent combat and in the acute emergencies that arose during it, the crew were all quietly precise on the interphone and decisive in action. The tail gunner, right waist gunner and navigator were severely wounded early in the fight, but all three kept at their duties efficiently and without cessation until the combat was over. . . . The burden of emergency work with the controls, oxygen, wounded men and reparable battle damage fell on the pilot, engineer, and ball turret gunner, and all functioned with rapidity, effectiveness and no lost motion. . . . The decisions, arrived at with care and speed, were unquestioned once they were made, and proved excellent. In the period when disaster was momentarily expected, the alternative plans of action were made clearly and with no thought other than for the safety of the entire crew. All at this point were quiet, unobtrusively cheerful and ready for anything. There was at no time paralysis, unclear thinking, faulty or confused judgment, or self-seeking in any of them.

The object of all this cooperation, skill, and unselfish, even heroic, behavior was to blow to pieces other human beings and their homes, in a war whose purposes the bomber crew—if it was typical—didn't believe in and indeed took little interest in. The domination of modern man by his own creations, his involvement in processes beyond his control and contrary to his desires, the contrast in our society between noble means and ignoble ends, and the dissolution of ends into means, so that the Marines fight for the honor of the Marines—all of this is summed up here.

It would be a cheerless outlook if this were all that can be said about the psychological reactions of men to modern warfare. Fortunately, however, these positive factors which make possible adjustment to war do not as yet seem to be dominant, at least not in the American armies. I have emphasized them because one tends to overlook them and therefore to expect more resistance to the process of war from soldiers than actually takes place. But the big fact is still that among American troops psychological disorders are running at a higher rate than in the last war. Although the army screens out at the induction centers as many potential psychiatric cases as possible—one out of every ten draftees is rejected for psychiatric reasons—the incidence of neuropsychiatric disorders in the army is *twenty times that in civilian life,* and within the army itself it is *ten times greater in combat areas than in non-combat areas.* A Presidential medical board which examined causes of army rejections last winter was "astonished" and "concerned" at the number of "N.P." (neuropsychiatric) discharges from the army, "particularly those occurring in the first six months of service." (*Time,* March 13, 1944.) What worried the Presidential board seems to me, on the contrary, cheering news. I should be concerned if the N.P. rate *failed* to increase sharply within the armed forces. Is it unreasonable to speculate that, blocked from political expression, outraged human nature seeks out this back door, so to speak, of protest?

It is good news, also, that the rate of N.P. rejections is running high. On July 10 last, General Hershey told a Senate committee: "Out of 4 million disqualified, over 1 million draftees were rejected because they were found mentally unfit, and though three-quarters of that number at first sight seemed to be sound, they showed on examination that their emotions were in such a state that they could not stand modern war." This seems to me a pretty good state to have one's emotions in. No doubt most of the million draftees rejected as "mentally unfit" were neuropsychiatric cases by any standards, but may we not assume that a good proportion of them were simply too sane to fit into the lunatic pattern of total war?

One would expect the degree to which the soldier believes in the war he is fighting to be an important factor in his morale (which is an old-fashioned term for his neuropsychological health). Ardent political convictions can enable the individual to survive experiences he might otherwise crack under. I have seen no studies of this rather delicate question. There is, however, a suggestive passage in the report which Col. Leonard G. Rowntree, chief of the medical division of the selective service system, gave before the American Psychiatric Association on May 14 last. Noting an increase in psychiatric rejections by the army examiners between December, 1942, and December, 1943, Dr. Rowntree added: "The most striking evidence is the marked increase in incidence of psychosomatic disease in the Negro, *who in peacetime appeared relatively immune.*" (My emphasis.) Rejections of Negroes for peptic ulcer, for example, have been running at 2½ times the peacetime rate, while neurocirculatory asthenia ("soldier's heart") doubled for the whole group of draftees (white and colored) between December, 1942, and December, 1943, but went up *five times* for the Negroes alone. "This may represent the influence of war stress and strain, and to some extent it may also reflect the desire of the registrants to avoid service." Thus the group which above all has the most reason to reject the democratic slogans under which the war is being fought is also the group which shows the greatest increase in psychiatric symptoms when confronted with conscription into the armed forces.

These psychiatric rejections indicate not only the individual's desire not to enter the army but also, often, *the army's desire not to accept the individual if he obviously does not want to serve.* From what I gather from people who have been through the army examination routine, as I have not, the doctors usually reject draftees whose general "attitude," personality or overt statements during the psychiatric examination indicate they may cause "trouble" in the army. And a marked unwillingness to enter the army seems to be regarded, reasonably enough, as threatening future "headaches." Here the authorities confront a nice question of morality vs. expediency. The draftee who clearly wants to avoid service is, of course, a socially reprehensible person, a "draft dodger" psychologically if not legally, who should be punished by being shoved into uniform at once. But this moralistic approach is not expedient, since a single cog with an antagonistic will of its own can cause all sorts of friction in a mass production machine like the army. So, "for the good of the service," it seems better to keep out such cogs. Thus we get the curious result that individual rebellion is in one sense hopeless but in another effective in causing a degree of friction out of all proportion to its size—and both for the same reason: because the military machine is so big and so well organized. Here we may have an important principle of action against the authorities in control of great totalitarian institutions like armies: the cooperation, whether willing or just submissive, of the individual is necessary if he is to be useful as a slave-citizen or as a soldier. It is just not worth the trouble to punish or to reshape individuals who refuse to fit into the pattern. Here is the last line of battle for the dissenter; he is of no use to the army if his dissent goes deep enough. In the total state, the issue cannot be avoided by "rejecting" the dissenter; there is no area to which to reject him. Prison or the firing squad has to be *its* 4F.

Too great willingness to serve, in some circumstances, may cause the authorities as much worry as too little. The good soldier Schweik found himself in jail, one recalls, when he had himself wheeled to the recruiting office in an invalid's chair, waving his crutches, and shouting "Long live the Emperor Franz-Joseph!" and "On to Belgrade!" That was in Prague in August, 1914, and the Austrian authorities seem to have suspected Schweik's patriotic ardor of a tinge of irony. A more modern instance is the story that is told of a well known Surrealist painter who escaped military service in Paris at the beginning of this war by excessive manifestations of military ardor and patriotism when he was called up for service. Entering his draft headquarters, where everyone was plunged in the deepest gloom, he threw out his chest and saluted smartly on all sides, shouting "Oui, mon capitaine!" and "Vive la France!" They rejected him as mentally unbalanced.

September, 1944

My Favorite General

1.

MY FAVORITE GENERAL is George S. Patton, Jr. Some of our generals, like Stilwell, have developed a sly ability to simulate human beings. But Patton always behaves as a general should. His side arms (a brace of pearl-handled revolvers) are as clean as his tongue is foul. He wears special uniforms, which like Goering he designs himself and which are calculated, like the ox horns worn by ancient Gothic chieftains, to strike terror into the enemy (and into any rational person, for that matter). He writes bloodcurdling poetry apostrophizing the God of Battles. He slaps shell-shocked soldiers and curses them for cowards. When Italian mules obstruct the progress of his staff car, he has them executed on the spot—doubtless with full military protocol, including bandaged eyes (optional). And now he has shown that he can turn even a routine affair like opening a new Anglo-American service club in London into something memorable. "The idea of these clubs," ruminated the general in the presence of reporters, "could not be better because undoubtedly it is the destiny of the English and American peoples to rule the world, and the more we see of each other the better." Once more the general was in the headlines, once more the army publicity staff wearily got to work. . . . Patton has only two rivals in my affections. One is General MacArthur, also a master of the grand military manner. (MacArthur's literary style is more impressive, but he lacks Patton's punch.) The other is Admiral William F. ("Bull") Halsey, who declared in a recent newsreel interview: "We are drowning and burning the bestial apes all over the Pacific, and it is just as much pleasure to burn them as to drown them," and who whimsically remarked at an "off-the-record" dinner of Washington newspapermen, "I hate Japs. I'm telling you men that if I met a pregnant Japanese woman, I'd kick her in the belly." Bull is a top-ranking naval officer, which gives him the privilege of talking in public in a way which would get civilians locked up in the violent ward of Bellevue. . . . A few more such generals and admirals, and militarism will be a dead issue in this country.

May, 1944

2.

THE OTHER DAY I saw a newsreel of General Patton's speech in the Los Angeles Stadium shortly after his return from Europe. Gray-haired and erect, "Old Blood and Guts" had a fine presence: paternal, gruff, a bit diffident, with a warm smile flashing every now and then as he talked. He told of what Germany looks like today from the air, solemnly, with awe: "You cannot imagine such destruction. It was the face of hell." Perhaps I was wrong about Patton, I thought. . . . Then the fatherly voice continued: "After that we flew over the ocean. It was disappointing. There were no Germans to kill down there." And the warm, shy smile spread slowly as he stooped over the microphone, waiting for the laughter and clapping of 70,000 people to subside. A friend whose job is putting together newsreels tells me they had difficulty getting enough footage for exhibition out of this speech of Patton's, it was so full of "goddamn" and other secular expressions. The few minutes of it I heard was thus probably only a mild echo of the real thing.

General Patton made another speech, to the men of his Third Army, on the day before they took off for the landing in Normandy last spring. OWI operatives recorded the historic utterance on the spot and rushed the precious disks across the Atlantic by air, for use at war-bond rallies and other consecrated gatherings. But the speech was never released. For when the records were played over here, with a dozen topflight OWI experts listening, pencils poised, despair settled down over the gathering. Speaking to his men, the good gray general was completely uninhibited (or at least played the part—I suspect Patton's toughness is mostly theatricalism and neuroticism). The four-letter words fell like rain: Molly Bloom and Studs Lonigan would have blushed. The speech was completely unusable: the general had, in his martial ardor, sabotaged the war effort.

Just what Patton said on D-Day-Minus-One will be known only when the OWI releases the speech; that is to say, will not be known. However, it is possible to construct a reasonable facsimile here, from two sources: an alleged text published by a N. Y. *Daily News* columnist on May 31, 1945, and some notes sent me by a friend who jotted them down from the OWI recordings. The two check pretty well. Patton's speech, shortened for space reasons, ran as follows:

GEORGE PATTON'S FAREWELL ADDRESS TO HIS TROOPS

Men! This stuff we hear about Americans wanting to stay out of this war—not wanting to fight—is a lot of bullshit. Americans love to fight, traditionally. All real Americans love the sting of clash of battle. America loves a winner. America will not tolerate a loser. Americans despise a coward. Americans play to win. That's why America has never lost and never will lose a war, for the very thought of losing is hateful to an American.

You are not all going to die. Only 2% of you right here today would be killed in a major battle. Death must not be feared. Every man is frightened at first in battle. If any man says he isn't, he's a goddamned liar. But a real man will never let the fear of death overpower his honor, his sense of duty to his country and to his manhood.

All through your army career, you've bitched about what you call "this chicken-shit drilling." That drilling was for a purpose: instant obedience to orders and to create alertness. If not, some sonofabitch of a German will sneak up behind him and beat him to death with a sock full of shit.

An army is a team. It lives, sleeps, eats and fights as a team. This individual hero stuff is a lot of crap. The bilious bastards who wrote that kind of stuff for the Saturday Evening Post don't know any more about real fighting under fire than they know about fucking.

Even if you are hit, you can still fight. That's not bullshit either. . . . Every damn man has a job to do. Each man must think not only of himself but of his buddy fighting beside him. We don't want yellow cowards in this army. They should be killed off like flies. If not, they will go back home and breed more cowards. We got to save the fucking for the fighting men. The brave man will breed more brave men.

Remember, men! You don't know I'm here. . . . Let the first bastards to find out be the goddamn Germans. I want them German bastards to raise up on their hind legs and howl: "JESUS CHRIST! IT'S THE GODDAMNED THIRD ARMY AND THAT SONOFABITCH PATTON AGAIN!"

We want to get the hell over there and clean the goddamn thing up. And then we'll have to take a little jaunt against the purple pissing Japs and clean them out before the Marines get all the credit.

There's one great thing you men will be able to say when you go home. You may all thank God that thirty years from now, when you are sitting at the fire with your grandson on your knee and he asks you what you did in the Great World War II, you won't have to say: "I shoveled shit in Louisiana."

Spengler often refers to the "style" of a period, an essential quality which may be detected in all forms of expression from mathematics to landscape gardening. The above speech, I venture to say, will be considered by later historians as typical of the style of this war as Caesar's and Washington's and Trotsky's set speeches to their troops were in *their* wars. At once flat and theatrical, brutal and hysterical, coarse and affected, violent and empty—in these fatal antinomies the nature of World War II reveals itself: the maximum of physical devastation accompanied by the minimum of human meaning.

These utterances of Patton's are atrocities of the mind: atrocious in being communicated not to a psychoanalyst but to great numbers of soldiers, civilians, and school children; and atrocious as reflections of what war-making has done to the personality of Patton himself. Patton, it is true, is an extreme case, noted in the army long before the war for his martial hysteria. (The racist demagogue, Representative Rankin of Mississippi, recently nominated him for Secretary of War.) But I cannot believe he has not been brutalized by the war. Certainly most of us have. I remember when Franco's planes bombed Barcelona for the first time what a thrill of unbelieving horror and indignation went through our nerves at the idea of hundreds—yes, *hundreds*—of civilians being killed. It seems impossible that that was less than ten years ago. Franco's air force was a toy compared to the sky-filling bombing fleets deployed in this war, and the hundreds killed in Barcelona have become the thousands killed in Rotterdam and Warsaw, the tens of thousands in Hamburg and Cologne, the hundreds of thousands in Dresden, and the millions in Tokyo. A month ago, the papers reported that over one million Japanese men, women, and children had perished in the fires set by a single B-29 raid on Tokyo. One million. I saw no expression of horror or indignation in any American newspaper or magazine of sizeable circulation. We have grown calloused to massacre, and the concept of guilt has spread to include whole populations. Our hearts are hardened, our nerves steady, our imaginations under control as we read the morning paper. King Mithridates is said to have immunized himself against poison by taking small doses which he increased slowly. So the gradually increasing horrors of the last decade have made each of us to some extent a moral Mithridates, immunized against human sympathy.

August, 1945

3.

SIR:

I have just read "Atrocities of the Mind" in the August POLITICS. Such speeches as you quote were never intended to be heard by the people back home. Men at the front speak a different language.

I am completely disgusted with your article. Must you completely cast down a man, without once looking to his better side? Certainly he must have something on the ball if he leads his men as he does.

As for your persecution of Bull Halsey—it is very unwarranted. I have served under this great admiral, and I am willing to square off for him any time.

A DISGUSTED MEMBER OF OUR ARMED FORCES.

ANN ARBOR, MICH.

SIR:

General George S. Patton, Jr., is not the only General Officer in the U. S. Army. His speeches, together with his mannerisms and cultural attitude, are not representative of all officers in the Army. True, he is very colorful, greatly publicized, speaks violently and uninhibited, but also he is a good general. As long as we remember that that is all he is, and do not expect his speeches to be profound declarations of dialectics or holy wisdom, we can dismiss his speeches as only those of a successful general who helped defeat the Jerries.

As General Patton is unqualified to tell Dwight Macdonald how to publish POLITICS, so is Mr. Macdonald very unqualified to tell General Patton how to fight a war, or how to address his men prior to entering battle. True his Sunday School and public utterances may not be in the best of taste or decency, but he is only a general, and his words are not those of an Angel, but of a militarist who thoroughly hates Germans as any one would who has fought against them.

But the D-Day-Minus-One speech wasn't for Sunday School kids, or for civilians, or for an evening gathering of "holier-than-thou" pacifists. No, he's addressing a particular group of men, a group of soldiers all over 18. How else would you talk to a group of men . . . who would soon be falling in battle. . . ? No, he wasn't talking to Dwight Macdonald or any of his creed, or to those of the OWI either, but an audience of whom a large percentage would soon be dead. And he wasn't talking to the graduating class at the University of Chicago, but to men of all cultural backgrounds, whose chief desire was to be back home out of this damn mess, but who in a few days would be killing Jerries and getting killed themselves.

General Patton's speech is the kind that would appeal to a bunch of GI's, that would make them want to do their best in combat, not because the GI's are of lower intellectual levels than the readers of POLITICS but because they've "shoveled shit in Louisiana" . . . No, Patton was talking the language of GI's, or doesn't Macdonald know many GI's?

I'm only sorry that now the war is over, Mr. Macdonald won't have a chance to enter the army and learn what it's all about. It would do him some good.

2ND LT. JOSEPH MINSKY.

CAMP MAXEY, TEXAS.

—These apologies for Patton are based on two arguments: (1) The war was a just one; therefore, it had to be won; to win it, good generals are needed; Patton is a good general; therefore, Patton is justified. (2) Army life is radically different from civilian life; therefore, it is foolish to criticize its values from a civilian standpoint. Both arguments raise the problem of means and ends.

(1) I never thought World War II was a just war. But accepting this premise for the sake of argument, I'd say that far from the justness of the war excusing Patton's barbarism, Patton's barbarism calls into question the justness of the war. There is something suspect about an end which calls for such means. As I have noted before, Patton is my favorite general because he expresses so naïvely the real nature of World War II.

(2) That life in the US Army is more brutal and inhumane than civilian life is true, but this fact would seem to be something to be criticized and changed rather than accepted as a law of nature. If it cannot be changed, then, if we are serious about our humane values, we must reject the war which requires such instruments to achieve its ends. Also: my correspondents would wall off military from civilian society, whereas I would do just the opposite: extend civilian values throughout the armed forces. What is actually taking place is, of course, something worse than either of these alternatives: a breaking down, indeed, of the wall between military and civil society, but in the sense that the former is reshaping the latter.

Recent events throw some light on both the above points. The behavior of many American soldiers in Europe shows just what, as Lt. Minsky puts it, our Pattonized army "is all about." And General Patton himself has shown what he "is all about" in what is, even for him, a definitive manner. I refer, of course, to his September 22 interview, in which he stated that "this Nazi thing is just like a Democratic and Republican election fight" and added that he had, personally, "never seen the necessity of the de-nazification program." As military governor of Bavaria, Patton had kept reactionaries and ex-Nazis in power and had treated Jewish refugees—according to a recent official report to President Truman—just about as the Nazis had, except for killing them. These facts—which of course were known to the press and the authorities for months—were brought out in public after Patton's de-Nazification interview, and General Eisenhower, on October 2, replaced him as military governor. The interesting question arises: can my correspondents, consistently, approve of Eisenhower's action? Any reply by them will be gladly printed here.

May I add that I do know quite a few members of the armed forces—a remarkedly large number of our subscribers are in this category—and that, just as Patton is not the only general, so my two correspondents are not the only soldiers and sailors?—D. M.

October, 1945

The Responsibility of Intellectuals

THE GERMAN PEOPLE have let Max Lerner down. There is no other way to put it—they have failed him and damn near busted his big progressive heart. It seems that Lerner, all dressed up in his War Correspondent's Uniform, was scooting along behind the advancing Ninth Army in his jeep when he came across a large group of German civilians. "It was a drizzly afternoon," he writes (*PM*, March 4), "and they were clustered under a cement shed open at one end. There was a woman with a several-weeks-old baby, and there was an old man of 87. Most were men and women in their middle 40's and above, with a scattering of children. They were almost all farmers." They had been hiding in cellars for three days while American guns destroyed their village in the course of "the war that they themselves had brought on." (How "they themselves had brought it on" not specified.)

Descending from his jeep, Lerner asked them: Are You Guilty? He records no reply from the baby, but the others answered that they had never trusted or liked Hitler, that they had always considered the Nazis criminals, and that they were Catholics and hence opposed for religious reasons to Hitler's policies. Why then, asks Lerner with that implacable logic he shows when he is baiting someone who can't hit back, Why then, did you allow the Nazis to do these things? "With one accord they answered that they had yielded to force and to force alone." But this doesn't go down with Lerner; he points out to the shivering, bomb-dazed farmers that the people of France, Belgium, Poland, and Russia didn't yield to German force; so why did they? * This was a block-buster: "They were silent." (Different interpretations might be put on this silence.) Even after this, some of these simple peasants apparently didn't understand the kind of animal they were dealing with; they had been accustomed, after all, to the civilized society of hogs. So they asked Lerner to put in a good word for their local police chief, who had used his official post (probably at the risk of his neck) "to shield them from the severity of the Nazi regime." We will omit Lerner's reaction to *that* one.

"I came away heartsick and discouraged," writes Lerner. "The crime of these people was cowardice and moral callousness rather than active criminality. . . . Nowhere did I find the moral strength to face the fact of guilt. Only protests that they were not responsible for what had happened." Even the baby apparently lacked a sense of responsibility for Hitler, which shows how deeply ingrained this moral callousness is in the German national character.

However, Lerner thinks there may be "better material among workers than among the farmers and middle-class." (You can't keep a *PM* editor discouraged for long.) "Indications in Aachen are that a substantial section of the working class is possibly salvageable." So—if I may apply logic to Lerner himself—since what discourages him about the Germans is that so many of them deny they were pro-Nazi, the moral superiority of the Aachen workers must reside in the fact that they admit they were not forced to back Hitler but did so of their own free will and are hence responsible for

* According to reliable sources, the above countries were all engaged in a war against Germany.

the Nazis' crimes. That the German working class was pro-Nazi thus becomes a source of satisfaction for Lerner. We may be pardoned for reacting to this novel information—hitherto unrecorded in studies of Nazi Germany—with less jubilation.

But Lerner was able to report in the same issue of *PM* a happier experience, one that seems to have restored his faith in human nature. He devotes a full page to describing, with a fullness of detail reminiscent of Cholly Knickerbocker, the thrilling visit of TWO SOVIET MAJOR GENERALS to the Ninth Army. These personages were as warming to Lerner's big progressive heart as the German peasants were depressing. They were much better dressed, for one thing: "resplendent uniforms with long field coats of a rich purplish material, tight green trousers and long black boots, and gold stars glittered on their shoulder insignia." Also they were much more Important. Lerner delightedly reports the trivia of their visit: how a "military crisis" occurred when it was found that General Suslaporov's name was spelled with a "t" instead of a "p"; how one of them "showed a rich command of American slang"; how the other patted a wall map as he passed it (significance not explained). Finally, they were Soviet generals, people's generals, democratic generals, very inspiring generals altogether, generals on the Right Side, the People's Side, the Yalta Side. Yes, they were clearly Max Lerner's kind of people—the progressive, democratic and victorious people, not like those wretched German farmers with their shabby clothes and shell-wrecked homes and hungry faces and their callous and cowardly refusal to lick the boots of an accredited *PM* war correspondent.

The same issue of *PM* reprints as an editorial an article from *Free World* by Thomas Mann. The 20th Century Goethe (pocket edition) pontificates about his fellow Germans (he doubts "the propriety of pity") and regales us with selections from his diaries for the years 1933 and 1934. The key passage:

"The lack of sense for evil that large masses of the German people have shown was and always will be criminal. The tremendous spree that this ever thrill-greedy nation imbibed from the poisoned gin of nationalism ladled out by fools and liars must be paid for. [*Not much of a sentence, that, for a Goethe, even pocket-size.—DM*] It is impossible to demand of the abused nations of Europe that they shall draw a dividing line between 'Nazism' and the German people. If there is such a thing as Germany as a historical entity, then there is also such a thing as responsibility—quite independent of the precarious concept of *guilt*."

Now Thomas Mann himself belongs to that "historical entity" called GERMANY, he uses the GERMAN language, he is a GERMAN. If we abandon "the precarious concept of guilt" and make an individual morally responsible for the deeds of the "historical entity" he gets himself born into, then I fail to see how Thomas Mann is not just as guilty as his fellow Germans trembling under Allied bombs and shells in the wreckage of their homes—those poor devils Mann has the bad taste and the inhumanity to judge in so Pharisaical a manner. If we abandon "the precarious concept of guilt," then Mann's position over here becomes precarious indeed. Is he or is he not a member of that "historical entity," Germany?

It would be sad if the above specimens represented the sum total of "our side's" thinking on the responsibility of the German people. But fortunately for the honor of the human race, there are many with contrary opinions. An especially dramatic instance is the Associated Press interview of March 8 with Sergeant Francis W. Mitchell, of New York City, who belonged to one of the first American units to enter Cologne. It has often been observed how much more brutal and bloodthirsty civilians are than those who do the actual fighting. Sergeant Mitchell's remarks bear this out. He tells how the Germans crawled out of their cellars and brought out beer, bread, jam and pretzels for the American troops. "They were mostly children and old people—just sort of helpless and glad they were not being killed. It's hard to keep that icy front when people act friendly; also we Americans used to have some respect for old folks." The order against fraternization with German civilians, added the sergeant, works only when the MP's are around. "We are supposed to hate people—to be very tough customers. But as soon as the fighting is over, it works just the other way—we begin to feel sorry for them."

It is a great thing to be able to see what is right under your nose.

April, 1945

Two Footnotes to History

1.

THE DEFINITIVE judgment on the Nuremberg Trial is to be found in the October 7 issue of *Barron's,* a financial weekly: "The difference between justice and vengeance is that the former applies equally to all." An enormous amount has been written pro and con the judicial validity of the trial. But *Barron's* seems to have cut to the heart of the matter. If aggressive warfare is a crime, then may we expect a Leningrad Trial in which the leaders of Russia's attack on Finland in 1939–1940 will be duly tried and executed? If "crimes against humanity" are to be punished, when may we look forward to the hanging of those who killed millions of kulaks, saboteurs, and other "enemies of society" in *their* camps; or to the execution of those who put to death without trial or ceremony some hundred thousand men, women and children of Hiroshima and Nagasaki? "The difference between justice and vengeance is that the former applies equally to all."

It is a little ironical that so much protest has arisen about the moral basis of the Nuremberg Trial and so little—in fact, I have seen none—about the morality of certain other executions we have been carrying out in Germany. Ironical because the defendants at Nuremberg had all of them committed or connived at unthinkable atrocities, while the defendants in these other trials were, in my opinion, guilty of no crime at all. I refer to the executions by the US Army of several score German civilians who were found by our courts martial to have taken part in the mob killings of American fliers forced down in Germany. Lynching is ugly anywhere, and as a pacifist I oppose the killing of anyone. But was it not perfectly natural and, in terms of the commonly accepted morality (I assume the US Army is not pacifist in philosophy), entirely justified for German civilians to kill the fliers who had killed so many of them? What should an airman expect who has been dropping blockbusters on helpless civilians, if he is unlucky enough to fall into the hands of his victims? He gave *them* no chance to surrender. Why should they accept *his* surrender? It would be unfortunate, of course, if civilians got the idea that they could with impunity strike back at the technicians who massacre them with scientific devices from two miles in the air. It is understandable why the army wants to "make some examples." But the justice is all on the side of the hanged, not the hangmen.

November, 1946

2.

SOME LIGHT on Roosevelt's claim to political progressivism, and also on his Administration's "hard peace" policy for the German people, is shown by a curious fact which *The Progressive* of July 31 last uncovered. In his speech accepting the Democratic nomination, Roosevelt quoted as follows from "the greatest wartime president in our history":

> With firmness in the right, as God gives us to see the right, let us strive on to finish the work we are in; to bind up the nation's wounds; to care for him who shall have borne the battle, and for his widow and orphan—to do all which may achieve and cherish a just and lasting peace among ourselves and all nations.

The Progressive pointed out that Roosevelt had omitted the first eight words of this passage from Lincoln, eight words which are the most famous of all, namely: "With malice toward none; with charity for all." The atrophy of progressive values in modern American politics appears strikingly in this deletion, just as in the omission, from the marble wall of the new Jefferson Memorial in Washington, of the words in the Declaration of Independence about governments "deriving their powers from the consent of the governed" and the revolutionary "Right of the People" to "alter or abolish" any form of government they feel is not serving them well. Freud wrote a whole book on the significance of slips of the tongue and other apparently trivial manifestations of "The Psychopathology of Everyday Life." Semantic alterations like the above have an equally profound meaning in what might be termed "political psychopathology."

November, 1944

LOOKING AT THE WAR

The Unconscious War

At the beginning of *La Chartreuse de Parme,* Stendhal has a memorable description of the liberation of Milan from Austrian rule. It is 1796, and the young Bonaparte, fresh from the brilliant victory at the Bridge of Lodi, has entered the city at the head of his revolutionary army "which, having just won six battles and conquered twenty provinces, was fully equipped except for shoes, trousers, coats and hats":

> At once a new and passionate social atmosphere materialized. An entire people realized on the fifteenth of May, 1796, that everything they had respected until then was utterly absurd, if not downright hateful. The withdrawal of the last Austrian regiment marked the downfall of the old ideas; to risk one's life became fashionable. Everyone began to live only to be happy after centuries of hypocrisy and dullness, everyone felt he must love something passionately and be prepared to risk his neck for it. The interminable, suspicious despotism of Charles V and Philip II

> had plunged the Lombards in deepest night; now their statues were overturned and suddenly everything was flooded with light. For half a century, while the Encyclopedists and Voltaire had been enlightening France, the monks had dinned it into the good people of Milan that to learn to read or any other worldly pursuit was useless bother, and that if one paid one's tithes punctually to the priest and confessed one's little sins, one was practically sure to go to heaven . . . The exaltation was so excessive and widespread that I can explain it only by this profound historical reflection: these people had been bored for a century.

So it was in the springtime of the bourgeois revolution. Last fall another army arrived in another land ruled by reaction. For the victory at Lodi, the deal with Darlan. For the ragged regiments commanded by a twenty-seven-year-old genius, the vast fleets bearing a formidably equipped host commanded by generals neither young nor geniuses. For the fresh breeze of freedom, the perpetuation of the stale atmosphere of Vichy. When Bonaparte entered Milan in 1796, the Marquis del Dongo fled to his country estate; when Eisenhower entered Algiers in 1942, the men of Vichy entertained his officers at their clubs. Bonaparte brought along a young artist who gave the delighted Milanese the first political cartoon they had ever seen: a drawing of a French soldier slitting the belly of a rich landowner, from which poured not blood but wheat. Eisenhower brought along Col. Darryl F. Zanuck, late of Hollywood. Eisenhower's army was as "non-political"—in the sense that the reactionary anti-Semite, Giraud, is non-political—as Bonaparte's was political. One might have expected an army of the Four Freedoms to begin with the liberation of the native population. But Eisenhower's first communiqué states: "The forces under my command bring with them a solemn assurance that the French North African Empire will remain French." His subordinate, General Patton, defined the modest aim of the American forces as the maintenance of "political as well as economic normality" in North Africa. Rarely before in history has so vast a physical force been deployed with such tragically—or comically, perhaps—small political results.

It is ironical that the first great American military venture in the war, a coup hailed by the liberals at the time as a "turning point," should have proven to be such indeed, but a turning away from their values. What the French collapse of 1940 revealed about European bourgeois democracy, the North African campaign revealed about its American counterpart.

The positive idealism which was dominant in the first part of the war, as expressed in the Four Freedoms, the Atlantic Charter, and Henry Wallace's "People's Revolution" speeches, has been superseded by a new line. As military victory comes closer, the philanthropic slogans can be honorably discharged: they have done their "bit," or tried to, and might prove embarrassing if permitted to survive into the peace-conference stage. There is also a broader consideration: the antagonism between actual policies and formal principles has become too acute to be bridged by even the most powerful propaganda. In England, since last summer the Tories have so consolidated their control of the Government that the Labour Party ministers dare not support the Beveridge Plan; Cripps has been squeezed dry and thrown aside; Gandhi has been jailed and the Congress Party has been temporarily defeated. In this country, the fall elections returned the most conservative Congress since 1933; the new taxes are regressive, food prices rise sharply, wages are frozen, profits enormous; the unions have become instruments of Governmental control, and the Administration and Congress are using the mine strike as an occasion for still further weakening labor; the Negroes are jimcrowed as much as ever in military and civilian life; big business is more powerful than ever, and its representatives have excluded almost completely both labor men and New Dealers from the policy-making level of the war agencies; foreign policy has been increasingly determined by the reactionary State Department. As a former radical leader remarked recently, "This time we're getting the postwar disillusionment during the war."

A nation fighting the kind of war the French Revolutionary armies fought, or the Red Army, in 1919, does all it can to *politicalize* the struggle. It is notable that everything possible is done by our leaders to *de-politicalize* this war. As it grinds automatically on, as it spreads and becomes more violent, the conflict becomes less and less meaningful, a vast nightmare in which we are all involved and from which whatever hopes and illusions we may have had have by now leaked out. Some weeks ago, the Office of War Information issued directives to its propagandists on "the nature of the enemy." He was described as a bully, a murderer, a thief, a gangster, etc., but only once in the lengthy document as a *fascist*. Soviet Russia has never pretended to be fighting for any international socialist ideals, but simply for national survival—"the Great Patriotic War," as the official slogan has it. The recent dissolution of the Comintern was Stalin's effort to wash his regime clean of even the smell of any general principles. With his usual cynical boldness, Dr. Goebbels expresses the new line: "To date, from the national viewpoint, we have fought only for illusory objectives—for the House of Prussia, or Hapsburg; for socialism and for national socialism; for questions of proletariat or bourgeoisie. But today it is for important things we are fighting: for coal, for iron, for petroleum, and above all, for daily bread." The German Army fights on because it is—an army. The people at home support the war—endure the war might be more accurate—because they rightly fear an even more terrible Versailles if the other side wins. The unreality of the "Democracy-vs.-Slavery" propaganda of the United Nations is exposed by their inability to appeal politically to the masses of enslaved Nazi Europe. The best wisdom of our war leaders is that it will take x tons of bombs to reduce y acres of European cities to rubble.

The increasing *unconscious* character of the war—in the sense that the policies of the United Nations express no positive ideology or principles but merely an opportunistic adaptation to a reactionary *status quo*—coming as it does on top of twenty years of defeat of democratic and radical forces, has had its effect on American intellectual life. "Le 2 décembre m'a physiquement dépolitiqué," wrote Baudelaire after Louis Napoleon's *coup d'etat.* "Il n'y a plus d'idées générales . . . Si j'avais voté, je n'aurais pu voter que pour moi." (I owe this quotation to Meyer Schapiro's "Courbet and Popular Imagery" [*Journal of the Warburg and Courtauld Institutes,* Vol. 4, Nos. 3 & 4, 1941] which is in part a study of the effect of 1848 on French writers and artists.) It is remarkable, by the way, how many of the issues of this period (and the intellectual reactions to them) anticipate those of our own time. "There are no more general ideas"—what better describes the intellectual atmosphere today? Most political thinking has abandoned not only the old optimism of progress, but also the very notion of any consistent attempt to direct the evolution of society in a desirable direction. Submission to the brute force of events, choice between evils rather than between positive programs, a skepticism about basic values and ultimate ends, a refusal to look too far ahead—this is the mood.

The system of values which has been built up slowly, painfully since the end of the Middle Ages and which has commanded general assent, in Europe and here, since the end of the 18th century, is today threatened as never before. These values, crystallized around the free development of the individual, first became political realities in the two great revolutions of the 18th century. The "LIFE, LIBERTY & THE PURSUIT OF HAPPINESS!" of 1776 was echoed by the "LIBERTY, EQUALITY, FRATERNITY!" of 1789.

What has happened is that these liberal values have come into conflict with the actual development of capitalism, and, as always, it is the values and not the productive system which are giving way. Worse, those developments which had seemed to be steps towards the realization of these values appear today as their executioners. The great liberating power of the last two centuries, the growth of the forces of production, which turned men's eyes from heaven to earth and created the material plenty out of which a humanistic culture and ethics could grow, this has now become, by a dialectical turn, the new enslaver. Man has learned to master nature so well that we use the most advanced technology to blast to bits the fabric of culture. Art museums, hospitals, vast industrial works, ancient churches and modernistic housing projects, whole historic cities like Warsaw, Coventry, Cologne and Nuremberg—all are being destroyed with the most admirable efficiency week after week, month after month. Everyone can read and write, popular education is a reality—and so the American masses read pulp fiction and listen to soap operas on that triumph of technology, the radio, and the German and Russian masses are the more easily indoctrinated with a lying and debased official culture. The freeing of man to develop himself has had the effects which Erich Fromm described in *Escape from Freedom:* craving to be rid of this empty "freedom," the masses turn neurotically to totalitarian leaders. The struggle for universal suffrage is won, and the result is the rise of plebescitary dictatorships, in which the State authority becomes sacred precisely because it claims to represent "the People" against the individual. Far from decreasing in power, as all progressive thinkers from Jefferson to Marx and Lenin hoped and believed it would, the State is becoming an end in itself, subjugating the human being as the Church did in the Middle Ages. In the new religion of the State, which has reached full growth in Germany and Russia and which is steadily growing here, the individual is once more frozen into the hierarchical, irrational pattern of a society based on status. The peoples of the world are being organized into vast power-States, military-socialist in form, which are devastating the globe in their internecine struggles.

Partisan Review, July-August, 1943

C.P.U.S.A. Liquidates Itself

THE SELF-LIQUIDATION of the American Communist Party is one of the more spectacular results of Teheran. "Any realistic dealing with national and world problems today must begin and end with an evaluation of the agreements of Teheran, Cairo and Moscow," said Browder. "The answer to all other questions will depend, in the final analysis, upon the judgment made of Teheran." For a long time, the CP has been a branch office of the parent firm in Moscow rather than an American political party. When Stalin and Roosevelt, therefore, come to an agreement on postwar policies as broad as that apparently reached at Teheran, there is no longer any point for the American branch office to keep up even the formality of political opposition to Roosevelt and the social system he represents. As far as the Communists are concerned, there is nothing more left to struggle for.

In announcing the decision to liquidate, the Party's Executive Committee took a very rosy view of the postwar future: "Not only a prolonged world peace without precedent in history, but also . . . a development of economic wellbeing and social reforms is the prospect open for the world." This can all be realized through "full use of the democratic political machinery under our Constitution" and "under the system of free enterprise . . . within the two-party system traditional in this country." Browder summed it up: "Capitalism and socialism have begun to find the way to peaceful coexistence and collaboration in the same world. . . . Our postwar plan is the continuation of national unity into the postwar period for a long term of years." That is to say, the indefinite extension into peacetime of the authoritarian, highly centralized kind of State capitalism which this country has adopted as a war measure. This Utopia will be reached through a National Front of all "decent"—Browder constantly uses the word as a political criterion—Americans, regardless of trivialities like class or economic status. "The policy of the supporters of Teheran must be to seek support from all classes and groups, with the working people as the main base, from the big bourgeoisie to the Communists." To show he really means this, Browder strews his speech with assurances of esteem for big business, quoting the National Association of Manufacturers at length to show how progressively minded American businessmen really are. Thus first we had the United Front, limited to working class parties. Then we had the Popular Front, which included the liberal bourgeois parties as well. And now we have the National Front, which includes exactly everybody—everybody that's decent, that is.

One cannot but admire the thoroughness with which the CP follows out the logic of their line of the moment. The perspective sketched above is essentially that of the majority of liberals today, including the optimism about Teheran, but what liberal would have the nerve to put it all down? There is a madman's consistency about Communist political behavior, as when last year the New Jersey Communists backed Boss Hague against the liberal Governor Edison because Hague was closer to Roosevelt, the Commander-in-Chief of the great people's war. This extremism is a relic of their Bolshevik past and produces comic results when it appears in conjunction with extremely un-Bolshevik actions.

Somewhat similar is their bizarre combination of Marxist ideology—in the midst of his speech which was a laborious repudiation of practically every tenet of Marxism, Browder dropped in "we Marxists"—with totalitarian political tactics. These last are characterized above all by extreme flexibility, since decisions are made wholly at the top. The Party can turn on a dime—overnight. But these sudden shifts must always be rationalized with the ponderous apparatus of Marxist historical thinking, which is a very long-range affair. Hence Browder has to develop a detailed theory of a new "period" and a new conception of class relationships—new to Marxist thought, that is—in order to explain what is after all not so very complicated: that Stalin made a deal at Teheran.

However comic from an intellectual point of view, this procedure is quite sensible as a practical measure. Only the most case-hardened Party member could make such sudden and extreme shifts in cold blood. The ranks have to get hopped up on Marxicology to endure the strain, and the dosage has to be increased precisely in proportion to the severity of the operation. Browder's speech was a massive dose. The papers reported that some of his audience walked out on him, but I will venture to predict that the great majority of Party members will follow the Party right out of the Party. The effect of this sort of thing on the human mind and spirit after a few years must be appalling.

February, 1944

Roosevelt's Labor Draft

THE VERY NEXT DAY after the Communists announced their decision to fight inside the two-party system for such goals as "a total removal of all anti-labor laws," their leader, President Roosevelt, came out with his unexpected proposal for a national labor draft. It was unexpected because the manpower shortage has been easing off since last summer, and already cutbacks in war production are throwing tens of thousands of war workers out of their jobs.

Roosevelt gave three reasons for a labor draft: (1) "most democratic way to win the war"; (2) speed up war production; (3) stop strikes. (1) is demagogy. (2) has been denied by almost all the engineers, business managers and labor leaders that have testified before congressional committees on the subject; they tend rather to think a labor draft would impede production because of the conflict and confusion it will cause. (3) disregards all previous experience, in this country and in England, with attempts to stop strikes through compulsion; they have never worked and have often stimulated strikes, as the Smith-Connally Act has.

What then is behind Roosevelt's proposal? It is partly 1944 politics, a gesture of appeasement to the increasingly powerful right wing. (Though perhaps the term "appeasement" should now be dropped in describing such maneuvers of Roosevelt, since it implies he is "really" on the left.) But there is something bigger involved: one more indication of the authoritarian character Roosevelt's war government has assumed. It is an attempt to extend the State power over labor relations, of the same nature as Roosevelt's ordering the army to take over the railroads. This order was actually issued several hours *after* all the unions had notified the White House they accepted the President's terms and had called off the strike. It was thus a political demonstration, pure and simple. Nor is it just a question of weakening the unions. It is significant that the railroads themselves opposed having the army take over, and that both the US Chamber of Commerce and the National Association of Manufacturers are on record as opposed to a national labor draft. (The only backing for a labor draft comes from the army and navy—and Roosevelt.) Business evidently fears the strengthening of State control of industry even more than it welcomes a blow at unionism. It is precisely to extend that control that Roosevelt plays with the idea of a labor draft, despite the political and economic dangers involved.

February, 1944

Internationale into Nationale

ALL FRIENDS of progress must be grateful to Marshal Stalin and President Roosevelt for going out of their way, within three days of each other, to dispel any liberalistic illusions about their policies. They were unsuccessful, but at least they must be given credit for making an honest effort.

On December 20, Radio Moscow announced that the *Internationale* has been replaced as the Russian national anthem because "it does not reflect the basic changes which have taken place in our country." Instead of the old-fashioned stuff about an "international Soviet" that will "free the human race" and the exhortations to "the wretched of the earth" to arise (what if they should respond?), the new song celebrates "mighty Russia" and "the one great Soviet Union." It promises nothing for the future beyond a succession of military victories. There is no question that this new song, as Radio Moscow claims, better expresses the present "socialistic context of the Soviet Union."

Three days later, Roosevelt remarked to a correspondent that he felt the "New Deal" was outmoded as a slogan and should be changed to "something like 'Win the war.' " This suggestion was repudiated with indignation by Republicans and liberals alike. The former denounced the President's attempt to evade responsibility for the horrors of his first two terms. "Can the leopard change his spots?" asked the Republican National Chairman—a little nervously, one suspects, for if spots *can* be changed, Roosevelt is the leopard to do it. The editors of *The New Republic*, on the other hand, insisted, "THE NEW DEAL MUST GO ON," stating flatly: "The President is wrong . . . wrong in fact and in strategy." They then proceeded to give Roosevelt one of those lessons in *realpolitik* with which liberal editors are constantly favoring the shrewdest and most amoral political strategist of our day. Their view is that the New Deal, far from being dead, is spreading all over the world: "Nothing can underline that fact better than the Cairo and Teheran conferences, which have given a new progressive impetus to the whole task of framing a people's century." If this is true, it seems odd that the first acts of Stalin and Roosevelt on returning from Teheran were to drop the *Internationale* and the "New Deal." The mystery clears up, however, if we remember that Roosevelt and Stalin were present at Teheran—and the editors of *The New Republic* weren't.

February, 1944

Monte Cassino

THE MONASTERY of Monte Cassino was not of much architectural interest. This is fortunate, for on February 15 the ancient structure was reduced to rubble in four hours by 226 American heavy and medium bombers. One of the many things I cannot get accustomed to in this war is the fact that the most ancient, famous and beautiful buildings of Europe may be blasted to bits in a few hours at any time. Rome, Paris, Assisi, Florence, Ravenna, Carcassonne, Venice, Beauvais—who knows when they will join Warsaw, Bath, Coventry, Nuremberg, Frankfort, Kiev, Cologne, Palermo, Naples, Rotterdam, Cracow, London and Berlin? It is like living in a house with a maniac who may rip up the pictures, burn the books, slash up the rugs and furniture at any moment.

"The present world war," wrote Rosa Luxemburg in the *Junius Pamphlet* (1915), "is a turning point in the history of imperialism. For the first time the destructive beasts that have been loosed by capitalist Europe over all other parts of the world have sprung with one awful leap into the midst of the European nations. A cry of horror went up through the world when Belgium, that priceless little jewel of European culture, when the venerable monuments of art in northern France, fell into fragments before the onslaughts of a blind and destructive force. The 'civilized world' that stood by calmly when this same imperialism doomed tens of thousands of Hereros to destruction, when the desert of Kalahari shuddered with the insane cry of the thirsty . . . when in China an ancient civilization was delivered into the hands of destruction and anarchy, with fire and slaughter, by the European soldiery . . . when in Tripoli the Arabs were mowed down . . . this civilized world has just begun to know that the fangs of the imperialist beast are deadly, that its breath is frightfulness, that its tearing claws have sunk deep into the breasts of its own mother, European culture."

What words could Luxemburg have found to express the

lengths to which this process has gone in the present war? The physical destruction of historic cities is matched by the extermination of their "civilian"—the word has become a mockery—inhabitants, some by bomb and bullet and rope, many more by the slow fire of starvation. The political and economic techniques used by the Nazis on occupied Europe have been borrowed from colonial experience: the substitution of direct force for market relations, the use of Quislings (that is, *compradores*), the reduction of the native populations to a slave labor force, to be "mined" as ruthlessly as their countries' material resources, the replacement of the judge's gavel by the rifle butt, the ballot by the gauleiter's (that is, pro-consul's) decree.

March, 1944

"Native Politics"

NOW THAT the United Nations are beginning to reconquer Europe from the Nazis, the "democratic" phase of colonial policy comes into effect—a milder application, it is true, but still . . . colonial. At the time of the American invasion of North Africa, Henri de Kirillis, who is a realistic reactionary —that is to say, a cynic—wrote a remarkable article in the French refugee paper here, *Pour la Victoire*. He described the methods used by "the illustrious Marshal Lyautey" to extend the French empire. "He practiced an extraordinary realism, using to the utmost the leaders on the scene, however stained their records. He took every advantage of their divisions and their quarrels to increase his own authority, encouraging or even provoking native intrigues where none existed. He used flattery, corruption and the bestowal of honors to attain his ends." But it seems that Lyautey has a worthy successor. "Let us not be afraid," continued M. De Kirillis, "to recognize in President Roosevelt a genial disciple of Lyautey. . . . It may be a trifle painful for the people of

Europe, especially the French, all of a sudden to recognize that what they used to refer to with a certain disdain as 'native politics' is now being applied to them. But it is only the result of their own frightful divisions, their terrifying defeats and the complete social, moral and intellectual disorder into which they have fallen."

"Native politics"! The phrase is just, even if "a trifle painful." But the sentiments of the Europeans are of very slight interest to those who are fighting the war. Nothing is more boring to the powerful than the feelings of the powerless.

The hypocrisy of the Anglo-American-Soviet promises of "liberation" for Europe was exposed by the simple fact that at the Moscow, Cairo and Teheran conferences there were no representatives from any of the Nazi-occupied countries, although their governments-in-exile are formally recognized by England and America. (As for the Soviet Union, one only has to recall the veto placed by Moscow on any movement towards federation of Eastern Europe—the one step that promises some economic and political hope for that region.) The pitiful complaints of DeGaulle about the exclusion of France from the Moscow conference fell on deaf ears. He was not supported by his former ally in the Kremlin, which naturally preferred a deal with the Anglo-American powers at the expense of France, and which has always suspected DeGaulle as too nationalistic for its purposes.

The Big Three Powers are evolving a very interesting pattern for controlling postwar Europe. To prevent revolution, they encourage the formation of the kind of "national front" regime DeGaulle heads, which embraces in its governing apparatus all parties, from extreme left to extreme right, thus making every one responsible for keeping "order." But the great danger of such a regime is that it may become *too* nationalistic, in which case it would tend to put the interests of its own country before those of the Big Three. DeGaulle's unpopularity with the State Department is due mostly to this uncomfortable trait in him. What is really needed by the Big Three is a series of "national fronts" staffed by Quislings, *their* Quislings. Beneš of Czechoslovakia is a fine example of the species; every fiber of his being thrills with a deeply patriotic love of—Russia. A slogan for postwar Europe: "BUILD THE QUISLING NATIONAL FRONT!"

March, 1944

Three Worlds

THE GLOW of world brotherhood induced in the press by the Teheran meeting has ebbed away into a spooky twilight in which prowl sinister shapes of power politics. Even the man-in-the-street is now beginning to realize that Willkie's "One World" is actually Three Worlds, whose imperialistic interests are already beginning to clash in World War III tempo before World War II is over. There is England, there is America—and there is the Union of Soviet Socialist Republics.

Public uneasiness has been increased by the general belief that the Allied invasion of Europe is close at hand. It is awkward that the period in which the ultimate military effort of the Allies is to be made should coincide with such a wave of popular anxiety over the purposes and consequences of the war, but such are the hazards which political leaders today face. No wonder Anthony Eden recently complained that never in his experience has foreign policy been so difficult to conduct.

The question which Americans are asking more and more is that which a group of Republican Congressmen recently put to Secretary Cordell Hull: Has the over-all international organization endorsed at Moscow and Teheran by the United States, England and Russia "been abandoned in favor of piecemeal arrangements on various topics now deemed to have importance in the post-war world?" Hull's answer did not satisfy the Congressmen, nor the nation. The Twohey Analysis of Newspaper Opinion, for example, shows an incredibly rapid drop in editorial support of Roosevelt's foreign policy: from 80% favorable at the beginning of February, to

20% only two months later. The columnists have been twittering ever more insistently. Dorothy Thompson: "If we enter Europe without a plan, while the Soviets have a clear one in reserve, we stand to become caught in situations for which we are completely unprepared." Arthur Krock: "If we have a postwar policy toward Europe, including the disposition of Germany, the time is overdue to state it." William Philip Simms: "Anglo-American policy has reached such an obscure, undecipherable stage that United Nations circles here [in Washington] regard it as the prize mystery of the war."

So great has been the clamor that the aloof State Department has put the unhappy Mr. Hull on the air twice in recent weeks with lengthy expositions of American foreign policy. His speeches produced little effect, perhaps because they consisted mostly of pious platitudes, reassuring only to the editors of *PM*, who urged their readers to clip out the sacred texts and preserve them "for permanent reference."

It will be noted that two things, by no means synonymous, worry the average American about his country's foreign policy. One is that the allegedly democratic war aims of the United Nations have turned out to be mere phrases, and the postwar world threatens to be an even ghastlier mess than the prewar world. The other, and I think more acute, anxiety is that in such a world his country's national interests will not be sufficiently protected, i.e., that American imperialism has not sufficiently worked out a strategy to get the upper hand over its Russian and British competitors. The failure of the liberal and labor movements in this country and England to dominate the war effort on both the domestic and the foreign-policy fronts, or even to hold their own against the reactionaries—this failure, predictable from the moment they gave "critical support" to the present war governments in England and America, has caused the man-in-the-street to lose interest in reform and progress, for the moment, and to put his faith in the victory of *his* imperialism over its competitors. Hence Willkie's defeat, hence the recent enthusiasm in the British Commons, from Tories to left Laborites, for the strengthening of the Empire after the war.

The anxiety of Americans is intensified by the curious fact that, of the three major powers, the one with the mightiest economy is the one with the weakest and most confused foreign policy. The situation after the last war promises to repeat itself after this: an unaccountable failure of what would seem to be by far the strongest imperialistic power to dominate the postwar world. It may even go so far as a repetition of the withdrawal movement of the twenties. Isolated behind their oceans, Americans seem to be still a provincial people. This psychology probably derives from the unique position of American capitalism, which has up to now had a domestic economy sufficiently broad and developed to sustain it with comparatively little intercourse with the rest of the world. It may be that this is no longer true, but at least the American domestic economy comes closer to it than is the case with either Russia, which needs the higher technology of Europe, or England, which needs the markets and raw materials of colonial and backward European areas. And whether true or not, most American businessmen apparently still believe it.

Russia's military success plus the relative ineffectuality of Anglo-American arms have given her the initiative in world politics today. Furthermore, Russia has a much more aggressive and definite foreign policy than either of her war partners. This fact, which has manifested itself with especial force in recent months, is the basic fact about world politics today.

The Teheran conference was held at the beginning of December. This was supposedly the final seal on the indissoluble brotherhood of the Big Three. No one proclaimed this more fervently than the Russians. The American Communists, for example, have in a few months created a mythos of Teheran which gives that Iranian city all the overtones of the Bastille or Bunker Hill. "Enemy of Teheran" has become the new anathema for housewives who buy on the black market.

It is, therefore, not surprising to find that since Teheran the Kremlin has taken a whole series of unilateral actions, without consulting her partners, which have shattered whatever unity and confidence once existed among the Big Three. It is these post-Teheran actions of Russia, indeed, which have been mainly responsible for her partners' present state of nerves. Rarely has the conflict between form and content of international power-politics been more ironically revealed.

"This cook will prepare peppery dishes," wrote Lenin about Stalin in his "testament." What the master chef of the Kremlin is now preparing for his allies the future will show. A Moscow dispatch in the N. Y. *Times* of April 30 is rather alarming, however, considering Stalin's habit of talking one way and acting in just the opposite way (maybe it's the dialectic in him). "The dominant themes for Russia's third wartime observance of May Day," it begins, "are that the Soviet Union is fully committed to the principles of the Moscow and Teheran conferences and is doing everything possible to fulfill the decision taken there; that Russia is seeking to strengthen its coalition with Britain and the United States and to anticipate the enemy's efforts to sow discord among the Allies; and that the Soviet Union aims at a diplomatic wall of military isolation for Germany." After this ominous report, Churchill and Roosevelt would do well to be prepared for plenty of pepper in the soup.

May, 1944

Mr. Churchill's Spades

CHURCHILL's speech in the House of Commons on May 25 was refreshingly outspoken. It provoked the usual moans and protestations from the liblabs. Even the N. Y. *Times* felt it necessary to raise an editorial eyebrow, and Roosevelt, who embargoed American aid to the Spanish Republic and has loyally supported Franco ever since, washed his hands of Churchill's too-blunt endorsement of the Franco regime. The English are traditionally considered the arch-hypocrites of imperialist politics, but in this war it is Churchill and Smuts alone among United Nations' statesmen who call a spade a spade.

What Churchill had to say has been evident for a long time, and was said long ago by many radicals, including myself—with the significant difference that we said it at the beginning of the war and he says it at the end. In the first years of the war, when idealism and big promises were needed, Roosevelt made the major speeches for the United Nations; for the past two years, Roosevelt has been discreetly silent, while Churchill has delivered the weighty policy speeches. It is a sensible division of labor: New Deal rhetoric to get us to accept the war and tough Tory talk to prepare us for the peace. Churchill seems to relish his role. He does not apologize for his Tory views, he trumpets them in the face of the liblabs, whom he knows have no fight left in them. "I am here today to speak kindly words about Spain." "The word 'Empire' is permitted to be used, which may be a great shock to a certain strain of intellectual opinion." One can almost hear the sarcastic growl, see the ironical side glance at the Labor benches.

The key sentence was: "As this war has progressed, it has become less ideological in character, in my opinion." By "ideological" Churchill meant two things. First of all, he meant revolutionary communism and "the other ideology," fascism. The latter he said, has already been overthrown in Italy and "as to nazism . . . we intend to wipe that out utterly." Nor does communism, in its Russian form at least, hold any more terrors for Churchill as a realistic Tory:

"Profound changes have taken place in Soviet Russia. The Trotskyite form of communism has been completely wiped out. [William Gallacher, Communist member, interposed: "There never was such a thing."] The victories of the Russian armies have been attended by a great rise in strength of the Russian state, and a remarkable broadening of its views. The religious side of Russian life has had a wonderful rebirth. The discipline and military etiquette of the Russian armies are unsurpassed. There is a new national anthem.

[Laughter and interjection by a member, to which Mr. Churchill replied: "The honorable gentleman had better be careful to keep in step."] The terms offered by Russia to Rumania make no suggestions of altering the standards of society in that country. . . . The Comintern has been abolished. . . . These are marked departures from conceptions which were held some years ago for reasons we can all understand. [Mr. Gallacher interposed: "On both sides." Mr. Churchill replied: "Certainly, on both sides."]"

The other sense in which the war is less "ideological" is that progressive principles play less part in it—less, that is, ideologically; they have never been important in reality. "The House will know that all questions of monarchy or republic or leftism or rightism are strictly subordinate to the main purpose we have in mind. In one place we support a king, in another a communist. There is no attempt by us to enforce particular ideologies. We only want to beat the enemy, and then in happy and serene peace, let the best expression be given by the will of the people."

How long this respect for the will of the people lasts will depend, of course, on what the people will. If they will socialism we may expect a different tune. For the moment, however, Churchill is banking on the fact that the Soviet Union has been sterilized as the center of communistic infection. (As a rival imperialistic power, the Soviet Union offers a very real and growing threat to Britain, but Churchill is too much of a gentleman to allude to such things—prematurely.) It is true that Churchill speaks of supporting a "communist" (Tito), but he evidently uses the word in a Pickwickian sense. For a few paragraphs earlier he states: "Marshal Tito has largely sunk his communistic aspect in his character as a Yugoslav patriotic leader. He has repeatedly proclaimed that he has no intention of reversing the property and social systems which prevail in Serbia." Churchill's present lack of interest in "ideologies," his broad tolerance for the popular will is based on the fact he thinks *one* of the two great ideologies has been removed as a revolutionary threat by the changes in Soviet Russia, while "the other ideology" still has a base on the continent: ("I am here to speak kindly words about Spain.").

The most important political aspect of the speech was the revelation that the Big Three intend to dominate the postwar globe by force of arms, with no nonsense about a democratic league of nations, or the "sovereign rights" of small powers. "We intend to set up a world order and an organization equipped with all necessary attributes of power in order to prevent future wars. . . . For this purpose of preventing wars there must be a world-controlling council . . . comprising the greatest states which emerge victorious from this war, who will be obligated to keep within certain minimum standards of armaments for the purpose of preserving peace. There must also be a world assembly of power whose relations to the world executive or controlling power . . . I am in no position to define."

Thus there will be a "world-controlling" council composed of the Big Three ("the greatest states") which will remain heavily armed ("for the purpose of preserving peace," of course). The lesser nations will participate, along with the Big Three in a "world assembly," which will *not* be world-controlling and will *not* be heavily armed. Although one might think it would be a crucial point, Churchill is "in no position to define" the relationship of the unarmed world assembly to the armed and controlling world council. One suspects that even so frank an orator as Churchill flinched from putting into words the exact degree of domination the Big Three plan over the rest of the world.

There is one rather startling idea in Churchill's prospectus which I have not seen commented upon anywhere: he speaks of the big powers being "obligated to keep within certain minimum standards of armaments." The word one would expect there is "maximum," that is, a limitation of armaments; this has been traditional peace talk for generations. But Churchill gives us the 1944 pattern: a floor *under* armaments instead of a ceiling *over* them. The Big Three will be compelled (in the interests of world peace of course) to build a *minimum* number of battleships each year, to produce a *minimum* number of tanks and war planes. The more they exceed that minimum, the greater will be, presumably, their contribution to international peace and harmony.

Footnote to history: Although making fun of the liberal weeklies these days is in the shooting-fish-in-a-barrel category, their reactions to Churchill's speech are irresistible. The *Nation* found the speech "as puzzling as it was shocking," which rolls into one tight phrase the two classic liberal attitudes of today: "I just can't believe it! They seemed such a devoted couple." And: "They can't do this to me." Churchill's main difficulty, it seems, is that he doesn't "understand" contemporary politics—as against, for example, the editors of the *Nation.* (My own dismal feeling is that he understands it all too well.) "British liberal and labor forces are outraged," reports the *Nation,* as I have no doubt they are, "and Edward Murrow of C.B.S. reports for the first time since 1940 national unity has been impaired." One visions a huge glittering mechanism, the Murrowmeter, testing hour by hour a specimen block of national unity and suddenly, the morning after Churchill's speech, recording the fatal tidings: IMPAIRED! Small wonder the editors of the *Nation,* aware of their tremendous responsibilities, should be concerned. The editors of the *New Republic* also rose to the occasion. "NO, MR. CHURCHILL!" they grandly entitled their editorial. They were disturbed to find in the speech "several hints" that Churchill thinks more in terms of power politics than of liberal ideals. But they are not the men to let Churchill get away with innuendoes. They put him squarely on the spot. "To put it bluntly," they write, "are you fighting to preserve the British Empire, and are we fighting to preserve capitalism, or are we really sincere about the noble abstractions we have together espoused?" This is blunt all right, positively brutal for an editor of the *New Republic,* but my impression was that on several previous occasions Churchill has replied to the question with equal bluntness. However, the British Prime Minister had better mend his ways. "This will not do, Mr. Churchill," warn Bruce Bliven, Malcolm Cowley, George Soule, Michael Straight and Stark Young in one thunderous squeak. And again, in conclusion: "No, Mr. Churchill, it will not do." He can't say he hasn't been warned.

June, 1944

The Prospects for Revolution

OUR BEST HOPE for a better, or even a humanly tolerable world after this war is for the common people to take things in their own hands in a series of popular revolutions which will be socialist as to economics and democratic as to politics. The chances of anything like that happening in this country in the foreseeable future would seem to be as close to nil as at any time in our history.

The war has brought national prosperity on an unprecedented scale; the cream has naturally gone to big business and the rich, but there has been plenty of milk left over for the workers and farmers; guns *and* butter have been produced, to the surprise of both leftist and conservative prophets. The most recent government figures show that the average weekly earnings of factory workers in March, 1944, were almost double (97% higher) those of January, 1939, and 71% higher than January, 1941. (*Monthly Labor Review*, June, 1944, p. 1271.) In cash terms, weekly earnings rose from $23.19 (1939) to $45.62 (1944). It is true that the cost of living has also increased—how much is in dispute. The Bureau of Labor Statistics says the rise has been 23%, while the CIO, on the basis of much research, says it is 45%. *But even if one accepts the CIO figures (as I personally do), there has still been a 52% rise in real wages. In addition, and even more important, practically everybody has a job.* By April of this year, unemployment had been reduced to the statistically incredible figure of 770,000—economists used to assume that, because of factors like labor turnover, unemployment could never sink below the 1,000,000 mark. Retail sales hit an all-time high in 1943, and in the first four months of 1944 were 6.1% above the same period in 1943, after allowing for a 2.9% increase in prices (*Survey of Current Business*, June, 1944). That much of this increase was due to buying by low-income families is suggested by the fact, reported in a study of "Consumption Expenditures, 1929–1943" in the same magazine, that by far the biggest increase in expenditures during the war period has been for food.

Politically, as one might expect, the temper of the American masses has rarely been more conservative. The American Civil Liberties Union recently reported: "Up to now there have been but 26 prosecutions by the Federal Government for 'utterances or publications alleged to obstruct the conduct of the war,' involving 130 persons, as compared to nearly one thousand such prosecutions involving more than fifteen hundred such persons in the corresponding period in World War I." The Union implies this is due to a more tolerant attitude by the authorities, but, with the imprisonment of the Minneapolis Trotskyists and the current Sedition Trial in mind, I should say it was rather to be explained simply by the much smaller amount of popular opposition to the present war. There was a real mass anti-war movement among the American working class last time, led by the Wobblies and by Socialists like Debs; this time the trade union leadership has met with only negligible opposition to its win-the-war drive. The differences between the two major parties, tenuous in the 1940 presidential campaign, are becoming positively spectral this year, with Roosevelt pledging no abatement of American sovereignty in postwar foreign relations and the Republicans, to the editorial dismay of the N. Y. *Times*, putting a labor plank in their platform which endorses the Wagner Act and threatens the Little Steel formula. An ideal opportunity for a Third Party movement. Yet the only sign that the common people have any ideas and interests of their own is the formation of the Michigan Commonwealth Federation, which ventured neither to repudiate Roosevelt as the common man's "man" nor to put forward so radical an economic program as its Canadian counterpart has been propagating, with sensational success of late, for a decade.

No, whatever leadership towards social progress may exist in the world, it is not to be found in this country. It is to Europe above all that we must look at present. There four years of war and unbelievable suffering under German occupation have at least cleared away the institutions, ideologies and property rights which Marx called "the muck of ages"; have at least forced the common people to think deeply—or "radically," i.e., in a going-to-the-root way—about how they can avoid these horrors in the future. Now that D Day has come and the liberation has begun, the question of Europe and the Anglo-American-Russian policies there has become crucial.* Already certain lines can be traced out.

Allied armies are now occupying parts of two major European powers, France and Italy. The experience of Amgot in Italy has shown what should have been understood in the first place: that it is very difficult, and takes a vast amount of manpower, to maintain complete military rule over a foreign country. The cooperation of some sort of native politicians and parties is essential. Even the Nazis, specialists in organized coercion, used Quislings wherever possible. It goes without saying that the Allies have endeavored to build up, as their native collaborators, the most reactionary possible leaders: the fascistic Darlan is preferred to the simple conservative Giraud, and Giraud is preferred to the more opportunistic DeGaulle; the fascist-monarchist Badoglio is preferred to the antifascist-monarchist Sforza, who in turn is infinitely preferable to the republicans and socialists. But another prime requisite for the "native chiefs" whom the Allied liberators support is a proper flexibility of the spine.

---

* I hope the authorities, especially the Department of Justice, will note that POLITICS has followed the President's suggestion that the term "invasion" be avoided and "liberation" used instead. It is a regrettable indication of the uncooperative and unpatriotic attitude of the rest of the American press that in no instance that has come to my notice did a single newspaper, in reporting the inva- that is, liberation, comply with the President's request. POLITICS, however, is always glad to oblige in such small matters.

It is because DeGaulle lacks this quality, and not because he is a potential authoritarian leader or because the French people have not been given a chance to choose "freely" their government, that Roosevelt's State Department looks so coldly on his movement. The business about protecting the right of the French people to choose their own government is the same kind of nauseating hypocrisy Roosevelt recently showed when he shed crocodile tears over Hitler's Jewish victims and proudly announced that the great generous American government has agreed to allow just one thousand (1,000) such refugees to enter this country, provided they stay within a special "free port" area and get the hell out the minute the war is over. The lizardlike insensibility, the triple-ply brass of a statesman who can advance such a proposal—and Roosevelt made it clear that the 1,000 refugees to be admitted are *all* that will be let in—with unctuous satisfaction as a great humanitarian action! So too with DeGaulle: where was our tender concern for self-determination in Italy, when our armies propped up with bayonets the unpopular monarchy, and only reluctantly allowed Badoglio to be kicked out after all but one of the Italian parties had repudiated him? No, that cock won't fight. It is DeGaulle's nationalistic intransigence—why is it always the conservatives these days who show boldness and guts?—which makes him *persona non grata* in Washington.

However, DeGaulle hardly needs our sympathy: he has the trump cards and he will probably win whether the Liberators like it or not. On D Day, the Allied command tried to ignore DeGaulle's Committee of National Liberation; the Committee was not informed of the date, and Eisenhower pointedly failed to mention the Committee in his first proclamation to the French people. DeGaulle reacted with characteristic vigor, withdrawing several hundred liaison officers his Committee had originally assigned to accompany the Allied forces. Within the next four days, the exiled governments of Belgium, Poland, Luxemburg and Czechoslovakia had all extended formal recognition to the Committee as the "provisional government of the French Republic." The issue was thus clearly drawn between the Big Three and the lesser European powers. On June 14, DeGaulle visited Normandy, landing from a French destroyer, and while there, without consulting the Allies, appointed a Commissioner for Civil Affairs in Normandy. Five days after this bold putsch, calculated to freeze out Amgot, DeGaulle's Committee was invited by the British to open negotiations about the civil status of the "liberated" areas of France. These conversations are by now academic: as things worked out, the Anglo-American military authorities on the spot cooperated closely with the local Gaullists simply because they had to have some kind of local authority running civilian affairs—this is not a revolutionary war, and so the people must not "get out of hand"—and the only alternative to Gaullism was Vichy, which was politically impossible. On June 22, Eisenhower capitulated and reached an agreement with DeGaulle, on the latter's terms, about the 230 administrative liaison officers who had been withdrawn on the eve of the invasion. As this is written, DeGaulle has just been received in Washington with honors "almost" those for the head of a state. "General DeGaulle," reports the N. Y. *Times*, "seems about to get the substance though not the form of the recognition he once expected."

The recent course of Anglo-American policy in Italy is also worth following a little. On June 5, as the Allied armies entered Rome, King Victor Emmanuel resigned in favor of his son, Prince Humbert, who became "regent," his father retaining the royal title. Three days later, Humbert and Badoglio arrived in Rome to form a new government. At once five of the six parties in Rome demanded the resignation of Badoglio. In Naples, the representatives of these parties, including the much-advertised Signori Croce and Sforza, had swallowed Badoglio; their Roman colleagues, however, representing a more progressive and politically conscious part of Italy, booted out Badoglio before anyone knew what was happening. The only support Badoglio got came from Togliatti, leader of the Communists, who was probably ordered to take this politically suicidal stand because at Teheran Stalin gave Churchill and Roosevelt a free hand in Western Europe in return for the same for himself in Eastern Europe. Italy is definitely within the British sphere of power, commanding as she does Britain's Mediterranean lifeline, and Churchill has been the chief backer of Badoglio-Emmanuel.

On June 9, twenty-four hours after Humbert and Badoglio had arrived in Rome, a new government had been formed—with the aged Ivanoe Bonomi as premier—which excluded Badoglio. The parties did not even inform Humbert about it until the deed was done. Furthermore, the new ministers refused to take the usual oath of allegiance to the throne, substituting an oath of "loyalty to the fatherland." They announced that a plebescite would be held after the war is over to determine whether Italy will remain monarchist. For ten days the Allies refused to recognize the new Bonomi regime, much as they had tried to ignore DeGaulle after the Normandy landings. But there was really no alternative, also as in Normandy, and on June 19 they recognized Bonomi & Co. (In the interim, the Italian people were rich in at least one commodity, governments, having three of them—Badoglio, Bonomi, and Amgot. They would probably have swapped them all for a plate of spaghetti.) Two questions delayed the recognition: the monarchy, and the armistice terms. The latter was much the more important. It is rather breathtaking, after the democratic rhetoric of our war leaders, to recall that the terms of the armistice on which Italy surrendered to the Allies have never been made public. One can imagine why not. The Allies wanted Badoglio, who had signed the armistice and accepted the terms, included in any new cabinet. This difficulty was apparently finally surmounted when the Bonomi government formally agreed to honor the terms—an act which it takes no great prescience to foresee will not help their political careers in postwar Italy. As for the monarchy, the Allies naturally insisted that this great democratic institution, so well loved by that Italian "common man" who in turn is so well loved by Roosevelt, should be maintained. What the outcome was is not, at this writing, known, although it is reported that Bonomi at least has backed down and taken the oath of loyalty to the king.

A certain pattern, of which the more farsighted Allied leaders are probably aware, has evolved in the French and Italian situations. Four years of war and German occupation have devastated both the prestige and the actual economic base of the old bourgeois ruling class in Europe. If Roosevelt-Churchill were sincere about letting the people of Europe choose their own forms of government, they would be running the gravest danger of socialist revolution. But of course they are not sincere. Instead, we have a system of "defenses in depth," so to speak, against such an eventuality.

The way it works may be seen most clearly in Italy. Most liberals have criticized the State Department's support of Badoglio and the king on grounds of *realpolitik* as well as morality: it was so frustrating to even the mildest democratic aspirations of the Italian people that it would force them into "anarchy" and "violence"; better to permit them to expend these dangerous energies in building an Italian New Deal. I think, however, the strategy was probably sound, given the State Department's aim of restoring the *status quo ante bellum.* Ever since the Allies landed in Sicily, the great political issue has been: should we keep the king and Badoglio or not? The real issue of "Capitalism or Socialism?" (or, if you will, "Status Quo or Revolutionary Social Change?") has been quite submerged while everyone battled it out on a secondary issue: "Monarchic Capitalism vs. Republican Capitalism." And so what we now have in Rome, to the delight of the American liberals (who themselves are also taken in by the maneuver), is a government which would under other circumstances be vigorously attacked from the left, appearing to be a great step forward simply because it has gotten rid of Badoglio and the king. Bonomi himself is a senile third-rate ex-socialist ("Leon Blum is a Lenin compared to him," remarked an Italian friend) who is typical of the political bankrupts who paved the way for fascism. He paved it, indeed, in a literal sense, joining with Giolitti in

1920 in giving legal status to Mussolini's Black Shirts, whom he hailed as preservers of law and order, as a counterweight to the workers who were then occupying the factories. On the crucial war issue, Bonomi stands with Badoglio. "We hope to be of real assistance to the Allies," he said on taking office, with the valet-like servility of his kind.

So too in France. By opposing DeGaulle, the Allies have modulated "Socialism or Capitalism?" into "DeGaulle or Amgot (or perhaps even Vichy)?" That DeGaulle is personally reactionary and power-hungry, the very type of military man-on-horseback that has periodically arisen in French politics from Napoleon to MacMahon and Boulanger; that his Committee is a sinister amalgam of militarists, big businessmen, and Stalinists, with socialists and labor representatives as window-dressing; that its policies are ultra-nationalistic and imperialistic, and its internal political organization extremely authoritarian—all of this is forgotten and only the fact that DeGaulle is the uncompromising protagonist of French interests against the rapacity of the Big Three is remembered. If the Allies had supported DeGaulle at once, as the liberals wanted, the primary question, "DeGaulle or Democratic Socialism?" would have at once moved up to the front. As it is, the French underground has been, up to now at least, successfully diverted from considering any such dangerous question, or even developing a critical consciousness of the fascist (nationalism plus authoritarianism) direction of the DeGaulle movement. As between DeGaulle and the State Department, or DeGaulle and Vichy, it has seemed necessary to support the former. Nor does the State Department, in the long run, object to such a strengthening of DeGaulle's hand when the revolutionary alternative to his movement is considered.

These delaying actions now seem to be concluding their first phase. Bonomi and DeGaulle are being accepted by the Allies despite the objections of Churchill in the one case and Roosevelt in the other. Considering the almost complete lack of popular support for the alternatives of Badoglio-Emmanuel and Vichy-Amgot, to have delayed this acceptance so long is a triumph of *realpolitik*. The beauty of the tactic is that it diverts the insurgent energies of the popular parties precisely in the most ticklish period: the transition from German to Allied domination.

With their usual "revolutionary optimism," the American Trotskyists celebrated the downfall of Mussolini last summer with lengthy treatises inscribed "THE ITALIAN REVOLUTION HAS BEGUN!" But the Italian Revolution had *not* begun, and has not yet begun. The Allies have merely, after almost a year, withdrawn to their second line of defense-in-depth: the Bonomi regime. This is not to say that this period will last as long as the first. The instantaneous rejection of Badoglio once the Allies reached Rome indicates the more progressive political temper of Central as against Southern Italy. And once the Allied armies get into the industrialized North, where the proletariat is dominant and where the masses have a living tradition of working-class socialism, we may hope to see Bonomi kicked out in Milan as unceremoniously as Badoglio was kicked out in Rome.

The Communists offer the worst stumbling-block to any popular revolutionary movement. These fifth columnists in the camp of revolution are much more dangerous than the open enemies. A N. Y. *Times* dispatch from Rome dated June 20 illustrates both the existence of a really revolutionary temper among the Italian masses and also the cynicism with which the Communists exploit this temper. It records the formation, under Communist auspices, of an Italian "Red Army" which claims 58,000 recruits and whose leader, Umberto Carminati, has asked "permission" from the Allied Command to help fight the Germans. When a reporter asked him why "Red Army," Carminati replied apologetically that "the name, 'Red Army,' was the only symbol that would attract volunteers from the masses and that that alone was the reason it was being used." Thus the party that supported Churchill on the retention of Badoglio uses the most extreme revolutionary symbol in order to recruit cannon fodder for the Allied armies. Why in God's name a "Red Army" should get itself killed fighting alongside imperialist armies which will be employed later on to fight precisely the kind of socialist revolution a "Red Army" ostensibly exists to defend—this is a problem for the dialecticians of the Kremlin to unravel. It is, however, in all probability an academic question, for it is impossible to visualize the Allied military command getting any closer to anything called a "Red Army" than the reach of the traditional ten-foot pole. (Later reports are that the Communists have given up their attempt to square the circle and have disbanded the "Red Army.")

What course the Italian revolution takes once it has begun depends largely on whether the Italian masses continue to be dazzled by names like "Red Army" and to cherish the illusion that the Soviet Union has a positive connection with socialism, revolution, and working-class interests. One small and encouraging sign is that the Italian Trotskyists recently issued a revolutionary manifesto, rejecting both sides in the war and calling on the Italian workers to fight for their own interests, which categorically rejected the idea that Russia is any kind of a socialist or workers' state, whether degenerated, shopworn, or slightly chipped.

July, 1944

Warsaw

THE TRAGEDY of Warsaw is over. For two months the Polish underground army, equipped only with light weapons, stood up to the mechanized fury of the Reichswehr's planes, tanks and siege guns. Betrayed passively by two of their "allies," England and the United States, and actively by the third, Soviet Russia, General Bor's underground fighters have surrendered—such of them as are still alive—after 63 days of heroic battle. The Warsaw tragedy is over. But the treachery, the brutal calculation of Russian policy which delivered the Warsaw underground into the hands of the Nazis—the reckoning for this has not yet been presented. Let us attempt a bill of particulars.

The facts may be briefly stated.

At the end of July, the Red Army was approaching the city of Warsaw at the rate of from five to fifteen miles a day. By August 1, its advance lines were within ten miles of the city. That day the Polish underground army inside Warsaw, commanded by General Bor, began open street-fighting against the German occupation forces. By August 3 they had captured strategic sections of the city and controlled perhaps 40 per cent of the total area. As this is written, over two months later, the Red Army has not yet entered the city proper. Between August 1 and September 15 it stood still, making no attempt to advance; in those six weeks there was furious activity to the North, in the Baltic region, and above all to the South in the Balkans, which were overrun by the Red Army in an offensive which rolled forward ten, twenty miles a day. But in the center: All Quiet on the Warsaw Front. No aid whatsoever, furthermore, was sent by Russia to the Warsaw Fighters during this six-week period.

On September 15 the Red Army resumed its drive on Warsaw, and began a battle for the suburb of Praga. After a few days this offensive seems to have been abandoned also, and at the moment of writing the Red Army has still not gotten inside Warsaw proper. In the two months' interval, General Bor's underground fighters have naturally suffered terrible losses and have lost most of the area they controlled early in August. The Germans have rounded up 200,000 "hostages"—old men, women and children—from the city and have sent them to a camp at Pruszkow, where they are being killed by slow starvation.

So much for the military story. One political fact must be added: General Bor and the bulk of his underground fighters are loyal to the present Polish Government-in-Exile in London; Stalin has refused to recognize this government and has set up in Moscow a rival government called the Polish Committee of National Liberation. The Kremlin states this is because the London Government is reactionary and has no popular support. In fact, however, the London Government is a "national front" of all shades of political parties, from socialists to reactionaries, and as for popular support, the Warsaw uprising itself shows a considerable degree of it. Much more, without question, than the Moscow Committee has yet commanded. One statement may be made quite definitely: the Moscow Committee is more subservient to Russian pressure than the London Government. It is, in fact, simply a Quisling outfit in no way different from those the Germans strewed about occupied Europe except that its allegiance is to Moscow instead of to Berlin.

What, then, lies behind these facts? Why did the Red Army fail to penetrate to Warsaw for two months, with devastating effects to the Polish underground?

The Russians and their friends say that the uprising was "premature" and against the wishes of Moscow and that General Bor wanted to make political capital for the London Government.

These claims are refuted by the following facts:

(1) According to the *Manchester Guardian*, the Union of Polish Patriots, a group with headquarters in Moscow, broadcast throughout July appeals to the people of Warsaw to arise and fight the Germans. As the Red Army drew near to Warsaw, these appeals, which went out over the Kosciusko radio station in Moscow, became more urgent. On July 28, for example, Radio Kosciusko exhorted the inhabitants of Warsaw: "Fight the Germans! Do not doubt that Warsaw hears the guns of the battle which is to bring her liberation!" July 30: "Warsaw trembles from the roar of guns! . . . People of Warsaw, to arms! The whole population of Warsaw should gather around the Underground Army! Attack the Germans!"

(2) A dispatch in the N. Y. *Times* of August 15 stated: "The rising of General Bor's underground forces in Warsaw two weeks ago had been designed specifically to frustrate a counterattack by four German armored divisions against the Red Army forces closing in on Warsaw from the East. . . .

Moreover, Premier Stalin, as well as the British and American High Command in London, had promised to send aid to the ill-armed Polish forces, and detailed plans for the delivery of arms and the bombings of German strongholds had been dispatched to Moscow."

(3) Premier Mikolajczyk of the Polish Government-in-Exile, as quoted in the N. Y. *Times* of Sept. 1, stated that (a) the Red Army was informed of the projected uprising through the British and American Combined Chiefs of Staff; (b) he himself told Molotov while he was in Moscow on July 21 negotiating with the Kremlin, that the Warsaw uprising was imminent; (c) detachments loyal to the Soviet-sponsored Polish Committee of National Liberation were fighting in Warsaw alongside General Bor's men. These allegations have not been denied by Moscow.

That the Kremlin knew of the uprising in advance and approved of it—or rather, a most important emendation, *gave the impression it approved of it*—would thus seem to be pretty conclusively established. But let us assume that all the above data is false, and that all the claims of the Stalinists are true as to the rising being "premature" and in conflict with the Red Army's plans. The flimsiness of this excuse appears if one considers the parallel case of the Paris uprising. Here the FFI started fighting while the Allied troops were scores of miles away from Paris, not ten. Nor is there any question (as there is in the case of Warsaw) that the Allied military plans did not at that time call for the capture of the city. The strategy was to cut off the retreat of the German armies, and the taking of Paris played no part in it. Yet, when the FFI appealed to Eisenhower for help, he diverted a division from the main military task and sent it into Paris. His decision was a political one, just as was that of the Kremlin not to help General Bor.

It is also interesting to note that some reports have it that the FFI was forced into its uprisings because of the large-scale arrests and executions by the Germans preparatory to evacuating the city. Either they fought for their lives, or they died before German firing squads. The same choice probably confronted the Polish underground in Warsaw, even more brutally, since the German terror in Poland far surpassed that in France. Thus, whether strategically "premature" or not, the Warsaw uprising was necessary from another viewpoint. However, since Stalin had the same aim as the German High Command, to exterminate the Polish underground, he could not be expected to appreciate this necessity.

For why, after all, did the Russians give no aid to the Polish underground fighters for a month and a half, despite repeated and frantic appeals from General Bor; and, even more, *why did they sabotage the attempt of the British to give such aid?* Vernon Bartlett, a liberal Member of Parliament, has revealed that the British and American high commands all through August made "repeated" requests that the Russians would allow RAF planes to land on Russian soil after having dropped munitions to General Bor in Warsaw. (For months now British and American planes bombing the Balkans have been shuttling between Italian and Russian airfields instead of having to make the round trip without landing.) The Soviet Government refused these requests up through the middle of September. Consequently, the RAF planes used to supply the Warsaw underground army had to turn around and make a non-stop return trip all the way back to their Italian bases, instead of landing behind the Red Army lines a few miles outside of Warsaw. By September 12, 250 RAF flyers had been lost on this hazardous route.

The Russians justified this incredible sabotage—and sabotage of their British allies, note, as well as of the Warsaw fighters—by claiming Bor's forces held such small areas that supplies could not be parachuted to them accurately and would fall into the Germans' hands. This excuse, however, was exploded by the Russians themselves in mid-September when they for the first time opened their airfields to the RAF planes and also sent their own planes over Warsaw to drop supplies to the underground. For obviously if it is true that Bor's forces held such small areas *in early August* that supplies dropped to them would be likely to land inside the German lines instead, then today, when Bor has lost most of the ground he once held, the likelihood is very much greater. The bogging down of the Red Army's offensive for six weeks, and its renewal (in token form, at least) in mid-September; the sabotage of aid to the underground during those same six weeks, and the reversal of this policy in mid-September—these events have nothing to do with military considerations, as the Stalinists and their liblab supporters claim, and everything to do with political considerations. The game that Stalin played here was as cool, brutal and treacherous a squeeze play as even that master of the doublecross has ever perpetrated.

The Poles, whatever their other defects, are magnificent fighters and passionate rebels. Poland was the only country in Europe, *including Russia,* which did not produce a single Quisling leader of any standing; the Nazis were unable to find *one* university professor, *one* important businessman, *one* labor leader, *one* high military officer in the whole of Poland who would enter a Quisling government. In Russia's imperialistic plans for postwar Europe, a Moscow-dominated Polish regime is essential. But the Warsaw underground, skilled in the use of arms, toughened by years of struggle against the Germans, stood in the way of such a regime. The Kremlin's game is thus clear. First it provoked the uprising by radio appeals and by interposing no objection to it when Premier Mikolajczyk revealed it was being planned. Then it called off the Red Army's offensive for six weeks at the very gates of the city and did its best to prevent arms reaching the insurgents, while the Germans mobilized tanks and heavy artillery to batter to pieces General Bor's ill-equipped fighters, and while 200,000 civilian inhabitants of Warsaw were slowly starved to death in Camp Pruszkow.

As a Marxist, Stalin is well aware of the principle of division of labor: he saw a chance to let the Nazis do his dirty work for him. Every Warsaw fighter killed by the Germans was one less for his own firing squads to liquidate. That the Kremlin finally sent aid and renewed, in token form at least, the Red Army's drive on the city in mid-September was because even the Kremlin has to make some concession to world opinion, and the Warsaw situation had become too rotten to be prolonged further (part of Bor's forces, after all, were actually followers of the Moscow Committee; they were sacrificed along with the rest as far as Stalin dared, but there must have been some serious repercussions among his tame Poles in Moscow). Also in six weeks of slaughter, the Nazis had "fulfilled" most of the plan anyway.

The press and the governments of this country and England behaved shamefully. Some aid had to be sent to Warsaw, if only because of the questions that might otherwise be asked in Parliament and the speeches that might be made in Congress. But the very minimum was sent—most of the RAF flyers detailed for the job, incidentally, were members of the Polish squadron—and not a word of criticism of the Kremlin's refusal to cooperate was made by any government official in either country. The American press has either passed over the whole affair in silence, or has accepted the Stalinist rationalization that the uprising was "premature." For not only are the Anglo-American authorities willing to condone almost anything to avoid a clash with Russia, but they must also regard the Warsaw street fighters with more alarm than enthusiasm. They, too, want an "orderly" postwar Europe.

But the tale is not told yet. On September 30, Chairman Osubka-Morawski of the Polish Committee of National Liberation (Moscow) held a press conference which seems to indicate still another turn of Kremlin policy. Attacking General Bor as "a criminal against the Polish people," he stated that evidence had come into his Committee's hands that . . . the London Polish Government had ordered the Warsaw uprising. (Thus the uprising now has become an actual crime, and to this Stalinist leader it seems sufficiently damning merely to "accuse" the London Government of something which to a normal mind might seem a matter for legitimate pride: that it stimulated a popular uprising against the Nazis.) "If this is substantiated," he continued, "these persons also would be tried as criminals, as Bor will be if he falls into the hands of the Red or Polish armies." Here we might add that the London *Tribune* of September 1 reports that the Moscow Committee had dropped leaflets from airplanes to the Warsaw insurgents "threatening punishment and execution of the men they described as the guilty leaders of the uprising."

The new turn of Kremlin policy would seem to be to call off once more the Red Army drive on Warsaw that began anew on September 10. It has been many days since reports have come of fighting around Warsaw, and Osubka-Morawski stated that the city could not be taken until sufficient forces were mustered completely to encircle it. "He admitted that those forces were not now available because they were tied up on other parts of the long Soviet-German front." When we add the facts that Osubka-Morawski gave his interview 24 hours after conferring with Stalin, and that his denunciation of General Bor as a "criminal" followed almost immediately on the announcement that the London Government had made Bor its war chief succeeding General Soskowski, the pattern begins to emerge. Stalin has declared all-out war on the London Government, probably because he has finally concluded he cannot make a deal. The Warsaw insurgents are therefore to be left to their fate, their leaders are threatened with execution, such token aid as they got from Russia two weeks ago will probably be no longer forthcoming (the Soviet press has, significantly, carried no news of this aid), and the heroic Polish underground is now smeared by Stalin's officials as "criminal" and "traitorous."

Comrade Osubka-Morawski ventured "the sad prediction that the people of Warsaw, of whom it was estimated 250,000 had already died in the uprising, must undergo still further suffering." This prediction will unquestionably be realized for it is simply a statement of future Kremlin policy. But—

250,000 dead—and the Red Army sitting ten miles away for two months!

250,000 dead—and the Soviet Government refuses to allow relief planes to land on its territory!

250,000 dead—and the leaders of this popular revolt against Nazi oppression are threatened with execution by the Soviet Government!

After Warsaw, whatever honest doubts one might have had as to the nature of the Soviet regime and the direction in which it is heading must be resolved. This butcher of popular insurrection, this doublecrosser of its own allies, this factory of lies and slander, this world center of counterrevolution can have nothing in common with socialism. We cannot compromise with it if we would achieve our aims as socialists. Our slogan must be, once more: *Ecrasez l'Infame!*

October, 1944

At this writing, it is just four months after the Polish underground began its heroic and tragic uprising against the Germans in Warsaw, under the illusion that the Red Army, which had arrived within ten or fifteen miles of the city, would join forces with them inside Warsaw in a few days. The Red Army has not yet taken Warsaw but with his customary energy in such matters, Stalin has already had his puppet "National Committee of Polish Liberation" appoint a puppet "Lord Mayor of Warsaw." (The taking of the city by the Red Army is a mere military detail; plenty of time for that later; the important thing is that the political interests of the inhabitants of Warsaw—if any—are now in reliable hands.) On November 22, Radio Moscow carried the following broadcast by this official, one Spychalski, describing the interview he had just had with Stalin as one of a delegation of citizens of Warsaw!

> Marshal Stalin and Foreign Commissar Molotov received us in an extremely friendly manner, and Marshal Stalin showed an almost brotherly interest in the condition of Warsaw and the needs of its population. He inquired

about the destruction wrought upon the city by the Nazis and assured us that the Soviet Union is prepared to assist her ally, Poland, in the reconstruction of our beautiful capital. In giving this assurance, he said: "And what the Soviet Union promises, it unfailingly carries out."

Our discussion lasted for more than two hours, and Marshal Stalin made many exceptionally valuable comments on the military as well as the political situation. While all of us were very grateful to the great leader of the Soviet people, we were hesitant to take up more of his time. But he insisted that he could "always find time for the brotherly Polish people."

In our conversations, Marshal Stalin stressed particularly the need for friendship and alliance between all people of Slav nationality. . . . Our visit in Moscow has given us new inspiration for our efforts towards the speedy liberation of our country and all other tasks.

The spinelessness and moral insensibility of present-day American liberalism appeared in the way those modern Pilates, our liberal editors, washed their hands of the whole business. The dailies, *PM* and the *Post,* ignored the issue when they didn't print the usual Stalinoid rationalizations. *The Nation* editorially took its notorious Moscow Trial Line —"We'll know the truth in a hundred years; until then, we must suspend judgment." In the September 23 issue appeared the only editorial I saw on the subject. Its classic beginning: "The full truth about the Warsaw patriots' uprising will not be known until after the war. Reports emanating from Moscow, from Lublin, from London and from beleaguered Warsaw itself simply do not jibe. [" 'What is truth?' said jesting Pilate, and would not stay for an answer."] The fate of the Warsaw fighters has been but dimly seen through thick clouds of political controversy." It used to be the job of an editor of a paper like *The Nation* to penetrate "thick clouds of political controversy" and to decide, in case of conflicting reports, where the weight of evidence lay. But that was B.K. —Before Kirchwey. It is evident now that the complexities of the modern world have become too much for the good lady. Especially when she confronts the horrifying situation of the report which has the least factual evidence behind it being also the one which has the most state power behind it. To preserve its liberal franchise, *The Nation* printed one excessively cautious article on Warsaw by W. R. Malinowski, an official spokesman for the London Committee who was so diplomatic that he ventured not a word of direct criticism of Russia; and two not at all cautious articles by the magazine's regular Moscow correspondent, the veteran Stalinist hack, Anna Louise Strong. *The New Republic* also had little to say editorially about the affair, and that on *The Nation* plane. Its regular contributor, Heinz H. F. Eulau, gave a perfect specimen of liblab evasion when confronted by crimes committed by the wrong people when he wrote in the September 25 issue: "The Soviet offensive may have been stalled before Warsaw, but aid by air might have been possible. Regardless of whether the Soviet refusal to support the underground is morally right or wrong, it emphasizes Russia's determination to have her own way in Poland." Regardless? But it is just the rightness or wrongness which should be the question. Why not: "Regardless of whether the Nazis' killing three million Jews in gas chambers is right or wrong, it emphasizes Hitler's determination to eliminate the Jews from Europe"?

December, 1944

'Twas a Famous Victory

"Now tell us what 'twas all about,"
Young Peterkin he cries;
And little Wilhelmine looks up
With wonder-waiting eyes;
"Now tell us all about the war,
And what they fought each other for."

"It was the English," Kaspar cried,
"Who put the French to rout;
But what they fought each other for
I could not well make out.
But everybody said," quoth he,
"That 'twas a famous victory."

. . . .

"But what good came of it at last?"
Quoth little Peterkin.
"Why that I cannot tell," said he,
"But 'twas a famous victory."

—Southey

NOW THAT ROOSEVELT has been triumphantly reelected by the forces of Progress, which have even won back complete control of the House from the Forces of Reaction (unless those awkward Southern Democrats make some more of their wicked deals with the Republicans), now that the victory is won and the field of battle lies quiet and deserted save for a few gruesome campaign photos of Dewey, it seems a fitting time to answer little Peterkin's question. It goes without saying that we shall try in so doing to avoid the deplorable negativism shown by Old Kaspar.

To begin with, a superficial observer might imagine, from certain post-election developments that all the hard work and splendid organization of PAC had been in vain, that once safely reelected, Roosevelt had forgotten what he owed to labor, and was behaving in much the same way as it had been gloomily predicted that Dewey would behave if, by some calamity, he had been elected. An unscrupulous writer could even draw up what would appear to be a rather imposing tabulation of reactionary moves by Roosevelt in the few weeks since his reelection. Something like this:

Item: Labor has been trying for some time to purge from the Administration two top officials: Byrnes, the War Mobilization Director, and Davis, head of the War Labor Board. After the election, both submitted their resignations to Roosevelt, and not as a matter of form, either. Both wanted very much to get out. Roosevelt refused to accept their resignations and "drafted" them for the duration.

Item: The unions have insisted, with elaborate statistical arguments, that the Bureau of Labor Statistics' Cost-of-Living Index, which is used by the War Labor Board in deciding on wage rates, understates by almost half the real rise in such costs since the war began. On November 18, safely after the election, Roosevelt is advised by his special Cost of Living Committee that the BLS Index is accurate.

Item: Breaking the Little Steel Formula has been allegedly the main concern of the CIO leadership for over a year. To the reaffirmation of the BLS Index was added, a week later, an even more crushing blow to any such hopes: the War Labor Board finally decided the long-pending application of Phil Murray's United Steel Workers for a general 17c-an-hour wage increase. It granted 5c an hour, and to night shift workers only. It also turned down the union's petition for a guaranteed annual wage.

Item: On November 28, Hull resigned as Secretary of State. Roosevelt immediately appointed as his successor the present Under-Secretary, E. R. Stettinius, former head of the U. S. Steel Corp. It is regrettable but a fact that in so doing Roosevelt ignored *The New Republic's* formal nominee for the post: Henry Wallace.

Item: To direct the Surplus Property Board, which will dispose of some $100 billions worth of war supplies and equipment, $15 billions of plant, and 10 million acres of land, Roosevelt appointed two Democratic lame-duck politicians, both conservatives. But it might have been worse. He had originally planned to give the job to two henchmen of Jesse Jones. After considerable liblab pressure, he choose the lame ducks instead.

Leaving Roosevelt himself aside for the moment, it is sad to report that one can also make out a plausible case for the thesis that the Great Progressive Victory in the Congressional elections was largely ballyhoo, and that the future of the country would have been about the same whichever set of candidates won. Nathan Glazer has made some computations on the voting records of the ten incumbent Senators whom PAC supported for re-election, and the four it opposed. "Since there were other Senators running," he writes, "we may assume that only sterling liberals or black reactionaries were selected for support or opposition. I took the voting records of these Senators as compiled by *The New Republic* on fourteen domestic issues which involved a liberal-conservative clash. A liberal vote counts + 1, a reactionary vote — 1, no vote nothing. The best possible score is + 14, the worst — 14. My calculations show that the median scores are:

PAC–endorsed Sterling Liberals............. + 4
PAC–opposed Black Reactionaries........... — .5
Difference..............4½ (out of a possible 28)

Why does *The New Republic* print those tables, anyhow?"

All of this, as you see, can be made to look pretty bad. But on closer analysis, one would probably find that the facts have been taken out of their context and that the figures are distorted; and that there are many offsetting factors on the other side. (I regret I haven't the time to make such an analysis, and I hope little Peterkin won't ask me what those factors are.)

In any case, it is becoming more and more clear from the post-election think-pieces of eminent liberal journalists that one would be awfully simple-minded, not to say crude, to expect anything much from the reelection of Roosevelt *itself*. They gave a rather different impression during the campaign, of course, but there is a time and a place for simplemindedness and also one for sophistication. We have now definitely entered the sophisticated era. As near as I can work out the new line, it is that it was necessary to reelect Roosevelt in order to continue to have a chance to put pressure on him from the left. The clearest formulation of this line was by I. F. Stone in a recent *Nation*. Apropos the latest outrage committed by the newly reelected People's Friend, Stone wrote: "This is exactly what we could have expected of Dewey, and it dramatizes the fact that progressives have a double task ahead. One is to support the President; the other is to fight him. . . . Unless we organize quickly, all will be as it was before." It is thus plain that the election settled nothing, and that Armageddon is now to be fought all over again.

Just as this goes to press, the White House announces a great shake-up in the State Department, the most complete since Roosevelt took power. Foreign policy is today the crucial sphere of American capitalism, and Roosevelt's reorganization puts the conservatives in full control. The new undersecretary is the career diplomat Joseph C. Grew, former ambassador to Japan, who wants to keep Hirohito after the war. The five new Assistant Secretaries will be: Will Clayton, big cotton broker and close associate of Jesse Jones, who will have charge of American economic relations with the world; James C. Dunn and Julius Holmes, veteran State Department officials (i.e., rabid conservatives); Nelson Rockefeller, who was a large impressive blank as "Coordinator of Inter-American Affairs"; and Archibald MacLeish, Librarian of Congress, who flopped badly as head of the Office of Facts and Figures. Doubtless Roosevelt intends this last appointment as a sop to the liblabs, and they could hardly have a fitter representative than this empty-headed rhetorician. The score is thus 5 to 1, and at least two of the conservatives—Grew and Clayton—are extremely able men. No wonder *PM* asked in frontpage headlines: WHO WON THE ELECTION?

If all of this leaves little Peterkin with a slightly confused feeling, and if little Wilhelmine's eyes are more wonder-waiting than ever, perhaps another post-election analysis by another eminent liberal will clear things up. Writing in *The New Republic* of Nov. 20, James Loeb, Jr., thus described the post-election liberal state of mind:

> No progressive could have listened to the radio or read the newspaper reports the following morning without a feeling of jubilation and a profound sense of relief. . . . Progressives fought hard and successfully to reelect an

administration they had sharply and justifiably criticized in the past, an administration whose State Department has followed an almost consistently reactionary policy in its dealing with the forces emerging from the chaos of Europe, an administration which has as yet put forth no workable program for solving the postwar economic problems in this country and has not even put up a fight for those proposals which have come from its own agencies or Congressional supporters. . . . Unless these issues are fought through, the significance of this electoral victory will diminish as the months and years pass. It is now the obligation of progressives to strengthen their own ranks. . . .

Does that make it all clear, Peterkin?

December, 1944

1919 v. 1944

After world war i, the objective factors for socialist revolution were less favorable than they are today and the subjective factors more favorable. In 1919, the old ruling class was relatively intact throughout Europe, even in Germany, as were the old economic and political institutions; the masses were not in a revolutionary mood. In 1944, the German conquest of the continent and the political warfare waged by the Nazis have combined to destroy or hopelessly compromise the old ruling classes and to liquidate the property interests, political parties, trade unions and other institutions which formed the framework of pre-1939 European capitalism. In consequence, capitalism is everywhere discredited with the masses, who are pressing forward along socialist—or at least collectivist—lines.

On the other hand, in 1919 a successful revolution had just been made in Russia by a party whose slogans and ideology were Marxian socialist, and whose leaders, whatever else one might say about them, were revolutionaries whose dearest hope was to pass on the torch of socialism from Russia to her more advanced European neighbors. In 1944 the epigones of this revolution, long since evolved into a new ruling class themselves, manipulate the revolutionary sentiments of the European masses to the best advantage of the nascent Soviet imperialism, blowing now hot and now cold (but never very hot), prepared to sell out any popular movement for a little ready cash in the great game of imperialist power politics. And outside the Stalinist ranks, there is in Europe today very little experienced revolutionary leadership, very little clear political consciousness among the masses. The long series of defeats for the Left between the two wars has discouraged the mass consciousness and destroyed the leadership which might have easily seized on the present unparalleled objective *opportunity*.

December, 1944

Old Judge Hull & the Refugees

THE MOST nauseating thing I've read in a long time in a left-of-center publication is the following little tribute to the retiring Secretary of State, which appeared in *The New Leader* for December 2:

> The resignation of Cordell Hull is a blow in more ways than one to the cause of democracy and freedom. The blow is softened somewhat by the fact that his successor as Secretary of State is his level-headed Undersecretary, Edward R. Stettinius, Jr.
>
> Judge Hull wasn't always right. And he'll be the first to admit this. He sometimes made mistakes. But they were honest mistakes, with no mean motives underlying them. But even so he made fewer mistakes than the totalitarian minds who so frequently assailed him because he couldn't be either coerced or cajoled into playing their game and because he insisted on working 100 per cent of the time for Uncle Sam instead of Uncle Joe.
>
> The totalitarian smear campaigns against "the Judge"

> may have obscured for some the fact that none surpassed him in helping to save the refugee labor leaders of Europe; the doomed Jews in the Nazi grip, the honest democratic elements who found it necessary to flee totalitarianism everywhere. . . .
>
> Judge Hull was a sober, steady force for good in the State Department. He served his country faithfully and to the best of his ability for 12 years.

Anyone whose brains have not been addled by the kind of simple-minded Moscow-baiting *The New Leader* goes in for (in which *any* anti-Communist personality or institution, regardless of other considerations, acquires superhuman virtues), I say anyone in possession of his wits knows that Hull is a narrow-minded, petty, pompous, provincial reactionary who has never made a speech that says anything; whose press conferences are models of bumbling and evasion; who has had just one idea in his entire career (to save the world and abolish wars forever through . . . reciprocal trade treaties); who found the State Department a nest of reactionaries twelve years ago and who has laid a few new eggs there himself; who carried out Roosevelt's imperialistic foreign policies, from the saving of Cuba for the Chase National Bank after Machado's downfall, to the support of Franco in the Spanish war and the current burking of popular movements in Europe, without so far as is known any complaint except that Roosevelt sometimes made leftward gestures; whose one discernible virtue is that he is personally honest, a distinction which he shares with some millions of his fellow-citizens.

As for "his level-headed Undersecretary," the photogenic Mr. Stettinius, I interviewed him some years ago when I was on *Fortune* and did a research job on his career which convinced me that he is an extreme type of "front man," devoid of any special knowledge or talents, who became first chairman of the US Steel Corp. and now the Secretary of State because he is a glad-hander and back-slapper with no ideas of his own; because he has prematurely white hair, thick black eyebrows, and the flushed, gross, handsome face of Hollywood's idea of a successful executive; and because his father was an important partner in the House of Morgan.

But the thing that really makes one unable to believe one's eyes is *The New Leader's* tribute to Hull for saving the Jews and labor leaders of Europe from Hitler and the statement that all criticism of his State Department on the score of refugees has been simply a "totalitarian smear campaign." This is especially abominable in a paper which is closely identified with the garment workers' union and other sections of the New York Jewish community.

I say that, far from being a matter for congratulations, Hull's refugee policy should be a cause of shame to every decent American. This is not a strikingly original idea: for years every publication with any pretensions to liberalism has been complaining about the refusal of the government to save the tortured Jews of Europe; the most conservative Jewish groups have kept up a running fire of criticism; in fact, *The New Leader's* extraordinary statement is the first I recall having ever seen in a left-wing publication which defended (in fact, eulogized) Hull on this score.

The most complete exposure of the State Department's failure to do anything about refugees (except keep them out of the country) is perhaps provided in two critical analyses of the testimony of Breckinridge Long, the Assistant Secretary of State to whom Hull entrusted refugee matters, before the House Foreign Affairs Committee on Nov. 26, 1943. The testimony is summarized in the New York *Times* of Dec. 11, 1943. The two analyses are: (1) a letter in the *Times* of Dec. 31, 1943, from Leibush Lehrer, president of the Yiddish Scientific Institute; and (2) the Dec. 24, 1943, issue of *Jewish Comment,* the organ of the World Jewish Congress.

Long appeared before the House Committee in order to persuade them (successfully) to kill two bills providing for a special government commission "to effectuate the rescue of the Jewish people of Europe." These bills reflected the dissatisfaction of the Jewish Community with the State Department policies, and Long's job was to show that these policies had been good and that for Congress to pass any such bill would amount to "a repudiation of the acts of the executive branch of your own Government." (Hull is notoriously unable to take the slightest criticism; rather than allow the policies of his department to be censured, even by implication, he was willing to block any "outside" effort to help the Jews.) Long's testimony was partly a smear campaign against American Jews, who he suggested were trying to help Jews at the expense of non-Jews. Sample: "The situation has come to such a state of publicity today where I think the Jewish interests have emphasized the fate of the Jews as such . . . the State Department's policy I think must be that we cannot exclude persons from our sympathetic attention if they are not Jews." He also intimated the Department felt the Jews were selfish and unreasonable in expecting any special treatment for their refugees. To these insinuations, *Jewish Comment* tellingly replied that (1) the Jews have a right to ask for special aid because they are specially marked out for death by the Nazis; (2) they have, naturally, never conceived of this aid as being *instead* of aid to non-Jewish refugees, but as a supplement *over and above* such aid.

Long's other strategy was the use of misleading statistics and actual misstatements. To give the impression of vast numbers of Jewish refugees entering this country, he states: "We have taken into this country since the beginning of Hitler's regime and the persecution of the Jews, until today, approximately 580,000 refugees." But Long was really talking about *visas issued,* and all visas are not used. Thus the actual number of aliens admitted *from all over the world* (including Canada, Mexico, etc.) in the period was only 477,000; of these 286,000 came from Europe; and of these 166,000 were Jews. Quite a drop from the half million alleged victims of Hitler. Furthermore, Long failed to specify how many were mere transit visas. He also defended the disgracefully small number of refugees admitted since Pearl Harbor—i.e., during the time, as we are now learning from the horrors uncovered at Maidanek and other Nazi death camps, that the Jews were being slaughtered on a scale not approached before then. (In the year 1943, for example, immigration was cut down so drastically that only 5.9% of the legal quota—low enough anyway—was filled.) This drop in admissions was explained by Long as due to lack of shipping facilities after the country entered the war. But *Jewish Comment* points out that the Spanish and Portuguese ships *alone* which made trips to this country in that period had a capacity of 1,000 to 2,000 persons a month—as against the average 200 who actually arrived in them each month. The real reason for the small number of refugees admitted in recent years is the restrictive regulations adopted by Good Judge Hull's State Department, under the pretext of keeping out Gestapo spies, notably the almost incredible provision that *no one with relatives in Axis-occupied Europe was eligible for admission.* The result was that while Hitler was slaughtering tens of thousands of Jews a day, the USA was issuing visas, according to Long's own testimony, at the rate of 100 a week, or about 5,000 a year.

The most recent instance of the Judge's concern for refugees was the admission of 1,000 extra-quota refugees last fall for internment in a barbed-wire enclosed camp at Oswego, N.Y. This was a cheap publicity gesture of the most revolting kind: the thousand admitted were taken from Rome and North Africa, where they were already under Allied protection, and not from Axis-occupied countries; and Roosevelt stated at once that the tiny band was *not* the first instalment of such extra-quota refugees but all that would be admitted.

Such is the record of the man whom *The New Leader* sentimentalizes over as the savior of "the doomed Jews in the Nazi grip." The shabby episode was worth going into at length, I think, because it shows (a) the fraudulency of the Roosevelt Administration's humanitarian claims, and (b) the corrupting influence of an editorial line whose major and often apparently sole criterion of value is anti-Stalinism.

January, 1945

Horrors—Ours and Theirs

By the time this appears, the Nazi Government will probably have formally surrendered and the European phase of World War II will be over, so far as large-scale military operations go at least. In its last years, the war became a war of annihilation, by mutual choice of both sides. The Nazis realized they had no hope of surviving defeat and calculated that their policies, if not themselves, had the best chance of being revived later on if Germany were devastated so thoroughly as to prove to every German that Hitler was right when he warned of the dire plots of international Jewish-Bolshevik-finance-capital. They also probably preferred to go down, if they had to go down, in the melodramatic glory of a Wagnerian *Götterdämmerung*. The Allies also wanted to prolong the war as long as possible so as to do the maximum damage to German cities and industry, and also to reduce the German people by intensive bombing to such a state of chaos, misery and impotent despair that no alternative revolutionary regime to the Nazis can come into existence.

The result has been a war which in destructiveness of lives, property, and civilized values has had no equal since the religious wars of the 17th century. To say that civilization cannot survive another such war is a truism; the question is whether it can survive this one. Two horrors confront each other in Europe: the dying Nazi horror and the surviving Allied horror; the horror of conscious, rationalized destruction of the fabric of Western culture and ethics; and the horror of vast technological power exerted in warmaking by nations with no positive aims and little social consciousness, the result being the maximum devastation and the creation of conditions in which another such phenomenon as Nazism seems all too likely to arise.

We have heard a great deal of late weeks, as the Nazis' main concentration camps are overrun by American troops, of the first horror. Without in any way minimizing the terrible significance of these reports, which confirm and elaborate the more fragmentary data which I summarized in "The Responsibility of Peoples," one must note that for many years camps like Dachau and Buchenwald operated entirely on the living flesh of *Germans*, both Jews and political opponents of the Nazis,* that in all those years the American press showed little concern about these atrocities.

Perhaps I read these reports with a prejudiced eye, but I have been struck with how often they confirm the point made in "The Responsibility of Peoples": that the atrocities were committed by specialized SS and Gestapo formations and were not in any sense actions of the German people.

"I found that German soldiers did not like this cruelty," said a French sergeant who had seen frightful things during his captivity. "It was the SS and Gestapo and Ukrainian volunteers who did the murdering." (N. Y. *Times*, April 10).

In *Time* for April 23 there is an account of how the citizens of Ohrdruf were taken on a tour by the Americans of a nearby camp which "few had ever been allowed to see." "The Germans found it hard to believe. Conceded one: 'It's the work of beasts.' That night the Burgermeister and his wife hanged themselves."

A German girl, member of the Hitler Maedchen, was taken on an enforced tour of Buchenwald. "She moaned, with tears running down her face: 'It is terrible what they have done to these people.'" The reporter comments, in evident disapproval: "The pronoun she used was 'they,' not 'we.'"

The other horror is also reported in our press, but with all the moral indignation left out: the horror of what Allied warmaking technology has done to the people of Germany. The destruction of Germany is on a scale which one simply cannot conceive. This morning's paper reports that since the war began British and American planes have dropped the incredible total of 2,454,000 tons of explosives on German

* Dachau and Buchenwald were the camps in which Bruno Bettelheim was confined and which he described in "Behavior in Extreme Situations" (*Politics*, August, 1944).

"targets" (the quotes are used advisedly). "For every ton the Germans hurled at Britain by bomber plane or V-bomb, they received 315 in return." A month ago, it was estimated that twenty million Germans had fled their homes, and that most of the 250 cities of Germany were in ruins; today the damage must be much greater. Cologne is more completely wrecked than Stalingrad.

These are general statistics which are hard to visualize. The human meaning of bombing on the scale the Allies are now able to inflict may be suggested by three specific instances:

(1) On March 3, planes of the RAF's second Tactical Air Force arrived over The Hague in the early morning hours for a routine bombing of German V-Bomb launching sites. "Because of an error in judgment," the bombs fell instead on the "peace city" itself. Result: 800 Dutch civilians dead, 1,000 injured, 20,000 homeless, and one-sixth of the city in ruins. This was, note, just a routine raid, not a specially mounted mass bombing.

(2) The British *New Leader* of March 3 summarizes a "reliable report from a neutral country" on the effects of the first great RAF raid on Dresden:

> It states that the bombers dropped thousands of incendiaries as soon as they were over Dresden and followed these up with high explosives. As in earlier raids on German cities, the incendiaries started immense fires which created such an intense heat that shelterers were driven from shelter. They were still rushing through the streets looking for fresh shelter when the explosives fell. They and the thousands of others for whom there was no shelter accommodation and who were crouching in shop doorways were blown to pieces.
>
> After the raid many streets were carpeted with corpses and fragments of corpses. Dozens of people, their clothes blazing, jumped into the river which flows through the city—floating bodies filled the stream.
>
> Shattered bodies lay everywhere. Many, killed by the heat, had shrivelled up to half their normal size.

(3) In the N. Y. *Times* of April 10, John MacCormac described the effect of 18 minutes of bombing on the German city of Hildesheim:

> In that 18-minute attack, and by the fires that burned for days after it, this town of 65,000 inhabitants had been destroyed. It had been a cradle of art in Germany. Its series of half-timbered buildings of late Gothic and Renaissance period design had been unrivaled in the whole of the Reich. The most modern buildings in it were 300 years old. The oldest—a Catholic basilica—had been built on a still older foundation in 1054–1079 by medieval craftsmen who gloried in their work. . . . Its Protestant Michaelis Church was rated as one of the grandest Romanesque basilicas in all Germany. . . . So Hildesheim, along with so much else in the Reich that was part of humanity's common treasure, was thrown into the scales of war. Weighed in that balance, Hildesheim was important only for its marshaling yards. Hence the 18-minute bombardment from 2:00 to 2:18 on the afternoon of March 22. . . . Hildesheim is 95% destroyed.

Another Dark Ages has come to Germany, to Europe. In Frankfurt, a correspondent found a pencil-scrawled piece of cardboard stuck up on the ruins of Goethe's birthplace: "HERE WAS THE HOUSE WHERE THE OLD GREAT POET GOETHE WAS BORN."

May, 1945

A Japanese Badoglio?

NOT THE LEAST ironical aspect of this ironical war is the fact that the war in the Pacific has always been more popular with all classes of Americans than the war in Europe. Ironical because the war against Germany had at least a certain moral ambiguity about it—even we who opposed it had to admit that fascism was the most terrible enemy of our ideals to emerge so far; our dissent was on the means employed to fight it. But the war in the Pacific is a straight imperialist conflict of the classic old pattern; even a *PM* editorial writer would scarcely have the heart to argue that we are fighting to prevent the spread of Japanese political ideas. This very fact, of course, makes that war popular with our businessmen. They have no interests in Europe so vital as those of Britain and Russia, which is one good reason for the ineffectuality of American policy there. But in the Pacific they have real interests: raw materials, cheap labor, and, in the densely populated regions of Eastern Asia, the last great commercial frontier. The general public, on the other hand, also responds more enthusiastically to the Pacific war because of simple racial hatred of the Japanese. The confinement of all West Coast Japanese, even those who were American citizens—a breach of civil liberties for which our history provides only one parallel: the treatment of the colored people of the South—is one index of this racism. The "no prisoners" policy of our troops in the Pacific is another, as are such statements from high public officials as the recent postwar plan for Japan that was publicly suggested by Paul V. McNutt, War Manpower Commissioner: "Extermination of the Japanese—*in toto.*" ("I know the Japanese people," added Mr. McNutt.)

Our press has been so busy hating the Japanese as an alien race that it has failed to provide us with any information as to what Japan and the Japanese are really like. A nightmare of 70 million bucktoothed grinning apes, whose totalitarian uniformity is only exceeded by their political fanaticism, this is the general picture we are given. If it is true, not only is the McNutt formula justified, but the Pacific war will last many years. It is, of course, not true. The Japanese are people, not apes. . . . Here I want to speculate on the possibility of a "Badoglio clique" taking over in Japan in the near future and accepting "unconditional surrender" terms. In considering this possibility, we shall perhaps get some idea of the general nature of Japanese society.

A nation may be taken out of a war from the top or from the bottom. The Bolsheviki did it from the bottom, inciting the people against Kerensky's war policy with the slogan, "Peace, Bread, Land." The failure of the junkers and businessmen to take Germany out of the war even in the last terrible months when all was obviously lost was due to the fact that the Nazis had organized a mass political party, with an ideology and program, with large and powerful armed forces (SS and Gestapo), and with several millions of adherents in the population. Even had the generals' attempt on Hitler's life last summer succeeded, it seems doubtful they could have made a coup of the Badoglio type: with a politically conscious mass organization at their disposal, the Nazis could probably have only been overthrown by a mass revolution. (That there were apparently not even the faintest stirrings of such a revolt would seem to be one more indication that Nazism was a far more serious affair than the "Bonapartist dictatorship of monopoly capitalism" which some unimaginative Marxists have thought it to be; that it rather resembled the kind of bureaucratic-collectivist alternative to *both* socialism and capitalism that Stalin has created in Russia.) In any event, it is obvious that Mussolini never was able to create in Italy the kind of totalitarian regime Hitler had—whether because of the national character of the Italians or the country's economic backwardness or both. Like a Latin American dictator, he ruled as the bravo and demagogue of the old ruling groups—the army, the Court and big business—with little popular enthusiasm for his program and ideology. His Fascist Party therefore never developed the mass roots which Hitler's did, and when the army and the Court decided to take Italy out of the war, they had a freedom of action in two directions: there was no other powerful group to block them, and there was no mass support for Mussolini. For better or worse, the decision could be taken at the top level, without worrying about the politically inert popular masses.

The situation in Japan is more like that of Italy than of Germany. At first glance (which is also last glance so far as most of our press goes) it would seem that the opposite is the case. For it is true that, from the standpoint of the control of the masses by the ruling class, Japan is the most totalitarian nation on earth, including Russia. As is well known, the Meiji Restoration which overthrew the old order and "Westernized" Japan simply laid a veneer of democratic-capitalist institutions over the old feudal social structure without seriously altering that structure. The Japanese people are even more docile, disciplined, and politically unconscious than the Russians are: their lives are regulated from above even more extensively and intimately. They reverence the Emperor as the living representative of the gods, an aberration that is fully exploited by the very ungodlike characters who rule them in his name. From these facts, it is usually deduced that the Japanese people will enthusiastically follow the Emperor's leadership to the grave and beyond, and hence that the war will be prolonged to the bitter end.

An instance of successful cultural conditioning is the frequency with which Japanese civilians on islands captured by American troops commit mass suicide. Several hundred destroyed themselves and their children on one of the Ryukyu islands recently, duped by propaganda tales of what awaited them if they fell alive into the hands of the "Western barbarians." Those who did not kill themselves, or who were not successful, were amazed when the Americans gave them food and medical treatment, and became extremely bitter against the leaders of the suicide movement. "A group of seventy refugees, munching food, stopped when a Japanese soldier was put in the circle with them. They turned on him and denounced him with such vehemence that the American soldiers removed him to a safer place—for him." (N. Y. *Times,* April 2, 1945.) *

* I might add that little was said in "The Responsibility of Peoples" about the Pacific war because the problem involved there is historically different from that of Germany. Japan is an

There is, however, another factor to be considered: the conflict within the ruling class. In this respect Japan is far from totalitarian: two distinct groups have for years existed, and still exist, with quite different approaches to the war question. There are the militarists of the Kwantung Army clique, dominant since they succeeded in forcing the occupation of Manchuria in 1931; their policy was a rapid and daring expansion of Japanese imperialist rule over Eastern Asia, regardless of possible military clashes with the Western powers; their policy now is war *à outrance*—preferring, like the Nazis, to see their country perish in flames rather than abate their fanatical (and, in bourgeois terms, irrational) ideology. On the other hand, there are the businessmen, led by the great family monopolies (Mitsui, Mitsubishi, etc.), the politicians, most of whom are even more intimately linked to big business than our own are, and the "moderates" of the older generation of nobles and Court advisers (Prince Konoye is the type). Frightened by the risks of shoestring-imperialism, and better informed about the industrial and military strength of the Western powers than the Kwantung Army fanatics, this predominantly bourgeois faction has tried in vain to slow down the pace of Japan's military expansion. They have no prejudices against imperialism as such, of course, nor against wiping out half the globe, including most of "their own" people, in total warfare. They simply calcu-

essentially feudal nation, with capitalist trimmings; the Oriental attitude toward individual moral responsibility, the infliction of death and torture, and the relationship of people and State proceeds from quite a different historical tradition than the Christian-humanitarian-bourgeois tradition of the West. Yet, as these few instances show, even here something of the same patterns can be traced. And so far as *our* side of the question is concerned, the animus of the average American towards the Germans as a collectivity is mild compared to his feeling, compounded of racial prejudice and dislike of a dramatically alien culture, against the Japanese people. It is notable, for example, that, while all Japanese *including American citizens* were deported to concentration camps in the interior, similar measures were not taken against Germans, not even those who were not American citizens.

late the risks and costs in a mean-spirited bourgeois way that is alien to the dashing spirits of the Kwantung Army.

It seems likely that at the present the businessmen and "moderates" are making some very dismal calculations indeed. The Japanese fleet has been almost eliminated as a military factor; the air force largely destroyed; the Greater East Asia Co-Prosperity Sphere is rapidly contracting; American bombers now have land bases comfortably near the Japanese mainland; and all this while the main weight of Allied military power has been occupied in Europe. Already the cities of Japan are being destroyed from the air almost at will.* The invasion of Japan can be made costly to the Allies, as the bloody fighting on the various Pacific islands has shown, and resistance on the Asiatic mainland, where big and effective Japanese armies exist and where the supply situation is better and there is more space to maneuver, might go on for years after the fall of Japan itself. But (1) there seems little prospect of ultimate success; (2) the destruction of Japanese industry and cities would be even greater than in Germany; (3) the longer the war goes on, the harder it will be for the big businessmen and the Court "moderates" to survive, in the Badoglio style, as a ruling class tolerated by the victorious Allies for fear of something worse (i.e., more left-wing). For all these reasons, it seems likely the non-militarist section of the Japanese ruling class is thinking in capitulation terms, and that the many rumors of peace

* In a single raid on the great industrial center of Nagoya recently, 500 Superfortresses dropped 3,300 tons of incendiary bombs, the biggest incendiary raid on record to date. The human horror of such raids on cities built largely of wood and paper hardly needs underlining. In Nagoya the heart of the city, where the population density was 75,000 to the square mile, was deliberately bombed. The military justification, or rather excuse, was that the Japanese "home industry" system makes every house in a working-class district a military objective. Such excuses are of interest only to military scholastics, and can be dispensed with if necessary: our air forces roasted to death tens of thousands of civilians in vast incendiary raids on Hamburg, Dresden and other German cities where "home industry" has been unknown since the 18th century.

"feelers" that have recently come out of Washington have some basis in fact.*

The very phenomenon which is often considered a guarantee of Japanese resistance to the bitter end—the hold of the Emperor over the people—might also be turned in the opposite direction. The Emperor is an institution without specific political content; for many centuries, those who have held or usurped the real political hegemony have done so "in the name of the Emperor"; the army fanatics who assassinated a number of leading "moderate" statesmen in 1936 in an unsuccessful putsch acted in the name of the Emperor even while shooting some of his most intimate counselors. Thus the Emperor could be exploited by a "capitulation cabal" just as readily as he is now exploited by the dominant militarist clique to rally the masses behind the war. Furthermore, there is no mass political party, with a definite program and ideology, of the Russian and German type. Thus all the obstacles to a reversal of policy are on the top level, not rooted in mass institutions and beliefs, and the issue will be decided, as it was in Italy, by the struggle of groups within the ruling class.

June, 1945

* Three months after this was written, the USA ended the war by dropping two atomic bombs. The excuse was that this shortened the conflict and so saved lives, Japanese as well as American. This kind of reasoning, of course, can be used to justify any atrocity. But it wasn't true anyway. It is now known that, as suggested here, the rulers of Japan were frantically trying to make peace for months before Hiroshima was atomized. Thus Admiral Halsey told the press on September 9, 1946: "The first atomic bomb was an unnecessary experiment . . . The Japs had put out peace feelers through Russia long before." And Admiral Blandy stated about the same time: "Japan had lost her means of resistance before the atomic bomb was dropped."

The Bomb

1.

At 9:15 on the morning of August 6, 1945, an American plane dropped a single bomb on the Japanese city of Hiroshima. Exploding with the force of 20,000 tons of TNT, The Bomb destroyed in a twinkling two-thirds of the city, including, presumably, most of the 343,000 human beings who lived there. No warning was given. This atrocious action places "us," the defenders of civilization, on a moral level with "them," the beasts of Maidanek. And "we," the American people, are just as much and as little responsible for this horror as "they," the German people.

So much is obvious. But more must be said. For the atomic bomb renders anticlimactical even the ending of the greatest war in history. (*1*) *The concepts, "war" and "progress," are now obsolete.* Both suggest human aspirations, emotions, aims, consciousness. "The greatest achievement of organized science in history," said President Truman after the Hiroshima catastrophe—which it probably was, and so much the worse for organized science. (*2*) *The futility of modern warfare should now be clear.* Must we not now conclude, with Simone Weil, that the technical aspect of war today is the evil, regardless of political factors? Can one imagine that The Bomb could ever be used "in a good cause"? Do not such means instantly, of themselves, corrupt *any* cause? (*3*) *The Bomb is the natural product of the kind of society we have created.* It is as easy, normal and unforced an expression of the American Way of Life as electric iceboxes, banana splits, and hydromatic-drive automobiles. We do not dream of a world in which atomic fission will be "harnessed to constructive ends." The new energy will be at the service of the rulers; it will change their strength but not their aims. The underlying populations should regard this new source of energy with lively interest—the interest of victims. (4) *Those who wield such destructive power are outcasts from humanity.* They may be gods, they may be brutes, but they are not men. (5) *We must "get" the national State before it "gets" us.* Every individual who wants to save his humanity—and indeed his skin—had better begin thinking "dangerous thoughts" about sabotage, resistance, rebellion, and the fraternity of all men everywhere. The mental attitude known as "negativism" is a good start.

August, 1945

2.

WHAT first appalled us was its blast. "TNT is barely twice as strong as black powder was six centuries ago. World War II developed explosives up to 60% more powerful than TNT. The atomic bomb is more than 12,000 times as strong as the best improvement on TNT. One hundred and twenty-three planes, each bearing a single atomic bomb, would carry as much destructive power as all the bombs (2,453,595 tons) dropped by the Allies on Europe during the war." (*Time*, August 20, 1945)

It has slowly become evident, however, that the real horror of The Bomb is not blast but radioactivity. Splitting the atom sets free all kinds of radioactive substances, whose power is suggested by the fact that at the Hanford bomb plant, the water used for cooling the "pile" (the structure of uranium and other substances whose atomic interaction produces the explosive) carried off enough radiation to "heat the Columbia River appreciably." *Time* added: "Even the wind blowing over the chemical plant picked up another load of peril, for the stacks gave off a radioactive gas." And Smyth notes: "The fission products produced in one day's run of a 100,000-kilowatt chain-reacting pile of uranium might be sufficient to make a large area uninhabitable."

There is thus no question as to the potential horror of The Bomb's radioactivity. The two bombs actually used were apparently designed as explosive and not gas bombs, perhaps from humanitarian considerations, perhaps to protect the American troops who will later have to occupy Japan. But intentions are one thing, results another. So feared was radioactivity at Hanford that the most elaborate precautions were taken in the way of shields, clothes, etc. No such precautions were taken, obviously, on behalf of the inhabitants of Hiroshima; the plane dropped its cargo of half-understood poisons and sped away. What happened? The very sensitivity of the army and the scientists on the subject is ominous. When one of the lesser experts who had worked on the bomb, a Dr. Harold Jacobson of New York, stated publicly that Hiroshima would be "uninhabitable" for seventy years, he was at once questioned by FBI agents, after which, "ill and upset," he issued another statement emphasizing that this was merely his own personal opinion, and that his colleagues disagreed with him.

The point is that none of those who produced and employed this monstrosity really knew just how deadly or prolonged these radioactive poisons would be. Which did not prevent them from completing their assignment, nor the army from dropping the bombs. Perhaps only among men like soldiers and scientists, trained to think "objectively"—i.e., in terms of means, not ends—could such irresponsibility and moral callousness be found. In any case, it was undoubtedly the most magnificent scientific experiment in history, with cities as the laboratories and people as the guinea pigs.

The official platitude about Atomic Fission is that it can be a Force for Good (production) or a Force for Evil (war), and that the problem is simply how to use its Good rather than its Bad potentialities. This is "just common sense." But, as Engels once remarked, Common Sense has some very strange adventures when it leaves its cozy bourgeois fireside and ventures out into the real world. For, given our present institutions—and the official apologists, from Max Lerner to President Conant of Harvard, envisage at most only a little face-lifting on these—how can The Bomb be "controlled," how can it be "internationalized"? Already the great imperialisms are jockeying for position in World War III. How can we expect them to give up the enormous advantage offered by The Bomb? May we hope that the destructive possibilities are so staggering that, for simple self-preservation, they will agree to "outlaw" The Bomb? Or that they will foreswear war itself because an "atomic" war would probably mean the mutual ruin of all contestants? The same reasons were advanced before World War I to demonstrate its "impossibility"; also before World War II. The devastation of these wars was as terrible as had been predicted—yet they took place. Like all the great advances in technology of the past century, Atomic Fission is something in which Good and Evil are so closely intertwined that it is hard to see how the Good can be extracted and the Evil thrown away. A century of effort has failed to separate the Good of capitalism (more production) from the Evil (exploitation, wars, cultural barbarism). *This* atom has never been split, and perhaps never will be.

The Marxian socialists, both revolutionary and reformist, also accept the potentialities-for-Good-or-for-Evil platitude, since this platitude is based on a faith in Science and Progress which is shared by Marxists as well as conservatives, and is indeed still the basic assumption of Western thought. (In this respect, Marxism appears to be simply the most profound and consistent intellectual expression of this faith.) Since the Marxists make as a precondition of the beneficial use of Atomic Fission a basic change in present institutions, their position is not open to the objections noted just above. But if one looks deeper than the political level, the Marxist version of the platitude seems at the very least inadequate. It blunts our reaction to the present horror by reducing it to an episode in an historical schema which will "come out all right" in the end, and thus makes us morally callous (with resulting ineffectuality in our actions against the *present* horror) and too optimistic about the problem of evil; and it ignores the fact that such atrocities as The Bomb and the Nazi death camps are *right now* brutalizing, warping, deadening the human beings who are expected to change the world for the better; that modern technology has its own anti-human dynamics which has proved so far much more powerful than the liberating effects the Marxist schema expects from it.

The bomb produced two widespread and, from the standpoint of The Authorities, undesirable emotional reactions in this country: a feeling of guilt at "our" having done this to "them," and anxiety lest some future "they" do this to "us." Both feelings were heightened by the superhuman *scale* of The Bomb. The Authorities have therefore made valiant attempts to reduce the thing to a human context, where such concepts as Justice, Reason, Progress could be employed. Such moral defenses are offered as: the war was shortened and many lives, Japanese as well as American, saved; "we" had to invent and use The Bomb against "them" lest "they" invent and use it against "us"; the Japanese deserved it because they started the war, treated prisoners barbarously, etc., or because they refused to surrender. The flimsiness of these justifications is apparent; *any* atrocious action, absolutely *any* one, could be excused on such grounds. For there is really only one possible answer to the problem posed by Dostoievski's Grand Inquisitor: if all mankind could realize eternal and complete happiness by torturing to death a single child, would this act be morally justified?

Somewhat subtler is the strategy by which The Authorities —by which term I mean not only the political leaders but also the scientists, intellectuals, trade-unionists and businessmen who function on the top levels of our society—tried to ease the deep fears aroused in everyone by The Bomb. From President Truman down, they emphasized that The Bomb has been produced in the normal, orderly course of scientific experiment, that it is thus simply the latest step in man's long struggle to control the forces of nature, in a word that it is Progress. But this is a knife that cuts both ways: the effect on me, at least, was to intensify some growing doubts about the "Scientific Progress" which had whelped this monstrosity. Last April, I noted that in our movies "the white coat of the scientist is as blood-chilling a sight as Dracula's black cape. . . . If the scientist's laboratory has acquired in Popular Culture a ghastly atmosphere, is this not perhaps one of those deep intuitions of the masses? From Frankenstein's laboratory to Maidanek [or, now, to Hanford and Oak Ridge] is not a long journey. Was there a popular suspicion, perhaps only half conscious, that the 19th century trust in science was mistaken . . . ?"

These questions seem more and more relevant. I doubt if we shall get satisfactory answers from the scientists (who, indeed, seem professionally incapable even of asking, let alone answering, them). The greatest of them all, who in 1905 constructed the equation which provided the theoretical basis for Atomic Fission, could think of nothing better to tell us after the bombings than: "No one in the world should have any fear or apprehension about atomic energy being a supernatural product. In developing atomic energy, science merely imitated the reaction of the sun's rays. ["Merely" is good!—DM] Atomic power is no more unnatural than when I sail my boat on Saranac Lake." Thus, Albert Einstein. As though it were not precisely the natural, the perfectly rational and scientifically demonstrable that is now chilling our blood! How human, intimate, friendly by comparison are ghosts, witches, spells, werewolves and poltergeists! Indeed, all of us except a few specialists know as much about witches as we do about atom-splitting; and all of us with no exceptions are even less able to defend ourselves against The Bomb than against witchcraft. No silver bullet, no crossed sticks will help us there. As though to demonstrate this, Einstein himself, when asked about the unknown radioactive poisons which were beginning to alarm even editorial writers, replied "emphatically": "I will not discuss that." Such emphasis is not reassuring.

Nor was President Truman reassuring when he pointed out: "This development, which was carried forward by the many thousand participants with the utmost energy and the very highest sense of national duty . . . probably represents the greatest achievement of the combined efforts of science, industry, labor and the military in all history." Nor Professor Smyth: "The weapon has been created not by the devilish inspiration of some warped genius but by the arduous labor of thousands of normal men and women working for the safety of their country." Again, the effort to "humanize" The Bomb by showing how it fits into our normal, everyday life also cuts the other way: it reveals how inhuman our normal life has become.

The pulp writers could imagine things like the atom bomb; in fact, life is becoming more and more like a Science Fiction story, and the arrival on earth of a few six-legged Martians with Death Rays would hardly make the front page. But the pulp writers' imaginations were limited; *their* atom bombs were created by "devilish" and "warped" geniuses, not by "thousands of normal men and women"—including some of the most eminent scientists of our time, the labor movement (the army "warmly" thanked the AFL and the CIO for achieving "what at times seemed impossible provision of adequate manpower"), various great corporations (DuPont, Eastman, Union Carbon & Carbide), and the president of Harvard University.

Only a handful, of course, knew what they were creating. None of the 125,000 construction and factory workers knew. Only three of the plane crew that dropped the first bomb knew what they were letting loose. It hardly needs to be stressed that there is something askew with a society in which vast numbers of citizens can be organized to create a horror like The Bomb without even knowing they are doing it. What real content, in such a case, can be assigned to notions like "democracy" and "government of, by and for the people"? The good Professor Smyth expresses the opinion that "the people of this country" should decide for themselves about the future development of The Bomb. To be sure, no vote was taken on the creation and employment of the weapon. However, says the Professor reassuringly, these questions "have been seriously considered by all concerned [i.e., by the handful of citizens who were permitted to know what was going on] and vigorously debated among the scientists, and the conclusions reached have been passed along to the highest authorities.

"These questions are not technical questions; they are political and social questions, and the answers given to them may affect all mankind for generations. In thinking about them, the men on the project have been thinking as citizens of the United States vitally interested in the welfare of the human race. It has been their duty and that of the responsible high Government officials who were informed to look beyond the limits of the present war and its weapons to the ultimate implications of these discoveries. This was a heavy responsibility.

"In a free country like ours, such questions should be debated by the people and decisions must be made by the people through their representatives."

It would be unkind to subject the above to critical analysis beyond noting that every statement of what-is contradicts every statement of what-should-be.

Atomic fission makes me sympathize, for the first time, with the old Greek notion of *Hubris,* that lack of restraint in success which invited the punishment of the gods. Some scientist remarked the other day that it was fortunate that the only atom we as yet know how to split is that of uranium, a rare substance; for if we should learn how to split the atom of iron or some other common ore, the chain reaction might flash through vast areas and the molten interior of the globe come flooding out to put an end to us and our Progress. It is *Hubris* when President Truman declares: "The force from which the sun draws its powers has been loosed against those who brought war to the Far East." Or when the *Times* editorialist echoes: "The American answer to Japan's contemptuous rejection of the Allied surrender ultimatum of July 26 has now been delivered upon Japanese soil in the shape of a new weapon which unleashes against it the forces of the universe." Invoking the Forces of the Universe to back up the ultimatum of July 26 is rather like getting in God to tidy up the living room.

It seems fitting that The Bomb was not developed by any of the totalitarian powers, where the political atmosphere might at first glance seem to be more suited to it, but by the two "democracies," the last major powers to continue to pay at least ideological respect to the humanitarian-democratic tradition. It also seems fitting that the heads of these governments, by the time The Bomb exploded, were not Roosevelt and Churchill, figures of a certain historical and personal stature, but Attlee and Truman, both colorless mediocrities, Average Men elevated to their positions by the mechanics of the system. All this emphasizes that perfect automatism, that absolute lack of human consciousness or aims which our society is rapidly achieving. As a uranium "pile," once the elements have been brought together, inexorably runs through a series of "chain reactions" until the final explosion takes place, so the elements of our society act and react, regardless of ideologies or personalities, until The Bomb explodes over Hiroshima. The more commonplace the personalities and senseless the institutions, the more grandiose the destruction. It is *Götterdämmerung* without the gods.

The scientists themselves whose brain-work produced The Bomb appear not as creators but as raw material, to be hauled about and exploited like uranium ore. Thus, Dr. Otto Hahn, the German scientist who in 1939 first split the uranium atom and who did his best to present Hitler with an atom bomb, has been brought over to this country to pool his knowledge with our own atomic "team" (which includes several Jewish refugees who were kicked out of Germany by Hitler). Thus Professor Kaputza, Russia's leading experimenter with uranium, was decoyed from Cambridge University in the thirties back to his native land, and, once there, refused permission to return. Thus a recent report from Yugoslavia tells of some eminent native atom-splitter being highjacked by the Red Army (just like a valuable machine tool) and rushed by plane to Moscow.

Insofar as there is any moral responsibility assignable for The Bomb, it rests with those scientists who developed it and those political and military leaders who employed it. Since the rest of us Americans did not even know what was being done in our name—let alone have the slightest possibility of stopping it—The Bomb becomes the most dramatic illustration to date of the fallacy of "The Responsibility of Peoples."

Yet how can even those immediately concerned be held responsible? A general's function is to win wars, a president's or prime minister's to defend the interests of the ruling class he represents, a scientist's to extend the frontiers of knowledge; how can any of them, then, draw the line at the atom bomb, or indeed anywhere, regardless of their "personal feelings"? The dilemma is absolute, when posed in these terms. The social order is an impersonal mechanism, the war is an impersonal process, and they grind along automatically; if some of the human parts rebel at their function, they will be replaced by more amenable ones; and their rebellion will mean that they are simply thrust aside, without changing anything. The Marxists say this must be so until there is a revolutionary change; but such a change never seemed farther away. What, then, can a man do *now*? How can he escape playing his part in the ghastly process?

Quite simply by not playing it. Many eminent scientists, for example, worked on The Bomb: Fermi of Italy, Bohr of Denmark, Chadwick of England, Oppenheimer, Urey and Compton of USA. It is fair to expect such men, of great knowledge and intelligence, to be aware of the consequences of their actions. And they seem to have been so. Dr. Smyth observes: "Initially, many scientists could and did hope that some principle would emerge which would prove that atomic bombs were inherently impossible. The hope has faded gradually. . . ." Yet they all accepted the "assignment," and produced The Bomb. Why? Because they thought of themselves as specialists, technicians, and not as complete men. Specialists in the sense that the process of scientific discovery is considered to be morally neutral, so that the scientist may deplore the uses to which his discoveries are put by the generals and politicians but may not refuse to make them for that reason; and specialists also in that they reacted to the war as partisans of one side, whose function was the narrow one of defeating the Axis governments even if it meant sacrificing their broader responsibilities as human beings.

But, fortunately for the honor of science, a number of scientists refused to take part in the project. I have heard of several individual cases over here, and Sir James Chadwick has revealed "that some of his colleagues refused to work on the atomic bomb for fear they might be creating a planet-destroying monster." These scientists reacted as whole men, not as special-ists or part-isans. Today the tendency is to think of peoples as responsible and individuals as irresponsible. The reversal of both these conceptions is the first condition of escaping the present decline to barbarism. The more each individual thinks and behaves as a whole Man (hence responsibly) rather than as a specialized part of some nation or profession (hence irresponsibly), the better hope for the future. To insist on acting as a responsible individual in a society which reduces the individual to impotence may be foolish, reckless, and ineffectual; or it may be wise, prudent and effective. But whichever it is, only thus is there a chance of changing our present tragic destiny. All honor then to the as yet anonymous British and American scientists—Men I would rather say—who were so wisely foolish as to refuse their cooperation on The Bomb! This is "resistance," this is "negativism," and in it lies our best hope.

September, 1945

THE NEW YORKER did a bold thing when it devoted its entire issue of August 31 to John Hersey's long reportage piece on Hiroshima. It was also a useful thing, judging by the popular sensation the issue seems to have caused. For what Hersey tried to do was to "bring home" to the American reader just what the bomb did to the human beings who lived in Hiroshima. The device he used was at once obvious (yet no one else thought of doing it) and journalistically effective: to interview a half dozen of the survivors some months later, and reconstruct in intimate human detail just what each of them did, felt and thought from the time of the dropping of the bomb until he interviewed them. As I say, his piece apparently affected a great many readers. But I must note that it didn't for some reason affect me; in fact, I found it so dull that I stopped reading it halfway through. For one thing, I don't like *The New Yorker's* suave, toned-down, underplayed kind of naturalism (it might be called "denatured naturalism," as against the cruder—and, to me, preferable—variety of Dreiser and the early Farrell). For another, Hersey is feeble as an artist, with no style, no ideas, no feelings of any intensity, and no eye for the one detail that imaginatively creates a whole; so he puts in everything, which gives a relaxed monotonous effect; I could not help thinking what the Hemingway who described the Caporetto retreat would have done with the theme, and in a fourth the space. These defects of art produce, and are produced by, what seems to me a moral deficiency: the dead-pan, keyed-down approach is so detached from the persons Hersey is writing about that they become objects of clinical description; the author appears like a specialist lecturing on some disease, with "interesting" cases on the platform. The "little people" of Hiroshima whose sufferings Hersey records in antiseptic *New Yorker* prose might just as well be white mice, for all the pity, horror or indignation the reader—or at least this reader—is made to feel for them. And yet Hersey's intention, which apparently was successfully communicated to many thousands of other readers, was to convey precisely such emotions. It is puzzling. Perhaps my feeling is simply that naturalism is no longer adequate, either esthetically or morally, to cope with the modern horrors.

October, 1946

The Late War: A Trial Balance

CHURCHILL's speech in Missouri, with its call for an Anglo-American military alliance and its open incitement of an ideological war against Russia, prompts me to some reflections on the late war. While it was in process, those eccentrics who opposed it were told by all sensible philistines that they were Unrealistic: granted that "our" side was far from perfect, was it not obvious that an Allied victory would be a lesser evil than a Nazi victory? I was myself the beneficiary of many such homilies. It made no impression on these sensible people to reply that the problems we faced were dynamic ones which could not be solved by a military victory of either side, that the triumph of the lesser evil would turn out to be merely the triumph of the greater evil in a different form, and that a choice between an Allied and a Nazi victory was a choice between being strangled or poisoned.

It is less than a year since the war ended in Europe, and already the world, having avoided being hanged by Hitler, is being poisoned by the victors. The gloomiest predictions of those of us who opposed the war are being fulfilled with a speed and on a scale which to me at least is quite unexpected.

What was the war fought for, according to the Realists?

The war was fought to secure freedom of speech and freedom from fear—i.e., freedom from political dictatorship. Russian totalitarianism has direct control of all Eastern Europe, has great influence in Western Europe through its disciplined Communist parties, and is expanding throughout the Orient.

The war was fought to secure freedom from want. A world food crisis, for which the American government is largely responsible, has materialized. Not for centuries have so many millions of people been faced with actual starvation. It is expected to be many months, perhaps years, before these famine conditions are mastered.

The war was fought to eliminate Racism. The newspapers

constantly tell us that anti-Semitism is more widespread in Europe today than it was under the Nazis; the tragic remnants of the Jews of Europe have one overwhelming desire—to leave their native lands, where they are despised, persecuted, threatened.

The war was fought above all to lay the foundations for a peaceful world. The Russian and the British empires have been clashing with mounting intensity, and now, with Secretary Byrnes' recent speech and his protests to Russia on Iran and Manchuria, this country enters the conflict. The UNO is already a bad joke; Russia fears the Anglo-American axis, which in turn fears Russian expansionism; both sides are exasperated, intransigeant, bellicose. The development of the atomic bomb adds the maximum technological force to the blind nationalistic antagonisms that are conducting us to World War III.

Already, Stalin's Russia has taken the place of Hitler's Germany as a ruthless totalitarian power that is out to upset the Anglo-American status quo; the parallels that can be drawn between 1945–46 and 1934–39 are really terrifying. Already, the Realists are making another lesser-evil choice, preparing to "defend" an admittedly imperfect Anglo-American "democratic way of life" against Russian totalitarianism. Already, the arguments are becoming horribly familiar: Isn't our imperfect democracy better than Stalin's (Hitler's) dictatorship? If Stalin (Hitler) is not "stopped," it will be our turn soon. Are you willing to face the prospect of a Communist (Nazi) world? There are only two Realistic alternatives: either "appeasement" or resistance, by force if necessary. Just *one* more war, and we shall have those famous Conditions for Democratic Progress at last firmly established!

It may be that there is little or no chance of the kind of revolutionary change in our own and Russia's institutions which would be needed to avoid a third world war; it may be we are once more in a blind alley, and this time with the actual extinction of human life on this planet as its ending. But let us at least face the real situation and not continue to deceive ourselves, and corrupt our values, by making another lesser-evil choice. From both the scientific and the ethical standpoint, it will be disastrous to think that "our" side will be any more successful in eliminating by force of arms the evils represented by Russian totalitarianism than it was in the case of the Nazis; even less so, in all probability. It may be there is no exit from the blind alley, but surely the first condition for finding one is to give up the superficial lesser-evil approach, with the support it implies for a future war against Russia, in favor of a more radical and basic approach, be it pacifist or social-revolutionary or perhaps some new combination of both.

March, 1946

Stalin's February Ninth Speech

STALIN'S SPEECH of February 9 was an important statement of policy. To the foreign ministries of Britain and the USA, it was a formal "resignation" from the wartime alliance. To the Russian people, at whom it was primarily aimed, it justified socialism (or rather "the Soviet social system" as Stalin termed it throughout—perhaps a significant verbal shift) as a good thing because it wins wars, which are assumed to be man's chronic fate because of the wickedness of all nations except the Soviet Union.

What Stalin said may be briefly summarized, since he always says everything at least three times. ("Moreover, after this war no one dared any more to deny the vitality of the Soviet state system. Now it is no longer a question of the vitality of the Soviet state system, since there can be no doubt of its vitality any more.") On the evidence of Stalin's barbarous oratorical style alone, one could deduce the bureaucratic inhumanity and the primitiveness of modern Soviet society. His main points, then, were:

(1) The war was "no accident" but rather "the inevitable result of the development of . . . monopoly capitalism." ("Our Marxists declare that the capitalist system of world economy conceals elements of crisis and war.")

(2) *We* won the war; not a word about Lend-Lease or any help from the Anglo-American military operations. ("Our victory implies that it was the Soviet armed forces that won. Our Red Army has won.")

(3) Our victory proves we have a good social system, the best in fact. ("The war has refuted all the assertions of the foreign press as without foundation. The war has shown that the Soviet social system is a truly popular system, issued from the depths of the people and enjoying its mighty support. . . . The Soviet social system is . . . fully viable and stable.")

(4) The military victory was possible because of the industrial base created by the first three Five Year Plans, which are presented as a historically unique achievement of the viable and stable Soviet system. ("In 1913 our country produced 4,220,000 tons of pig iron . . . in 1940, 15,000,000 tons of pig iron. . . . As you see, the difference is colossal . . . an unprecedented development in production.")

(5) This achievement was possible because while "in capitalist countries industrialization usually starts with light industry," "in our country the Communist Party reversed the usual path and began . . . with the development of heavy industry."

(6) The past Five Year Plans were justified by the victory won in World War II and the future Plans will, by implication, be similarly justified by victory in World War III. ("The party intends to organize a new mighty upsurge of national economy, which will enable us to increase the level of our production threefold . . . 50,000,000 tons of pig iron a year. . . . Only under such conditions will our country be insured against any eventuality. Perhaps three new Five-Year Plans will be required to achieve this, if not more. But it can be done, and we must do it.")

Thus the Five Year Plans are admitted to have had nothing to do with a better way of life but to have been simply military measures. This to Stalin appears entirely natural: making war successfully has come to be the acknowledged aim of Soviet "socialism," and the supreme test of a social system, for the Stalin bureaucracy, has nothing to do with Life, Liberty and the Pursuit of Happiness, nor with Liberty Equality and Fraternity, nor with Marx's Kingdom of Freedom, but quite bluntly: can it win wars? Even on this level, one must reject as unfounded the claim that only Sovietism could have industrialized Russia so quickly. Capitalism in America produced comparably speedy results in the decades 1850–1870; and in Russia itself a similar growth took place after the liberation of the serfs. (Cf. Engels' letter to Danielson of Sept. 22, 1892, on "the hothouse process of fostering industrial revolution" in Russia after 1861 "which . . . crams into twenty years a development which otherwise might have taken sixty or more years.") But it *is* true, as Stalin boasts, that the Communists have "reversed the usual path" of capitalist development and begun with heavy instead of light industry. What a world of human misery in that dry economic formulation! Light industry means consumers' goods, heavy industry means steel and dynamos and other inedible and unwearable things. The only way to *begin* with heavy industry is for the mass of workers to live like beasts, as they have in fact been living for a generation under Stalin. No wonder the Red Army soldiers would commit any crime for the possession of a watch or a bicycle. But all of this is, of course, necessary because the Soviet fatherland is encircled by wicked "monopoly capitalist" nations—the similarity to what Hitler told the German people is striking—and "our Marxists declare that the capitalist system of world economy conceals elements of crisis and war." Therefore, the Russian people may look forward to three more Five Year Plans "if not more," and the Red Army, in the Order of the Day which Stalin issued on February 22, is enjoined during "the new [i.e., post-Hitler] conditions" to "vigilantly guard the peaceful, creative labor of the Soviet people . . . and make the borders of our motherland impregnable against enemies."

March, 1946

Truman's Doctrine, Abroad and at Home

THE "TRUMAN DOCTRINE" has two aspects, foreign and domestic. Foreign: it is a declaration of economic and ideological war against the Soviet Union. Domestic: it calls for unprecedented security measures against Communism inside this country. With the recent passage through both houses of the initial appropriation for military aid to Greece and Turkey, the Doctrine has now progressed from a proposal to a reality. The temper of Congress leaves little doubt that the funds will also be appropriated for its implementation at home.

On March 12, 1947, Harry Truman, president of the United States by the act if not the grace of God, changed the face of postwar world politics when he asked Congress to appropriate $400 millions for military loans to Greece and Turkey. He made no secret either of his general or his specific purpose, apparently not realizing that these were in deadly conflict. The latter was to prop up the present reactionary governments of those countries so as to contain the expansion of Soviet imperialism. The former could be more eloquently expressed: "I believe that it must be the policy of the U.S. to support free peoples who are resisting attempted subjugation by armed minorities or by outside pressures. I believe that we must . . . help free peoples maintain their free institutions."

As a move to counter Russian imperialism, Truman's proposal has its points. The Soviet Union plays in world politics the same role Nazi Germany did in 1936–1939: that of a totalitarian, militarized "have not" power using aggressive tactics to upset the status quo in its favor. Appeasement—as practiced by Roosevelt at Teheran and Yalta and by Truman at Potsdam—has been no more effective in moderating the dynamism of Stalin's drive to world power than was the Munich appeasement with Hitler. Only a firm stand, backed by a show of force, will be effective. It can even be argued—I think with justice—that such a policy is more likely to postpone World War III than a "soft" policy. But only to postpone it; the show of force must sooner or later come to a show-down of force, i.e., war. Thus at best, the Truman Doctrine is no more than a detour on the road to World War III.

As a means of "helping free peoples maintain their free institutions," it is grotesque. Turkey is just another military-police state like Spain or Yugoslavia, and the entire $100 millions allocated there is to be spent on the army. The present monarchist government was imposed on the Greek people by force after the British Army had crushed the party that had the support of the great majority, the Communist-dominated EAM (see POLITICS, January-May, 1945). This government has refused to impose rationing or price control: the rich live better and the poor worse than in almost any other European country. There is no income tax. There are no exchange controls: since the Germans left, rich Greeks are estimated to have sent out over $50 millions in cash to American banks. No sensible import-export controls: "the first consignment of imports the Greek government allowed to be purchased abroad included 7 tons of chocolate, 3 tons of cosmetics, nearly 19 tons of combs, and *several thousand tons* of picture magazines" (Raymond Daniell, N. Y. *Times,* April 5, 1947). These figures may explain why the Greek military forces, estimated by the *Times* at almost 150,000, have been unable to suppress the tiny outlawed EAM bands in the North, estimated (maximum) at 13,000. The Greek army, states Truman, "needs supplies and equipment if it is to restore the authority of the government throughout Greek territory." In short, American funds are to be used to enable a monarchist oligarchy to deal with popular opposition. If, as Truman and Marshall insist and as is on the whole true, misery is world Communism's best ally, this would seem to be a peculiar way to "help free peoples maintain their free institutions."

Ten days later, on March 22, Truman made a comparably great alteration in domestic politics when he issued an executive order calling for an investigation of the political beliefs and activities of every one of the 2,200,000 employees of the Federal Government. This purge, of unprecedented scope, is to dismiss from the Government service every employee guilty of any one of a long string of offenses, including (besides "treason" and "sabotage") such cloudy matters as "performing his duties . . . or in any way acting in a manner which better serves the interests of a foreign government than the US." Further, the Attorney General is instructed to draw up a list of "totalitarian, fascist, communist or subversive" groups which "seek to alter the form of government of the United States by unconstitutional means." This list may or may not be made public, at the discretion of the Attorney General. Any Federal employee who is found to be connected with such a group may be summarily dismissed. Further, the "Loyalty Board" which will decide his fate is not required to reveal the source of any accusations against him. Thus the domestic aspect of the Truman Doctrine provides that an individual may be purged (a) on the charge of an accuser whom he is not permitted to confront, or (b) for connection with a group whose identity he is not told.

That this is a proposal to fight a totalitarian group—the American Communist Party—with its own methods is clear: punishment on anonymous denunciations for unspecified crimes is the essence of Nazi-Stalinist jurisprudence and the antithesis of what was once foolishly thought to be basic American procedure. That Congress will appropriate the considerable sums necessary for this witch-hunt ($25 millions is the initial appropriation asked for by Truman) also seems clear: its temper was accurately shown when the House Appropriations Committee on May 5 voted deep cuts in all Federal budgets except one—that of the FBI, which will play a key role in the Truman purge and whose director got the full $35 millions he asked for after he had delivered a speech to the committee on "the spread of Communism in the United States." Of those who argue that such measures are justified in order to "defend democracy," it may be asked what kind of democracy will result from such measures?

All "practical" politics today tends to be reduced more and more to the conflict between the USA and the USSR. These are the two remaining Great Powers; their friction is constantly more intense and irreconcilable; it magnetizes the class struggle in advanced nations like France as well as the colonial revolt in Asia, reducing both to skirmishes in the major battle; domestic politics are increasingly trivial, foreign policy swallows up everything, either—in the case of the Big Two—as preparation for eventual war, or—in the lesser nations—as maneuvering between the Big Two.

In terms of "practical" politics,* we are living in an age which constantly presents us with impossible alternatives. That is, alternatives which *both* appear to lead us away from the direction we want to go in. Such an alternative, it seemed to me, was posed in the recent coal strike, as well as in the last world war. This is not to deny that a choice was possible *if the existing alternatives alone were to be consulted:* Lewis was quite definitely a "lesser evil" to the Government in the strike, just as an Allied victory was a lesser evil to a Nazi victory in the war. But the miners' cause was so flawed and corrupted by the one-man dictatorship that controlled their union, just as the Allied cause was by the nature of the American and Russian social systems, that the only choice one

* By this I mean a politics which works in terms of the effective forces now existing. The term would include not only the bourgeois liberal or conservative, working within the limits of the status quo, but also the classic Marxian revolutionary, who saw in the oppressed workers an existing effective force to overthrow this status quo. The last flicker of this Marxian hope, in this country, was the "Third Camp" position in the last war: opposition to both sides on behalf of a revolutionary "Third Camp" of the masses—which turned out to be tragically non-existent.

could make with a clear head and a whole heart seemed to be—not to make a choice. However realistic it may have appeared at the time to back an Allied victory as "better than Hitler," it now looks like pure romanticism to have expected from the military defeat of Germany by the Allies anything more than the military defeat of Germany by the Allies.

The Truman Doctrine poses another such impossible alternative. America or Russia—or, more accurately, American imperialism or Russian imperialism? If these be the only alternatives—as they are in terms of practical politics—my own choice would be for the former, no doubt partly because I happen to live here, but also because we have not yet reached, by far, the degree of totalitarian horror that Russia has. But, for the reasons expressed above, the Truman Doctrine appears to be more a competitor than an opponent of the Kremlin Doctrine. Nor do I think this is either a "mistake" or a policy peculiar to "reactionary" politicians, which could be set right if "progressives" were put in their places. It seems rather the kind of policy suited to the kind of economic and social system we have, and I think that if Henry Wallace had won out over Truman in Chicago in 1944, he would by now have evolved a "Wallace Doctrine" along much the same lines.

If we admit there are only two alternatives in world politics, USA or USSR, and if we find it impossible, from the standpoint of our own values and hopes, to choose either, where are we? However logically and morally valid, our position is not an easy one. It raises some distressing general questions. Is it any longer possible for the individual to relate himself to world politics? Can these vast and catastrophic events be any longer conceived of in terms of radical choice and action? And if they cannot, must we not regard them as part of natural rather than human history, affecting us for good and ill like the weather—and also, like it, something everybody talks about but nobody does anything about?

On May 12, the N. Y. *Times* published a detailed survey of the military forces now being maintained throughout the world, after two years of "peace." This shows that there are almost 19 million men under arms, at a cost—in a world three-quarters of whose population gets too little to eat—of $27,400,000,000 a year, which is over ten times the yearly budget of UNRRA. This is about $10 billion more than was spent in 1938, when the world was preparing for World War II—and this despite the elimination of Japan and Germany. The USA spends a third of its budget on its army and navy; the USSR keeps 4 million men under arms; smaller nations, war-shattered and bankrupt, starve their people to maintain big armies; thus France has 430,000 men under arms, of whom almost half are in North Africa and Indo-China.

Even a statesman can see that all this is something close to insanity. Nor is it hard to show, in a general way, that the remedy must be as radical as the disease, stopping short of nothing less than pacifism and libertarian socialism. The data on which to base such a conclusion becomes more abundant every day, the arguments more convincing, but the scale and complexity of world politics has also become such that it seems to be a process uncontrollable by man's will and consciousness.

Superior insight into history used to be exhilarating for radicals: if we can see more clearly than the Enemy what is really going on, then we can use this knowledge to advance *our* values. But now the clearer one's insight, the more numbed one becomes. Thus during the war, some of us wrote articles in this magazine predicting that the conflict would *not* solve anything, that Potsdam would have tragic consequences, that the methods used by the Allies were infecting the moral atmosphere, that Russia and America would clash violently as soon as Germany was disposed of, etc., etc. Almost all the rest of the press, from liberal to conservative, was more optimistic. It turns out we were more right than they. This should make us feel prescient, confident.*

* Indeed, certain sectarian groups do now express such an attitude, so that one imagines, in the awful moment after the globe

Instead, it is discouraging. For our positive ideas have not worked out, either: the world seems farther than ever from either pacifism or socialism. As one brought up in the Progressive tradition, which assumes that if we only "know enough" about any situation, we can master it, and which further assumes, in its scientific innocence, that for every problem there *is* a solution and it is just a question of finding the appropriate road to it—I say that as one brought up in this tradition, I find it disconcerting to be confronted with a problem that shakes this assumption. We radicals are faced with a split between knowledge and action; we may overcome it, but we cannot any longer assume that we will; and meanwhile, in any case, there it is and it's not at all comfortable.

In the above, I am discussing only the dilemma which big-scale politics (and especially its ultimate, world politics) presents to the radical of today. On this scale, the situation indeed appears desperate. But on a more limited scale—that in which the individual's own thought, action and feelings can "make a difference"—political problems are more tractable, and there is some connection between knowledge and success. There, too, "practical politics" is possible: "effective forces now existing" (both emotional and rational) may be called into play. The slim hope left us is that in this limited, small-scale kind of activity some seeds may be planted now which will later produce larger changes. This kind of activity, also, can be rewarding in itself. But on the world scale, politics is a desert without hope.

May, 1947

---

has been split apart by atomic bombing, a thin voice floating down the wind of dissolution: "Capitalism means war. We told you so."

The Pacific Dilemma

SHOULD *the Western powers withdraw their troops from Berlin?*

To do this as part of a general pacifist program would be good. But if it is done, it will not be a symbol of pacifist-socialist revolution but simply a tactical move by militarist-capitalist governments. It would mean just what Munich meant: not peace-in-our-time but appeasement, and would thus strengthen, not weaken, the Stalin regime. Furthermore, such a move would not awaken any reaction in the Russian army or people, and would hand over to the Russians for punishment thousands of Berliners who have so courageously indicated their preference for the West's imperfect democracy against the East's perfect tyranny. This betrayal, aside from its moral aspects, would hardly encourage the rest of Europe to resist the spread of Communism.*

Assuming a pacifist revolution in the West, would this not merely insure the world triumph of Russian totalitarianism?

First, let me say that pacifism to me means to resist Stalinism, not to submit to it. The resistance is non-violent because

---

* This reply is not very satisfactory, from a pacifist standpoint. The fact is that there is no pacifist (or socialist) answer to the question of Berlin, just as there wasn't to Munich. As a pacifist, I cannot say, Don't Yield, since the consequences might be war—though I think they would not be—and it is irresponsible to support an action without being willing to support its possible consequences. On the other hand, a pacifist for the reasons given above cannot recommend getting out of Berlin either (any more than he could have recommended, though many pacifists mistakenly did, giving Czechoslovakia to Hitler as a step towards either peace or justice). Such situations, and they are increasing, are dilemmas for the pacifists or socialists. They call into doubt, in my mind at least, the political validity of a "Utopian," or ultimatist, position today.

I think it is immoral to kill or injure others, and because, on the political level, warfare has become too destructive and ghastly to hope for good results from it, and war means killing precisely our best allies against Stalinism, namely the people of Russia, who are the chief victims of Stalin's system, but whom the fires of war would weld closer to the Kremlin.

Pacifism does assume that not in the leaders but in the ranks of the enemy there is something similar to itself to which it can appeal, whether innate human feelings or an ethical-cultural tradition. That is, that we pacifists can count on a so-to-speak fifth column of brotherly love and reason and respect for truth and justice working for us behind the enemy lines. And that this fifth column can be stirred into action if we reveal unmistakably that it has already conquered in our own minds and hearts. Does this fifth column exist in the Russians today? That is a very speculative question.

Let us dismiss, first, the illusion of some of the more innocent pacifists that it exists in comrades Stalin, Molotov, Vishinsky, et al. These gentlemen would interpret any showing of brotherly love by the West as simply weakness, and would take advantage of a pacifist revolution to occupy Europe and the USA preliminary to instituting a People's Progressive Order. But would the Red Army march? And, if it would, what prospects are there that its soldiers, and the population back home in Russia, would be won over to our side by pacifist tactics?

Human beings do respond to love; they do have a feeling for truth and justice; they do dislike authority and repression; they do have prejudices against murder. They also have the reverse of these instincts, of course, but at least *both* tendencies exist, and one can choose which to appeal to. The Stalin regime has done its best to bring out in the Russians the reverse of the feelings listed above. How successful has it been? On the one hand, there is the barbarous behavior of the Red Army in Germany and Eastern Europe; the absence of rebellion inside Russia; the cynicism and apathy shown in the documents on Russian life. On the other, there is the fact of large-scale desertions from the Red Army, of episodes like the Kosenkina case, of the distaste for the regime also shown in the documents. The current defiance of Russian totalitarianism by large numbers of Berliners—quite unexpected by the Western authorities and newspapermen there—may be a sign that twelve years of Nazism have not too profoundly reshaped the German people. But Stalin has been in power for twenty years, and has enjoyed a much more complete and intimate control than Hitler did. The very completeness of his control makes it hard to evaluate its effects on the Russian people, since they are deprived of all possible outlets of self-expression. Except the jokes. Perhaps here is a sign of the existence of our fifth column!

In any case, we can say that the political leaders of USA have made no effort to see whether this fifth column exists or not. Their policy is static, unimaginative, niggardly, unfeeling. As their "unconditional surrender" policy plus the saturation bombings forced the German people to stick to Hitler to the end, so they are now solidifying the Russians behind Stalin. Except for the happy inspiration of the Marshall Plan —and even that is now in danger of being superseded by military expenditures—the US Congress and State Department have made no appeal to the imagination of the peoples of Europe and USSR. A nation which refuses to permit more than a token immigration of DP's, and that only under the most humiliating conditions, offers little encouragement to such dissident potentialities as there may be inside USSR today.

What about the chances of the American people adopting, in the face of the Soviet threat, an attitude of non-violent resistance?

Slight. The practice of loving, non-violent resistance towards one's enemies is a difficult discipline which even Gandhi, despite his leadership of a great mass movement, proved to have been unable to implant in the Indian masses. As he himself—unlike our own pacifist sectarians—recognized in the last year of his life, the communal massacres showed that his life work had been a failure in this respect. The

American temperament would seem to be less receptive to non-violence than the Indian; certainly there is no such popular tradition of it as in India. Also, the British authorities were themselves bound by a moral code which had some similarity to that of Gandhi's, whereas the Soviet authorities are not so bound.

If your chief political objective today is the overthrow of Stalinism, and if you do not think either pacifism or socialism can give answers to the specific political issues—such as whether the US Army should get out of Berlin or not—which arise in the course of the fight, and if war seems the most likely final upshot of the kind of resistance the West, as now constituted (and you see little hope of a basic change before World War III), offers; then will you not support World War III when and if it comes?

No.

Why not?

Because I agree with Simone Weil that the methods that must be used in fighting a modern war are so atrocious and clash so fundamentally with the ends I favor as to make impossible the achieving of those ends. Specifically, the mass slaughter of the enemy population by atomic bombing and bacteriological warfare, and the destruction of the fabric of Western civilization if not of the globe itself.

The usual argument for supporting war today is that if someone comes to burn down your house and kill your family, you have a right to kill him in order to prevent this. But this analogy, so persuasive to the popular mind, is misleading because it leaves out of account the chief difference between such a situation and the wars of our time. If you kill someone to prevent him burning your house and killing your children, the result is that your house is not burned and your children are not killed. But war today seems to bring about just what it is allegedly fought to prevent. After Hitler is defeated, the same evils reappear with the hammer and sickle on their caps instead of the swastika. And the moral and physical destruction employed to defeat Hitler has mounted to a total comparable to the hypothetical damage which the war was fought in order to avoid. A better analogy would be: The proprietor of a china shop battles a gang intent on breaking his china. But the encounter is so furious that most of the china is broken anyway; in fact, the proprietor himself seizes some of the most precious items in his stock to smash over the heads of the attackers.

Then if both violence and non-violence, for different reasons, seem impractical today, you are in a dilemma?

Yes.

Summer, 1948

"I Choose the West"

[*In the winter of 1952, I debated Norman Mailer at Mt. Holyoke College; my position was summed up: "I choose the West"; his: "I cannot choose." This is the gist of what I said.*]

I CHOOSE the West—the US and its allies—and reject the East—the Soviet Union and its ally, China, and its colonial provinces, the nations of Eastern Europe. By "choosing" I mean that I support the political, economic, and military struggle of the West against the East. I support it critically—I'm against the Smith and McCarran Acts, French policy in Indo-China, etc.—but in general I *do* choose, I support Western policies.

During the last war, I did not choose, at first because I was a revolutionary socialist of Trotskyist coloration, later because I was becoming, especially after the atom bomb, a pacifist. Neither of these positions now appear valid to me.

The revolutionary socialist position assumes there is a reasonable chance that some kind of popular revolution, a Third Camp independent of the warring sides and hostile to both, will arise during or after the war, as was the case in Russia in March, 1917. Nothing of the sort happened in the last war, despite even greater destruction and chaos than in 1917–18, because the power vacuum was filled at once by either Soviet or American imperialism. The Third Camp of the masses just doesn't exist any more, and so Lenin's "revolutionary defeatism" now becomes simply defeatism: it helps the enemy win and that's all.

As for pacifism, it assumes some degree of ethical similarity in the enemy, something in his heart that can be appealed to—or at least something in his traditions. Gandhi found this in the British, so his passive resistance movement could succeed, since there were certain repressive measures, such as executing him and his chief co-workers, which the British were inhibited from using by their traditional moral code, which is that of Western civilization in general. But the Soviet Communists are not so inhibited, nor were the Nazis. So I conclude that pacifism does not have a reasonable chance of being effective against a totalitarian enemy. Pacifism as a matter of individual conscience, as a *moral* rather than a *political* question, is another thing, and I respect it.

I choose the West because I see the present conflict not as another struggle between basically similar imperialisms as was World War I but as a fight to the death between radically different cultures. In the West, since the Renaissance and the Reformation, we have created a civilization which puts a high value on the individual, which has to some extent replaced dogmatic authority with scientific knowledge, which since the 18th century has progressed from slavery and serfdom to some degree of political liberty, and which has produced a culture which, while not as advanced as that of the ancient Greeks, still has some appealing features. I think Soviet Communism breaks sharply with this evolution, that it is a throwback not to the relatively humane middle ages but to the great slave societies of Egypt and the Orient.

Nor are the Communists content, or indeed able, to confine this 20th-century slave system to Russia or even to the vast new provinces in Asia and Eastern Europe added since 1945. Like Nazism, Soviet Communism is a young, aggressive, expansive imperialism (as against, for instance, the elderly

British imperialism, which since 1945 has permitted India, Egypt, and Iran to escape from its grip). Also like Nazism, it represses its own population so brutally that it must always be "defending" itself against alleged foreign enemies—else its subjects would ask why such enormous sacrifices are needed. The rulers of Soviet Russia will consider they are encircled by threatening invaders so long as a single country in the world is left that is independent of them. A reader asked the Moscow *Bolshevik* recently: "Now that we control a third of the world, can we still speak of capitalist encirclement?" The editors replied: "Capitalist encirclement is a political term. Comrade Stalin has stated that capitalist encirclement cannot be considered a geographical notion." (Thus the existence of a UN army on the Korean peninsula constitutes a *political* encirclement of Communist China.) Furthermore, precisely because the bourgeois West is so obviously superior, in most of the spiritual and material things that people value, to the Communized East, the mere *existence* of a non-Communist country is a danger to Communism. This was shown in 1945–46 when the Red Army troops returned from their contact with Europe "infected with bourgeois ideology" —i.e., they had seen how much more free the masses outside Russia are and how much higher their standard of living is—and had to be quarantined in remote districts for a while.

In choosing the West, I must admit that already the effects on our own society of the anti-Communist struggle are bad: Senator McCarthy and his imitators are using lies to create hysteria and moral confusion in the best Nazi-Communist pattern; building a great military machine cannot but extend the power of the State and so encroach on freedom. In short, we are becoming to some extent like the totalitarian enemy we are fighting. But (1) being on the road is not the same thing as being there already (though one might think it was from certain Marxist and pacifist statements), and (2) this malign trend can be to some extent resisted.

After all, here and in Western Europe there still exist different political parties, free trade unions and other social groupings independent of the State; varied and competing intellectual and artistic tendencies; and the protection, by law and by tradition, of those individual civil rights on which all the rest depend. Ours is still a living, developing society, open to change and growth, at least compared to its opposite number beyond the Elbe.

When Ulysses made his journey to the Elysian Fields, he saw among the shades his old comrade-in-arms, Achilles, and asked him how are things? Achilles' answer was: "I would rather be the slave of a landless man in the country of the living than the ruler of the kingdom of the dead." This is my feeling. I prefer an imperfectly living, open society to a perfectly dead, closed society. We may become like Russia, but we may not—the issue is not settled so long as we are independent of Moscow. If Moscow wins, the door is slammed shut, and to open it again would be a more difficult and brutal business than is now required by the measures to keep it open.

[*The following was written in 1953.*]

If it comes to another world war, I think we are done for, all of us. In supporting measures of opposition, including military ones as in Korea, against the Communists, I reason that the best chance of postponing war and perhaps avoiding it altogether is for the West to keep up its military strength and to be prepared to counter force with force. Appeasement didn't work with the Nazis and it won't work with the Communists. I admit that the results of the Korean war have been disastrous, especially for the Korean people; if I were a South Korean, I'm not sure I should have not preferred to have just let the North Koreans take over peacefully. Yet perhaps, in terms of world politics, the results of not making a fight to defend the Korean Republic would have been even more disastrous, like the results of letting Hitler absorb the Rhineland, Austria and Czechoslovakia without a fight.

Perhaps there is no solution any longer to these agonizing problems. Certainly the actual workings of history today yield an increasing number of situations in which *all* the real alternatives (as against the theoretically possible ones) seem hopeless. The reason such historical problems are insoluble now is that there have been so many crimes, mistakes, and failures since 1914, and each one making the solution of the next problem that much more difficult, that by now there are no uncorrupted, unshattered forces for good left with which to work. A decent social order in Europe after the first world war, for instance, would have made Hitler's rise impossible; even after he took power, a Loyalist victory in the Spanish Civil War or some radical reforms in France by Leon Blum's *Front Populaire* would have made his position very difficult. But none of these things happened, and when the *Reichswehr* marched into Poland, what solution was possible? Some of us felt it was our duty as socialists to "oppose the war," i.e., to refuse to fight the Nazis under the flags of existing governments; we also had illusions about the historical possibility of a "third camp" of the common people arising and making it possible to fight the Nazis with clean hands, so to speak. But this alternative, it is now clear, existed only on the ethical and ideological plane; it had no existence on the historical level. The only historically real alternatives in 1939 were to back Hitler's armies, to back the Allies' armies, or to do nothing. But none of these alternatives promised any great benefit for mankind, and the one that finally triumphed has led simply to the replacing of the Nazi threat by the Communist threat, with the whole ghastly newsreel flickering through once more in a second showing.

This is one reason I am less interested in politics than I used to be.

THE CULTURAL FRONT

Kulturbolshewismus & Mr. Van Wyck Brooks

In the period of reaction we are living through, it is peculiarly unfortunate that, as Dos Passos remarks in the introduction to his latest book, "Americans as a people notably lack a sense of history." For the modern intellectual needs a sixth sense if he is to survive—the historical sense. Confronted by a frustrating historical situation—the breakdown of the political, social and cultural values of the bourgeois order, and the simultaneous impotence of any progressive revolutionary force to sweep clear the debris—our intellectuals have for the most part either tried to find their way back to the long discredited values of the bourgeoisie, or else have begun to move towards a totalitarian "solution." But for the values they instinctively want to preserve, both roads lead to historical dead ends.

The swing back to bourgeois values has been up to now much the stronger. It has caught up almost all the old intellectual leaders of the left wing. Lewis Corey, whom we once looked to as the outstanding Marxist economist, has discovered "the industrial capitalist virtues—however imperfectly realized—of production for welfare, democracy and peace" (*Nation,* May 19, 1941). Louis M. Hacker, once the "coming" Marxist historian, has also discovered the virtues of "industrial" as against "finance" capitalism (as Hitler did years ago) and now regards Rockefeller as "a great industrial innovator" who "conformed to the pattern of the enterpriser of classical economics" (*Nation,* Dec. 7, 1940). Sidney Hook, once the leading Marxist philosopher, has swung away from Marx towards John Dewey and celebrates all kinds of extremely vague beauties in capitalist bourgeois democracy (*New Leader,* passim). John Dos Passos, the "irresponsible" chronicler of the last war, flies to England, fittingly accompanied by Thornton Wilder, to help the bellicose P.E.N. Club win this one. Max Eastman, the hero of the old *Masses* trial, the gay rebel, the original American Trotskyist, writes war propaganda and publishes an attack on socialism which Wendell Willkie implores every good American to read and which is the low-water mark to date in such affairs for vulgarity and just plain silliness (*Reader's Digest,* June, 1941).

This tendency is nothing new, nor is it of itself especially dangerous, since the values these writers are trying to revive are quite beyond the aid of their oxygen tanks. In this article I want to analyze the other and newer and much more ominous tendency, which seems to me most significantly expressed to date in a recent paper of Van Wyck Brooks—the tendency to rally to the concepts of Hitler's (and Stalin's) "new order."

Van Wyck Brooks' speech * was a Dadaist gesture in reverse. Dadaist in the furious invective, the wild statements, the general air of provocative hyperbole; only the madly ringing alarm clocks to interrupt the speaker and the stench bombs to drive out the audience were lacking. In reverse

* "Primary Literature and Coterie Literature," a paper delivered at the Second Annual Conference on Science, Philosophy and Religion, at Columbia University, New York City, on September 10, 1941. I am indebted to Dr. Louis Finkelstein, of the Conference, for a copy of the paper and of Thomas Mann's letter of comment.

because the apparatus was turned *in defense of* bourgeois-Philistine values. The comparison is unfair to the Dadaists, whose antics were both logical and deliberate. Brooks was apparently serious in his clowning.

The paper is built around an antithesis between "primary" and "secondary" writers. The former is "a great man writing," "one who bespeaks the collective life of the people" by celebrating "the great themes . . . by virtue of which the race has risen—courage, justice, mercy, honor, love." He is positive, constructive, optimistic, popular. He believes in "the idea of progress." Above all, he is primary. The "secondary," or "coterie," writer, on the other hand, is a thin-blooded, niggling sort of fellow, whose work reaches "a mere handful of readers." His stuff has brilliant "form" but lacks "content." He is "a mere artificer or master of words," who perversely celebrates the "death-drive" instead of the "life-drive." He is a doubter, a scorner, a skeptic, expatriate, highbrow and city slicker. His work is pessimistic and has lost contact with The People and The Idea of Greatness. He is, above all, secondary.

Brooks does not hesitate to name names, as follows.* *Primary:* Tolstoi, Milton, Erasmus, Dickens, Rabelais, Dostoievski, Socrates, Goethe, Ibsen, Whitman, Hugo, Emerson, Whittier and Thomas Mann. (Critics: Arnold, Taine, Renan, Sainte-Beuve.) *Secondary:* Joyce, Proust, Valéry, Pound, Eliot, James, Dryden, Nietzsche, Rimbaud, Mallarmé, Farrell, Hemingway, Dos Passos and Gertrude Stein. (Critics: Eliot, Richards, Winters, Pound, Tate, Ransom.)

This is childishness, ignorance, nonsense, what you please, but it is unhappily symptomatic of much more than Brooks' own mentality. It is the boldest statement to date of that cultural counterrevolution opened by Archibald MacLeish's attack on the "irresponsibles." And what are we to make of Brooks' side remark in his speech that Edmund Wilson, of

* For this list I have also drawn on a speech Brooks gave a year ago at Hunter College (published as "On Literature Today") in which he first developed his thesis, though in much more genial and cautious terms.

all people, "partially agrees with me"? Or of Thomas Mann's extraordinary comment on the paper, which I think worth reproducing in full:

> It strikes me as a piece of daring, intelligent and aggressive criticism; I have been well entertained by it without considering myself justified to give it a Yes or No. Above all I must admit that I am not sufficiently familiar with Eliot's work to be able to judge whether the extraordinary hostility which Van Wyck Brooks feels for this author is justified or not. I am tolerant by nature and look at things with an eye to gain from them the best for my own education; I would never have the courage to express such contempt for Joyce, Valéry, etc., as the author does.
>
> In the main, he is undoubtedly right when he says that in our present epoch only a few primary and truly great poets and authors represent and embody the spirit and the experience of our time. The others do work which probably also has to be done, but is not creative in the true sense, and they are certainly not entitled to lack respect for the great representatives of tradition. I believe, however, that this difference between the real leaders of a culture and its average servants and carriers has existed at all times, and is no particular sign of our epoch.

It is clear that Mann is somewhat uneasy about Brooks' paper; his comment is the most shameful kind of equivocation. He is "not familiar" with Eliot's work—what amazing ignorance in one who aspires to be the 20th century Goethe! He is "tolerant" of Joyce, Valéry, "etc."—what impudent condescension! The second paragraph of his letter is pure doubletalk: of course there are only "a few primary and truly great" creators in every age, but the question is precisely does Mann agree with Brooks' definition of who these are today? The implication, which he lacks courage to state openly, is that he does. But Mann read Brooks hastily when he speaks of "a few" great creators. Brooks mentions *only one* of our age, and that one happens to be none other than . . . Thomas Mann. So we see Mann accepting the flattery and assenting to Brooks' barbaric attack on all the other great writers of our age.

The most obvious comment on the two lists of writers given above is also the most important: all the primary writers except Mann * are of the past, while the scope of the "coterie" classification includes practically every significant modern writer, of every school from Paul Valéry to James T. Farrell. Now it would be logically *possible* that many writers in the past and no writers today might measure up to a given esthetic standard. But Brooks is not making an esthetic judgment—in fact one of his chief quarrels with the coterie writers is their preoccupation with "mere" esthetics. He is making a *historical* judgment: he claims that Eliot, Joyce and the rest are bad writers because they don't truly render the "sense of the age." This is the point at issue. For, if we overlook the crudity of Brooks' formulations, we can agree with him that the coterie writers don't believe in progress and the "march of humanity," that they are inclined to be skeptical and critical, that they are not at all popular and that they represent the end and not the beginning of a culture. But the real questions are: Is their skepticism justified? Are their audiences small because popular cultural values are debased or because they perversely prefer to isolate themselves from "humanity"? *Is* bourgeois society—which I assume Brooks would grant is the society of the period and writers in question—dying, or is it entering on a new life?

For all his boldness, Brooks nowhere dares to assert that bourgeois society in this century is in a flourishing condition. He simply *assumes* this crucial point—or, more accurately, doesn't seem aware it *is* crucial, and that writers can be expected to exhibit his "primary" virtues only in a "primary" historical period. Here his historical illiteracy stands him in

* This exception is in appearance only. Brooks dubs Mann "primary" not because of his *work*, which is patently "secondary" in its pessimism, skepticism and world-weariness, but because of his *ego*, because "the Goethe-intoxicated Mann" alone of modern writers is preoccupied with "the idea of greatness." What irony, that the foible of a great creative talent, which leads him to pose as *Goethe redivivus*, should be to Brooks precisely Mann's passport to the ranks of the "primary" writers!

good stead. For he is actually able to believe that the specific values of the last century are eternal values, and that Homer, Rabelais, Erasmus, Milton and Dostoievski all wore the spiritual costume of Victorian humanitarianism. "Tradition," he states flatly, "implies that mankind is marching forward." And: "This mood of health, will, courage, faith in human nature is the dominant mood in the history of literature."

"Thirty years ago, when I began to write," remarked Brooks wistfully in his Hunter College speech, "the future was an exciting and hopeful vista. Everyone believed in evolution as a natural social process. We took the end for granted. Mankind was marching forward." Facing a world in which such beliefs are violently in conflict with reality, and unable or unwilling to change them, Brooks is forced to denounce as somehow responsible for this reality those writers whose work most truthfully reflects it. It is a particularly neat example of how an originally progressive ideology becomes reactionary when it is carried over into a later period. Van Wyck Brooks has become, doubtless with the best intentions, our leading mouthpiece for totalitarian cultural values. For the spirit in which such great creative works as *Ulysses, The Golden Bowl, Death in Venice, Swann's Way* and *The Waste Land* are conceived is that of free inquiry and criticism, and it must always and in every instance result in exposing the overmastering reality of our age: the decomposition of the bourgeois synthesis in all fields. The final turn of the screw is that Brooks, like MacLeish, in attacking those whose work exposes this decomposition, himself expresses its farthest totalitarian reach. We can now understand his close relations with the Stalinist literary front, his chauvinistic leanings of late years, and his famous proposal that "committees be formed in towns to make house-to-house collections of objects made in Germany, which might be destroyed in public bonfires. . . . If these mass demonstrations were on a scale sufficiently large, they would suggest that democracy has something to say." (Letter to *Time,* Dec. 5, 1938) Hitler also has something to say, in these terms, and has said it.

To explain how it is that the greatest writers of the age

don't possess the "sense of the age," Brooks constructs the theory that a clique of mediocrities have somehow seized control of modern literature and imposed on it a set of "secondary" values which effectively prevents anyone (except Van Wyck Brooks) from perceiving that they themselves are just not up to the "primary" standard. "That certain minds are dominant does not mean that these are the minds which possess the sense of the age. They may be only the most articulate. . . . These coterie writers have expressed a moment in which they have caught humanity napping." It is all a tragic historical *accident*—like an automobile smashup. In an incredibly venomous and silly passage he calls James and Eliot "little Jack Horners" who sit in a corner and gloat over their little plums of style. "Meantime they forget that they are in a corner, while the center of the room is occupied by someone else. But the someone in the center sits in the place of humanity, and he has the final word." The object of the grand conspiracy—he actually refers to "James Joyce, who conspired with Eliot to destroy tradition"—is to "cut away the standard by which they can be measured as the minor poets and novelists they most assuredly are." Elsewhere he refers to "international mystagogues"—this note of xenophobia recurs throughout the paper—"concerned, above everything else, for their own prestige; for, as maladjusted persons they are insecure, and, being insecure, they develop a morbid will-to-power." This is an eminent literary critic writing in the year 1941! *

At one point in his tirade, Brooks recalls, a bit uneasily one suspects, that his subject matter is after all literature. "But

* In the same Chamber-of-Commerce spirit, Brooks asks: "What was Proust's sickness if not an excuse for dropping out of the common life, to which he was not superior but unequal?" Cf. Eastman's *Readers Digest* article on Marx: "While telling a planet how its future business was to be run, he threw up his hands at the comparatively simple task of earning his own living. He had to be supported throughout life like a baby, and as though to compensate he grew an enormous beard." Such judgments tell us nothing pertinent about Proust or Marx, but much about their critics and even more about the state of our culture today.

are not some of them beautiful writers? Who can deny this? I enjoy their artistry as much as any man living." But what shall we say of the sensibility of a literary critic who reacts to the playful and wonderfully skillful parody section in *Ulysses* in these terms:

> Has he not in the "Oxen of the Sun" episode run through the whole of English literature, depreciating with his parodies its greatest authors, deforming every one of them—Gibbon, Burke, Goldsmith, Lamb, De Quincey, Dickens, Ruskin, Burns and a dozen others? What fools he makes them seem as he fills his travesties of their styles with trivial and salacious implications!—and all for the glorification of James Joyce. For what a big boy he must be to put all these authors in their places!

Here we have the accusation of petty vanity—so often repeated as to appear to be an obsession—and the insensibility to specifically *literary* values already noted, combined with a Victorian squeamishness ("salacious implications") and a feeling that any adverse criticism of the great writers of the past is *irreverent* and a blow at "tradition." Brooks is shocked by Joyce's paraphrase of Newman's hymn, "Lead, kindly foul!" and his: "Greater love than this no man hath than that a man lay down his wife for a friend. Go thou and do likewise." He is shocked by the freedom with which Pound and Eliot comment on established authors. When, after the lecture, someone asked him whether Wagner and Dostoievski were "primary," Brooks replied in all solemnity, according to the N. Y. *Times*, "that although Wagner had streaks of meanness in his character and Dostoievski was morbid, their other qualities entitled them to be termed great men." Shades of Edmund Clarence Stedman! *

* The Brooks of 1941, in fact, has joined hands with that vestal guardian of the bourgeois *convenances* he so acidly depicted in his *Ordeal of Mark Twain:* Olivia Clemens, who made her husband delete from his manuscripts such words as "stench," "offal" and "breech-clout." Brooks quotes one of her marginal notations: "P. 1038—I hate to have your father pictured as lashing a slave boy." "It's out, my father is whitewashed," noted Twain. He also took

Everything is reversed in the looking-glass land Brooks mentally inhabits. He objects that Eliot and Joyce are destroying "tradition," but he himself would kill the living tradition of our age for the sake of a sapless respectability. He scolds the coterie writers for their "negativism" and "death-drive" but what could be more Nihilistic than his own rejection of the whole body of significant writing of our time? This apostle of the positive, the "life-drive," recommends to the contemporary American writer that he nourish his art on . . . Whittier. No, the shoe is decidedly on the other foot. It is true that the approach of the coterie writers to the specific historical values of modern society is negativistic, cynical, skeptical, destructive, etc. But in an age of social decay, it is only by rejecting the *specific* and *immediate* values of society that the writer can preserve those *general* and *eternal* human values with which Brooks is concerned. What blindness to see in *Ulysses,* a work overflowing with genial delight in the richness of human life, a *rejection* of life. What is rejected is a specific historical social order, and it is only by making that rejection that Joyce was able to survive as an artist and to preserve and defend those general human values on which culture depends. Brooks does not mention a single contemporary "primary" writer, because to do so would have given the whole show away. For there *are* such writers today, plenty of them. They put into practice what Brooks preaches, they accept modern society, they are positive, constructive, optimistic, popular, and they are firm believers in progress. Their work, however, turns out to be worthless as literature and also profoundly anti-human. It is printed in, among other periodicals, *The Saturday Evening Post.**

---

out the offending words, protesting, "You are steadily weakening the English tongue, Livy." Isn't all this just the operation Brooks would perform on modern writing?

* In *Letters and Leadership* (1918), Brooks quotes these words of a popular writer of the day: " 'Modern life is full of problems, complex and difficult. . . . The newspaper poets are forever preaching the sanest optimism. . . . That's the kind of poetry the people want, and the fact that they want it shows that their hearts and heads are all right.' " Brooks commented: "This doctrine is that

Where have we heard all this before? Where have we seen these false dichotomies: "form" vs. "content," "pessimism" vs. "optimism," "intellect" vs. "life," "destructive" vs. "constructive," "esthete" vs. "humanity"? Where have we known this confusion of social and literary values, this terrible *hatred* of all that is most living in modern culture? Where have we observed these methods of smearing an opponent, these amalgams of disparate tendencies, this reduction of men's motives to vanity and pure love of evil? Not in the spirit of abuse but as a sober historical description, I say these are the specific cultural values of Stalinism and the specific methods of the Moscow Trials. Brooks' speech could have been delivered, and was in essence delivered many times, at Stalinist literary meetings here and in Russia during the crusade against "formalism" and for "social realism" which began with the Popular Front turn in 1936 and remains the characteristic Stalinist approach to esthetics. Proust to him is a "spoiled child," Joyce "the ash-end of a burnt-out cigar," just as Radek could describe *Ulysses* as "a microscope focused on a dunghill." And aren't we right at home in that poisonous atmosphere again when we read that John Crowe Ransom's literary criticism "suggests the joy of Bruno Mussolini hunting out the Ethiopians"? Or when Brooks retorts to Mann's "toleration" of T. S. Eliot: "Dr. Mann is not tolerant of Hitler, and there are certain people about whom I am not tolerant."? Is it farfetched to bring in the Moscow Trials? Their stage-managers, like Brooks confronted with unanswerable historical objections to their frame-up, also had to seek motivations for the accused in personal vanity and sheer diabolism. And just as they found it convenient to amalgamate

---

the function of art is to turn aside the problems of life from the current of emotional experiences and create in its audience a condition of cheerfulness that is not organically derived from the experience but added from the outside." Brooks' evolution might be summed up thus: up to 1920 he urged American writers to be more critical of bourgeois society; in the twenties they followed his advice, found society rotten, said so; today, although (or perhaps because) society is incomparably more rotted, Brooks wants the verdict reversed.

fascists, Bukharinists, Trotskyists and bourgeoisie into a single block, so Brooks makes no distinction between the critical values of Eliot, Richards, Tate, Pound and—actually—Logan Pearsall Smith. We are only just beginning to appreciate the terrible significance of the Trials for our age. The more closely integrated Stalin's Russia becomes into the Anglo-American war effort, the more threatening will be a recrudescence of its cultural values. We may have to fight the old fights of the thirties all over again. On the basis of this paper, Brooks is the logical successor to Dashiell Hammett as president of the League of American Writers.

But this outburst by an eminent American critic suggests even more than this. Here we have that *official* approach to culture which has spread far beyond the confines of the Stalinist movement. Brooks' thesis is essentially an amplification of the attack on the "irresponsibles" made a year ago by Archibald MacLeish, Librarian of Congress and intimate of the White House. And would not Goebbels, the foe of "degenerate" modern art, applaud not only the particular cultural tendency attacked but also the very terms of the argument: "Primary literature somehow follows the biological grain; it favors what psychologists call the 'life-drive'; it is a force of regeneration that in some way conduces to race survival." "Kulturbolschewismus," "formalism," "coterie writing," "irresponsibles"—the terms differ for strategic reasons, but the content—and The Enemy—is the same.

The official approach to art has for its aim the protection of a historically reactionary form of society against the free inquiry and criticism of the intelligentsia. It is an attempt to impose on the writer *from outside* certain socio-political values, and to provide a rationalization for damning his work *esthetically* if it fails to conform to these *social values*. The mechanism is exposed with particular crudeness in Brooks' paper, which simultaneously damns coterie writing in social terms because it has a *bad* content ("pessimistic," "negativistic," etc.) and also damns it esthetically because it has *no* content ("mere artificers of words . . . for whom only the manner exists and not the substance"). We may also note that the official critic, since he is attempting to defend what is historically indefensible, is forced at every turn to attribute petty and base motives to the serious writers of his day, and to elevate pure theological *wickedness* into a historical principle.

The recent growth of this tendency over here is an ominous sign of the drift toward totalitarianism. It is a matter of cultural life and death to resist this tendency, regardless of one's specific political beliefs. Looking over back issues of this magazine, I am struck with how continuously we have been fighting a rear-guard action against this growing official esthetic, first as it manifested itself in the Stalinist writers' front, then, after the Nazi Pact disillusioned the main body of American writers with Stalinism (unfortunately, purely on the political level, without raising the broader cultural issues at all), as it has cropped up in the swing behind the government in the war crisis. The irony is, of course, that it *is* a rear-guard action, that the new social and political forces which alone can bring into being a new esthetic tendency are still frozen and impotent. Eliot, Joyce, Proust, James, Valéry—these represent, as Brooks says, an end and not a beginning. Their school had done its work, fought and won its battles by the end of the twenties. But it is still the most advanced cultural tendency that exists, and in a reactionary period it has come to represent again relatively the same threat to official society as it did in the early decades of the century. The old battles must be fought again, the old lessons learned once more.

"*'Well, in* our *country,' said Alice, still panting a little, 'you'd generally get to somewhere else—if you ran very fast for a long time, as we've been doing.' 'A slow sort of country!' said the Red Queen. 'Now* here, *you see, it takes all the running you can do to keep in the same place.'*"

Partisan Review, Nov.-Dec., 1941

Homage to Twelve Judges

AN EDITORIAL

THE FELLOWS are aware that objections may be made to awarding a prize to a man situated as is Mr. Pound. In their view, however, the possibility of such objection did not alter the responsibility assumed by the jury of selection. . . . To permit other considerations than that of poetic achievement to sway the decision would destroy the significance of the award and would in principle deny the validity of that objective perception of value on which any civilized society must rest."

This seems to me the best political statement made in this country for some time, just as the action of the Fellows in awarding the 1948 Bollingen Prize to Ezra Pound's *The Pisan Cantos* is the brightest political act in a dark period. Let me explain why, despite the disclaimers of the Fellows themselves, I consider their award a political, as well as a literary, event.

As is well known, Mr. Pound's situation is disreputable and hopeless to a dramatic degree. For many years, he has articulated fascistic and anti-Semitic sentiments; during the war, he made radio propaganda from Italy for Mussolini's regime and against his native country; he is now under arrest in a Washington mental hospital and will be tried for treason when and if he is pronounced mentally competent. The very book for which he is now honored was mostly written in a US Army prison in Pisa, nor is it by any means free of its author's detestable social and racial prejudices.

The prize committee is a distinguished one. Its members are: Conrad Aiken, W. H. Auden, Louise Bogan, T. S. Eliot, Paul Green, Robert Lowell, Katherine Anne Porter, Karl Shapiro, the late Theodore Spencer, Allen Tate, Willard Thorp, and Robert Penn Warren. These constitute the Fellows in American Literature, a board appointed by Luther

Evans, the Librarian of Congress. Thus we have a committee composed of eminent American writers and appointed by a high Government official, giving an important literary prize to a man under arrest for treason. I think there are not many other countries today, and certainly none East of the Elbe, where this could happen, and I think we can take some pride as Americans in having as yet preserved a society free and "open" enough for it to happen.

Whether *The Pisan Cantos* is the best poetry published by an American last year or not, I am incompetent to judge. Nor is this the point considered here, which is rather that by some miracle the Bollingen judges were able to consider Mr. Pound the poet apart from Mr. Pound the fascist, Mr. Pound the anti-Semite, Mr. Pound the traitor, Mr. Pound the funny-money crank, and all the other Mr. Pounds whose existence has properly nothing to do with the question of whether Mr. Pound the poet had or had not written the best American poetry of 1948.

"That objective perception of value on which any civilized society must rest"—this seems to me a formulation difficult to improve. Is not one of the most repellent aspects of the present Soviet system—or, for that matter, of the fascist system which Mr. Pound was so foolish as to admire—precisely that any "objective perception of value" is impossible under it? For such a perception is possible only under two closely related conditions. The first is that no one sphere of human activity is exalted over the rest. The second is that clear distinctions be maintained between the various spheres, so that the value of an artist's work or a scientist's researches is not confused with the value of their politics.

The horror of Soviet communism, of course, is that it reduces the individual to one aspect, the political. The consequence is the obliteration of the boundary lines between the various aspects of culture—or better, the imperialist conquest of all the rest by politics—so that the fifteen members of the Politburo decide, *ex cathedra*, literally all questions, including the most abstruse problems of esthetics and science. Is not the literal meaning of "totalitarianism" just this pretension of the political power to control the *totality* of human life?

Such imperfect democracy as we of the West still possess depends on our continuing ability to make the kind of discrimination the Bollingen committee made, to evaluate each sphere of human activity separate from the rest instead of enslaving them all to one great reductive tyrant, whether it be The Church, The Proletariat, People's Democracy, The Master Race or American Patriotism. Such limping justice as our courts produce likewise rests on their ability to distinguish the defendant's total behavior and personality from the specific action he is accused of having committed. And such cultural achievement as we are still capable of is nourished by "that objective perception of value on which any civilized society must rest."

The wave of the future is rolling in the other direction, as the warmaking centralized State becomes more powerful. It is ironical that it is precisely those who are misnamed "liberals" and even "socialists" who seem to be least enthusiastic about the Pound award. What bothers them is the very thing that is healthiest, politically, about it: the fact that Pound's treason and fascism were not taken into account in honoring him as a poet.

An extreme reaction was that of Albert Deutsch (whose liberalism has a Stalinoid tinge) writing in the liberal N. Y. *Post* of February 28. After a virulent column, in which he denounces Lowell and Eliot as "friends of the turncoat poet" and criticizes them because they have not turned *their* coats ("they have been faithful visitors to Pound's ward in St. Elizabeth's"), Deutsch concludes: "There is something unholy in the act. To bestow honor in any form on the man who broadcast Fascist propaganda under the auspices of the Fascist enemy of his native land smacks, to me, like Benedict Arnold's American contemporaries awarding him a medal for his undoubted military ability—after his betrayal of West Point. . . . Regardless of the protestations of the prize committee, the prize given to the turncoat poet is likely to be regarded not only as a literary event but as a political act in many parts of our world."

On which: (1) such a medal to Benedict Arnold would have been, in my opinion, a noble gesture; (2) the award is indeed, as argued above, a "political act"—and one which should demonstrate to "many parts of our world" that at least some Americans have a right to oppose Soviet totalitarianism in the name of freedom.

Winter, 1949

Bureaucratic Culture: Nicholas I and Josef I

Let me begin with two anecdotes from Herzen's My Past and Thoughts. *The first:*

As a student, Polezhaev was renowned for his excellent verses. Among other things he wrote a humorous parody of *Onyegin* called *Sashka* in which, regardless of proprieties, he attacked many things in a jesting tone, in very charming verses.

In the autumn of 1826, Nicholas, after hanging Pestel, Muravyov, and their friends, celebrated his coronation in Moscow. For other sovereigns, these ceremonies are occasions for amnesties and pardons; Nicholas, after celebrating his apotheosis, proceeded again to "strike down the foes of the fatherland."

The secret police brought him Polezhaev's poem.

And so at three o'clock one night, the rector woke Polezhaev, told him to put on his uniform and go to the office. There the director was awaiting him. After looking to see that all the necessary buttons were on his uniform and no unnecessary ones, he invited Polezhaev without any explanation to get into his carriage and drove off with him. He conducted him to the Minister of Public Instruction. The latter put Polezhaev into his carriage and he too drove off with him—but this time straight to the Czar. . . .

Polezhaev was summoned to the study. The Czar was standing leaning on the mantelpiece and talking to Lieven. He flung a searching and malignant glance at the newcomer.

"Did you write these verses?" "Yes." "Here, prince," the Czar continued, "I will give you a specimen of university education, I will show you what young men learn there. Read the manuscript aloud," he added, addressing Polezhaev.

The agitation of the latter was so great that he could not read. Nicholas' eyes were fixed immovably upon him. I know them and know nothing so terrible, so hopeless, as those colorless, cold, pewtery eyes.

"I cannot," said Polezhaev.

"Read!" shouted the imperial drum-major.

That shout restored Polezhaev's faculties: he opened the manuscript. Never, he told us, had he seen *Sashka* so carefully copied and on such splendid paper.

At first it was hard for him to read; then as he got more and more into the spirit of the thing, he read the poem in a loud and lively voice. At particularly startling passages, the Czar made a sign with his hand to the Minister and the latter covered his eyes with horror.

"What do you say to that?" Nicholas inquired at the end of the reading. "I will put a stop to this corruption; these are the last traces, the last remnants. I will root them out! What is his record?"

The Minister, of course, knew nothing of his record, but some human feeling must have stirred in him, for he said: "He has an excellent record, your Majesty."

"That record has saved you, but you must be punished, as an example to others. Would you like to go into the army?"

Polezhaev was silent.

"I give you a chance of clearing your name in the army. Well?"

"I must obey," answered Polezhaev.

The Czar went up to him, laid his hand on his shoulder and, saying to him, "Your fate is in your own hands; if I forget, you can write to me," kissed him on the forehead. (I made Polezhaev repeat the story of the kiss a dozen times; it seemed to me so incredible. He swore that it was true.) . . . Polezhaev was led off to the camp and handed over to the army as a common soldier. . . .

Years and years passed. His hopeless, dreary position broke him down: become a police-poet and sing the glories of Nicholas he could not, and that was the only way of escape from the army. There was, however, another means of escape, and he preferred it: he drank to win forgetfulness. There is a terrible poem of his, "To Vodka."

After his death, his poems were published, and his portrait in a soldier's uniform was to have been included in the edition. The censor thought this unseemly, and the poor martyr was portrayed with the epaulettes of an officer—he had been promoted in the hospital.

The second extract from Herzen is the following:

What, one may wonder, is the significance of two or three pages published in a monthly review? And yet such is the strength of utterance, such is the power of the spoken word in a land of silence, unaccustomed to free speech, that Tchaadayev's "Letter" shook all thinking Russia. That letter was a shot that rang out in the dark night. Whether it was something perishing that proclaimed its end, whether it was a signal or a cry for help, whether it heralded the dawn or foretold that it would never be—anyway, it forced all to awake.

And well it might. There had been nothing written since *Woe from Wit* which made so powerful an impression. Between that play and the letter there had been ten years of silence, the Fourteenth of December, the gallows, penal servitude, Nicholas. It was the first break in the national development since the period of Peter the Great. The empty place left by the strong men who had been exiled to Siberia was not filled up. Thought languished, men's minds were working, but nothing was reached. To speak was dangerous, and indeed there was nothing to say. All at once a mournful figure quietly rose and asked for a hearing in order calmly to utter his *lasciate ogni speranza.*

In the summer of 1836 I was sitting at my writing table in Vyatka when the postman brought me the latest number of the *Telescope*. One must have lived in exile and in the wilds to appreciate a new periodical. I abandoned everything, of course, and set to work to cut the *Telescope*. I saw "Philosophical Letters Written to a Lady," unsigned. In a footnote it was stated that these letters had been written by a Russian in French—i.e., this was a translation. This rather put me against them, and I proceeded to read the rest of the magazine first.

At last the turn came for the letters; from the second or third page, I was struck by the mournfully earnest tone. Every word breathed of prolonged suffering, by now grown calm but still bitter. It was written as only men write who have been thinking for years, and who have thought much and learned much from life and not from theory. I read further; the letter grew and developed; it turned into a gloomy denunciation of Russia, the protest of one who for all he had endured longs to utter some part of what is accumulated in his heart. Twice I stopped to take breath and collect my thoughts and feelings; I read on and on. And this was published in Russian by an unknown author! I was afraid I had gone out of my mind. Then I read the letter aloud to Vitberg, then to S——, a young teacher in the local high school, then read it again to myself.

It is very likely that exactly the same thing was happening in all sorts of provincial and distant towns, in Moscow and Petersburg and in country gentlemen's houses. . . . Long cut off from the people, part of Russia had been suffering in silence under the most stupid and prosaic yoke, which gave them nothing in return. Everyone felt the oppression of it, everyone had something weighing on his heart, and yet all were silent; at last a man had come who told them in his own way what it was. He spoke only of pain. There was no ray of light in his words, nor indeed in his view. Tchaadayev's letter was a merciless cry of reproach and bitterness against Russia. . . . For a moment, all, even the drowsy and the crushed, were roused, alarmed by this menacing voice. All were astounded, most were offended, a dozen men loudly and warmly applauded its author. Talk in the drawing rooms anticipated government measures, provoked them. . . .

The magazine was at once prohibited; Boldyrev, the censor, was dismissed; Nadyezhdin, the editor, was sent to Ust-Sysolsk. Nicholas ordered Tchaadayev himself to be declared insane, and made to sign an undertaking to write nothing. Every Saturday he was visited by the doctor and the police-master. They interviewed him and made a report—i.e., gave out over his signature forty-two false statements as per the command of the Most High. . . . Neither the doctor nor the police-master ever hinted what they had come for. . . .

"In Moscow," Tchaadayev used to say, "every foreigner is taken to look at the great cannon and the great bell—the cannon which can never be fired and the bell which fell down before it was rung. It is a strange town in which the objects of interest are distinguished by their absurdity. Or perhaps that great bell without a tongue is a hieroglyph symbolic of that immense dumb land, inhabited by a race calling themselves Slavs as though surprised at the possession of human speech." *

WHAT STRIKES ONE, at first glance, is the similarity of atmosphere: the fate of Polezhaev is recapitulated from Yessenin to Mandelstamm; and what could be more apropos than Herzen's summary of Nicholas' "ten years of silence" (Stalin already has enforced twenty): "To speak was dangerous, and indeed there was nothing to say."

* "Slav" is derived from "slovo"—"word," "language." (Translator's note)

In fact, the parallels between Stalin's regime and that of Nicholas, most autocratic of the 19th century Czars, are numerous. Herzen's epigram about Nicholas' police state could be applied to Josef's: "Genghiz Khan plus the telegraph." It was Nicholas who instituted the Third Section, which has persisted, under Czars and Commissars alike, uneasily changing its name like a criminal his aliases: Okrana, Cheka, GPU, NKVD and now MVD. Like Stalin, only less successfully, Nicholas tried to prohibit "Western" ideas. He restricted travel abroad; Stalin abolished it. His censorship was rigorous, being designed, in one official's phrase, "to make printing harmless"; works on logic or philosophy were forbidden; during one year, there were said to be more different censorships than books published. Like Stalin, who in 1936 admonished Soviet composers to produce only tunes the people could whistle on their way to work, Nicholas was not modest about giving esthetic advice: according to Pares, he "recommended to Mr. Pushkin" that he rewrite *Boris Godunov* "with an elimination of superfluous material, as a novel after the manner of Sir Walter Scott."

But here one takes a second glance, and finds that the similarities of kind are overshadowed by the differences in degree. What Czar Nicholas, with the very best will in the world, was able to do only partially, Czar Stalin has done almost completely. Thus, Pushkin did *not* rewrite *Boris Godunov* in the manner of Sir Walter Scott, but the most eminent Soviet composers did alter their manner after Stalin's 1938 *obiter dictum,* just as the whole musical world of Russia has been thrown into a tailspin by the fact that Stalin recently found an opera distasteful. The very thing which is usually thought to establish the identity of the 19th century Czarist regime and that of Stalin turns out, on closer inspection, to show almost the opposite: I refer to the censorship and the use of exile and imprisonment to punish dissident thought.

The difference between Nicholas' and Stalin's censorship (as Herzen's story about Tchaadayev shows) is that between abortion and contraception. The former tried to kill ideas before they reached the public, but the latter prevents their inception in the first place; the former is applied from outside, but the Soviet system resembles our own in that there is no formal censorship at all (except for foreign correspondents) since the whole publishing business is so thoroughly organized by the State, mobilizing the pressure of "public opinion" behind it, that it simply could not occur to a Russian writer to buck it. (In America, the commercial market performs this function; the difference—and it is an important one, to journals like the present one, at least—is that dissident opinion *can* be expressed, to a rather small audience it is true, if a not impossible amount of cash can be raised.)

As for punishment, Nicholas' treatment of Polezhaev and Tchaadayev was mild compared to what the Soviet rulers have done to writers for far less open gestures of defiance—in most cases, indeed, for none at all. Herzen himself only suffered periods of exile to the provinces which were boring and inconvenient but nothing more. And the later Czars were sentimental bunglers, compared to the Commissars, in their treatment of disaffected intellectuals. Chernyshevski was able to write *and publish* from prison his novel, *What Is To Be Done?*, which expressed radical ideas that for a whole generation inspired anti-Czarist actions. Under Alexander II, a pamphlet appeared—or, more accurately, was intercepted by the Okrana—which contained such sentiments as: "The dynasty of the Romanovs and the St. Petersburg bureaucracy must perish. . . . That which is decaying and dying must itself fall into the grave. We have only to give them the last push and throw dirt upon their stinking corpses." The authorship was traced to the well-known Nihilist journalist, D. I. Pisarev. His punishment: four years' imprisonment, during which he was allowed to read, write and even to publish. Lenin wrote important political pamphlets in exile, and Trotsky, in *My Life*, tells how he studied and wrote in Czarist prison and exile. In short, the Czars permitted their prisoners books, writing materials, and enough food to keep alive—a policy of bourgeois softness which their successors have rectified. Small wonder that Jerzy Gliksman's fellow-prisoner in a really up-to-date Russian prison camp, when he tries to cheer her up by telling how his brother in 1913 escaped from Siberian exile, replies impatiently: "Oh, in those sentimental Czarist times . . ."

"Nothing is more remarkable in the history of the 19th century revolutionary thinkers," writes Maynard, "than the vast amount of thought, dangerous to the existing order, which they succeeded in publishing. Nothing more strikingly illustrates the comparative efficiency of the present regime than the success with which subversive doctrines, as distinct from mere criticism of methods and details, are kept away from the public."

IT IS NOT, however, only or even primarily a question of efficiency of repression. Repression implies coercion from outside, which in turn implies some overt resistance. But in Russia since 1928 a much subtler form of authoritarianism has been developed: an "inner censorship" which makes the old-fashioned police state of Nicholas or Metternich look . . . old-fashioned. For all Nicholas' efforts, his thirty years' regime saw a vigorous literary and intellectual movement which produced such figures as Pushkin, Gogol, Lermontov, Herzen, Bielinsky, Tchaadayev, Granovsky and Bakunin. But twenty years of Stalin's rule has reduced Russian thought and literature to a Balkan level. It is not a case of subversive doctrines being "kept away from the public"; so far as one can tell, no such doctrines—and in Soviet Russia, any idea arrived at independently of the official line is deemed, *ipso facto*, subversive—are produced at all. The "inner censorship" sees to that.

Under the 19th century Czars, the Russian intelligentsia were on the offensive; they felt they had reason, justice and the people on their side. The State bureaucrats were on the defensive; they had a bad conscience; they knew they were laughed at and widely despised; they didn't really believe in the justice or rationality of the system they enforced. Hence the mild treatment of political opposition (Vera Zasulitch, who shot the Governor of Moscow, was not only given a public trial in the regular courts but was actually acquitted, amid general rejoicing!). Hence the fact that Herzen's émigré newspaper, *Kolokol,* could be circulated by the thousands throughout Russia, and read by the highest State officials, including the Czar.

Today the situation is just the reverse: it is the artists and writers who are on the defensive, who feel guilty and absurd; and it is the bureaucrats who take the offensive because they feel that reason (historical materialism), justice and the people are on their side. Where Bielinsky criticized Nicholas' police rule, an Eisenstein or a Shostakovitch denounce . . . their own failure to conform completely to Stalin's police rule. The oppressors have a good conscience; the victims are ashamed.

In all the years that the Soviet bureaucracy has been giving orders to Russian writers, composers, film directors, artists and philosophers, there has not been a single case of open resistance. Similarly, during the Moscow Trials not one defendant found the moral courage—or, more accurately, the good conscience—to speak out against the regime that was framing him up. Not even the courageous Rakovsky, whose behavior so shook Trotsky, not even the bold Civil War commander, Muralov. In Nazi Germany during the war, Ernest Junger could write and publish *The Marble Cliffs,* a thinly disguised satire on Nazism. No such thing happened, or could conceivably happen, in Russia. Something new in the way of authoritarianism has developed there—new in the modern world at least.

The novelty comes from the fact that the Stalin group has been able to destroy *all* other competitors. In 19th century Russia, the State bureaucracy had to take into account both the nascent bourgeoisie and the old landed aristocracy—the "repentant nobleman" was a stock figure, from the Decembrists through Bakunin and Herzen to Count Tolstoi and

Prince Kropotkin. Nor was Hitler able to eliminate the junkers and the military, as appeared in the July 20th plot against his life.

What has happened in Russia might be outlined roughly as follows: (1) the 1917 revolution eliminated the old aristocracy and the private capitalists; by 1928 Stalin had eliminated the only competing group: the Trotsky opposition. The powerfully organized bureaucracy, controlling all the levers of economic, social and political power, then confronted only the atomized, undifferentiated masses. (2) The method of dealing with these masses was partly the old repressive police-terror system, but it had two other resources not open to the old-fashioned police states: (a) effective demagogic propaganda which mobilized the pathos of the 1917 revolution and the great tradition of Marxian socialism to persuade the masses that they were the rulers and beneficiaries of the first socialist society in history; (b) the possibility of offering to the more energetic and insensitive members of the submerged masses a chance to become part of the bureaucracy themselves—the career open to talents, Pareto's free "circulation of the elite."

The aristocratic culture from which Herzen and Tchaadayev and Pushkin drew their strength has been replaced by "popular" culture which has no taste, no sense of reason or fair play, but is simply the mediocrity and the "practical" cynicism of the man-in-the-street raised to complete state power. It is as if the norms of Hollywood were imposed by force on all American artistic and intellectual production. Since Col.-Gen. Zhdanov and the Central Committee of the CP represent this level of taste and intellectual integrity better than Zostchenko or Prokofieff or Eisenstein—just as Louis B. Mayer and the National Executive Committee of the AFL represent it better than, say, William Faulkner or Alfred North Whitehead—the latter have neither a social nor a cultural base from which to draw moral courage for a struggle. They feel just as guilty and contemptible as the old Bolsheviks felt at the Moscow Trials.

The main characteristics of this kind of "official" mass culture are high quantity, low quality, and the interference of the political bureaucracy in the most intimate details of artistic creation. On the last point: this interference takes the form of periodic "purges." The one that has been going on now for almost two years represents a great advance in bureaucratic pretensions over the 1936–37 purge. *Then* it was journalists and critics who initiated the purge and elaborated its rationale (acting, of course, on orders from above); *now* it is Col.-Gen. Zhdanov, a big political boss, who personally opened the ball with an hour-long address to the writers of Leningrad. *Then* it was the music critic of *Pravda* who took the composers to task; *now* it is the Central Committee of the Communist Party which issues a decree about technical points of musical theory. The most influential Russian literary magazine today is *Culture and Life,* which the Central Committee itself recently founded "to promote criticism of deficiencies in ideological work." The Committee also promoted, after Zhdanov's speech, a new philosophical organ: *Questions of Philosophy,* complete with a masthead motto: "TO MASTER MARXIST-LENINIST THEORY MEANS TO KNOW HOW TO DEVELOP AND ADVANCE IT."—STALIN. Thus the logic of bureaucratized culture has been carried to its climax, far beyond the simple censorship of Nicholas, all the way to the direct control by a purely political body—the Central Committee of the Communist Party—of esthetic technique as well as content. A culture has developed—or rather, an anti-culture—in which Col.-Gen. Zhdanov is the most influential literary critic, and Marshal Stalin the most important philosopher. This, I think, is something new in the world.

Spring, 1948

The Eisenstein Tragedy

1.

WAS IT ONLY a dozen years ago that, with pious excitement, we went to "little" movie houses—the very term has disappeared—to see the new films from Russia? Is it so short a time since many of us were writing on the cinema as *the* great modern art form, the machine art whose technique was most in harmony with the dynamism of the machine age, the art that most powerfully affected such peculiarly modern areas as Freud's subconscious and Pavlov's reflexes, the only art that could sometimes bridge the gap between serious creation and mass taste, so that *Birth of a Nation,* Chaplin's comedies, *Potemkin* and a few other films might be said to have been the only works of our time that have been both popular and great? Our enthusiasm was not misplaced, our theories were not unfounded. And yet the wonderful possibilities that lay before the cinema ten years ago have withered into the slick banality of Hollywood and the crude banality of the post-1930 Soviet cinema. The potentialities, which really existed, which, for that matter, still exist and in even richer profusion, simply were not realized, and the cinema gave up its own idiom and technique to become once more what it was before Griffith: a mechanical device for recording stage plays. Like so much else in the last decade, it crept back into the womb, into unconsciousness. It has been many years now since, anywhere in the world, a film has been made which, esthetically speaking, is cinema at all.

These depressing reflections are suggested by Eisenstein's new book, *The Film Sense,* which reads more like a conscientious and not too inspired Ph.D. thesis than like the work of the creator of *October* and *Potemkin.* The only valuable part of the book is the Appendices, which reprint some Eisenstein scenarios and articles and give a bibliography of his writings, films and unrealized projects.

I think *The Film Sense* may best be understood as an attempt by its author to adopt the protective coloration of official Stalinist culture. This explains the platitudes: the distinguishing mark of "an emotionally exciting work" is that it causes "inner creative excitement in the spectator" (p. 35); "the technique of creation recreates a life process, conditioned only by those special circumstances required by art" (p. 43); repetition "may well perform two functions"—(1) "to facilitate the creation of an organic whole," (2) to develop "mounting intensity" (p. 95); etc. It also accounts for the citations from Walt Whitman, Sir Joshua Reynolds, Lewis Carroll, Pliny the Elder and practically everybody else that strew the pages, apparently to show that Eisenstein has the authority of all past culture on his side. (Time was when that would have worried him!) And it also accounts for the ghastly "official" style in which the book seems to have been written—possibly Mr. Jay Leyda, the translator, is here partly responsible—so very different from the expressionist fireworks of Eisenstein's earlier writing. In fact, I would almost venture to say that Eisenstein has modeled his prose on Stalin's; there is the characteristic turgidity; the lingering over the obvious; even the familiar catechism form—isn't this a perfect echo: "What was the distortion in our attitude at that time to this indisputable phenomenon? The error lay . . . etc."

Above all, this hypothesis accounts for the remarkable change in Eisenstein's conception of montage. "There was a period in Soviet cinema," he begins his book, "when montage was proclaimed 'everything.' Now we are at the close of a period during which montage has been regarded as 'nothing.' Regarding montage as neither nothing nor everything, I consider it opportune at this juncture to recall that montage is just as indispensable a component of film production as any other element of film effectiveness." Thus montage, once the distinguishing principle of the Eisenstein school, has become simply one among many technical devices. Eisenstein has furthermore broadened his definition of montage until the term now merely describes any relation of elements in art. He has converted his old battle cry into a platitude. We are told that the "basic aim and function" of montage is "connected and sequential exposition of the theme, the material, the plot, the action . . . the simple matter of telling a connected story." This, he frankly remarks, is, of all aspects of montage, "the one really immune to challenge"—as indeed it is, since not even a Soviet commissar would deny the need for "a connected story." This is a complete reversal of Eisenstein's former theory. In his article, "The Cinematographic Principle and Japanese Culture," in *transition* for Spring-Summer, 1930, Eisenstein denounced the idea that montage is "a junction of elements" as "a most pernicious method of analysis." He continued: "By what then is characterized montage . . . ? By collision. . . . By conflict. By collision. . . . From the collision of two given factors arises a concept. Linkage is, in my interpretation, only a possible *special* case. . . . Thus, montage is conflict. The basis of every art is always conflict."

Eisenstein gives no explanation for this reversal, in fact does not mention that a reversal has taken place. Soviet culture doesn't build on the past, any more than Stalinist politics do. The Party line, in art as in politics, changes overnight into a flat contradiction of yesterday's line, so that the present is related to the past only as good is to evil or black to white; the past is simply scrapped, buried, forgotten. Soviet artists have no tradition; they must wipe off the past, as one wipes off a blackboard, the day the line changes. They are unable to learn from the past, and their culture is shallow and undeveloped since it is constantly uprooted.

Eisenstein's change of mind about montage has nothing to do with esthetic theory; it is simply an adaptation to the political pressures which have crushed all Soviet art in the last decade, and whose impact on the cinema I described in a series of articles in *Partisan Review* several years ago. The outlawry of "formalism," i.e. avant-garde experiment, in favor of "social realism" was partly an expression of the Philistine taste of the new-rich Stalinist bureaucracy, partly a move to harness art to the immediate service of mass propaganda (cf. Stalin's famous directive to Soviet composers to produce tunes the people can whistle on their way to work). In the triumph of the "linkage" over the "conflict" concept of montage these factors are involved—"linkage" is the Hollywood method, after all—and also another principle. The cinema is a dramatic art form, and dramatic structure depends largely on the tension created by conflict; but there cannot be conflict in a totalitarian state, since there is only one principle, one set of values authorized to be publicly expressed. I suggest, somewhat tentatively, that there is an intrinsically revolutionary quality to the conflict-montage of Eisenstein's *October* (1927), while the linkage-montage of *Alexander Nevsky* (1938), which robs it of any dramatic interest and makes it a static kind of masque or pageant, is in itself counterrevolutionary.

The grandeurs and the miseries of the modern artist find high expression in Eisenstein's career. In the decade following the October revolution, his three great films—*Potemkin, October* and *Old and New*—were perhaps the supreme expression of the remarkable flowering of avant-garde art in the springtime of the new society. By 1929 the Stalinist bureaucracy had consolidated its hold on the State apparatus, and the great period of creativity in the arts was over. That year Eisenstein got permission to travel abroad. Whatever hopes he may have had of finding a more congenial milieu in the capitalist world—his difficulties with Stalin had begun as early as 1927, when he was forced to eliminate Trotsky's figure from all scenes of *October*—were frustrated with remarkable thoroughness. In Paris the police forbade the showing of *Old and New* to a private audience at the Sorbonne. He traveled on to Hollywood, where Paramount put him under a six-month contract with much publicity, and frustrated his attempts to make any movies. There followed the tragi-comedy of the Mexican film he made for a group of liberals headed by Upton Sinclair, which ended in Sinclair's asserting his property rights in the unedited film (which he later turned over to a Hollywood hack to chop into shorts) and Eisenstein returning empty-handed to Russia. The first indication many of us had as to what was going on in the

Soviet cinema was the failure of Amkino to back up Eisenstein's efforts to get his Mexican film—said by many who saw the raw material to be potentially his greatest achievement —out of the hands of Sinclair.

I am told that when Eisenstein returned to Russia he was a beaten man, disillusioned with both the capitalist and the new Stalinist world. There followed a long and heartbreaking series of unrealized projects: a cinematization of Marx's *Capital;* of the careers of Ivar Kreuger and Sir Basil Zaharoff; of Vandercook's *Black Majesty;* the Hart-Kaufman comedy, *Once in a Lifetime;* Malraux's *La Condition Humaine;* a comedy called *MMM;* a big historical film covering four centuries of Moscow's history; above all, the humiliating treatment of the only project that got beyond the scenario stage, his half-completed film on peasant life, *Bezhin Meadow,* which was branded "formalist" and officially suppressed in 1937. The only projects Eisenstein has been able to realize since *Old and New* (1929) are *Alexander Nevsky* (1938) and the present book. Although in this book Eisenstein analyzes *Nevsky* as though it were a masterwork, devoting many pages to the technical strategy of a tiny section, the film has always seemed to me empty and boring. It is a slow-paced historical pageant, devoid of any content other than a posterlike kind of patriotism, and quite conventional in its cinematic technique. I think it may be referred to the same strategy of cultural camouflage that produced the book: a patriotic pageant is about as "safe" an art work as it is possible to create in Russia these days. Eisenstein's next film is also to be a historical one, based on Ivan the Terrible. It is immensely significant that the one project Eisenstein was able to complete in the last decade is *Nevsky,* while all the rest, dealing with themes in which there is contemporary life, came to nothing. Back to the womb.

Eisenstein's career has been a tragedy without a hero. He has foresworn his most cherished esthetic theories when they met with official disfavor; viz., his abject behavior when his "formalist" heresy was attacked at the 1935 Film Conference (*Partisan Review,* Aug.-Sept., 1938, pp. 42-45); his confessional article, "The Mistakes of *Bezhin Meadow*" (*International Literature,* No. 8, 1937); his use of big-name "stars" in *Nevsky,* and his acceptance as collaborators in that film of D. Vassilev, the leading "social realist" director, and Teleshiva of the Moscow Art Theatre. (In the twenties he wouldn't have wiped his feet on the Moscow Art Theatre.) He has also issued from time to time the kind of political statements required of Stalinist intellectuals, and with a grossness bordering on the cynical. Examples are "My Subject is Patriotism" (*International Literature,* No. 2, 1939) and the preface to the present volume, in which he envisions "the definitive rise of an art of the cinema" as a result of Anglo-Soviet-American victory in the present war, and in which he writes: "I have long been tied to America both by a deep love and by the great tradition of film-art. Now these feelings are heightened by the warm friendship in which our people are together delivering powerful blows to the scourge of darkness, blood and savagery, in the fight for the ideals of mankind, culture, humanity and light." * So excessive, indeed, has been Eisenstein's capitulation to the demands of the Stalinist bureaucracy that a friend of mine thinks he is satirizing Stalinist culture by wholly conforming to it. He cites the case of Ernst Jünger, who several years ago satirized the Nazi blood-and-race ideology by publishing, in Germany, a work carrying it to extreme conclusions. This theory is psychologically possible, from what I know of Eisenstein's personality. Two considerations, however, seem to make it unlikely: (1) Eisenstein's failure to produce anything of interest in the last decade (which argues that he made a sincere, opportunist effort to conform); (2) the fact that this mode of behavior, fantastic to our eyes, is the norm in the

* "MOSCOW, Feb. 18 (UP): Sergei Eisenstein, one of the most prominent Soviet film directors, today launched a Soviet-German cultural cooperation program over the Comintern Radio Station. Broadcasting especially to Germany, Mr. Eisenstein said that friendly Russian-German relations established last year formed a solid base 'for increased cultural cooperation between the two great peoples.'"—N. Y. *Times,* Feb. 19, 1940.

Soviet Union today, as was shown in the Moscow Trials and in the esthetic capitulations of artists like Pudovkin and Shostakovich.

There is a modern sentimentality about the artist and intellectual which pictures him as a Prometheus defying the gods of totalitarianism in the name of Art and Culture. Such defiances are not unknown, but they are generally delivered from a safe distance—California is an ideal location. When, as in Russia, the artist-intellectual has remained within the totalitarian borders, he has reacted pretty much as Eisenstein has, submitting in esthetic as well as political matters. About the only heroes in the tragedy of Stalinist culture were Mayakovsky and Yessenin, who instinctively chose suicide to creative death. The Nazi order is by now old and extensive enough for some further evidence to begin to appear. Braque has accepted a high artistic post in occupied France, and Vlaminck, de Segonzac and Derain are reported to have toured Germany on a "cultural mission." In an interview in the N. Y. *Herald Tribune* of Aug. 16, Dr. John Altmann revealed that the greatest of German film directors, G. W. Pabst, famous for the anti-war films, *Westfront*, 1918 and *Kameradschaft*, and for his wonderful cinematization of Brecht's *Dreigroschenoper*, edited the Nazi documentary terror film, *Victory in the West*. According to *Pic* for Aug. 18, Pabst was secretly working for Abetz while he was in Paris before the war, ostensibly an artist-refugee from Nazism. Such reversals cannot but shock us, just as a book like *The Film Sense* is shocking coming from Eisenstein. But I think we had better get used to such shocks; there are probably more unheroic tragedies to come.

Partisan Review, Nov.-Dec., 1942

2.

There seems to be a natural hostility, incompatible with the best will on both sides, between modern totalitarianism and artistic creation. Capitalism perverts art or makes its practice more difficult, but totalitarianism simply liquidates it. In a predominantly private-capitalist society like our own, there are crannies in which the artist and intellectual can survive, as well as conflicting forces of which he can take advantage. Frick, the steelmaster, used to sit on a Renaissance throne underneath a Rembrandt reading the *Saturday Evening Post,* but the middle-class intellectuals, for all their economic impotence vis-à-vis Frick, were able to provide an audience for Joyce and James and Proust and Eliot. The "contradictions of capitalism," that bourgeois anarchy at which generations of Marxists railed, now turn out in our present ghastly period to have their advantages. For in the kind of society that has developed in Russia, there are no crannies, no contradictions, no conflicting forces—at least none of a growth sturdy enough to give shelter to the artist. There is only one culture, one conception of art, one criterion of taste and achievement; and if, as seems to be fatally the case, the one standard is that of Frick reading the *Satevepost* (without the Rembrandt), then the most dignified way out for the artist is Mayakovsky's.

The news comes, for example, that Eisenstein is again in trouble with the authorities—Part II of his new trilogy, *Ivan the Terrible,* has been found to be ideologically defective and will not be released. Although since 1929 Eisenstein has made every possible effort to adapt his genius to the base and vulgar uses required of it—and a few efforts one might think not possible, such as presenting the half-crazy, murderous Czar Ivan as a progressive Leader of the People—he has been in almost continual difficulties; in the last seventeen years he has completed only two films, both of them much inferior to the three he produced in the five years before 1929. Most of the other talented Soviet artists have also tried faithfully to follow "party directives," but have been little more successful than Eisenstein in avoiding constant harassment. One difficulty, perhaps the chief, is simply that they *are* men of talent—conscious, perceptive individuals who are mentally alive, who cannot help thinking freely, experimenting, seeing things in an original way, and so, despite their earnest wish not to, cannot help threatening Stalin's leaden dictatorship of mediocrity and lifeless conformism. One thinks of the writer in Henry James' *The Next Time,* who all his life tried to write something commonplace, cheap, vulgar that would sell but who kept producing one uncommercial masterpiece after another. Or of the remark of the Prince—another leaden despot—in Stendhal's *Charterhouse of Parma:* "It seems that this is a man of intelligence who comes to us from Naples, and I do not like that tribe. An intelligent man follows in vain the best precepts, even in good faith; always in some way he is cousin to Voltaire and Rousseau."

Another difficulty is that serious artists, especially in a still primitive country like Russia, naturally are influenced by the ideas and techniques of more advanced countries. There is a spontaneous internationalism about good art. The current campaign against "alien" Western influences is the most extreme but by no means the first. As I noted in 1939: "It was precisely this international character of the Eisenstein cinema that most alarmed the Kremlin. If the masses are to accept the present totalitarian dictatorship as a fully realized socialist society, they must be cut off from contact with more advanced cultures. And so, in the last ten years, the Soviet Union has been slowly isolated. . . . This campaign is designed to reinforce, not to combat, those characteristic defects of backward cultures: provincial smugness, the ignorant acceptance of inferior, banal art forms as 'healthy' and 'normal,' and a corresponding suspicion of more advanced forms. This is what, esthetically, the theory of 'Socialism In One Country' has meant." There is an added motive today: to prepare for war against the West. In the "collective security" period and after Germany had attacked her in 1941, Russia looked on the Western powers as allies, potential and then actual. Her cultural policy, therefore, could not reach the degree of hermetism it is now attaining. Eisenstein made *Nevsky* in 1938 and *Ivan* was projected and largely finished during the war period. For all their faults, they are sophisticated films, and extremely "formalistic" in the stylization of costumes, acting and setting and in the elaborate composition of each individual shot. They are not at all the sort of home-grown provincial films—a blend of stodgy realism and naïve melodrama—we generally get from Russia these days. When *Culture and Life,* therefore, criticizes *Ivan the Terrible* for its "failure to portray contemporary reality" and its "cold and passionless historicism" and calls for fewer films about literary and historical figures and more about "the simple Soviet people who are the real creators of history," one can assume that even a Soviet editor would not criticize a historical film for not dealing with contemporary life, and that what is meant is that the stylized, ornate technique is now considered "formalistic," "decadent" and "Western." It is also just possible that Eisenstein took advantage of the historical pageant to escape from that Contemporary Reality which both Russian artists and audiences seem to wish to forget. This suggests in turn another speculation: why is it that the dominant classes in America feed the masses dreams, romance, "escape" culture while their peers in Russia adopt just the opposite policy, although both have the same end in view?

October, 1946

3.

"It exhibited ignorance of historical facts by portraying the progressive army of the *Oprichniki* [Ivan's equivalent of the OGPU] as a band of degenerates, similar to the American Ku Klux Klan, and Ivan, a man of strong will and character, as weak and spineless like Hamlet." Thus the Central Committee of the Communist Party of the Soviet Union explained its suppression of Eisenstein's *Ivan the Terrible, Part II,* in the course of its decree of September 4, 1946, which gave marching orders to the cinema. This was part of the great "culture purge" that began in 1946 and whose rationale received its supreme expression in the famous 10,000-word speech that August by Andrei Zhdanov, who up to his death in 1948 was second only to Stalin in the Soviet hierarchy. Declaring war on all contemporary non-Soviet culture as decadent, corrupt, anti-human, reptillian, cannibalistic and generally not quite the thing, Zhdanov demanded that "our comrades, both as leaders in literary affairs and as writers, be guided by the vital force of the Soviet order—its politics." The Central Committee responded with decrees that, in addition to the one on the cinema, criticized current practice and laid down detailed "directives" for reform in literature (August 14, 1946), in the theater (August 26, 1946) and in music (February 10, 1948). The Central Committee also, in its decree of August 4, 1948, officially repealed the Mendelian Law in genetics in favor of a new theory, by a home-grown biologist named Lysenko, which held that acquired characteristics can be inherited.*

The Central Committee's supression of the second part of his *Ivan* trilogy must have been all the more upsetting to Eisenstein because up to then he seemed to have, at last, squared the circle and come to terms with the Soviet bureaucracy. After the premiere, in 1938, of *Alexander Nevsky,* Stalin himself is said to have clapped him on the back and declared, "Sergei Mikhailovitch, you're a good Bolshevik after all!" † And the following year, one Vsevolod Vishnevsky

* For the text of these decrees, of Zhdanov's speech and for much other fascinating and invaluable material on post-1945 Soviet culture, see *The Country of the Blind* by George F. Counts and Nucia Lodge (Houghton Mifflin, 1949). The effect of these "marching orders" from the political bureaucracy to those actually engaged in artistic and scientific work was, of course, not motion but paralysis. In 1947, for example, just six feature films—full length, non-documentaries—were released in the USSR, and the average per year in the five-year period 1948–1952 was exactly ten. The surrealist nature of these statistics may be appreciated if one compares the nine movies made in the USSR in 1951 with that year's production not only in the USA (432) but also in Japan (215), Mexico (102) and Egypt (96). Nor, on the basis of what one has seen of recent Soviet films, is there any reason to suppose that the USSR has gone in for quality instead of quantity.

† So Marie Seton reports in her biography of Eisenstein (Wyn, 1952), a peculiar volume whose rich documentation on Eisenstein's career, feelings and ideas conflicts constantly with her political line, which is favorable to the Stalin regime. Her data clash with her interpretation perhaps because of her close identification with her subject, and friend, who also, at least in public, always converted the thistles of political interference into the figs of socialist idealism.

signalized Eisenstein's return to official favor with a biographical pamphlet which blamed his ten-year eclipse on certain unnamed "enemies and saboteurs" (as, for example, Boris Shumiatsky, installed by the Kremlin in 1930 as top boss of the cinema and given a free hand up to 1938 in reducing Eisenstein, Pudovkin, Dovzhenko and the other great directors of the twenties to Hollywood-type hacks) who "prevented the realization of various projects and suggested to Eisenstein ideas which were invalid, confused his goals and offered useless material" until finally "the party and the government, and Stalin in particular, came to his aid." It would be gilding an already refulgent lily to comment on this Tartuffian document, which continues: "We can only imagine what Eisenstein and other great artists could have created if not hampered by these obstacles."

Eisenstein's response to the Central Committee's rejection of *Ivan, II* was a confession of error that was a macabre echo of his apology, ten years earlier, when *Bezhin Meadow* was suppressed:

> I must admit that we artists . . . forgot for a time those great ideals which our art is summoned to serve . . . the honorable, militant and educational task . . . to build a communist society. . . . In the light of the resolutions of the Central Committee, all workers in art must . . . fully subordinate our creative work to the interest of the education of the Soviet people. From this aim we must take not one step aside nor deviate a single iota. We must master the Lenin-Stalin method of perceiving reality and history so completely and profoundly that we shall be able to overcome all remnants and survivals of former ideas which, though long banished from consciousness, strive stubbornly and cunningly to steal into our works whenever our creative vigilance relaxes for a single moment. This is a guarantee that our cinematography will be able to surmount all the ideological and artistic failures . . . and will again begin to create pictures of high quality, worthy of the Stalinist epoch.

Is all this perhaps irony? Did Eisenstein, by carrying the Stalin-Zhdanov line to its logical extreme, thus attempt to express his personal despair and cry a warning to the outside world? Was there perhaps some justice, from the Soviet point of view, in the Central Committee's reaction to *Ivan, II?* (Even *Ivan, I,* which was not banned, is full of a sinister, neurotic atmosphere quite discordant with the surface political "line.") What can Eisenstein mean by those "former ideas" which, though sternly repressed, "cunningly steal into our works whenever our creative vigilance relaxes for a single moment"? What can they be but the artist's vision and energy which, whenever he is off guard, persist in shattering the crude, wooden formulae of "socialist realism" with effects that are subtle, original, living, hence unpredictable and hence politically anathema in a totalitarian state? Or, alternatively, was Eisenstein so neurotically dependent on identification with Soviet power that he never allowed its actual evil to come to consciousness, even when he was himself the victim? Eisenstein died in 1948, long before the post-Stalin "thaw" in Soviet culture. One can only speculate.

Problems of Communism, Jan.-Feb., 1955

Alien Corn

LIKE *War and Peace,* Mikhail Soloviev's *When the Gods Are Silent,* is long and full of Russian history; unlike *War and Peace* it is tripe. In this last fact lies its significance. Exposing the evils of Stalin's Russia, which was a handicraft in the thirties, has now become a mass industry. *When the Gods Are Silent* is what the Germans call *kitsch* and we call corn—a literary commodity manufactured for the mass market. Soloviev, who was an *Izvestia* correspondent up to his capture by the Germans during the war and who now lives in this country, has taken the same theme—the corruption of the Bolshevik revolution by Stalinism—which was treated with artistic seriousness and integrity by Arthur Koestler (*Darkness at Noon*), Victor Serge (*The Case of Comrade Tulayev*) and Godfrey Blunden (*A Room on the Route*), among others, and has exploited it to make a best-seller, or at least what his publishers hope will be a best-seller. (They have publicly threatened to make it "the No. 1 novel" of 1953.) Such an enterprise is a sign of the times; it will be interesting to see if it succeeds.

No one can complain about Mr. Soloviev's coverage of his theme, quantitatively at least. He takes his hero from the 1905 revolution through World War II. Like Upton Sinclair's Lanny Budd, Mark Surov skims through the historical tempest like a stormy petrel, always in the center of great events, beloved of all including women, and somehow combining a high moral tone with the ability to function for twenty years as a member of the corrupt and brutal Soviet officialdom. Leaking sawdust at every pore, he appears, successively and conveniently, as a Red partisan fighter in the Civil War, a student at Moscow University, a party official in the Far East, a member of the Kremlin staff, a major in the Red Army in the war, a prisoner of the Germans and finally a guerrilla leader fighting both Hitler and Stalin. The publishers believe the result is "a great imaginative recreation of the mightiest upheaval of our time," and if blood, sweat and tears, plus plenty of Getting Around, could turn the trick, turned it would surely be. Unhappily, something more is needed.

After I had read ten pages of Mr. Soloviev's prose, I began to suspect he lacks talent. But as I read on, a deeper truth glimmered: he is without doubt untalented, but the special kind of badness of his novel is not due to that. No merely unskilled writer could so consistently strike the banal note. He would sometimes, however ineptly, put in something which he himself had thought, or felt, or observed; he would occasionally deviate into reality. But *When the Gods Are Silent* runs along the well-worn grooves of stock melodrama from beginning to end. Literally. "Steppe, immeasurable steppe," it begins, and it closes with Mark climbing a hill to "brood over the vast expanse of plain." ("'What are you looking for?' Korovin finally asked. 'I am looking for a sunrise. I have faith that God will bring forth another sunrise in the East.'" *Cut, slow dissolve, The End.*) In between these termini, the steppe—vast, immense, immeasurable, endless, in a word, Big—periodically reappears, to be well brooded over by one or another character. As I read the text, the author intends to suggest by this image that Russia is large in a cosmic sort of way, that the soil is eternal, and that, Stalin or no Stalin, Old Man Steppe jest keeps rollin' along. The other *dramatis personae,* animate and inanimate, are equally predictable. Bullets sing, refugees swarm, faces are fixed like masks, mouths are twisted in bitter smiles, while other smiles play over other faces that are often weatherbeaten. The eyes are especially expressive—in fact, often they alone give a clue as to what the dialogue is supposed to express. They glitter feverishly, glow warmly, burn (or, in extreme cases, blaze) with hatred, light up with amusement, become narrow, steely, hard, etc. "'So our inevitable meeting has taken place, Major Surov,' the Gestapo man said, and a smile played on his lips." ("So we meet again, Lionel Strongheart!") On page 397 another villainous German actually purrs, and there is a Japanese villain who is polite, smiling and hard to make out, in fact, inscrutable. These would have been fat parts for Von Stroheim and Sessue Hayakawa thirty years ago, but will be hard to fill today, that sort of acting not being practiced much any more. But in general, little will need to be changed to make it all into a super-colossal Grade B movie. Certainly not the chapter endings: "Tears burned in Mark's eyes, and he went to the open window. 'Look, Simon! Outside that window is Moscow [*the characters are forever taking each other to windows and pointing out obvious things*] and beyond Moscow lies all our country, flooded with the blood of our fathers, washed with the tears of our mothers. It's worth living, for her sake, Simon.' Outside, dawn was breaking." (*Lots of dawn-breakage, too*) Or this: "Then he smiled more broadly, to the corners of his eyes. [*Close-up*] He would live, he knew it. And someday he would go to Maria." (*Cut!*) Or this: "Yes, Mother; we'll go away. We'll go home . . . to the steppe!" (*Camera pans to long shot of Old Man Steppe.*)

If the artist's task is to induce a willing suspension of disbelief, Mr. Soloviev is no artist. My doubt was unsuspended through all 506 pages. I doubt that a starving man, offered a piece of bread, would remember to remark, "Stalin took everything away." I doubt that a man alone in the wild Siberian *taiga,* under whatever stress of emotion, would clutch his head and cry out, "I can't! I mustn't!" And among the mutters I doubt ever got muttered is: "You cur! You'll pay dearly for this!" I also doubt that the life story of any human being could so consistently and unremittingly illustrate a thesis as Mark Surov's does. The long arm of coincidence has a boarding-house reach in this novel. Even in the depths of the *taiga,* Mark can't help finding a notebook thoughtfully left behind by a Soviet engineer which gives a full account of a forced-labor camp. The poor fellow gets no rest at all. On page 213 he recognizes an elderly prisoner as none other than Borodin and at once has an edifying discussion with him on political ethics; a couple of pages later on, he runs into an old girl friend from Moscow U., also now a prisoner, with more edification and more mutual rumination on the evils of Stalinism; and so it goes, all work and no play, and Mark becomes a very dull boy indeed. The author works hard, too, conscientiously giving the public its $3.95 worth of Intimate Glimpses of History. "Have you heard that Vishinsky's being assigned to the University?" a Trotskyist classmate of Mark's asks. "He'll be a tower of strength to us." Two pages later, Mark runs into Stalin and we get a peep into Stalin's domestic life. (" 'How's it going, Nadia?' he asked in his gutteral tones. 'Quite well, Joseph Vissarionovich,' she replied.") When some of Mark's friends are about to escape into Manchuria, they ask him to come along. He refuses: "My place is here, on this soil. . . . Life is driving us in different directions, but you are my friends." "Come with us," implores Lena, his old flame at Moscow U. "I've always loved you, Mark." "No, my place is here," he repeats, with a bitter smile. His real reason for not leaving with them, of course, is that it is only page 248 and he still has to get a job in the Kremlin so we can have some Intimate Glimpses of the 1937–38 purges.

The curious, and disturbing, thing about a book like this is that it precisely reverses the function of art: instead of making something imaginary seem real, it makes the real seem imaginary. Mr. Soloviev obviously hates what Stalin's regime has done to Russia, and he has good reason to hate it. His intention was to demonstrate fictionally the horrors of Soviet Communism; instead, by conveying them in the terms of journalistic cliché and of wooden melodrama, he has assimilated them to something we know is false and so has actually made it harder to believe in their reality. Only a master of *kitsch* could take the whole sweep of the Bolshevik revolution, the agony of the Russian people under twenty-five years of a brutal totalitarianism and two world wars and make it all as flat, contrived and implausible as *Forever Amber*. Such a master is Mr. Soloviev, so great a one indeed that he has surmounted even the fact that his book is written largely out of his own first-hand experience—at least, I am told that he, like Mark Surov, fought in the Civil War, studied at Moscow University, spent years in the Soviet Far East, was first a Kremlin reporter and then a war correspondent of *Izvestia*, was captured by the Germans and took part in the resistance behind the lines. It takes a bit of doing to transmute a real-life experience like that into *kitsch*.

But, master of corn though Mr. Soloviev is, there is one factor which may, providentially, prevent his book from having the popular success his publishers hope for—the fact that he learned his trade in Soviet Russia. His book is corny enough, but it is Soviet corn, alien corn. As the citations already given show, it is a cruder, more old-fashioned kind than ours. He has put in a few religious touches for the American market ("'A great sorrow has brought you here,' the priest murmured.") but he has fallen down badly on sex, Soviet corn being puritanical. Not only are there pitifully few sexual interludes but also such as there are are miserably scamped. "She laughed happily and clung to him with her whole body." No, this won't do at all, our public expects much more. Above all, he has not realized that Soviet corn is heavily didactic while the American kind is strictly for entertainment. What kind of a way is this to begin a chapter: "Who would maintain that there is any limit to the power of the human heart? If that were true, Mark Surov's heart would have broken that night when Yoshima presented him with Katya's brooch. But the human heart has an unlimited potential." Sounds like ore reserves. Working in the Soviet tradition, the author shapes his material to make a political point and reduces his characters to wooden puppets acting out a morality play, while American *kitsch* is rarely tendentious, treats its characters as individuals (however falsely observed) and tries to get at least a surface impression of variety and liveliness. In brief, the American mass audience wants to be amused by its corn, the Soviet masses, whether they want it or not, are instructed by their *kitsch*. Perhaps *When the Gods Are Silent* will not, after all, be "the No. 1 novel of 1953." Let's hope so.*

UN World, January, 1953

Liberal Soap Opera

During the Roosevelt-Truman era, there were two kinds of liberals in America: the "practicals," who made the New Deal—politicians like Ickes, labor leaders like Reuther, college professors like Berle and Tugwell—and the "intellectuals" (the quotes are also in order here) who wrote and argued about it—Max Lerner, Freda Kirchwey, Bruce Bliven and the like. The "practicals," who in a decade wrought a social revolution which took generations in Europe, were not much affected by Communism, indeed not much interested

* It wasn't. (*1956*)

in it; they had power, they were changing things right here, they were pragmatists rather than idealists or doctrinaires. The "intellectuals," however, were often drawn to Communism because they felt impotent and the idea of "one-sixth of the globe" going their way was comforting, because they were more internationally minded than the "practicals" and so desperately hoped in the Soviet Union as the axis of world anti-fascism, and because they needed an ideology. The work of the "practicals" has endured; Eisenhower's victory has chipped the New Deal but has not shattered or even cracked it. But the faith of the "intellectuals" has turned sour as Soviet Communism has emerged as a totalitarian system like Nazism. But, although this kind of liberalism has disappeared as a political force, it survives as a nostalgic myth, so that in most liberal-intellectual circles it is still risky to say a good word for Whittaker Chambers or a bad one against Owen Lattimore. The myth survives because the liberals have never honestly confronted their illusions in the thirties and forties about Communism but have instead merely counterposed a disingenuous defense, a blanket denial to McCarthy's equally sweeping attack. One does not learn from experiences which one refuses to examine. The survival of the liberal myth, which glosses over Soviet Communism's shortcomings and correspondingly exaggerates those of American capitalism, is a big factor in delaying that political reorientation that our liberal ideology has so long needed.

Charles Wertenbaker's *The Death of Kings,* although of less than no interest as a novel, is of considerable significance in the above context. For it presents the liberal myth with an enthusiasm that is all the more extreme precisely because the author has never been a practicing liberal, who might by now have lost a few illusions by sheer dint of unhappy experience, but rather a Virginia-type gentleman who wears his liberalism as his ancestors might have worn their plumed hats. That even today he finds this intellectually tattered and morally bedraggled garb a respectable, even dashing costume is a tribute partly to his innocence—he has written a period piece without knowing it—and partly to the curious vitality of liberal mythology.

The story begins one evening in 1938 when Louis Baron, who resembles Henry Luce right up to his shaggy eyebrows and who is the new publisher of *Beacon,* a news magazine not wholly unlike *Time,* confers with five of his top editors. They are liberals—using the term as the novel does, as meaning *pro* TVA, labor, Spanish Loyalists, and *anti* lynching, Huey Long, big business, and appeasement (of Hitler's Germany, that is, appeasement of Stalin's Russia being just good common sense)—and they have come to talk politics with their new boss. They leave reassured. The rest of the book takes the story up to 1950, telling how Baron's increasing conservatism wrecks the lives and careers of the five who met with him in 1938. *The Death of Kings* is thus a political novel, a novel of ideas.*

To write a successful novel of ideas, an author must have (1) ideas, or at least the ability to deal with them, and (2) a level of consciousness superior to that of his characters. As to (1), the following is a fair sample of Mr. Wertenbaker's intellection, which is as woolly as his Harris tweed prose:

> The bright dome had passed from his sight, and so had the other domes of the Pantheon and Val de Grace, squashed by a perspective that stunted even Notre Dame, and he thought it was a sacrilege to look down on Paris, as it would have been a sacrilege for God to look down on the hopes of men knowing their unfulfillment. But no. If God was the sum of human hopes (and what else could

* Even the sex, of which there is a saleable amount, is heavily politicalized. Two lovers talking in bed sound like a branch meeting. "Don't you believe the world will have to go socialist?" asks the girl. "Something like that, eventually," concedes the man, but adds that he prefers the 1776 kind of revolution to the Marxist kind. "And what about the colonial people?" counters the lady. "If I ever have to choose between the people anywhere and what I think is good for me as a privileged American, I hope I choose the people," he replies with the smugness the author often confuses with political virtue. "Then you're one of us," his inamorata sums up, "and that's why I'm in your bed."

> He be?), then He *had* looked down, as the war was ending, and had glimpsed the dimmest reflection of Himself—enough to keep men believing and striving, as they had been put on the face of the earth to do.

As to (2), when Stendhal anatomized obscurantist reaction in post-Napoleonic Parma or when Dostoievski made Nihilism the theme of *The Possessed,* they stood apart from and above their characters and so were able to penetrate into the ideas those characters lived by and demonstrate them clearly. But Mr. Wertenbaker flounders around in the bog of liberal mythology just as blunderingly as his characters, following with them the *ignes fatui* that beckon in the foggy air. Consider, for example, the crucial 1938 conference. Baron convinces his liberal editors that he is one of them by delivering a pompous and banal lecture on revolutions, which he believes always aim at "the liberation of mankind" but are always corrupted by power, winding up with a line of malarkey that a *Life* editorialist might hesitate to perpetrate (though he would probably overcome the hesitation). "What are we fighting for?" asks Baron—(They are always asking each other questions like, "What do you mean, *really,* by principles?") "We're fighting for that line in the Declaration of Independence that says all men are created equal; it's just as simple as that. . . . And since the ideal of equality can never be reached, this revolution of ours will go on as long as there are men to fight it." His five listeners, whom the author presents as not only competent journalists but also men of serious political principles, are wowed:

> He had won them; Berkeley saw it; and Louis, lifting the heavy brows to stare each one in the face, could not fail to see it, too. He pushed on to seal it into speech.
>
> "We're the kings of the present time—and I'm not mixing my political metaphors because, remember, it was the early kings who led the people against the nobles. We're kings because we wear the crown and wield the scepter of truth. So I'll tell you what to call our principle. I'll tell you what to call *us.*"

> He paused until the last ripple of sound had been smoothed into silence, then into it cast his words: "Call us kings of the revolution!"

The reader is supposed to feel sympathy and respect for grown-up men who are deceived by this sort of bombast. The misadventures of such addlepated heroes might be presented successfully in terms of farce or of pathos, but not, as Mr. Wertenbaker does, as matter for high tragedy.

The Death of Kings stresses two main tenets of the liberal myth: that the main trouble with our press is ideological, i.e., that it reflects the reactionary views of its owners; and that Communism is no worse than a bad cold.

It is interesting to note that the fictional Baron's magazines grow more reactionary as they grow older and more powerful, which is what the liberal myth would lead one to expect, but those of the real Henry Luce have developed the other way: the turning point was around 1937 when Luce, impressed by the viability of the New Deal and alarmed by the military threat of Nazi Germany, kicked upstairs the late Laird Shields Goldsborough, whose incredible Foreign News section had built up Mussolini and Franco. For many years now the Lucepapers, while they have favored Chiang Kai-shek, General MacArthur, and the Republicans, have also been consistently favorable to civil liberties and racial equality and have opposed McCarthyism. The real trouble with *Time* and *Life*, as with other big-circulation organs, is cultural rather than ideological. They are edited according to superficial formulae designed to sell not capitalism but papers. In a sense, they are *too* democratic: they try so hard to titillate and entertain a mass audience that they cannot tell much of the truth. Not because they suppress it, but because it hardly ever happens to fit the Procrustean bed of their technique. How can *Time* get very close to reality when every story has to be tailored and tortured into a little drama, with an angle, a climax, an arresting lead and a "kicker" at the end? Or when, to make the news "vivid," issues are systematically reduced to personalities, so that one learns that Eden wore a derby and Dulles chain-smoked but not what the conference meant.

The chief evidence, however, that Mr. Wertenbaker gives of Baron's fall from grace is his mean-spirited suspicion of Soviet Communism. When the publisher asks Berkeley, the "point-of-view" character in the book and as mutton-headed a progressive as I have encountered since the Wallace campaign, apropos a colleague accused of having been a Soviet spy, "How do you know what a traitor is?" Berkeley replies: "In your guts. That's what they're for." This reply is a stylistic and intellectual epitome of the book. A clause beginning with "in" doesn't quite fit as an answer to "how." And guts are to digest food, not to think with. It was the Nazis who did their thinking with their blood, and it isn't much better to think with one's stomach. Viz.:

> Berkeley's attitude toward Russia, like that of many of his countrymen in high places and low, had developed less through the intellect than through the generous emotions. He had little real knowledge on which to base an intellectual judgment; all he could believe with certainty was that Russia's leaders would go to any length to preserve what they had won by revolution. When he compared the noble professions of that revolution with its assault on man's painfully built moral structure, he could not but feel that the ideal had been degraded almost past redemption. But when he read how bravely millions of people were suffering and dying to save it, when he read into the actions of the Russian rulers a greater tolerance of democratic ways, he could not but hope that the ideal might yet be redeemed, and that the two great revolutionary nations [i.e., the USA and the USSR] might pursue similar ends, if not in similar ways, at least with a similar regard for human dignity.

What a museum of outworn liberalistic clichés! And how extraordinary that a political novel expressing the crudest illusions of the "Popular Front" psychology of the thirties should today be reviewed sympathetically and seriously even in so sophisticated a journal as *The New Yorker!* The liberal myth is indeed a tough old bird. Myself, I found the deplorable Louis Baron generally right on Communism as against his progressive but woolly-witted antagonists. He shocks them in 1939 by wanting to criticize *both* Hitler and Stalin, and in 1945 by suppressing a story by Berkeley about "democracy and Communism working together in Czechoslovakia" and by damning the Yalta conference. I can even sympathize with his annoyance over "the pressure of 'Communist' members of the New York Newspaper Guild," for I remember that when I worked for Luce in the early thirties, there *were* Communists in the Guild, notably one who helped me organize the Time-Fortune unit.* "Even if the great majority of the Chinese people are for the Communists—the ignorant Chinese people, mind you—that's no reason for us to be for 'em," Baron sensibly observes to Berkeley, who replies with his usual fatuity, "It strikes me as a pretty good reason." According to liberal mythology, The People are always right, except for the Germans under Hitler.

It's not considered sporting for a reviewer to comment on a writer's professional competence—at least I assume this is why so few reviewers pay any attention to the matter—but the fact is that Mr. Wertenbaker, although a journalist since the age of twenty-one and the author of nine books, is a most amateurish writer—clumsy, long-winded, bumbling and pretentious. He overloads his descriptive passages with details, but somehow omits the one that would make the scene vivid. He can linger longer over lighting cigarettes, pouring drinks and the exchange of allegedly significant looks than any author I know and with less result. He expresses the sensibility of cheap women's-magazine fiction in prose as turgid as the most high-falutin' avant-garde writing, an unhappy combination. His ear for dialogue is of purest tin—"Oh what comic

* That Mr. Wertenbaker puts "Communist" in quotes shows simple ignorance of the left-wing milieu, I think, rather than bias. He just doesn't know his way around there, as when he makes the girl in bed already cited, allegedly a party-liner, refer to "the colonial people" instead of the standard Marxist usage, "the colonial peoples."

ingredients our sadnesses are made of!" one character remarks—and he has no ear at all for plain English, the phrasing being so chronically "off" as to give the effect of a bad translation, as: "Berkeley had grown deeply fond of Dick without getting through his reticence, which often summoned youthful banter to the defense of a nature almost solemn." Or: "Although he had no other job as yet, he refused to accept a technical discharge, which would have entitled him to five thousand dollars in severance pay. Such was his integrity." No skilled writer would juxtapose these sentences, or indeed write the second at all.

Political mythology rarely produces good novels, as Soviet literature since 1930 has amply demonstrated, and this, in addition to the author's tin ear, is doubtless responsible for the artistic defects of *The Death of Kings.* We took ourselves pretty seriously, I suppose, when I worked for Luce on *Fortune,* but not in the elegant, portentous way of Mr. Wertenbaker's characters. Like them, we talked a lot, but how differently! Mostly gossip, shop talk, or arguments in rough-and-ready language about limited, concrete matters. Not these lofty Socratic dialogues—without a Socrates—about what are principles, really, or whither the Chinese revolution? I do recall such dialogues, but earlier in my life—to be exact, at college, and we called them "bull sessions." There was indeed much conflict on *Fortune* between liberalistic writers and conservative editors—I left in 1936 partly because I lost a crucial battle over the final installment of a series I wrote on the US Steel Corp.—but again it took a more modest form, that of grubby little arguments about data rather than of grandiose expositions of cosmic philosophy. I was also involved, as a Trotskyist, in the left-wing movement of the thirties, and probably at some time asked someone, "Why did you fight in Spain?" But damned if I can recall any such scene as that on pp. 230-31 when Berkeley asks Dick Elgin this question. After a page of portentous meandering, we get, "'I had to do something, and going to Spain was the easiest thing.' . . . Berkeley refrained from asking what the alternatives had been; trust had not gone that far." Finally Dick, after "looking up at the sky above the chasm of Fifth Avenue, as though searching there for the words to give meaning to an adventure an older man might think meaningless," reveals he was sore about Franco. " 'So I had to do something, and of the two things that might have helped'—he paused while their heels rang in unison on the sidewalk—'the other thing I couldn't do.' " Berkeley, of course, delicately refrains from asking what "the other thing" was, and it is not until two hundred pages later that we find it meant spying in the State Department for Soviet Russia. (The author does not conceal his admiration for such lofty integrity.) I'm afraid the people I knew on the left, whether Trotskyists or fellow-travelers, would not have discussed the issue of Spain in this vague and gentlemanly way, but of course we were real people and not characters in a liberal soap opera.

Partisan Review, May-June, 1954

Memo to Mr. Luce

TO: Mr. Luce

FROM: Dwight Macdonald

SUBJECT: William S. Schlamm's "Notes on the New Magazine"

Although you have not formally asked my advice on this new TIME Inc. project, I know you will be pleased by this evidence of continued interest by a former employee. Perhaps you will also profit by an expert's advice, particularly in view of Mr. Schlamm's amateur standing in the field you now propose to invade, that of intellectual journalism. (Not that I have the slightest objection to Mr. Schlamm's amateurishness in itself; in fact, as I shall show, it is an essential quality for the editor of the kind of magazine you project.) Also, as a stockholder of TIME Inc., I have a natural interest which you will, I am sure, be the first to appreciate, in seeing that my corporation's funds are wisely invested.

The Schlamm memo is preceded by a short note, dated May 21, 1945, stating: "The attached memorandum has been considered by TIME Inc.'s Executive Committee. The Committee's decision: to go ahead, tentatively." This decision, I think, should be reconsidered (and, I venture to predict, *will* be reconsidered). For the Schlamm memo purposes to square the circle: to publish an anti-cultural cultural magazine. Our civilization is still not historically ripe for such an enterprise. Let me explain.

The proposal is for TIME Inc. to publish a cultural monthly which will depend for contributions on such intellectuals as—to name a few listed as "candidates for possibly sustained contact"—W. H. Auden, R. P. Blackmur, T. S. Eliot, Reinhold Niebuhr, George Orwell, and Lionel Trilling. It will thus compete not with any of the categories of existing magazines Schlamm lists—the liberal weeklies, the "serious" monthlies like *Harper's* and the *Atlantic*, or journals like *The New Yorker* and *The Saturday Review of Literature*—but rather with a category which, with his usual prudence, he does not list: such "little magazines" as *Partisan Review, Kenyon Review, Sewanee Review* and *Politics*. This invasion of a field hitherto, because of its notoriously unprofitable nature, left to irresponsible intellectuals is part of that present-day tendency toward a merging of commercialized culture and serious (or "high-brow") culture which I analyzed in "A Theory of Popular Culture" (*Politics*, February 1944). Schlamm expresses very well the weighty considerations that must have moved TIME Inc.'s Executive Committee to undertake such an invasion at this time:

> No matter what *we* do, new magazines are bound to appear. Towards the end of this war, a lot of people will want to articulate concerns, attitudes and ideas for which none of the established magazines seems to provide the proper amplification. . . . Our limited problem is merely: do we want to take out an option? We do, and not only because it may be fun to participate in one of the great

> mutations of journalism. In this case, fortunately, fun is identical with an objective responsibility: to prevent, with wisdom, a new growth from getting wild and pernicious. There is no historical law that new departures of journalism, following the hysterics of the war, have to end in Menckenism, "debunking" and adolescent despair. If civilized respect for fundamentals, and mellowing experience, could be combined with a sense of urgency and an understanding of the "new" [these quotation marks are a masterly touch—DM] the resulting magazine might just as well be adult, constructive and readable. . . . Left to themselves, the prospective new magazines of a "disillusioned" [again, masterly!—DM] postwar period will spread gloomy *Weltschmerz.* Started by men who recall the past and don't dislike it entirely, our magazine might provide the moderate climate that is so essential for any intellectual venture.

These formulations could hardly be improved on. Hitherto, the problem which the existence of a body of intellectuals, with their characteristic irresponsible insistence on criticizing the existing order from the standpoint of their own personal values, has been dealt with mostly by the unsubtle and ineffective method of counterattack. But such well-meant polemics as those of Van Wyck Brooks and Archibald MacLeish have had the opposite effect from that intended: they have sharpened the lines and driven waverers over into the intellectuals' camp precisely because the issue was posed too nakedly. Now that the atomic bomb and other features of present-day society are lending a dangerous plausibility to the intellectuals' criticisms, more effective measures are necessary. Instead of attacking the intellectuals, Schlamm proposes to join them in order to gently guide them, aided by three-figure pay checks, away from the rocks of despair and the shoals of disillusionment into the safe harbor of constructive Respect for Fundamentals. It is a project worthy of TIME Inc.'s Executive Committee.

There is also another purpose, more mundane but, to us stockholders, perhaps even more attractive. As Schlamm puts it:

> It seems appropriate that TIME Inc. publishes such a magazine. TIME Inc. is the protagonist, if not the inventor of group journalism. Evidently, group journalism presupposes personal journalism which it puts to more objective use. If this well dries up, the growth goes with it. Clearly, TIME Inc.'s enlightened self-interest should encourage the emergence of mature personal talent. In cultivating it . . . TIME Inc. might solve its grave strategic problem of intellectual supply.

Thus the new magazine will be a kind of fattening-pen from which a constant supply of fresh talent will be supplied to the TIME Inc. abattoirs. Already TIME Inc. has put a good deal of promising talent "to more objective use"; with a pool like this to draw from, the results should be spectacular. Considering the probable returns on this investment, I think we should caution Schlamm against a parsimoniousness which may be penny-wise and pound-foolish. Thus he writes: "Our magazine wouldn't know what to do with a big editorial staff. It needs three editors, four assistants, three secretaries and one office boy." It is true that cultural monthlies hitherto have usually scraped along with a couple of part-time and generally unpaid editors, plus one secretary if they were lucky; and that the *Politics* editorial staff consists of just one editor. But these hole-in-the-wall methods are inadequate for a project of the scope of this one, whose editorial staff, whatever the pennypinching Schlamm may think, should above all be BIG. That is one editorial virtue, at least, which our resources can make absolutely certain.

The objectives of the new journal are thus well worth an effort. Nor can I regard Willi Schlamm as anything but an ideal choice for the editor of such a magazine. It has long been a principle of TIME Inc. journalism that the less a writer knows about a field the more he may be trusted to avoid the expert's tedious complexities and niggling discriminations. Schlamm, whose whole previous career has been devoted to a rather crude kind of political journalism, is thus well equipped for his new post. As his memo itself shows, he not only fears and distrusts all "advanced" ideas, but even better, all ideas *per se*. His ignorance on music, philosophy, political theory, literature and the fine arts—the subject-matter of the new magazine, in short—is of satisfactory proportions. And above all, he shows in every sentence that common (or vulgar) touch which has been such an important ingredient in the success of our magazines.

His description of the *tone* of the new magazine, which occupies a number of pages, is a masterpiece of prudence. The magazine "cherishes personal style" (but not "affectation" or "freakishness"); it is "thoughtful" (but "abhors pomposity"); it has "definite opinions" (but "does not sell a social nostrum"); it is controversial (but "in the spirit of an earnest disagreement, not of an unconcerned whimsicality"); it will favor "manly cussing" (but "won't stand for the rudeness that nowadays goes for polemical wit" and will "discourage boring *literati* feuds"). In short, the magazine will have all the virtues and none of the drawbacks of every conceivable editorial attitude. Its readers, hopefully described as an "elite," will be equally impressive in a vague sort of way, "neither the partisans who read only to see their bias confirmed, nor the jaded who look for an occasional helping of hot pepper." In a word: "It is a magazine for grownups."

The shrewd avoidance of any definite ideas, one way or the other, in the memo is perhaps carried a little too far in Schlamm's 3-point "CODE OF EDITING": "good thinking, good writing, good manners." Also, as a stockholder, I should like to know more about the magazine's contents than that each issue will contain articles, "excerpts from books (new and old)," and a feature "that we might call *Editor's Notebook*." But these are minor complaints. The great good thing is that Schlamm's approach to culture reminds one of those ruddy-faced tweedy men in the whisky ads holding a highball and surrounded by old masters, maps, morocco-bound volumes and other cultural apparatus, the whole ensemble suggesting Casual Distinction and Good Taste. Those ads, I am told, sell a lot of whisky.

On Important Matters, Schlamm is more daring: "We feel satisfied that the standards we have inherited from the Scriptures and the Declaration of Independence are pretty good guesses of what decent people will accept as self-evident truths in another 200 years." The magazine abstains "from political partisanship," but: "Far from sneering at the Tweedledum-Tweedledee nature of our Two-Party system, the magazine sees in it a chance for assured American continuity." Under "(4) Philosophy and Religion," Schlamm does not hesitate to stand Marx on his head in the interest of Soundness: "Even if it had not planned it that way, this magazine would very soon see itself deeply involved in religious matters. . . . Disguised as political, 'ideological,' economic feuds, all the battles of our epoch come finally down to a desire for religious reorientation. The Church is no longer on the defensive. . . . Theology is about to become once more an immensely practical public concern." This is Very Important. I am aware, as no doubt Schlamm is also, of your own keen personal interest in religion as a bulwark against "wild and pernicious" growths in these troubled times. I note that the faculty of our *alma mater,* Yale, has lately decided to emphasize religious instruction, to mention only the most recent of many similar instances. If it can make religion—of the responsible Episcopalian variety, of course—intellectually respectable, the new magazine will by that alone have justified itself. I imagine that Schlamm agrees with me—and you.

This is all very well. Furthermore, Schlamm's career, even if we did not have the evidence of the memo, shows he is the man for the job we have in mind. His evolution from the editor of the Austrian Communist paper, *Rote-Fane* through the editing of the liberal-pacifist journal, *Weltbuhne* (whose founder, the impractical and rather pernicious Karl von Ossietsky, was obviously not responsible enough to be entrusted with so influential a journal) and then, over here, first to the featured columnist of the Social-Democratic *New Leader* and finally to your own confidential adviser, maintained in a private office simply to Think and Correlate—this development at every point reveals a flexibility of spine and a nose for the Main Chance which are absolutely essential for our purposes. I recall with admiration his *New Leader* columns which were unique in left-wing journalism, outside the Stalinist press, in exploiting the polemical tone and method of Westbrook Pegler. My only quarrel with his selection is that we should not give well-paid jobs to European hacks if qualified Americans are available. Would it not be possible to find an American citizen equally well-equipped as to ignorance, vulgarity and adaptability? On the other hand, perhaps only a foreigner could so completely ape the attitudes of American Philistinism.

And yet, despite the suitability of editor and editorial "formula" to the end in view, it remains to add that the project has slight chance of success. The difficulty lies—as always!—with those skittish creatures, the intellectuals. To put the matter crudely: can they be roped in? The urgency of the problem is suggested if we examine the 59 names listed as "candidates for possibly sustained contract." Of these 59 names, we find that 15 are regular contributors to *Partisan Review* (which I take simply because I am familiar with it), and that, if we eliminate some 20 names of economists, scientists and philosophers whose work falls wholly outside PR's field, we find that almost half of the literary-cultural names on the list are PR contributors. Some of the others are closely identified with other "little" cultural magazines. Now these magazines, despite certain counter-tendencies, are on the whole actively opposed to the Philistine "constructiveness" and timid banality with which the new magazine will approach cultural matters. Assuming some personal sympathy on the part of their contributors for the values these "little" magazines attempt to further, what reaction may we expect to Schlamm's reference to "a tasteful thinker like Professor Hocking"? Or his section on "The Arts," which begins: "The magazine . . . is resolved to take art seriously." And continues: "The editors and contributors will easily agree on a few simple stratagems in their dealings with the arts. For one, this magazine does not promote *avant-garde* . . ." How will they react to this: "Though it didn't help her a lot, Europe kept producing a sort of historico-political essayism that, possibly unimportant otherwise, at least is significant for the troubles of the Old World (Julien Benda, Croce, Ortega y Gasset, Silone, Koestler, et al.). Applied in cautious dosages, this pretty special punditing might add an important dimension to our knowledge of Europe."

The dilemma seems fatal: sentiments like the above are calculated to alienate precisely those who are appealed to as contributors; while sentiments of a different order would alienate you, sir, and your Executive Committee. I note that Margaret Marshall, in a recent *Nation*, complains that our new magazine "will appeal to those liberal readers who are more or less vague, undiscriminating or confused" and that it will "serve to blur even more the line that divides right from left"—a line that "has already become difficult enough to distinguish." This is comical because it is precisely magazines like *The Nation* that have blurred this line and have rendered their readers as confused and undiscriminating as possible. In this fact, indeed, lies the one slim chance for our venture's success. However, it does not seem enough: the intelligentsia are demoralized, confused, even a bit frightened, but I doubt that they are yet ready for Schlammism. I chance to know personally three people recently approached by Schlamm with an invitation to collaborate; two, after reading the memo, refused; the third thought it pretty much of a joke.

The conclusion seems inescapable: TIME Inc.'s Executive Committee has made a historical miscalculation. Another generation or two of the kind of progress we are now making, and it may be possible to attract the intelligentsia to a magazine whose editorial criteria are drawn partly from Edmund Clarence Stedman and partly from Bernarr Macfadden. But the time, in my opinion, is not yet ripe. I therefore suggest that TIME Inc. wind up the enterprise at once, take its losses, and again confine Mr. Schlamm's flow of ideas to that audience to which they are best suited: you, sir.

October, 1945

A Way of Death

SEVEN YEARS AGO, Houghton Mifflin published an illustrated book that was either a novel, a poem, an autobiography, a sociological study, a muckraking pamphlet or a work of reportage, depending on how you wanted to take it. In the first year of publication, it sold less than 600 copies; its total sale to date has been—as near as I can fix it—something less than 4,000, the bulk of which was sold at remainder prices. The reviews were either cool or hostile almost everywhere except in *Kenyon Review* (Lionel Trilling), *The Saturday Review of Literature* (Selden Rodman) and the Memphis (Tenn.) *Times-Scimitar* (George Marion O'Donnell). Although it still enjoys some word of mouth reputation, it is rarely mentioned any longer in print, including the "little" magazines. It was, in a word, as bad a publishing failure as could be imagined: neither a commercial success nor a *succès d'estime*.

I am talking, of course, about *Let Us Now Praise Famous Men,* by James Agee, with photographs by Walter Evans. The book came out of an assignment to write and illustrate an article for *Fortune* about Southern sharecroppers. Agee and Evans spent two months in the South, one month living with the Gudgers, a family of sharecroppers in Alabama. *Fortune* didn't print the article after all, I don't know why but suspect because Agee's approach fitted into neither the "liberal" nor the "conservative" category, being pessimistic, unconstructive, impractical, indignant, lyrical and always personal. After a similar rebuff from Harper & Bros.*, the authors found a publisher, with the results noted above.

* The story is that Harpers' was very enthusiastic until they saw the MS, after which a deep silence ensued. Finally one of the Big Shots wrote the authors that Harpers' would print the book if certain deletions were made in the interests of "good taste." Agee and Evans replied they would gladly make the deletions on one condition: that they might reproduce, in an appendix, the complete text of the Big Shot's letter. That was the end of Harpers'.

I find all this very curious because *Let Us Now Praise Famous Men* seems to me one of the most interesting and important American books of the last fifteen years. True, it appeared at a bad time: the year that both Russia and America entered the war. Also true that so original a book could not hope for a mass circulation. But there is some audience for "experimental," "serious" writing, and when one sees the number of "little" literary magazines, most of them desperately serious and grimly experimental, when one sees how a feeble "highbrow" novel like, say, *Under the Volcano* is treated respectfully by even the daily reviewers, then one gets the impression that times have changed since *Moby Dick* sold only 500 copies its first year (not the only similarity with Agee's book) and all the other classic injustices. Not so. All that has happened is that the avant-garde has been institutionalized, the little magazines have developed their own editorial formulae and the highbrow audience feels the same ease in the presence of the mediocre and the same aversion to anything that breaks the familiar categories as the *Satevepost* readers. The neglect of Bartok's music until the last few years is a case in point; the reception of *Let Us Now Praise Famous Men* is another.*

The book is written in a great variety of styles—I know no American writer more talented with words than Agee; his virtuosity, indeed, is often a defect, leading him farther rhetorically than his thought and emotion will carry him—from straight reporting ("At a normal price, a half-sharing tenant gets about six dollars a bale from his share of the cottonseed.") to such passages as "the slow, silent, sweet, quiet yet so profoundly piercing enlargement of the physical sensual emotional world whereof, as we have said, not the least detail whose imposture and power to trench and habituate is not intense beyond calculation."

---

* Oddly enough—or perhaps not at all oddly—the book is being revived in Paris. When Simone de Beauvoir was over here, I lent her my copy. She read it, was impressed, and has had some of it translated for *Les Temps Modernes*. A French edition might do better than the American.

If Agee's book has some of the best prose of our time in it, it also has some of the worst—which also must have confused and therefore irritated the critics. As with all artists whose work is alive, Agee's "defects" seem not only inseparable from his "virtues" but also essential to them, which is another reason the book annoyed everybody so much. An example of Agee's writing close to its best is:

> All over Alabama, the lamps are out. Every leaf drenches the touch; the spider's net is heavy. The roads lie there, with nothing to use them. The fields lie there, with nothing to work in them, neither man nor beast. The plow handles are wet, and the rails and the frogplates and the weeds between the ties: and not even the hurryings and hoarse sorrows of a distant train, on other roads, is heard.

The content is as varied as the style. Much of it is close, minute description which blends lyricism with naturalism in an extraordinarily effective way. Everything, literally, the Gudgers see, touch, taste and smell is described. Two pages are devoted to the texture of the unpainted boards of their house—"these wild fugues and floods of grain," and four pages to a definitive account of overalls, how they look, how they feel on the body, how they age and decay. Their shoes, hats, dresses, shirts, knives, forks, etc., etc., are all described in sensuous terms. Also sociologically, as "The towels in such farmhouses are always floursacks. Kitchen towels are of another world and class of farmer, and 'face' and 'turkish' towels of still another."

Some of it is satire (as the section on the Gudger children's schoolbooks), some of it is savagely deadpan description of class and race relations (as the wonderful encounter with the young Negro couple outside the church, or the scene by the sawmill), much of it is devoted to Agee's personal relations with and reactions to the members of the three sharecropper families he and Evans spent most of their time with.

It is interesting to compare *Let Us Now Praise Famous Men* with *Moby Dick*. Like Melville, Agee is telling a moral parable in terms of a specific way of "making a living" (farming, whaling). There are other similarities: the Elizabethan exuberance of rhetoric, the whimsical variety of structure which packs in everything from poetic drama to drily naturalistic description, the alternation of grand romantic fortissimo passages with how-to-do-it expositions that could appear in *Fortune* if they were done less imaginatively (as Agee found out). This is not to put the two works on the same esthetic level: *Moby Dick* seems to me superior. The elements of its superiority tell us something about the degeneration of America since 1850. Melville's people are "bigger than life," they have will, consciousness and passion, they struggle and act; but the Ricketts and the Gudgers and the Woods, as presented by Agee, are passive, beaten, without much will or consciousness, victims of life with no more ambitious aim than to keep going from day to day. Ahab's defeat is tragic, George Gudger's is only pathetic. Melville had the creative force to give his theme a dramatic form; Agee's book is a series of notes from which such a drama might be worked up but which is not fused into a whole; Melville's worldly, objective, often humorous approach also seems to me superior to Agee's oversweet, sometimes mawkishly personal manner —one feels that Melville was more at home in his sea world than Agee is among his farmers, more the actor and observer and less the self-involved victim, so that somewhat the same difference exists between the authors as between their characters.

These differences are, of course, related to the different quality of our whole life today: we are all of us trapped in an incomprehensible organization of society which denies us human satisfactions like interesting work and comradeship, and which hurries us all along in its vast mechanism to war and destruction; we are all, in Camus' phrase, either victims or executioners—until an atomic war makes us both simultaneously.

"How did we get caught?" Agee's people ask. "Why is it things always seem to go against us? Why is it there can't ever be any pleasure in living? . . . How were we caught?

What, what is it has happened? What is it has been happening that we are living the way we are? The children are not the way it seemed they might be: She is no longer beautiful. . . . How was it we were caught?"

The great thing about Agee's text and Evans' photographs is that they dare to state the truth about these trapped people, without the usual Progressive-superficialities about "solving problems" (All They Need is a TVA). They have given us a *Works and Days* of our times, a chronicle of decay instead of growth, where the land does not nourish those who labor on it but destroys them. Perhaps the highest compliment one can pay their book is to say that it can be read, without too much of a wrench, after reading Rousset or Gliksman on the extreme expression of the modern entrapment: the Nazi and Soviet concentration camps. Hesiod chronicled a way of life; Agee and Evans, a way of death.

Spring, 1948

POLITICAL PATHOLOGY

ULTRA-LEFT

On the Proletariat as a Revolutionary Class

THE VALIDITY of Marxism as a political doctrine stands or falls on its assertion that the proletariat is the historical force which will bring about socialism. The reason political Marxism today is of little interest, save to a few romantic or pedantic sectarians (and of course to the Communists, but in a form so debased and distorted as to bear about the same relation to Marx's teachings as the "Christianity" of the Catholic Church in Franco's Spain bears to the teachings of Christ), the reason is that the proletariat has not been the motive force in either of the two great revolutions of our century, the Bolshevik and the Nazi, but has been as much the passive victim or, at best, accomplice of the organized elites which have made those revolutions, as the bourgeoisie themselves.

The Marxist idea was that just as the bourgeoisie developed inside the feudal system for centuries and finally became strong enough to replace it with capitalism, so the workers are developing their power within capitalism and will finally "burst asunder" the bourgeois integument. Writing a half-century ago, in his crabbed, doctrinaire, original and prophetic *Two Pages from Roman History,* Daniel De Leon put his finger on the peculiar weakness of the proletariat: "The working class, the subject class upon whom depends the overthrow of capitalism and the raising of socialism, differs from all previous subject classes called upon by History to throw down an old and set up a new social system." The difference is that other classes *first* gained "the material means essential to its own economic system" and *then* made their revolution. But the proletariat, by definition, is propertyless. "Holding the economic power, capital, on which the feudal lords had become dependent, the bourgeois was safe under fire. . . . Differently with the proletariat. It is a force every atom of which has a stomach to fill, with wives and children with stomachs to fill, and, withal, precarious ability to attend to such needs. Cato the Elder said in his usual blunt way: 'The belly has no ears.' At times this circumstance may be a force, but it is only a fitful force. Poverty breeds lack of self-reliance. Material insecurity suggests temporary devices. Sops and lures become captivating baits. And the one and the other are in the power of the present ruling class to maneuver with."

If the American working class were ever going to make a revolution, it would have done so, or at least tried to do so, during the 1929–1933 depression. Instead, it voted in Roosevelt, who proceeded to captivate it with "sops and lures" of reform. One of the most tragi-comic documents in our social history is the pamphlet, *Culture and the Crisis,* which the League of Professional Groups for Foster and Ford put out in the fall of 1932. It was signed by an extraordinarily wide range of intellectuals, among them Sherwood Anderson, Newton Arvin, Erskine Caldwell, Lewis Corey, Malcolm Cowley, John Dos Passos, Theodore Dreiser, Waldo Frank, Granville Hicks, Sidney Hook, Sidney Howard, Alfred Kreymborg, James Rorty, Frederick L. Schuman, Lincoln Steffens and Edmund Wilson. "As responsible intellectual workers," they proclaimed, "we have aligned ourselves with the frankly revolutionary Communist Party, the party of the workers." They rejected Roosevelt because his election would result in nothing more than "changes here and there in the machine of government"; they rejected Norman Thomas because the Socialists "do not believe in the overthrow of capitalism" and hence "are the third party of capitalism." Nothing less than the real thing would satisfy these incipient Robespierres, nothing less than "the revolutionary struggle against capitalism under the leadership of the Communist Party," which is alleged to stand for "a socialism of deeds not words." But when these deeds are named, the heady wine of revolution turns into very small beer indeed. "There is only one issue in the present election—call it hard times, unemployment, the farm problem, the world crisis or simply hunger." This issue is to be met by the Communist Party's program of "immediate demands," viz: (1) State-financed unemployment and social insurance; (2) no more wage-cuts; (3) emergency farm relief and a debt and mortgage moratorium for farmers; (4) equal rights for Negroes; (5) defense of workers' rights against capitalist terror; (6) "a united front against imperialist war; for the defense of the Chinese people and the Soviet Union." Except for (4), on which little progress was made until the Truman Administration, Roosevelt's New Deal put into effect this entire program (if his recognition of the Soviet Union and his "collective security" crusade against Nazi Germany may be taken as implementing the rather vague sixth point) as well as adding several dozen other similar measures such as TVA, the SEC and the Federal housing program. What price revolution?

Or compare the aftermath of the Great French Revolution and the 1917 Russian Revolution. Both degenerated from their initial promise of democracy and liberation into the one-man dictatorships of Napoleon and Stalin. This political regression, however, did not mean that the old ruling class regained its economic power. Napoleon did not restore their estates to the nobles but, on the contrary laid the legal and governmental foundations for 19th-century French capitalism. Stalin did not call in foreign capital or restore private property and the capitalist market, as Trotsky expected him to do, but on the contrary pushed Trotsky's own policy of state-owned industrialization and of farm collectivization ahead at a brutally fast tempo. There is, however, one significant difference: Napoleon did not turn against those in whose name the 1789 revolution had been made, the bourgeoisie, but rather acted as their representative. But Stalin smashed the working class and reduced them to subjection. Napoleon and his generals and officials ruled without disturbing the economic power of the bourgeoisie, but under Stalin the workers lost such slight economic power as they had had, including even the protection of their trade unions, for not they, but the Stalin bureaucracy was the new ruling class put into power by the 1917 Revolution. They were all the more easily subdued since Lenin and Trotsky, in the early years of that revolution, had broken the workers' own instruments of political and economic power: the Soviets and the workers' committees which for a brief time ran the factories. The workers were easily dispossessed by Lenin and Stalin because they had never possessed in the first place.

This chronic impotence of the working class has forced latter-day Marxists into apologetics whose metaphysical nature contrasts amusingly with Marxism's claim to being a materialistic doctrine. When one is indelicate enough to refer to the great mass of evidence by now available on the subject, one is met with indulgent smiles. First of all, the Marxists explain, the trade union bureaucrats and/or the Communists are traitors, *mis*leaders of labor, their policies are anti-working class, and they maintain their control through force and fraud. If one presses the matter and asks why, if the workers have been successfully gulled and coerced for a century, they will be able to assert themselves in the future, one discovers that when a Marxist talks about "working class aims" and "working class consciousness," he means nothing so vulgar as the actual here-and-now behavior of workers but rather what the workers *would* want and *would* do if they knew what their "real" interests were. Since the proletarian rarely does know his "real" interests and constantly tends to identify his interests with those of his exploiters, the result is that his "real" behavior Marxistically speaking is usually in conflict with his really real behavior, so that socialism becomes an ideal which the workers are assumed to cherish in their hearts but which they rarely profane by putting into action. (As Alfred Braunthal has put it: "the mystic cult of The Masses, who always feel the right way but always act the wrong way.") A metaphysical distinction between two kinds of reality is involved here. Thus a Marxist exults over the rise of the British Labor Party because it is a labor party (metaphysical reality) and at the same time denounces its entire leadership as traitors to the working class (materialistic reality). This produces a position as theoretically impregnable as it is practically sterile. The rank-and-file—suppressed, passive, coerced—is always judged on the basis not of what it does but of what it is assumed to want to do, while the leadership, which is seen as the active, coercive party, is always judged by what it does. That perhaps the leadership is a true expression of the needs and desires of the ranks, if we look at the matter only from a historical-materialistic standpoint—this idea is much too simple for a Marxist.

I have no objection to basing one's politics on a metaphysical, unprovable value judgment that people *should* want certain things—in fact, that is just what I think one ought to do. But I object to metaphysical assumptions being smuggled into a doctrine which affects to be materialistic. This is confusing both intellectually and practically, and is simply a way of avoiding the unpleasant reality. The real reality, that is.

From "The Root Is Man," 1953

Trotskyism I: "The Only Really Moral People"

STUDENTS of political pathology would do well to put aside the *Daily Worker* for a few minutes and read a remarkable document which appears in the February issue of *Fourth International,* organ of the Socialist Workers Party. "How the Trotskyists Went to Jail," by Joseph Hansen, explains many things about the American Trotskyist movement.

Hansen doesn't fall into bathos, he positively seeks it out. Under his treatment, his party's leader, James P. Cannon, takes on the corny dignity of Warner Baxter playing Abraham Lincoln. Nothing escapes this Bolshevik Boswell, this proletarian sob-sister. Cannon's watch—"a present from Local New York." His cigar—"a present from seagoing Trotskyists." His suit: " 'When America's No. 1 socialist exchanges his clothes for prison garb, he will get a receipt for that gray suit the Los Angeles comrades gave him,' I thought. 'When he gets out, it will be the first thing he puts back on—that suit is party harness, so to speak.' " Cannon's wife bids him good-by at the station: "In my mind . . . came the image of Natalia Trotsky, the great woman hero of the Marxist movement." Cannon's train passes Harlem: "The lines in Jim's face grew deep and grave." Cannon passes the Palisades: "The pillars of a famous geologic formation moved in stately procession into the past. . . . The sun fell on his hair as the train leaned around a curve and the iron gray waves lighted up luminously. Jim's lips moved: 'The Palisades are beautiful.' " Ever *le mot juste.*

This pious sentimentality towards the leader of the in-group is coupled with an arrogance towards the out-group (in this case, roughly 129,999,500 of the 130,000,000 inhabitants of the United States) which verges on paranoia. The compensatory role of this attitude hardly needs stressing: it is a classic psychological symptom of sectarian groups, whose arrogance is generally in direct proportion to their powerlessness. Thus Hansen reports the talk of some of the Trotskyists at a "last supper"—he calls it just that—before entering prison:

"Our movement is historic," said Dunne. "Take our press, for instance. The first volume of *The Militant* is a collector's item, worth I don't know how much. Compare it with other radical publications. Who cares about the first volumes of *The Call* for example?"

To which Hansen adds his inimitable touch:

> As I listened to these native American socialists, I could not help but conclude: When the history of our country is written by future historians, they will not look for material at Hyde Park where Roosevelt employs a staff to file away minutiae about himself. They will dig painfully into . . . the files of Trotskyist publications, to find out what the real figures of American history were like.

Evidently Roosevelt will be lucky to get a footnote in future histories of the period 1930–1950. The chapters compiled from the files of Trotskyist publications promise to be epic: CHAPTER IX: 1929 DEPRESSION BEGINS, JAMES P. CANNON AND MAX SHACHTMAN LEAVE COMMUNIST PARTY. CHAPTER XII: CIO LAUNCHED, LITTLE STEEL STRIKE, JAMES P. CANNON AND MAX SHACHTMAN LEAVE SOCIALIST PARTY. CHAPTER XV: NAZI-SOVIET PACT, WORLD WAR II BEGINS, JAMES P. CANNON AND MAX SHACHTMAN LEAVE EACH OTHER.

But the high point comes in Hansen's report of his conversation, on the train, with Cannon about how John Dewey came to head the commission that investigated the charges against Trotsky made in the Moscow Trials. They were probably passing the Great Lakes at the time, but Hansen unaccountably omits to record his Leader's reactions to those famous geologic formations. ("The Great Lakes are big," said Jim simply.)

Considering that Dewey disagreed strongly with Trotsky's whole political outlook, and considering the pro-Stalin climate of liberal opinion then, it might seem rather a fine gesture for an aged philosopher to assume the active chairmanship of the commission and make the long trip to Mexico City to give Trotsky a chance to prove his innocence. The credit, however, is miraculously shifted to . . . James P. Cannon. "I wouldn't let him go," says the Leader, "until he agreed to do something for justice. That was how he came to serve on the Commission." And a casual, generous remark of Dewey's is quoted as though it were his entire motivation: "He [Cannon] appealed to my better nature." Thus it is not Dewey who deserves credit (except that he is conceded to have a "better nature") but Cannon, who sternly shepherded Dewey into the paths of righteousness. ("Jim smiled warmly at the memory.")

Nor is this all. Cannon goes on:

> But even John Dewey was not wholly impartial. As a judge, it would have served the cause of justice to simply announce the verdict of not guilty, without interjecting his own personal views on politics. He took advantage of the occasion to attack the theory of socialism; in that he departed from strict morality. *When the history of this epoch is written . . . they'll discover that the only really moral people were the Trotskyists.* (Emphasis mine)

It was perfectly moral for Trotsky to deliver before the Commission an exposition of his revolutionary socialist views (and a superb speech it was), but it is immoral for Dewey to state that, as is well known, he has a different political philosophy. (Assuming he did so, that is. I have just looked up the two volumes put out by the Commission, and I can find no such statement of Dewey; nor is there any in his "Truth is on the March" speech—at least there is none visible on a cursory reading.) And words almost fail one before the colossal impudence, the *nerve* of Cannon's final remark about the Trotskyists being the "only really moral people" in this epoch. From what I know of Cannon and his followers, which is considerable, and from what I know of Dewey's public behavior, which is less but sufficient, it is not Cannon who has the right to talk about morality.

The above was written with some hesitation. Cannon and the rest are serving prison terms, victims of a monstrous frame-up by the Roosevelt Administration. They are in jail for their socialist convictions, and one must respect them for that and support every effort on their behalf. As far as their political program goes, furthermore, except for their support of Russia in the war, the Cannon group stand for many of my own convictions. It is, therefore, rather tragic when some of its leadership shows such pathological symptoms. These symptoms are not new, of course, and grow from the Bolshevik organizational tradition—but that is another and larger story.

May, 1944

Trotskyism II: Revolution, Ltd.

THE DEPARTMENT of Justice indicted the leaders of the Socialist Workers Party under the wrong law: instead of the Smith "Gag" Act, the Sherman Anti-Trust Act should have been invoked. The firm of Revolution, Ltd. (and "limited" is just the right word) owns the famous Trotsky patents on the revolutionary process. Its octopus tentacles stretch out from 116 University Place just like the Trust in the old cartoons. Its board of directors, headed by that Rockefeller of revolution, James P. Cannon, are frankly out to create an airtight monopoly (and "airtight" is also just right) not only of revolutionary-socialist action but also of political virtue and intelligence. Fortunately, their aspirations would seem to have slight chance of being realized—the picture of our national political and intellectual life were the SWP Trotskyites ever to "take power" is about as gruesome a nightmare as one can dream up—Cannon and his lieutenants resembling the Rockefeller crowd only in monopolistic ambition and not at all in energy and mental powers.

Last winter Cannon's Eagle Scout leader, Joseph Hansen, staked out a claim to a monopoly on political virtue in his "How the Trotskyists Went to Jail." Now the party boss himself—"Trotsky's Truman," a wit calls him—has filed papers for an exclusive patent on political intelligence, in his "Notes on the Party Discussion" in the party's *Internal Bulletin* for April. These notes are partly concerned with some criticisms of the boss's regime which have been raised within the party by a small group the boss contemptuously refers to as "the thinkers' faction," and partly with James T. Farrell's criticisms of the Hansen article in his letter to the *Fourth International* (never printed there; see POLITICS for December, 1944, for text). A selection will give the gist:

A Party for Workers

The principal reason why I am less tolerant now than before of the "Kibbitzers' Club" theories of organization is precisely the good prospect of an influx of new, politically inexperienced worker militants. I know that such workers will not stay in a kibbitzers' club. They won't talk back to the articulate smart alecks, and they won't write letters to the N.O. either. They "vote with their feet." But the new workers are more important than the old incorrigibles who think the party is a hospital for sick souls and a forum for unrestricted and unlimited self-expression. . . .

The prejudices against leadership and the fear of discipline are characteristics of the petty bourgeois who doesn't want to be tied down to anything definite. To the militant worker, however, who has an instinct for organized struggle, strong leadership and firm discipline are the most attractive features of a party. Such a party, in his eyes, is serious; it means business—and that is what he wants.

Self-Confidence and Skepticism

The objections we hear to our practice of praising our party, its institutions and—once in a while—its individual members, is at bottom an expression of the capitulatory skepticism of the petty bourgeois; his deep-seated lack of confidence in the proletariat, in the party and in himself. All petty bourgeois parties, groups and tendencies, no matter how much they may quarrel among themselves, make it an article of their creed that "no one party" can be trusted with the leadership of the workers' movement. The main lesson they deduce from the Russian revolution is that the "monopoly" of leadership by the Bolsheviks was the source of all evils. . . .

We think we are important because our ideas are going to change the world. Without this conviction we could never build the combat party which is destined to be the instrument of this historic mission. See what Trotsky wrote in 1914 when reaction was triumphant everywhere and "the death of Marxism" was being universally celebrated. "We feel ourselves to be the only creative force of the future."

Leadership and the Leader Cult

The "leader cult" theory, as we have heard it explained lately, is a version of the anti-leader prejudice of the syndicalists which was shared in part by menshevism. A nihilistic attitude toward leadership ("iconoclasm") is absolutely fatal to the design to organize a combat party; without a *firm, authoritative* and *continuing* central leadership the combat party must remain in the realm of daydreams. . . .

Lenin, who was in dead earnest about organizing a revolution, exalted the concept of leadership higher than anyone had ever done before. Perhaps that was his most distinctive, his most *Leninist* contribution to the theory of organizing the party and the revolution. . . . Our strength is in our combination. The "machine" (human) is stronger than any individual can be.

An Insult to the Party

The leaders of the opposition showed a great deal of disrespect for the opinions and sentiment of the party membership. Perhaps the worst manifestation was the demand that James T. Farrell's letter be published; the attempt to impose his pompous strictures on the party as some kind of authority which the party was bound to recognize. That was a coarse and brutal insult to the party. The party would not be a party if it had not learned to rely on itself and to reject out of hand every suggestion of guidance from outside sources.

We Leninists have studied the art of revolutionary politics and organization and our decisions receive the constant corrective of the workers' mass movement. We *work at it* every day. Such individuals as James T. Farrell, whose main interest and occupation lie in other fields, haven't yet started even to think about it seriously. His banal letter alone is sufficient proof of that. We take our ideas and our work far too seriously to welcome instruction from people who haven't the slightest idea of what they are talking about; who mistake vague impressions and Philistine prejudices for professional competence.

It is remarkable how politics lures the amateur. Every other art and science, every profession and occupation, has its own recognized body of knowledge and its own rules and standards which amateurs and laymen respect from a distance and take for granted. But in the art of revolutionary politics and organization any dabbler feels free to pontificate without the slightest sign of serious preparation. Dwight Macdonald is the archetype of these political Alices in Wonderland.* But Farrell, as the most cursory reading of his childish letter shows, is not much closer to the real world. There is nothing we can do about it. We can't prevent such people from committing their half-baked notions to paper as soon as they pop into their heads and then waiting for the earth to quake.

But we have people in our ranks—worse yet, in our leadership—who excitedly demand that we set aside our rules and suspend our business to listen to these preposterous oracles and even to heed their revelations. We

---

* Footnote by D. M.: An apt description. It will be recalled that Alice is presented in Carroll's book as a normal and reasonable person who is constantly being amused, bewildered or distressed by the fantastic behavior and logic of the inhabitants of Wonderland. During the years I was associated with the Trotskyist movement, I must confess I often felt like Alice. Comrade Cannon has some resemblance to the Caterpillar Alice found sitting on a mushroom serenely smoking a hookah:

"Are you content now?" said the Caterpillar.

"Well, I should like to be a *little* larger, sir, if you wouldn't mind," said Alice. "Three inches is such a wretched height to be."

"It is a very good height indeed!" said the Caterpillar, angrily, rearing itself upright as it spoke (it was exactly three inches high).

should in all conscience object to that. That is downright offensive. . . .

First, a few words on the reaction to Farrell's criticism. For years James T. Farrell has been a loyal and devoted fellow-traveler of the Trotskyists. Although personally I think he was *too* loyal, in the sense that he should have been more awake to the undemocratic ideology whose effects he has now himself experienced, one can only admire the moral courage with which he has stuck to his revolutionary-socialist convictions while most other American intellectuals have been abandoning them. When the leaders of the Socialist Workers Party were persecuted in such a disgraceful fashion by the Department of Justice, Farrell not only lent his literary prestige to the defense committee, of which he was chairman, but also gave much time and work to it—speaking, writing pamphlets, carrying on correspondence. His letter to the *Fourth International* objecting to Hansen's article (and also to what he considered an unfair polemic against Max Shachtman in the same magazine) was obviously intended as a *friendly* criticism, not as a breaking off of political relations. Not only did the *Fourth International* refuse to print the letter, but now we see the party boss considers that Farrell has insulted the party by presuming to write it. Result: Farrell has now transferred his allegiance to the rival Shachtman group, the Workers Party.

Obviously only the weightiest possible considerations caused the SWP leadership to handle Farrell's letter in this manner, which not only violates the most elementary notions of free thought and decent human relations but also deprives the party of its best-known sympathizer. The ethical aspect, we may presume from the above document, was not too vividly present to the SWP leadership, but certainly the *practical* drawbacks of their policy must have suggested themselves. Anyone who has followed the Stalinist movement at all closely has seen similar examples of a refusal to make even the most modest concession to freedom of criticism regardless of the practical consequences. Neither the Stalinists nor the SWP Trotskyists are usually very idealistic in their political maneuvers; they do not often sacrifice expediency for principle. Why, then, always in such cases? The reason, I think, is that these parties are organized on so totalitarian a basis that their whole structure would be imperiled by any concession to free thought. The dissenter must be eliminated —physically, when they have state power as in Russia; morally and intellectually, when they don't.

By what road do politicians who at one time were sincere socialists, dreaming of liberating mankind, arrive at so drastic a repudiation of freedom? The main elements seem to be:

(1) The mystique of the workers, who are allegedly for "strong leadership and firm discipline" as against the "articulate smart alecks" who want "unlimited self-expression." This is the classic ideology of the conservative trade union leader, especially in America, and also of the CP bureaucrat. (The fight against Trotsky himself was waged by the Stalinist apparatus precisely on this basis, Trotsky being obviously an "articulate smart aleck.") It is a means of discrediting in advance all criticism of the leadership's policies—and even all *consciousness*. To some extent it is true that workers are more easily disciplined and less insistent on free expression than petty bourgeois intellectuals, but this is precisely one of the evil effects of capitalism on the working class which socialists presumably should try to moderate, not intensify.

(2) The justification of one-party monopoly on the grounds that not to insist on eliminating all other parties is a sign of lack of self-confidence and seriousness. (The logic leads also, of course, to the elimination of dissident tendencies *within* the single party.) Leaving aside the obvious ethical objections to such a doctrine, I should say that it shows lack of self-confidence to insist on suppressing competing organizations; and also that, scientifically, it seems dubious that any party, even the SWP, can have a monopoly on political wisdom.

(3) The confusion of a belief in the importance of one's activity with a belief that all other people's activities are unimportant. Personally, I take revolutionary socialist doctrines

very seriously, but cannot take seriously the claim of any group to have a monopoly on an exclusive patent on socialism. A left-wing party which must deny importance to all other tendencies on the left in order to feel important is not very sure of its own importance.

(4) The most serious *weakness* of Lenin's political method (and of Trotsky's after he embraced Bolshevism too enthusiastically after 1917, forgetting the penetrating criticisms he himself had once made of its organizational ideas) is selected as precisely the *strength*, the main "point" of the method. "A firm, authoritative and continuing leadership. . . . The 'machine' (human) is stronger than any individual can be . . . permit no anarchistic individuals . . . to disrupt the 'machine.'" How does this differ from Stalinism? Even if leaders of great ability and sincere socialist convictions, like Lenin and Trotsky, are at the controls, they cannot withstand the immanent logic of a centralized power-machine, which is to crush all dissident tendencies regardless of the content and motivation of their policies.

(5) Finally, the party boss develops a theory which, so far as I know, not even the Stalinists have ventured to put into writing: that socialist politics is a science like physics on which only the technical expert may presume to think seriously. According to this remarkable notion, individuals "whose main interest and occupations lie in other fields" (i.e., about 95% of mankind), are presumptuous if they dare to criticize the policies and ideas of those "who work at it (politics) every day." It is unnecessary to labor the authoritarian nature of this concept: it is really a form of technocracy, or of Burnham's "managerialism," reducing the masses to the role of passive, trusting followers of the "professional revolutionaries." Lenin described the future socialist society with the formula: "Every cook will be a politician." But the party boss tells the cook to stick to his pots and pans, the novelist to stick to his typewriter and leave serious matters like politics to the technicians. Socialists in the past have labored to awaken the consciousness of the people, to break down the distinction between "expert" and "layman" in poli-

tics—which, after all, has to do with the most vital interests of every man—but this bureaucrat masquerading in Trotsky's garments, this dwarf in a giant's robe would reverse the process.

Justly enough, the concept cuts both ways. For if Farrell had behaved according to its logic, he would not have lifted a finger to defend the SWP leaders, letting the opposing "experts" (the indicted Trotskyists and the Department of Justice) fight it out between themselves. How could a mere novelist have any valid opinion on these deep matters? Indeed, the logic may be pressed further: if Farrell is a mere amateur (a "dilettante" Burnham would call him) with no right to be heard on political matters, what shall we say of the workers to whom the party boss refers with inconsistent respect? We may presume they have done much less reading and thinking about socialist politics than Farrell has; so what do they know about the art? Aren't they even ranker amateurs? Why, then, have they the ability to know whether the Trotskyists are right, or whether, let us say, Congressmen Rankin and Connally (who also "work at it every day," who are also experts) are right? The proper course of action for them, according to this logic, would be to let the SWP fight it out with American capitalism and not concern themselves with questions on which they cannot presume to have a sensible opinion.

We have not even yet exhausted this remarkable conception. Not only has the "outsider" no right to criticize any political aspect of the party; he cannot even make non-political observations. Farrell's criticisms involved no political *expertise* but simply the ability to detect, in his own words, "gross sentimentality, unbending rigidity, unfair attacks on opponents." He stated explicitly that he agreed with the SWP on the main *political* points involved: Shachtman's theory that Russia is a "bureaucratic collectivist" society, and my own low opinion of Bolshevism. Thus an "outsider" has no right to have a serious opinion even on non-political matters; he has, in short, no right to think; he has, even shorter, no rights. Like the shaman of a tribe, the party boss preaches distrust of and disdain for all outsiders simply because they *are* outside the in-group. "The party (read: "tribe") would not be a party if it had not learned to rely on itself and to reject out of hand every suggestion of guidance from outside sources." With such an attitude toward the profane outside world (everyone except the few hundred True Believers), it is hardly surprising that the SWP Trotskyists have become the Jehovah's Witnesses of the left-wing world. They make a principle out of not learning anything from anybody.

I don't see how it is any longer possible to regard such a party as anything more than a variant of Stalinism. This does not mean that if the SWP leadership get into trouble with the Government again—perhaps unlikely considering the excessive caution with which they have moved of late—one would not feel obliged to support them, just as one supports Harry Bridges against the Government's efforts to deport him. But it does mean that one would feel no greater obligation and no greater enthusiasm than in the case of the Stalinists.*

I have maintained that the question of party organization and party democracy is as important as that of program. This view, which is rejected by practically all Trotskyists, seems to me to be strikingly confirmed by the evolution, or rather devolution, of the Socialist Workers Party in the last five years.

July, 1945

A Historic Moment

I have always had a sneaking admiration for the editors of a tiny mimeographed journal called *Proletarian Outlook* who

* The document cited above is, of course, not the only evidence for this conclusion. See also, for example, the extraordinary data presented in "From the Bureaucratic Jungle" by Max Shachtman ("The New International," Nov. 1944 and Feb. 1945).

once asked the usual leftist question, "What can be done?" and answered it unexpectedly: "Nothing, absolutely nothing." That was June, 1940, and the editors showed they were in earnest by folding up their paper. It was a historic moment in left-wing history. The smaller the sect, the more grandiosely optimistic it usually is. The Revolution, like Mr. Hoover's Prosperity, is always just around the corner. The other day, for example, the current issue of *International News* (mimeographed) came into the office. *International News* bears on its flimsy cover the following awesome inscription: *"Issued by the Revolutionary Workers League for the International Contact Commission. Affiliates: Central Committee of the Red Front of Greater Germany; Revolutionary Workers League of the US; Leninist League of Great Britain."* Its lead article was headed, quite simply: "May Day Manifesto, 1944, of the International Contact Commission for a Fourth (Communist) International." This history-heavy document began: "TO THE WORKERS OF THE WORLD, TO THE OPPRESSED IN ALL COUNTRIES, TO THE SOLDIERS AND SAILORS." It ends in the usual spume of slogans: "THROUGHOUT THE WORLD ALL POWER TO WORKERS' COUNCILS! HANDS OFF ITALY! DEFEND THE SOVIET UNION DESPITE AND AGAINST STALINISM! FOR A NEW FOURTH (COMMUNIST) INTERNATIONAL!" The experienced manifesto-reader can easily fill in the text between these termini for himself.

July, 1944

THE LIBERALS

The Death of F.D.R.

Of all the reactions to Franklin Roosevelt's death—including the little girl in Spartansburg, N. C., who said, "Mummy, I believe that with President Roosevelt up there with God, we'll soon win the war"—none struck me as more significant than the remark someone told me one liberal journalist made to another: "Now we'll have to grow up."

The unexpected, to me at least, violence of the public reaction to Roosevelt's death seems to show that he had indeed become the Father of His Country, using the term in the Freudian rather than the Fourth-of-July sense.

A reader sends in a letter from an Ensign in the Navy, which reads in part:

> The word of our President's death still shocks me, three days later. . . . It is not the shock of familiarity suddenly disappearing, nor is it the sadness of seeing people cry. It is a deep and terrifying distress, both at the personal loss and of the consequences. Roosevelt believed in us—as we believed in him. He fought for us, as we fight for him. This is the greatness of democracy.
>
> He is dead. The steps he made forward must now be marched again, step by step. We and other Americans spent time arguing fine points of ideas. . . . The fine points must now be forgotten. . . . We must mass behind Truman. . . . How much did Roosevelt mean? He was a great friend, and his loss has murdered sleep. It is the end of an era. It is the beginning of a refrigerated, bathtubbed, toastered, newsreeled society that runs on electricity alone, without a soul, without a leader, without life.
>
> I have been amazed at my sorrow. Suddenly I see the collapse of Liberalism, the end of a United World, the death as well of Henry Wallace, of Labor, of Human

> Rights. We must fight—harder and more sincerely than ever before. And we must try harder to understand, because we are more alone. . . .

In its sentimentality and its panicky Leader-worship, the Ensign's letter is a naïve expression of the liberal reaction to Roosevelt's death. For Roosevelt had become the Father especially of the left-of-center section of American society. This was an unhealthy state of affairs, both politically and psychologically, and would have been objectionable even had Roosevelt been a far wiser and more benevolent Father than he was. Rebellion against paternal authority is the road to maturity for society as for the individual; in this sense, while one naturally is sorry to see anyone die, one must regard Roosevelt's death as a gain. Perhaps the American labor movement will now grow up—though the removal of Father by sudden death seems a little too easy a solution.

The "New Deal" ended in 1937, when three great turning points occurred: (1) the defeat of the "Little Steel" strike when the CIO foolishly relied on Roosevelt's support—and didn't get it—against the terrorism of the steel companies, a defeat which crippled the union movement until the outbreak of war caused a labor shortage; (2) the severe depression which began that fall and lasted until the war refloated the American economy, a depression which came about when Roosevelt, yielding to right-wing pressure, drastically cut down Government spending earlier in the year; (3) Roosevelt's "Quarantine the Aggressor" speech a few weeks after the first stock market break, in which he announced a pro-war, interventionist policy. After 1937, with the exception of the Wages & Hours Act the following year, no more major social legislation was enacted. Maneuvering the country into the war (which was, of course, essential for America's national interests under a capitalist system), preparing for war and then fighting the war—these made up the content of Roosevelt's policies in the last eight years of his life. By the time he died, he had emerged as the Commander-in-Chief, the implacable executioner of the Enemy peoples (his last

State document, appropriately enough, dealt with the necessity for punishing and controlling Japan for generations), the originator of the appalling "unconditional surrender" policy, which he forced on the reluctant Churchill at Casablanca. He is often compared to Lincoln and Wilson, but there was in him little of that humanity which the former, for all his unscrupulous politicking, often showed, or of the genuine liberal idealism of the latter. In the last few years, he had even grown cynically weary of the pretense of humane and progressive aims, declaring the New Deal was dead, and the Atlantic Charter not to be taken seriously.

Yet when he died, he was mourned as a great humanitarian and the Father of the common people. The myth was still intact. By this, we may measure the deterioration of our politics in the last two generations.

May, 1945

"People's Capitalism"

The Liberty League was the last expression of what might be called the "pure" ideology of Free Enterprise: that the system automatically spreads blessings if the legal owners are allowed complete freedom in making use of their property as they think best. The contemporary conservative doctrine is expressed in a recent ad by the great business publishers, McGraw-Hill: "Free enterprise does not imply the freedom to use any or all means to make a profit. It does not mean the right to monopolize. It means the opportunity and the obligation to compete." At the annual meeting of the National Association of Manufacturers, President Crawford formalized the new big-business line when he stated that the NAM no longer stood for "unqualified free enterprise" but rather for "free, private and competitive enterprise . . . the absence of all uncontrolled monopoly and special privilege wherever they may have been found in the past."

The left has also made concessions. The Communists have formally adopted "Free Enterprise" as their 1944 slogan, insisting that the reactionaries have no right to monopolize so inspiring a concept. Stuart Chase has lost much of his faith in nationalization of industry, and now urges that a large sector of the economy be reserved for private enterprise. Vice-President Wallace has confided to the press his vision of a postwar America "where all can become members of the middle class. . . . The spirit of competition will and must continue to be one of our main driving forces. We can have full employment without destroying private enterprise. . . . Horatio Alger is not dead in America and never will be."

The whole trend is epitomized in the intriguing idea of a "people's capitalism" recently put forward by Eric Johnston, the president of the U. S. Chamber of Commerce. This is the theme of his new book, *America Unlimited,* as also of his article in the September *Reader's Digest* with the wonderful title: "Three Kinds of Capitalism: Which Offers a Poor Boy the Best Chance?" At first glance, it seems daring of Mr. Johnston to say "capitalism" right out loud. (It is an interesting sidelight on capitalism that the very word has come to have a pejorative flavor. Thus I remember Ralph McA. Ingersoll, in his pre-*PM* period, when he was Luce's gauleiter on *Fortune,* citing, among other instances of my alleged smuggling of radical propaganda into my articles, my frequent use of the word "capitalism.") * However, the way that Mr. Johnston defines capitalism takes all the curse off the word.

"From a strictly economic angle," he begins, "there is

* "When this book first appeared (1926)," writes R. H. Tawney in the preface to his "Religion and the Rise of Capitalism," "it was possible for a friendly reviewer, writing in a serious journal, to deprecate in all gravity the employment of the term 'capitalism' in an historical work, as a political catch-word, betraying a sinister intention on the part of the misguided author." One is also reminded of the story, perhaps apocryphal, that President Butler of Columbia told his faculty member, Louis M. Hacker, that he liked everything about the latter's "Triumph of American Capitalism" except one thing—"Why, Mr. Hacker, was it necessary to use *that word* in the title?"

capitalism everywhere." He lists three types: (1) bureaucratic (Russia, Germany and "seedling growths" in Washington); (2) "capitalism of monopoly and special privilege" (flourishes most in . . . England); (3) "Then there is a *people's* capitalism. I come from it. I want to see it survive for every poor boy and girl in America after me. . . . Only America, I think, can light the world toward an ultimate capitalism of *everybody*." So we now have a "people's capitalism" as a fitting companion to the "people's war" and the "people's century." I suppose next we shall be hearing about "people's cartels" and "the imperialism of the common man."

All these formulae should be considered under the head of psychiatry rather than economics. The compensatory mechanism is obvious: the more monopolistic industry becomes, the more the State intervenes into capitalism, the more the middle classes are squeezed out of the control-sector of the economy, the more all this happens, the more powerful the compulsion to believe in the possibility of a future reversal of these tendencies. Some of the "Free Enterprise" ideologues are doubtless aware of this, but I think most of them are the dupes of their own rhetoric. Otherwise, one would expect some more plausible program to be evolved for securing Free Enterprise than the enforcement of the Sherman and Clayton Anti-Trust Acts.

For it is a fact that all of them, from Willkie and Johnston to Wallace, put all their hopes on trust-busting. One really thinks one is back in the days of the Boy Orator from the Platte when one reads Wallace's anti-monopoly speeches. His Dallas speech against the railroads, for example, showed with copious documentation—lately buttressed by the testimony of Assistant Attorney General Berge before the Kilgore Committee of the Senate—that railroad rates have never been competitive, that the ICC has failed for fifty years to regulate them effectively, that discriminatory rail rates have kept the South and West in a state of semi-colonial dependency on the Northeast, that "new restraints have appeared with the outlawing of the old," etc.

It was an impressive performance. But Wallace proved too

much. For if all this is true, two questions arise: (1) Why has half a century of Government regulation, including ten years of Wallace's own New Deal, failed to make any headway? (2) Why is it reasonable to expect the same method to work in the future? On the contrary, it is clear that the trusts to be "busted" have been getting bigger all the time, and that the present war is concentrating American capital at a specially rapid rate. These facts at once refute the trust-busting ideology and make it psychologically all the more necessary for supporters of capitalism to cling to it.

April, 1944

Curiouser and Curiouser

OUR READERS may have noticed that the "fillers" at the end of articles have been getting steadily wackier. The promising new department, "With the Heavy Thinkers," in particular has contained some remarkable specimens from the works of Samuel Grafton, Archibald MacLeish, and, in this issue, alas, my friend James Agee. The success with which James Burnham has impersonated a thinker and theoretician is another instance, as is the recent appearance of Orson Welles in the role of a political columnist, or any issue of that journalistic curio, *Free World* magazine. I don't mean simply that I disagree rather strongly with the above writers (as I do). It is possible to disagree violently with someone's conclusions and still recognize they have been reached by methods of thought, and in accordance with ethical assumptions, which one holds to one's self. Two cases in point, for me, would be John Dewey's political philosophy and Trotsky's conception of the Soviet Union. But in the above cases, and in many more I run across in books and the press these days, the *methods* by which conclusions are reached seem to me so irrational—and in some though not all cases the ethical assumptions so antipathetic—that one simply cannot even discuss the question. Agee, for example, may be right in asserting that Roosevelt was a hero and saint who died for suffering humanity. But the sentimental mush he unloads to prove it has nothing to do with the question one way or the other. In fact, I'll show my fair-mindedness by saying that Agee's eulogy of Roosevelt does not necessarily show that Roosevelt was *not* a modern saint, any more than the fact that fascist and Stalinist rhapsodizers have praised *their* Leaders with the same kind of "blood-thinking" necessarily proves that Hitler and Stalin are not exemplary characters.

What I mean is that the kind of wild stuff we used to associate, in the innocent old days, with the "yellow press" has been cropping up in the highbrow and middlebrow press with rather alarming frequency of late. *PM* is perhaps the prime example: here is a paper that crusades for the causes we leftish intellectuals have always considered "good"—labor unions, better housing, progressive education, socialized medicine, democratic racial relations, etc.; a paper which is typographically modern and whose writers use the jargon of "advanced" circles; and yet a paper which has even less respect for objective truth than the great bulk of our commercial press (a poll among Washington correspondents, for example, showed that only the Chicago *Tribune* was considered by them to more consistently color the news to fit its editorial line); which is uncritical to the point of irrationality on the big political issues of our time, such as the war, the Soviet Union, Roosevelt's leadership and the New Deal, and which uses methods that are Hearstian in their grossness to cover up unpleasant reality, smear every critic and induce in its readers a hypnotic assent to the use of any means toward what its editors consider a good end. The liberal weeklies still irritate me, which means I feel *some* contact, *some* common intellectual and moral ground. But *PM* simply depresses me—or did until I stopped reading it some time ago—because I feel, as with the *Daily Worker*, that the gap has become simply too great between our respective methods of thinking and behaving. What makes it all confusing, and rather ominous for the future of the left-of-center movement, is that one agrees with a paper like *PM* to a large extent on ends and even on values, and disagrees on *methods* only—that is, on the war as a means to advance social progress; or, on hysteria and halftruths and evasions and suppressions as a means of propagating democratic values. It is easy enough to see where one stands with Colonel McCormick, the type of the old obscurantist and demagogue. But the growing tension between a world organized more and more along the most brutal imperialist lines and a liberal creed which rejects imperialism and brutality seems to be forcing liberal thinking (which of course is too "realistic" to buck the tide) into increasingly pathological forms.

June, 1945

What Is Totalitarian Liberalism?

People often ask what one means by "totalitarian liberalism." The expression sounds like a simple term of abuse. It has a definite meaning, however, which may be suggested by the following examples of "totalitarian liberal" thinking, drawn from recent issues of *The New Republic:* *

* The other great source, of course, would be *The Nation.* There is a perceptible difference, however, between the two: *The Nation* is more fuzzy minded, naïve and "idealistic" than its colleague; it adopts approximately the same attitudes towards the Big Three, the Great Experiment of Comrade Stalin and World War II, but its betrayal of liberal principles is performed with a virginal innocence, a do-gooder enthusiasm which is quite foreign to the more cool and sophisticated tone of *The New Republic.* The editors of the latter magazine seem to have arrived, consciously, at a "totalitarian liberal" philosophy which the editors of *The Nation* still reject on the conscious level (while constantly forced to accept it in practice and piecemeal). The result is that *The Nation sometimes* prints honest articles and still has a crevice open to the impact of reality, while *The New Republic* is almost hermetically sealed against critical protest. The result is also, taken another way, that *The New Republic* is *intellectually* the better magazine, just as *The Nation* is *morally* the better.

1.

Words should not intimidate us. Compulsory labor is not always slave labor; neither is it, of course, the free labor of peacetime. Compulsory labor becomes slave labor only when it is used in the interest of enriching private individuals and groups. But compulsory labor at critical moments in the life of a nation, used in the interests of society, is not slavery.

It is true, of course, that the use of compulsory labor poses the problem of the social order in all its sharpness. From this point of view, in the USSR, where there is no private profit and where all labor is performed in the service of society . . . the compulsory labor of both the Soviet citizens and the German workers will be most efficient.

(A. Yugow, "Shall German Labor Rebuild Europe"; *The New Republic,* May 7, 1945.)

2.

Facts do not mean much to the Germans, who live in a world of unreality shaped in accordance with their wishful thinking, their "ideology." . . . Nazi education heightened this attitude by frustrating—under pain of punishment—every attempt at independent political thinking. . . . Hitler knew the Germans and how to influence them. . . . Our approach must be . . . to hammer home the truth that it was Germany which started the war and plunged the whole of humanity into unspeakable misery—the Germans, not the "Jews" or the "Bolsheviks" or the "plutocrats" or the "British imperialists." . . . They must be faced continuously with the basic fact of their collective guilt. As Hitler said: "The most brilliant propaganda technique will yield no success unless one fundamental principle is borne in mind constantly and with unflagging attention: it must confine itself to a few points and repeat them over and over . . ." We must never forget that our propaganda—or educational effort—is directed toward Germans, not toward Americans.

(Alfred Kantorowicz, "The OWI in Germany"; *The New Republic,* May 14, 1945.)

3.

The hue and cry is ever more frequently raised nowadays that the plan for an international security organization drafted at Dumbarton Oaks institutionalizes a system in which the so-called small nations are at the mercy of the big powers. . . . The point really at issue, however, is not the big powers' ability to intervene in a small country's internal affairs, but the wise use of the power of intervention when a small country's domestic policies seem to endanger peace. . . .

A genuinely democratic and peaceful country need not fear the intervention of a well-intentioned big power. The recent Finnish elections are interesting in this connection. The issue at stake was Finland's readiness for peaceful cooperation with Russia. A few days before the elections, Premier Paasikivi had warned his people that "new men must be elected to the Diet instead of those who during the past years followed the wrong policy" so that "a cooperation policy can be followed which will arouse confidence in the Soviet Union and the other United Nations." The Finnish people took this advice to heart. The new pro-Soviet Democratic Union made a decisive show of strength. . . .

What would have happened if the elections had strengthened the anti-democratic and anti-Soviet forces? They were certainly a test of a big power's sincerity in abiding by the results of a free expression of the people's will. *Pravda* bluntly stated the alternative on March 12, saying that "under the present circumstances, the elections in Finland cannot be considered as Finland's exclusively internal affair." In other words, no country, big or small, can be permitted to have just any government it pleases. As it is the responsibility of the big nations to use their power wisely in their relations with the small ones, so the latter are equally obligated to conduct their internal affairs in a way which arouses confidence on the part of the big powers.

(Editorial: "On War and Politics"; *The New Republic,* April 2, 1945.)

From these texts, some basic features of "totalitarian liberalism" may be generalized:

1. *Principles yield to circumstances.* Here we find anti-liberal policies advocated in order to arrive at "practical" solutions. The "practicality" of these solutions is not in the sphere of human interests but in that of the existing power structure. Slavery is abhorrent to liberal principles, but not when used "in the interests of society." The "interests of society" would seem at first to be a general principle (however open to question), but closer inspection reveals that by it is meant the interests of the existing state systems of the United Nations, especially Russia, and that Hitler's use of forced labor is not intended to be included thereunder. So, too, irrational demagogy is abhorrent to liberalism, but in dealing with *Germans,* it is permissible to use Hitler's propaganda methods. This leads us to:

2. *A double standard of political morality is employed.* "We" may do things with impunity and even approbation which become crimes against humanity if "they" do them. Slave labor, demagogy, imperialist domination of small nations smell to heaven in Nazi hands but give off sweet perfume in "ours."

3. *Effective power carries its own justification; to be weak is the only unforgivable crime.* Here No. 3 is especially striking. The big powers have *rights* (which they are exhorted to exercise "wisely"), the small ones have *responsibilities.* Even if we accept this weighting of the scales, who is to determine when the big fellows are "wisely" exercising their rights, and when the small fry are living up to their responsibilities? Not only is it left up to the big powers to decide when a small nation's domestic policies—*domestic,* mind you—are "endangering peace," but no principles are laid down by which the big powers are supposed to be guided; their only criterion is to be—actually!—whether the small nations' policies "arouse confidence" in them. But what if, say, Sweden, feels no "confidence" in, say, Russia's domestic policies, feeling they are undemocratic and peace-endangering? It is not hard to guess the reaction of *The New Republic's* editors to

such a situation; nor Stalin's. He would instantly lose *his* confidence in *Sweden,* we may be sure, just as Hitler lost *his* confidence in Czechoslovakia, Poland, Holland, etc. If "confidence" is the point, it is hard to see why *The New Republic* got so excited about Nazi Germany; and if the editors reply that the Nazis violated certain general principles, then one may ask them why they no longer refer to these principles.

4. *Abstractly put: the form is liberal, the content totalitarian.* Slave labor, Nazi propaganda methods, and imperialism are justified, respectively, in the name of social progress, democratic re-education and world peace.

5. *Concretely put: Soviet Russia is the repository of all political virtue.* Here we have a nation whose governmental system is so democratic, progressive and peace loving that it can transmute the base metal of slavery into "service for society," and is praised for its devotion to peace and democracy when it threatens to intervene in a weak neighbor's elections.

6. *Society is the end: human beings the means.* Hence, no concern for the Rights of Man (or of nations), for even-handed justice or the freedom of the individual, but simply for the effective perpetuation of the existing social systems. The editors praise the Finnish people not for progressing towards a richer democratic life in their elections but for "arousing confidence" in their great imperialist neighbor by electing pro-Moscow representatives. And Yugow actually makes the *efficiency* of Soviet compulsory labor an argument in its favor.

August, 1945

The Truth about the UN

IT IS TIME that someone stated the truth about the United Nations, now getting under way again not far from here. The liberal weeklies consecrate special issues to this "last, best hope" of the democratic peace-loving peoples of the world; the daily press gives us columns of eyewitness reports on the smile (or was it a smirk?) observed on the face of Molotov at a certain point in a recent debate; the President of the United States "WARNS UN DELEGATES WAR FEAR EXAGGERATED"; the Committee for Non-Violent Revolution pickets a UN luncheon with placards denouncing it as a cover for imperialist war.

All these reactions appear to me excessive. The UN is not a parliament of peace-loving peoples; it is not an arena of history-in-the-making; it is not even what the CNVR pickets think it is: a way of lulling the masses with talk of peace while war is prepared behind the scenes. It is, quite simply, a bore.

Before denouncing this as the judgment of an intellectual snob, the reader should consult the newspaper reports of the reaction of the people of New York—the masses, if you please—to the 96-car cavalcade which bore the UN delegates from the Battery to City Hall for the official welcoming ceremony. The people in the streets were "polite but notably unenthusiastic"; no torn paper or ticker tape fluttered down from the Wall Street skyscrapers; the crowds were "insignificant" compared to those which had turned out to welcome Nimitz and Eisenhower. So apathetic, indeed, was the public response that the president of the UN, in his speech at City Hall, felt obliged to note that the reception "was not quite as enthusiastic as we could have wished for." Everybody cheered up, however, after the next event: a luncheon in the grand ballroom of the Waldorf-Astoria, where a "distinguished" audience provided a "much more cordial atmosphere." All of which goes to show, as has been often observed in these pages, how much more intelligent people who cannot afford to pay $12 a plate for lunch are than those who can. Also how much smarter, in some ways, the average citizen (or, if you prefer, "the masses") is than most of us intellectuals, who get so accustomed to reacting to abstract concepts—which is what the UN is—that we forget to ask whether there is anything much underneath.

The reason the UN is boring is that it is an extreme example of the kind of abstraction—*the* proletarian revolution is another—which means nothing one way or another to any specific human being. As though a "nation" (i.e., 140 million Americans, including myself) were not meaningless enough, now we have a lot of individuals "representing" the governments which "represent" the nations. The delegates to this fiction superimposed on two other fictions appear to be as bored and impotent and baffled as the rest of us are. The UN shows why it is difficult for a radical today to place himself in relation to international affairs, or to any kind of thought or action which goes beyond his own personal experience, whether as an intellectual living in New York City or a member of a cooperative group farming some acres in Georgia. Speaking as the former, I cannot see that the UN is either a hope or a menace; just a bore.

November, 1946

A Note on Wallese

WALLACELAND is the mental habitat of Henry Wallace plus a few hundred thousand regular readers of *The New Republic*, *The Nation*, and *PM*. It is a region of perpetual fogs, caused by the warm winds of the liberal Gulf Stream coming in contact with the Soviet glacier. Its natives speak "Wallese," a debased provincial dialect.

Wallese is as rigidly formalized as Mandarin Chinese. The Good people are described by ritualistic adjectives: "forward looking," "freedom loving," "clear thinking," and, of course, "democratic" and "progressive." The Bad people are always "reactionaries" or "red-baiters"; there are surprisingly few of them, considering the power they wield, and they are perversely wicked, since their *real* interests would best be served by the Progressive and Realistic policies favored by the Good people. Wallese is always employed to Unite rather than to

Divide (hence the fog), and to Further Positive, Constructive Aims rather than Merely to Engage in Irresponsible and Destructive Criticism. As George F. Babbitt of Zenith City, who had his own brand of Wallese in the twenties, used to say: "It's Easy Enough to Criticize!" There are other conventions in Wallese. Issues are always Clarified, Events invariably Exert Pressure, Problems are Faced (good) or Not Faced (bad), and the World is either On the March (good) or At the Crossroads (neutral) or Facing a Crisis (bad). No article may be composed in Wallese unless it includes at least one of the following terms: "grass roots," "integration," "horizon," "general welfare." The frequent use of the "should and will" or "can and must" construction is also obligatory, as in the (imaginary) sentence: "The American people can and must free the forward march of technology from the dead hand of monopoly." The adjective "new" is much used, as: "new horizons," "new frontiers," and "the new democracy" (which means the old democracy minus all democratic elements). Like "adventure," another important word in Wallese, it suggests something Different (and God knows we're sick of what we've got now), Positive, Exciting; something, in short, to which the old critical categories, which have proved so lethal in the hands of Irresponsible and Destructive critics, cannot be applied. Thus many of us are by now somewhat leery of both democracy and *The New Republic*, but how about the new democracy and the new *New Republic*? Perhaps the greatest sentence ever composed in Wallese is the following, from the hand of the master himself: "New frontiers beckon with meaningful adventure."

Wallese is not, of course, Henry Wallace's personal idiom. There is nothing personal about his writing—indeed, alienation from his own individual interests, values and enjoyment is the most striking thing about Wallace's whole "style" as a political figure. Unlike Churchill or Roosevelt, for example, who clearly got a big kick out of exercising power and hurling around the thunderbolts of political rhetoric, Wallace is lumpish, depressed, weighed down by a sense of duty (or of guilt?). His political personality curiously resembles Herbert

Hoover's. "The words that spring from his mind," writes an admirer, "sometimes stumbling, sometimes leaping, are those of a man troubled, deeply troubled by the far-reaching sickness of these strange times. He takes little pride in his writing. . . . 'Strangely enough, I don't like to write,' he says." As literary criticism, nothing could be wider of the mark: Wallace's words don't spring, they don't leap, and they don't even stumble; they just ooze. But it is true that his writing is that of a sick and troubled man, a man not at peace with himself, alienated from his own individuality, a man who doesn't enjoy writing because he senses obscurely that it has nothing to do with his own pleasure and convictions.

Wallese is a collective product, a style that has developed in liberal journalism more or less instinctively as a drapery for the harsh political realities of our time. The justification for calling it "Wallese" is that Henry Wallace has parlayed it into a career.

This is not to say that Wallace is an accomplished rhetorician, as, for example, Churchill is. On the contrary, he is a ghastly stylist by the most modest journalistic standards; dull, vague, repetitious, humorless, with a fatal affinity for the cliché. His rule is never to use one word where ten will do the job. Mrs. Roosevelt has said that Wallace reads better than he sounds in person; I have not heard him speak publicly, but I hope, for his sake, this is not an accurate statement. His tone is that of the principal of a progressive school addressing a parent-teacher meeting: "The job of reconciling Jeffersonian democracy to the impact of machine civilization is one which is going to take the most imaginative resources of all of us." He begins a series of lectures, which were published in 1938 under the Wallesian title, *Paths to Plenty:* "In these lectures, I propose to consider the way in which the best elements in capitalism, democracy and religion can cooperate to lay a foundation for the long-term general welfare."

As the above sentence shows, the defects of his style are not only esthetic. Wallace never analyzes a problem; he barges around inside it, throwing out vague exhortations. The sentence quoted above could have meaning only if Wallace defined the abstractions which comprise its entire content. But he continues: "Throughout this book, I have used the phrase, 'general welfare' liberally. . . . Nowhere have I defined 'general welfare' . . . because I believe that in a democracy every individual ought to define the general welfare in his own way." This is perhaps the most revealing statement Wallace ever wrote. Aside from the absurdity of refusing to define one's terms on the grounds that this would violate the democratic right of each citizen to read his own definition into them—a right which Hitler always respected—it shows us why Wallace represses his own self in politics. The self-alienation is evident: if every individual has a right "to define the general welfare in his own way," then Wallace has the right. But he gives it up, as he gives up other personal rights and pleasures (such as the right to speak the truth and the pleasure of sticking to one's principles) because he wants to make himself an instrument through which "the common man" (i.e., everybody) expresses himself. If he defined terms, some people would be antagonistic; but Wallace wants to be loved, and followed, by *everybody,* just as he wants to believe every doctrine all at once. This tendency reaches its height in the matter of "the general welfare," for here is the key Wallese concept: a noun no one could possibly object to (for who but a fascist or a red-baiter could be perversely *against* welfare?) wedded to an adjective that is . . . general. The whole suggests a bold stand for the common man against his enemies, thus combining the maximum of safety with the maximum of emotive force. It is understandable that Henry Wallace would not want to endanger such a concept by defining it.

May-June, 1947

THE COMRADES

Remarks on the Constitution of the Mongol People's Republic

THE BUREAUCRATIC PRINCIPLE has reached its purest expression in the USSR. Its essence is that all life is ordered according to certain formulae, which are imposed without regard to individual or historical circumstances. The result is a kind of automatism which is funny or frightening depending on whether one is an observer or a victim. Its grotesque aspects come out perhaps most strikingly in the so-to-speak prefabricated political institutions which are exported from Moscow for erection in the more distant and primitive provinces. The effect is not unlike a Nedick orange drink stand in the depths of the African *veldt*.

Consider, for example, the Constitution of the Mongol People's Republic, adopted at Ulan Bator on June 30, 1940. Outer Mongolia has, to say the least, no tradition of democracy; it has from time immemorial been ruled by khans, vans, lamas, dzasaks, and other varieties of local autocrats. The Czars or the British, with the naïve frankness of old-style imperialism, would simply have put their own Governor General at the top of the pyramid. Not so the Kremlin, which has revised Marx's dictum to read: "The subjugation of the workers must be the work of the workers themselves." Therefore, the Mongols have received an up-to-date constitution, of the same model as was recently exported to Czechoslovakia, complete with social security, a judiciary, and a conscript army ("Article 90: Compulsory military service is the law of the land"). This document gives complete *formal* power to popular assemblies elected by universal suffrage. But since the present inhabitants of the Kremlin have even less intention than their

Czarist predecessors had of permitting the Mongols, or anybody else, to run their own lives, they have rigged the Constitution in a series of articles which fit into each other like those wooden *babushkas* Russian peasants used to make, so that, as one shell after another is removed, the effective power finally resides in the tiny *babushka* in the inmost center: one man, the President of the Presidium of the Little Khural.

This is how the trick is done (italic comments mine, rest direct quotes) *:

ARTICLE 1: The Mongol People's Republic is an independent state of workers (Arat cattle raisers, workers and intelligentsia), who have annihilated the imperialistic and feudal yoke, ensuring a noncapitalist approach to the development of the country to pave the way to socialism in the future.

ARTICLE 3: In the Mongol People's Republic, all power belongs to the urban and rural workers as represented by the workers' Khurals.

ARTICLE 14: The Great People's Khural is composed of deputies of the urban workers, the aimaks (*provinces*) and the armed forces of the People's Revolutionary Army, elected by the urban and aimak Khurals on the basis of one deputy for every 1,500 of the population.

ARTICLE 15: The Great Khural is convened by the Little Khural once in three years.

ARTICLE 16: The exclusive jurisdiction of the Great People's Khural extends to: (*here follows a list of functions which boil down to the election of the Little Khural*).

ARTICLE 17: In the intervals between sessions of the Great People's Khural (which meets once every 3 years) the highest authority in the Mongol People's Republic is vested in the Little Khural.

---

* Text from the Russian periodical, "Soviet Government and Law," No. 8, August 1947, as translated in "Soviet Press Translations" for Jan. 1, 1948.

ARTICLE 19: The jurisdiction of the Little Khural extends to: (*nothing of importance*).

ARTICLE 20: Regular sessions of the Little Khural are convened once a year. . . .

ARTICLE 21: For the conduct of current business, the Little Khural elects from its own members a Presidium consisting of seven members: a President, Vice-President, Secretary and four members.

ARTICLE 22: The Presidium of the Little Khural, in the intervals between the sessions of the Little Khural (*which meets once a year*), is the highest organ of State authority.

ARTICLE 23: The Presidium of the Little Khural: (*does practically everything*).

ARTICLE 25: The President of the Presidium of the Little Khural presides over the Little Khural and exercises jurisdiction over its internal organization.

Thus, by easy stages, the journey is completed from a popularly elected Great Khural which meets every three years and has no powers to the President of the Presidium of the Little Khural, whose powers are vast, who is on the job all the time, and who is given formal GPU-control over the Little Khural ("exercises jurisdiction over its internal organization"). This is what is known as Soviet democracy.

Even the elections to the phantasmal Khural are not what a Western observer might assume. For there is Article 71:

All citizens of the Mongol People & People's Republic who have reached the age of eighteen have the right to participate in elections and to be elected, irrespective of their sex, nationality, religion, education, nomadic or settled mode of life and property status, WITH THE EXCEPTION ONLY OF:

exploiters who hire workers for profit
usurers
former khutukhta, khubilgans and higher lamas
active dzasak and nadzasak
khans, vans, beili, beisi and guns,

AND ALSO
those who have had slaves and cruelly oppressed their slaves
government officials who managed the khoshun and shabin institutions
influential shamans
active participants in the White Army and counter-revolution
AS WELL AS the insane and persons convicted by the court whose sentence includes deprivation of electoral rights.

It is only fair to add that, four years later, the Presidium of the Little Khural decreed that all the above characters, including the khans, vans, guns, dzasak and nadzasak, but excluding the insane and those legally deprived of electoral rights, should have their rights restored. It is also fair to add the grounds given: (1) such persons "do not at present constitute a threat to the people's revolutionary order," (2) "the overwhelming majority have for more than ten years been occupied in useful public work and are in reality workers" (thus six years of useful public service do not reclaim a khubilgan but ten years do—an instance of the second law of the dialectic), and (3) "local organs of authority have in many cases acted without due consideration in depriving citizens of their electoral rights." This decree is "to be submitted for approval to the regular sessions of the Little Khural and the Great Khural." The Russian article, published three years later, does not bother to mention whether the Khurals approved, but we may venture a guess that they did.

The spirit of the Mongol People's Constitution is captured in a report from *Pravda* of September 1 last, describing a meeting of Turkmen shepherds (a region so primitive that, as the report notes, before the revolution it contained only 35 iron plows):

Recently shepherds of the Kizyl Dihqan *kolkhoz* gathered in a pasture not far from Kushka. Comrade Jumayev

Nruli, chairman of administration, had brought a propaganda brigade here from the district center. Comrade Jumayev opened the proceedings with a report:

"Our *kolkhoz* has won the Red Banner of the Council of Ministers and the Central Committee of the Communist Party of Turkmenistan . . . for success in animal husbandry. . . ."

Then Comrade Propagandist Sadkhanov, the second secretary of the Komsomol *raikom,* was granted permission to speak. He said:

"During the years of the Soviet regime, more than 1,500 irrigation projects have been constructed in our Republic. We have the Tashkeprin reservoir with a capacity of 150 million cubic meters of water, the Kolkozbent reservoir which holds 50 million cubic meters, the Kaushutbent Hydrological Station. . . . A century-old dream of the Turkmen people is being realized. . . ."

When the propagandist fell silent, happy exclamations of approval were heard from the shepherds. And at the end of the meeting, the *bakhshi* who had come along, the bards Mamedorazov Batyr and Bakhshiev Mukhy, gave a performance. They sang a song of the Turkmen people about the great Stalin:

> Enveloped by the love of all the people,
> In the hearts of the Turkmen—thou art forever
> one of us.
> May thy noble deeds be glorified!
> Father, we bow to the earth before thee.
> Both young and old, and the children,
> We all praise thee in our songs.
> There is nothing more precious in the world to us
> Than thy radiant name.

As I remarked above, this sort of thing is either funny or frightening depending on whether one is involved or not. The trouble is that we are all of us involved.

Summer, 1948

USA v. USSR

THE SUPERIORITY of Communism over Nazism as an ideology for export is manifest if one compares Hitler's speeches with Stalin's. The former are hysterical: full of violent emotion, self-contradictory, convincing only to those within the circle of the speaker's neurosis. The latter, paranoid: sober, ploddingly consistent, entirely convincing so long as the central delusion is not questioned. And it has been hard for us to question because it preserves the *means* of 19th-century Progressivism—such as rational planning, scientific advance, democracy, popular education, industrialization—while quietly dropping overboard the humanitarian *ends* which led both Marxism and bourgeois liberalism to accept these means. Unlike the Nazis, whose ideology was consistent with their practice, the Communists' practice sharply contradicts their ideology. Hitler said frankly that he was going to exterminate the Jews and make the Germans the master race of Europe; Stalin urges the economic rationality of collectivization (i.e., the extermination of the kulaks) and the building of people's democracy (i.e., the subordination of Europe to Russia). It is the SS man in his raven black uniform with the death's head insignia as against the Commissar—or, more lately, the People's Minister—in his business suit with a fountain pen clipped in his breast pocket. We are slowly learning that the Commissar is even more deadly than the SS man.

Our education has been slow because our Communists and fellow travelers have until recently been generally accepted as part of the liberal-labor movement. Compare, for example, "America First" (1938) with the Wallace campaign (1948). The historical situations are similar: an "unsatisfied," expanding young empire in conflict with the older, sated imperialisms of USA and England; totalitarianism against democratic capitalism; native movements which pretend to be seeking world peace, and enroll their mass following on that basis, but actually advocate a policy of appeasement of the imperialist competitor, whose leaders are, furthermore, not too unsympathetic with that competitor's government. Yet consider how widely the two movements differ.

America First was defensive on Nazism: its leaders felt obliged constantly to reiterate their opposition. But Wallace and his backers openly denounce the USA as the main threat to peace and constantly defend Russian acts of aggression (as in the Czech putsch). America First was not run by Bundists, nor was it closely correlated to German foreign policy; such tactics would have been politically absurd: only home-grown fascism, of the Long-Smith-Coughlin variety, has ever had a mass base in USA; Nazism appealed only to German-Americans. But the Wallace movement is run by veteran Stalinoids and is intimately correlated to Soviet foreign policy (cf. the 24-hour reply Stalin gave to Wallace's recent "open letter"; or the campaign to block the Marshall Plan). Wallace devotes one-fifth of his current campaign book, *Toward World Peace,* to a detailed defense of Russian foreign policy and a mendacious whitewash of such internal Soviet scandals as the suppression of the Trotsky opposition, the forced-collectivization famines, the Moscow Trials, and the forced-labor camps. Can one imagine the America Firsters issuing a similar campaign document defending the concentration camps and the Reichstag fire trial?

In short, Communism is on the offensive, morally and ideologically, while fascism was on the defensive even ten years ago and today—since, after all, Hitler lost the war—is negligible as a force in American politics.

Millions of sincerely democratic-minded Americans still regard an exposé of the truth about Stalinism as "red-baiting," though it never occurred to them to call the critics of Nazism "fascist-baiters." The really frightening thing is that even in the USA, which came out of the last war unscathed, prosperous and well fed, the Communists have been able to mount a campaign like the Wallace movement, and to attract to it in general the very people whom the non-Stalinist left must look to for any serious challenge to the status quo: the younger generation—college students and veterans—plus the more rebellious and idealistic of the older generations, including, alas, many pacifists.

In the thirties, some of us became—or thought we had become—fairly well-educated about the Soviet Union. The 1932–33 famines plus the Moscow Trials plus the Communist tactics in the Spanish Civil War plus the partition of Poland and the attack on Finland—the accumulation seemed conclusive. Yet I have recently come to think that I seriously underestimated the evils of Stalinism and the degree of continuity between it and the Bolshevism of the first revolutionary decade. Current books like Shub's *Lenin* and Gliksman's *Tell the West!* have been responsible for this change of mind; as also a review of the whole literature I recently undertook. "What a swindle!" I kept thinking as I read the first-hand exposés of Soviet Russia that were published in the twenties and early thirties—books like Emma Goldman's *My Disillusionment in Russia* (1923); *Letters from Russian Prisons* (1925), Malcolm Muggeridge's *Winter in Moscow* (1934) and Vladimir Tchernavin's *I Speak for the Silent* (1935)—and recalled how, in my Trotskyist days, I dismissed them as bourgeois fabrications. Has there ever been a political imposture on this scale?

The younger generation in America, on the other hand, seems to be not even at the level of sophistication I had reached in 1938. The experience of the thirties is not theirs; USSR to them is the wartime ally of the "peace-loving democracies" against fascism. This winter I spoke on Wallace on several campuses—NYU, CCNY, Brooklyn and the New School in New York, as well as Chicago, Wisconsin, Minnesota and Antioch; when I compared Wallace's demagogy to Hitler's or spoke of Communism and Fascism as similar political formations, a perceptible shudder ran through the audience.

A "scissors" seems to be developing: we middle-aged former fellow-travelers of the Bolsheviks are coming to believe, as evidence accumulates, that things are even worse with USSR than we had thought ten years ago. While "the youth" today is more ignorant than we were then; and even less critical of the Potemkin Villages of Stalinism.

The scissors gape even wider because of a difference in moral atmosphere. We of the thirties were idealists and enthusiasts, ardently believing in certain general principles; when we realized that these were being negated in practice, we turned against Soviet Communism. As long as we could either deny or overlook the terrible facts, we accepted the Soviet Myth; when the facts mounted too high to be ignored, we gave up the Myth. After all, we came out of the fat and peaceful twenties. But the younger generation, which grew up in an atmosphere of war, death camps and saturation bombings, is both more cynical than we were and more sentimental; they seem to have developed a peculiar combination of idealism and pragmatism. They don't deny the facts; they simply retort (a) we're just as bad, which is not true, and even if it were true, would not be to the point; and (b) how could they have done anything else, encircled by imperialist enemies?—an excuse which applies equally to Hitler's system.

Attacked on the level of socialist principles, the neo-Stalinist of the younger generation brushes aside such arguments as abstract idealism. But when the attack is pragmatic, and the facts are insisted on, he justifies the worst horrors as allegedly necessary steps to a highly abstract and speculative future end: the building of a socialist society. A good pragmatist would define USSR by what it does; a good idealist by how it measures up against some ethical norm; either procedure would puncture the Soviet Myth. But the neo-Stalinists work both sides of the street.

LET US admit at once—let us, indeed, insist on the point—that all the criticisms made of USSR could also be made of USA. Ours, like theirs, is an unjust society, where the few have too much and the many too little. Ours is an imperialist State, like theirs, whose leaders lie like troopers and equivocate like lawyers; a militarist State, like theirs, busily preparing for World War III; a repressive State, like theirs, which is about to draft its youth, in peacetime, against their will. The American common people, like their Russian brothers, are kicked around from cradle to grave by their Betters, and are inhibited from leading satisfying lives by a massive structure of ingenious and irrational institutions. Our culture, too, is a debased mass culture, ruled by commerce as theirs is by the Central Committee. Etcetera, etcetera.

The difference is partly one of degree: in USSR all the above unpleasantnesses are carried a great deal farther than they are in USA. The rich are richer and the poor, poorer. Imperialism is more vicious: USA bribes nations with massive capital exports (Marshall Plan), but USSR either absorbs them by force (the Baltic nations) or subjugates them by installing a Communist police state (the rest of Eastern Europe). Militarism is more blatant: USSR spends more of its national income on war preparation than USA, has four or five times as many of its citizens under arms, indoctrinates its children more systematically with militarist ideas and dolls up its generals more resplendently. Repression is much more severe: the American common people have too few civil liberties, the Russians have none at all. Social institutions are more massively impenetrable to popular pressures: the American school system is run by locally elected bodies, the Russian direct by the State. Political institutions are less democratic: Congress and the President do not truly represent the people, but at least they can be thrown out every two or four years, and at least they exercise power within the limits of written rules and after public debate; the 15 or 17 members of the Central Committee rule so far beyond public knowledge and legal control that they could tomorrow order all redheads to be "resettled" in Kamchatka—and they would be obeyed. Culture is more totally debased: in USA, artists, writers and intellectuals with the determination or the cash can ignore the commercial market and produce decent work; in USSR, there are no loopholes—the artist cannot create independently of the Central Committee's directives since the State controls the art galleries, the orchestras and concert halls, the theatres and the publishers.

There are, further, certain ways in which USSR is not comparable, even in degree, to USA or to any other civilized country today. Is there any other major nation where slave labor exists on a massive scale? Where all strikes are forbidden by law? Where over half the State budget is raised by the most regressive form of taxation: sales taxes, which fall most heavily on those least able to pay? Where colonels get thirty times the pay of privates? Where no figures on national income have been published since 1938 and no price indices since 1931? Whose soldiers, in foreign lands, go crazy at the sight of such luxuries as bicycles, watches and leather shoes? Whose DP's open their veins rather than return to the motherland? Whose secret police have their own secret courts, which try and sentence without appeal? Where children are officially applauded as patriots for denouncing their parents to the authorities? Where the political authorities instruct writers on prose style, movie directors on montage and composers on the proper use of polyphony and dissonance? Where citizens may be imprisoned for talking to foreigners? Where emigration is forbidden, and the families of illegal émigrés are punished whether or not they had knowledge of the attempt?

But the differences go deeper. Not only is Reaction, as it was called in the simple old days, carried much farther in USSR than in USA. But this is not done there, as here, furtively and apologetically, but rather as a matter of principle, in the name of Socialism, People's Democracy and other high notions. The powerful workings of ideology transmute these ugly realities into their opposite: they become the principles of a New Order which is asserted to be the glorious reverse of the undoubtedly wicked Old Order.

This is the Big Lie which Hitler once amateurishly peddled, but which the Communists are really putting over. It is not just the absence of truth; it is the very reverse of truth. Black is not called Blue or Dark Brown, but White. The political system which has gone far beyond Bismarck or Louis Napoleon in authoritarian repression is proclaimed as the realization of the program laid down in the Communist Manifesto. The society in which strikes are outlawed and workers are legally tied to their jobs is presented as the workers' fatherland. The world's most chauvinist and militarist government is sincerely believed by millions of Americans to be striving for world peace against the evil machinations of the State Department and the British Foreign Office. The empire that has added vast new satrapies since 1945, while its two chief rivals have either confined themselves to Pacific atolls or (reluctantly) freed their richest subject domains, is gilded by ideology with the moral splendor of anti-imperialism. Most striking of all, a double standard of international morality has been insinuated into the minds of millions of non-Communist workers and intellectuals. Truman is denounced for his Doctrine, which is indeed an evil thing; but the more far-reaching interference of the Communists in other nations' affairs is passed over in silence. The American Legion is properly excoriated for its flag-waving jingoism, but the same thing in USSR becomes transmuted into People's Patriotism in Defense of the Socialist Fatherland.

The list could be extended. The point would remain the same: the most militarist, imperialist, anti-democratic and reactionary nation in the world is precisely the one on which millions of Americans and Europeans have fixed their aspirations for world peace, national independence, democracy and human progress. This is a Fact of Life today, and one that must be faced, whether one is a liberal, a Marxist socialist, a conservative, or, as in the case of the present writer, an anarchist and pacifist. The way to face it, in my opinion, is to tell the truth about USSR, without suppression and without compromise. If there is a chance of avoiding World War III, it must be based on truth and not on lies. And certainly not on The Big Lie.

Spring, 1948

The Great Thaw

I MUST ADMIT that the extent of The Great Thaw has taken me by surprise—it's by no means the first time that the locomotive of history has run on a different timetable from the one I'd been using. I never expected to hear the top Soviet leaders denounce Stalin in the same terms we Trotskyists used in the thirties: dangerous madman, criminal bungler, betrayer of the revolution, etc. The polar rigors of Stalin's system have moderated since his death, until now the climate has warmed up to the level of Northern Greenland.

The question comes down, essentially, to whether this thaw is merely seasonal—a strategic retreat—or whether it is, so to speak, geological—a permanent shrinking of the Stalinist ice-cap. It is too soon, by ten or twenty years, to give even an approximate answer, but my guess is that the change is geological and that something new has happened.

In *The Origins of Totalitarianism,* Hannah Arendt gave brilliant and persuasive expression to the theory that totalitarian systems like those of Hitler and Stalin cannot be modified in a more humane direction, that their long-range tendency (granting temporary retreats) must be toward an ever more extreme reduction of humanity to atomized, helpless, subhuman masses whose reflexes can be manipulated as freely as were those of Pavlov's dogs. Her theory emphasizes the irrational, neurotic aspects of totalitarian behavior, denying that it can be explained in terms of Marxian economic interest or even of a Machiavellian drive to power, and insisting that the paranoiac will to exterminate all obstacles in the way of reshaping the actual world in the form of a monstrous and illusory ideal—even if the easily predictable result is ruinous, as in Stalin's decimation of his own military and industrial leaders just before the war, or in Hitler's terroristic policy in occupied Russia, which forced the population to become his enemies instead of his allies against the hated Stalin—that the free exercise of this will is more important to the totalitarian leaders than success, or even survival. This theory, I think, explains the actual behavior of Hitler and Stalin better than the kind of rational and materialistic interpretations we are used to. However, like Marx, Arendt is an enthusiastic generalizer, a system builder, and she, too, believes in an inherent logic, a big basic pattern which cannot be violated. Although Hitlerism did perish only in the ruins of Germany, as her theory would suggest, it seems to me by no means sure that Khrushchev & Co. are fated either to resume the Stalinist road after a temporary retreat or else to go down in the flames of war or revolution.

A strong case can be made, historically, for the temporary-retreat thesis. The alternation of crisis and relaxation is striking in Soviet history: the rigors of War Communism finally producing the Kronstadt revolt, to which Lenin reacted with the NEP; Stalin replacing NEP, once he had consolidated his power, in 1929 with the First Five Year Plan and the forced collectivization program; his retreating in turn, when the severity of Plan and collectivization had become unendurable, in 1932, with the "dizzy from success" speech; the "Indian Summer" of 1933–1936, when the political climate grew milder, art and letters had a breathing spell and the new, super-democratic "Constitution" was drafted by a committee headed by Bukharin; and then the Moscow Trials and the great purges bursting on the Soviet world like a thunderclap out of a clear blue sky, Bukharin and the majority of his fellow Constitution-drafters being executed as traitors. In Stalin's Russia it was always not only darkest before dawn but also lightest before sunset.

But the question is, precisely, whether Khrushchev's Russia is Stalin's Russia. Was Stalin, as Arendt's theory implies, a normal expression of the Soviet system or was he a peculiar individual who cast his morbid shadow over a whole period of Russian history? Granted that his death found Russia in a severe crisis, compounded of the tough Zhdanov postwar domestic policies, the discontent of workers over the resumption of the prewar guns-not-butter economic policy and of peasants over the attempt to still further extend State control over farming, the fears of the bureaucracy at the hints, in the last year of Stalin's life, of a new series of purges and the rearming of the USA as a result of the Soviet-backed invasion of South Korea—granted this crisis, I think the reaction of Stalin's heirs has gone farther than a mere strategic retreat. Some of their concessions were indeed comparable to the kind Stalin made when forced to: the easing of pressure on intellectuals and artists, the increase in consumer goods, the giving up of the unpopular super-collectives, the execution of the MVD head, Beria. But others have no parallel under Stalin: the public admission that the charges against the doctors in the "Kremlin poison plot," made in the last months of Stalin's life, were phony; the softening of the labor camp regimen and the release of many prisoners; the avoidance of wholesale bloodshed in dealing with the East German revolt; Khrushchev and his colleagues "going to Canossa," i.e., traveling to Tito to apologize to him for Stalin's expulsion of Yugoslavia from the Third International.

Above all, there is the current full dress attack on the Stalin myth. Had Khrushchev & Co. had merely in mind a temporary retreat, they would have made such concessions as they felt necessary without raising any general issues, which would only make it harder to reinstate the old system later on. Instead, they have launched a frontal attack on the ideological keystone of Stalinism, the Great Leader principle, and on the reputation of Stalin himself. In his speech to the Party congress (which has not yet been published, but of which the N. Y. *Times* of March 17 last, via "diplomatic channels," gave a full report), Khrushchev said: "We never knew when we entered Stalin's presence whether we would come out alive; he kept us all in terror; no one knew upon whom the next blow would fall." Here, I think, is the nub of the matter. As Arendt has observed, the totalitarian system means that the personal interests—and even the lives—of everyone right up to the very top of the pyramid may be sacrificed at any moment "for the good of the cause." But to endure such a system takes fanatics. Trotsky used to call Stalin the man of Thermidor; he was wrong, as speedily became apparent when Stalin, having exiled his great opponent, proceeded to put into effect Trotsky's basic program of collectivization and industrialization; Stalin was a Jacobin like Trotsky, not a restorer of the old order. Only now has Thermidor come to the Bolshevik Revolution—and a very good thing, too.

As Barras and his fellow members of the Directoire—another substitution of collective leadership, by the way, for the Great Leader—were scared for their own skins by the Jacobin proscriptions, as they were weary of bloodthirsty principles, monstrous idealisms, the boring repression in the name of revolutionary virtue of all human, lively instincts, and simply wanted a chance to enjoy their power safely, selfishly and corruptly, so with Khrushchev and *his* Directoire. There is something touching about his ebullient public behavior since Stalin died, his back slapping and joking with Western diplomats and reporters, his wearing of funny native hats on his Asiatic tour, his expansive vulgarity in the style of a Chicago ward politician. He is like a boy let out of school; this is his real style—the coarse geniality of a *nouveau riche*—and this is the real style of his colleagues. Even Molotov has loosened up a little.

Totalitarianism bends human nature, puts a terrible strain on the normal, mediocre man. When the pressure is removed, when Robespierre, Hitler, Stalin die, then human nature springs back to its normal shape, which is perhaps not very inspiring but is certainly preferable to the nightmare form given it by the totalitarians.

As for the future. So long as the essentials of Stalinism remain, there will be, of course, a possibility that another Great Leader will find them ready to his hand. To date, these essentials have not been touched. There is still only one party, and candidates for election all put forward the same program. The trade unions are still organs of the State rather than independent representatives of the workers, strikes are still forbidden and workers cannot shop around for the best wages and conditions. The peasants are still forcibly collectivized. Art and letters are still under the direct control of the political bureaucracy. The secret police still enjoy unlimited and undefined powers of arrest, and the right of every citizen to a public trial conducted according to a written code of law is still not recognized. The dilemma facing the Thermidoreans is that if they don't institute such reforms, a new Great Leader may take advantage of the system, as Stalin did; while if they do, the attempt to modulate away from totalitarianism may release such popular unrest as to give some aspiring Great Leader a chance to take over. It is not clear yet what the reaction has been to the first big step toward reform, the destruction of the Great Leader myth. When this is known, one can speculate on the probable effects of further advances toward the *status quo ante* 1917—the modest degree of freedom achieved under Czar Nicholas II and swept away by the Bolsheviks in the name of the socialist liberation of humanity. Meanwhile, one can only say to comrade Khrushchev, echoing Hamlet (and Marx): "Well dug, old mole!"

Encounter, July, 1956

FAR INTO THE RIGHT

The Neo-Non-Conservatism, or Notes on a Career

1.

LAST OCTOBER, Yale celebrated its 250th anniversary. Various notables, including the Chancellor of Oxford and the Chairman of US Steel, comported themselves on the campus with appropriate decorum. Not among those present was a brisk, brash, indecorous young man who, like the bad fairy not invited to the christening, cast a pall over the proceedings. His witchcraft was modern: a book, diabolically timed to coincide with Yale's anniversary.

It was an earnest, extreme and irreverent book, a book that, in its mockery of authority, its impetuous logic, its relentless hewing to the line of Reason, letting the sacred cows fall where they might, followed the old familiar script: CAMPUS REBEL FLAYS FACULTY. But the script was all balled up, for the author was more reactionary than any of the dignitaries in their black robes, and his book damned Yale as a hotbed of atheism and collectivism.

The essential point of *God and Man at Yale,* by William Buckley, Jr., is that Yale "derives its moral and financial support from Christian individualists and then addresses itself to the task of persuading the sons of these supporters to be atheistic socialists." This swindle is perpetrated "under the protective label 'academic freedom.'" The author believes that the alumni of Yale, whom he assumes to be Christian free-enterprisers, have the right and indeed the duty to require the professors they employ to indoctrinate the students along those lines, and to fire forthwith any professor of irreligious or "collectivist" * tendency.

God and Man at Yale sold 12,000 its first month, to date has sold 23,000 and is still selling about a thousand a month —a remarkable sale for a nonfiction work by an unknown author put out by a small publisher (Henry Regnery, Chicago) and dealing with no broader or livelier topic than the Yale curriculum. Apparently there is a big market today for anti-liberal polemics: Lait and Mortimer's guttersniping *USA Confidential* is currently a top nonfiction best-seller; and Senator McCarthy's diatribe against General Marshall, put out by another small house, has sold 30,000 copies.

Interestingly enough, three leading spokesmen for the neo-conservative tendency that has arisen among the younger intellectuals were hostile to Buckley (who, strictly speaking, is a reactionary rather than a conservative): August Heckscher (Yale '36) in the New York *Herald Tribune*, Peter Viereck in the New York *Times* and McGeorge Bundy ('40) in the *Atlantic*.

One of the wriest twists in the whole comedy is that, although Buckley is an ardent Catholic, the Catholic press has almost unanimously damned his economic views, which are Calvinist in their social irresponsibility. "He quite unwittingly succeeds in contravening Catholic moral doctrine as applied to economics and politics on almost every topic he takes up," *America* editorialized, concluding, "Mr. Buckley's own social philosophy is almost as obnoxious to a well-instructed Catholic as the assaults on religion he rightly condemns." Father Higgins in the Boston *Pilot* rebuked "his attempt to identify the heresy of economic individualism with Catholic or Christian doctrine," and a Catholic news service stated: "His analysis

* Precise terminology is not a fetish with Buckley, who uses "collectivist," "socialist," "Statist," "liberal" and "New Deal" as roughly synonymous, observing they are all stages on the road to Communism. It must be said, however, despite a widespread impression to the contrary, that he does *not* use "Communism" as synonymous with the other terms, and that his book does *not* charge there are pro-Communists on the Yale undergraduate faculty, possibly because there aren't.

is nineteenth century liberalism, which has been explicitly rejected by the Church and clearly identified by the social encyclicals of Leo XII and Pius XI as one of the principal causes of the development of modern socialism."

Although a number of reviewers agreed with Buckley's attacks on irreligious and/or collectivist teaching, very few went along with his proposal to replace academic freedom with alumni control. Such friendly critics as Max Eastman and Felix Morley parted company there. Even Bruce Barton: "What could be more terrifying? Are these noisy perennial sophomores, who dress up in silly costumes and get drunk at reunions, to be the nation's mentors? They are good lads, but certainly not scholars." In fact, Buckley's assault on academic freedom seems to have stimulated a widespread defense reaction.

"Bill's book," as the more tolerant at New Haven call it—the others call it "that book"—burst over the campus like a bomb, a delayed-action bomb whose ominous ticking had been heard long before it went off. "A brilliant boy named Buckley came to Yale in 1946," the Yale *Daily News* editorialized shortly after the explosion. "He came steeped in stifling orthodoxy, dogmatic, a child of the Middle Ages. . . . For four tempestuous years, he successfully battled education. Crouched behind walls of dogmatic preconceptions, blind and deaf but never dumb, he fired volley after volley from his crossbow into the roaring multitude." The battlement from which Bill sped his arrows was the loftiest on the campus: the chairmanship of the *News*. Almost no one agreed with him, but everybody read him.

In Buckley's senior year, the *News* gave a banquet for the university's retiring president, Charles Seymour. Chairman Buckley, having secured the attendance of the presidents of Harvard, Princeton, Columbia, M.I.T. and Penn, arose after dinner and, instead of the expected eulogistic pleasantries, gave President Seymour a fatherly lecture on his fainthearted support of Christianity and free enterprise. "The guests," understated the *Daily Princetonian*, "were shaken." Later that year, the college authorities, tolerant to the point of masochism, asked Buckley to give the undergraduate address on Alumni Day. He prepared an appropriate discourse picturing Yale as sinking into a godless, collectivist morass due to over-indulgence in academic freedom. The authorities felt this was hardly the right note; President Seymour, an optimist of heroic scale, expressed himself as "deeply disappointed"; futile efforts were made to persuade the campus Savonarola to modify or, better, omit his strictures; finally Buckley offered to withdraw and, reluctantly, the long-suffering President Seymour agreed this might be best. The alumni were temporarily left in the dark.

Despite all this advance warning, Bill's book seems to have caught the Yale authorities flatfooted. They have reacted with all the grace and agility of an elephant cornered by a mouse.

Though many of Buckley's specific charges are exaggerated, distorted, or just not true, he is clearly right when he points out that Yale has changed a lot since the eighteenth century, and that its teaching and textbooks do not indoctrinate the students with a faith in either Christianity or free-market capitalism. All this means, of course, is that Yale is a large American university, that America in 1952 is not very religious or free-enterprising and that Yale reflects the predominant culture of the nation it serves.

Instead of simply admitting this, the Yale authorities have behaved like Owen Lattimore and others who are attacked by Senator McCarthy and who now deny ever having been anything but simple bourgeois patriots. So Yale's reaction to Buckley's exaggerated charges is an equally exaggerated defense. It must be admitted that Buckley's medieval lance struck Yale officialdom in the most vulnerable joint in its armor: the gap between ideology and practice. Yale's official pronouncements, like those of most American universities, are far more pious and free-enterprising than its actual teaching is. This rudimentary fact of life Buckley is rude enough to dwell on for 240 pages. Thus he quotes his favorite pincushion, President Emeritus Seymour—"I call on all members of the faculty . . . [to upbuild] the Christian religion as a vital part of university life"—and laboriously demonstrates that the call has been largely unheeded. Thus, too, the dignitaries who presided over Yale's 250th anniversary often sounded not unlike Buckley in their speeches. Lord Halifax, the Chancellor of Oxford, deplored "the slow attrition of [our] religion and cultural foundations," and Chairman Olds of US Steel observed that "freedom of enterprise and freedom of education are the same thing" and noted "a growing popular belief that our universities are not adequately fulfilling the responsibility" of teaching this identity.

This showing up of the discrepancy between ideology and practice, which is practically all there is "to" Buckley's book, embarrassed the Yale authorities because they feared it might cause some alumni to stop giving money. Their administrative reflex was simply to deny everything. But they could have risked a more honest approach. Whether from sentimental loyalty to alma mater or from the bad conscience that nineteen years of New and Fair Deals have given the American business class, the alumni have not responded to Buckley's tocsin of revolt: "Alumni of Yale, unite! You have nothing to lose but your faculty!" True, there was Harry L. Bim ('06, Sheffield), who said (in part): "If this is the kind of Russian hogwash that is being taught our undergraduates it is high time to scrap the University, or at least delouse the faculty, and take a fresh start with the stink off."

This is the old Eli spirit, but one Bim doesn't make a revolution. No Alumni Committee to Save Yale has been formed; two direct-mail solicitations extracted only 1,000 orders for the book from 62,000 alumni; about fifty have written to Buckley, mostly approving, and about 125 to Yale, mostly disapproving or merely curious. Buckley himself has sternly rejected appeals of his class agent to kick in, but only five or six of his alumni brethren—according to the Yale authorities—have followed suit, and contributions in this year's Alumni Fund drive are running ahead of last year's, which topped one million, an all-time record for any American university. If anything, Buckley's attack may well have provoked a defensive reflex in the alumni as unreasoning as the administrative reflex already noted. It is discouraging for a devotee of Reason and First Principles.

William Buckley, Jr., comes from Sharon, Connecticut, where his family owns a big estate. His father is a wealthy oil man of pronounced illiberal views, with "interests" in Canada and Latin America; his mother is a devout Catholic—a landmark of the estate is her private chapel; he has three brothers, all Yale (and Bones) men like himself, and six sisters. After graduating from Millbrook School in 1943, he studied at the University of Mexico for six months, spent two years in the army as a second lieutenant and attended Yale from 1946 to 1950, where, besides studying, debating, campus-politicking, running the *News,* promoting religion and baiting President Seymour, he found energy, of which he has enough, to teach Spanish.

The year after his graduation he also spent at Yale, teaching Spanish and working on his delayed-action bomb. Most of last fall he spent in Mexico trying to start an export-import business; the success of his book led him to abandon business for a career as a publicist. Several right-wing journals offered him jobs: he chose the *American Mercury,* of which he is now an editor, because it had the biggest circulation.

It was a characteristic choice: Bill Buckley combines opportunism and conviction in a sometimes bewildering way. He has the outward and visible signs of the campus radical, and the inward and spiritual qualities of the radical's wealthy grandfather. Earnest-eyed, grim-lipped, lanky and ascetic, he is passionate about first principles, articulate to an almost frightening degree and would obviously rather argue than eat. He has the narrow, logical bigotry of youth (wherever did the notion originate that the young are more open-minded than the middle-aged?). "It stands to reason, if the word doesn't offend you . . ." he began a recent letter. He never went through a leftist phase, though he admits he wrote "some stupid things" in the *News;* in 1948, he even defended academic freedom ("before I'd really thought it through").

But these were youthful lapses. In his maturity, he damns

"equalitarian tax laws," especially the progressive income tax, and believes it immoral for the government to hand out unemployment relief unless people are "actually starving," a situation he does not think obtained in 1930–1933.

Something happened to swivel round the guns of this rationalistic fortress to bear on liberal positions. What? We can only speculate. A Freudian might mutter "father fixation"; a Marxian might note it is "no accident" that a rich young man, married to a Canadian heiress, has such views. But then there are such modern instances as Michael Straight, Corliss Lamont and Frederick Vanderbilt Field to confound these explanations. Perhaps it is simply that Bill Buckley is very argumentative and very ambitious. Since the New Deal there has arisen in academic and intellectual circles, where the best arguments take place, a new liberal orthodoxy, what Peter Viereck calls "the Babbittry of the Left," while of late years a countertendency, a reaction against liberalism, has gone far in the country as a whole. The line Buckley has taken permits him to enjoy the pleasures both of unorthodox rebellion (within Yale) and of conformity (outside Yale).

This may seem a cynical explanation, but Bill Buckley is a "realistic" young man. A year ago he published an article in the *Freeman* that argued that "we must support McCarthy" despite his "manners" because his demagogic methods are the only effective ones in a mass democracy in which the "non-university crowd," ignorant and easily bamboozled, is dominant. The Senator's use of the Big Lie was justified because (a) Roosevelt and Truman lied too, and (b) it has been effective.

Presumably in line with this last thought, Buckley recently appeared on "The Author Meets the Critics" supporting the authors of *USA Confidential* in a stormy debate with James Wechsler, editor of the New York *Post*. When a friend asked him how he could identify himself with that sort of gutter journalism, he replied: "I don't like the way the book is written any more than you do. But it's on *our* side. . . . And anyway, you've got to write that way to reach a big public."

Young Mr. Buckley is getting into low company. But so

did the youthful ideologues of the 1930's—the Communists and the *Daily Worker* being about on the same moral and intellectual level as McCarthy and *USA Confidential.* It is to be hoped that, as he grows up, he will become at once less fanatical and less "practical."

The Reporter, May 27, 1952.

2.

YOUNG Mr. Buckley is getting into low company," I wrote several years ago apropos the career up to then of William F. Buckley, Jr., Yale '50, and expressed a fatherly hope—from the vantage point of Yale '28—that he would straighten out when he grew up. He hasn't done either. *McCarthy and His Enemies* (Regnery, $5), which he and his brother-in-law, L. Brent Bozell, also Yale '50, have just published, is intended as a defense of the most unscrupulous demagogue in American public life today. If it is ingenuous, it is absurd, and if it is disingenuous, it is—at least in intention—vicious. It is written in an elegantly academic style, replete with nice discriminations and pedantic hair-splittings, giving the general effect of a brief by Cadwallader, Wickersham & Taft on behalf of a pickpocket arrested in a subway men's room. And it massively confirms the principal charge against the Junior Senator from Wisconsin, that he is a chronic, perhaps a pathological, liar.

This comic conflict of intention and result emerges with special force in Appendix F, which is devoted to "The George Marshall Episode." Until the invitation to army officers to break the law and disobey their superiors by feeding McCarthy classified material, the Senator's 60,000 word speech on June 14, 1951, denouncing General George Marshall, quondam Chief of Staff and at the time Secretary of State, as a traitor working for the Kremlin was the most dramatic example of McCarthy's demagogic impudence. The crucial passage in McCarthy's speech ran as follows:

> How can we account for the present situation unless we believe that men high in the Government are concerting to deliver us to disaster? This must be the product of a great conspiracy, a conspiracy on a scale so immense as to dwarf any previous such venture in the history of man. A conspiracy of infamy so black that, when it is finally exposed, its principals shall be forever deserving of the maledictions of all honest men. . . . What can be made of this unbroken series of decisions and acts contributing to the strategy of defeat? They cannot be attributed to incompetence. If Marshall were merely stupid, the laws of probability would dictate that part of his decisions would serve his country's interest.

With their customary show of pained rectitude, the authors quote this classic example of paranoiac demagogy, worthy to stand with efforts by Hitler and the Kremlin along the same line, and admit that, McCarthy's later disclaimers to the contrary notwithstanding, "it is unreasonable to conclude . . . that McCarthy was charging Marshall with anything less than pro-Communism." They go on to cite seventeen actions of Marshall which in their opinion worked for the benefit of Russia and against that of this country (I agree with them in many instances, my admiration for Marshall's brains not being excessive), but conclude that, since each can be explained on grounds of incompetence, since each was approved at the time by many indubitable anti-Communists, and since McCarthy presented no other evidence, there is no reason to believe General Marshall was a traitor. "In studying the record of General Marshall, McCarthy failed to take into account man's irrationality; he forgot that more often than not men stumble into patterns," they loftily chide, which is like saying Hitler was a careless historiographer when he accepted as authentic the Protocols of Zion. "As regards his imputation of treasonable motives to Marshall, McCarthy deserves to be criticized. . . . McCarthy's judgment here was bad." As if the essence of the Senator's method were not the attribution of disloyalty to his opponents! As if, like Hitler and the Communists, it were not a matter both of neurotic compulsion and of demagogic expediency always to smear his opponents as not just mistaken or stupid but as wicked, conspiratorial, traitorous! And as if such tactics were not largely responsible for McCarthy's success in getting headlines! If he had confined himself to the truth about Owen Lattimore, which is that, as the sober and painstaking reports of the McCarran Committee copiously document, Lattimore was a devious and energetic pro-Communist propagandist—if he had stuck to that, instead of charging (without ever adducing any evidence) that Lattimore was "the No. 1 Soviet espionage agent in this country," how many headlines would that particular gambit have reaped? Throughout their book, the authors are constantly admonishing their client—not their hero, for, as Richard Rovere has shrewdly pointed out, they obviously regard McCarthy with considerable distaste, personally that is, as against politically—to stick more closely to the facts (the chariot race in *Ben Hur* could take place in the space between McCarthy and any given fact), not to impugn people's loyalty without proof, and in general to behave in a slightly more civilized manner. There is something very droll in the spectacle of these two young doctrinaires teaching an old pro how to get ahead.

As for the delicate matter of McCarthy's lies, the authors grimly admit no less than 34 instances of what they call "inaccuracies," "exaggerations" or "misstatements," ranging from such big lies as his famous "57 card-carrying Communists in the State Department" to such peccadilloes (for McCarthy) as his smearing Drew Pearson as a Communist agent.* It is

---

* The count would be doubled if we include the 38 (out of a total of 81) cases of alleged security risks in the State Department in which the authors admit, on page 60, that their client was "guilty of exaggeration." And there are, of course, many, many other lies McCarthy has told to date which either occurred outside the rather narrow scope of this book or else are not admitted to have been lies by the authors. For the curious, or the skeptical, the 34 lies mentioned are described on the following pages: 51, 52, 58, 60, 65, 79, 80 (2), 81, 89 (2), 90 (2), 101, 109, 117, 118, 127, 130, 153, 209, 276 (2), 277, 291, 295, 296, 297 (2), 298 (2), 313, 388 (2).

to the authors' credit that they admit so many lies, but it would be more so if they called them that and if they showed any indignation or even concern about them. In fact, their tactic vis-à-vis McCarthy's wholesale lying reminds me ironically of the method developed by the liberal weeklies in the thirties for dealing with the seamier side of Soviet Communism: admit the facts when you have to, but always reprove them gently as "mistakes" or "excesses of enthusiasm" and never damn them as something evil. Freda Kirchwey could go on for columns that way about the Moscow Trials—wasn't it just too obtuse of that nice old Stalin not to understand that if he hoped to convince the Western mind, weakened by centuries of Anglo-Saxon common law, he would have to produce some evidence? It never occurred to the dear lady that maybe Stalin just didn't have any evidence to produce, just as it never occurs to the dear boys that maybe McCarthy commits so many "inaccuracies" not out of carelesssness but on the contrary from the most deliberate, and to date highly successful, calculation.

The authors' apologies fall into roughly three categories. (1) *Tactical Error:* "McCarthy got off on the wrong foot"; "McCarthy . . . took an unnecessarily hard row to hoe." (In the *Nation* this used to run, "It is doubtful whether such severe repressions of the peasantry in the long run serve the interests of the Kremlin as well as a more moderate policy would.") (2) *Over-Enthusiasm:* "Early in 1952, Senator McCarthy learned that copies of Edmund Wilson's *Memoirs of Hecate County* were being forwarded to Europe at government expense. Impulsively and absurdly, McCarthy denounced government sponsorship of books which 'follow the Communist Party line'—although it is notorious that Wilson turned his back on the Communists in the thirties and . . . the book is no more pro-Communist than the author. . . . Here McCarthy was reckless." ("Excess of revolutionary zeal," the *Nation* used to put it, never failing, however, to concede that "you can't make an omelette without breaking eggs.") (3) *It's a Wicked World:* "Such interpolations [i.e., putting his own words as direct quotes by his victim], to be sure, pay scant heed to the rules of scholarship. But to condemn McCarthy on the strength of these rules is to judge him by unusual standards . . . to demand . . . a norm of behavior not subscribed to by other politicians and, for better or worse, not expected of them." (The *Nation:* "It would be a mistake to let our abhorrence of the Communists' putsch overthrowing the Beneš government blind us to the fact that political morality is rarely on the level of personal ethics. Nor should we forget England's long and shameful record in India.")

At several points, the authors rebuke McCarthy for his "exaggerations" and "misstatements," on grounds not of morality but of expediency. Such tactics, they correctly maintain, make it harder to get rid of the Communists. Thus, apropos McCarthy's "blunder" in lying himself blue in the face about the mythical 57 card-carrying Communists in the State Department, they ponderously opine: "McCarthy's blunder would prove costly. His specific charges, just to the extent they were incautious [!], would make a cleanup more difficult because attention would be drawn away from loyalty *risks* (the real problem) to Communist Party card holders (a marginal aspect of the real problem)." Such blindness to the No. 1 Fact of Life about Senator McCarthy—that his aim is not to focus attention on security risks or on Communists but on Senator McCarthy, so that exposing Communists is a means *ad majorem gloriam McCarthii* and not an end in itself, hence can be sacrificed when it conflicts with the end—this might lead unkind persons to conclude the boys are a couple of shysters. I prefer to think them honestly naïve.

Like Gogol's Chichikov, McCarthy is a dealer in dead souls. His targets are not actual, living, breathing Communists but rather people who once were or may have been or were not but may be made to appear to have possibly once been Communists or sympathizers or at any rate suspiciously "soft" on the question. Like some D.A.R. who has dreamt over her (alleged) eighteenth-century revolutionary ancestors until they are more real to her than her butcher, McCarthy has brooded over *his* (alleged) revolutionaries of a past era until they are more real to him than, say, Howard Fast. (Not that Mr. Fast or his comrades are revolutionaries, quite the contrary indeed, despite McCarthy's best efforts to confer that respectable title on them.) Are there, indeed, any flesh-and-blood Communists extant today *besides* Mr. Fast? Reason and evidence say yes, but at times McCarthy's operations almost persuade one there aren't. Singlehanded, he has wrought a great change in our political atmosphere. Before he began to expose Franklin D. Roosevelt's Twenty Years of Treason, in that idyllic era of the Hiss case when tangible evidence was frequently produced, there were times when one wondered if anyone in New Deal Washington had been really anti-Communist. By now, one wonders whether anyone had been really pro-Communist. In each instance, a series of startling revelations exploded, like a string of firecrackers, with cumulative effect though with opposite political meanings. Where each day used to bring its startling vindication of some fantastic charge by Bentley or Chambers, today each morning sees another McCarthy exposé of Communist activity pop like a pricked balloon. If McCarthy keeps on much longer, one will begin to doubt the very existence of the Soviet Union.

Chichikov had his Gogol, but McCarthy has yet to find his. Meanwhile, Messrs. Buckley and Bozell will do very well as minor comic characters in the mock-heroic epic of McCarthyism, an interlude in our political history so weird and wonderful that future archaeologists may well assign it to mythology rather than history.

Partisan Review, July-Aug., 1954

3.

LAST FALL a self-confident young man named William F. Buckley, Jr., announced that he had raised $290,000 from 125 "investors" to publish "a new conservative weekly of opinion." He said he had put in only $10,000 himself, but had majority control. On November 19, 1955, the first issue of *National*

Review appeared without causing undue public agitation. Nor have the ten following issues I have seen set any rivers aflame.

However, *NR* seems worth examining as a cultural phenomenon: the McCarthy nationalists—they call themselves conservatives, but that is surely a misnomer—have never before made so heroic an effort to be intellectually articulate. Here are the ideas, here is the style of the *lumpen*-bourgeoisie, the half-educated, half-successful provincials (and a provincial may live within a mile of the Empire State Building as well as in Kokomo or Sauk Center) who responded to Huey Long, Father Coughlin and Senator McCarthy. Anxious, embittered, resentful, they feel that the mainstream of American politics since 1932 has passed them by, as indeed it has, and they have the slightly paranoiac suspiciousness of an isolated minority group. For these are men from underground, the intellectually underprivileged who feel themselves excluded from a world they believe is ruled by liberals just as the economic underdog feels alienated from society.

It is interesting to note that, of the score of "names" who sent in greetings to the first issue, the only ones that can be called intellectuals, by the most generous standards, are Ludwig von Mises and Raymond Moley. The others are a weird mixture: Admiral Ben Moreel and Adolphe Menjou; Gene Tunney and J. Howard Pew, the Pennsylvania oil magnate; Mrs. Preston Davie, of "Only x Days to Save the Republic" fame, and Father James M. Gillis, C.S.P.; René A. Wormser, counsel to the Reece Committee in its crackpot "investigation" of foundations, and Vivien Kellems, the Joan of Arc of our own Poujadist tax-resistance movement; the aged Edward F. Hutton of Wall Street and the venerable Cecil B. DeMille of Hollywood.

Young Mr. Buckley is editor-in-chief as well as publisher of *NR*. There are five other editors: James Burnham, a spectacular backslider from Trotskyism who signalized his departure from the movement in 1940 by publishing *The Managerial Revolution* and whose intellectual horizon has steadily narrowed to a kind of anti-Communism as sterile and doctrinaire as the ideology he fights; Willmoore Kendall, a wild Yale don of extreme, eccentric and very abstract views who can get a discussion into the shouting stage faster than anybody I have ever known; Jonathan Mitchell, who I think used to write a dullish column for one of the liberal weeklies long ago, and writes another one now for *NR;* Suzanne LaFollette, whose boiling point is even lower than Kendall's, and who was an associate of Albert Jay Nock on the *Freeman* of the twenties, was later active on the Trotsky Defense Committee and was recently associated with John Chamberlain in editing another *Freeman* (a pseudo-conservative job, like *NR*—Nock's old *Freeman* was the real thing, and an excellent magazine it was); and, finally, William S. Schlamm, who around 1939 did a column in the *New Leader* which regularly denounced the German people as Nazis and Jew killers in Peglerian accents, and who later became an idea-man for Henry Luce.

WE HAVE long needed a good conservative magazine. (We have also long needed a good liberal magazine.) This is not it, any more than its predecessor, the LaFollette-Chamberlain *Freeman*—which deployed much the same forces—was. And for the same reasons: because it is neither good nor conservative.

Like Senator McCarthy, whom it admires, the *NR* is "anti-liberal" (though, like him, it never bothers to define very clearly what it means by "liberal") but not conservative. Culturally, a conservative is someone like Irving Babbitt or Paul Elmer More, not always the liveliest company in the world but a respecter and defender of tradition. The *NR's* editorials —as I shall presently show—are as elegant as a poke in the nose, as cultivated as a camp meeting, as witty as a prat fall. ("After You, Gaston!" for instance, is definitely not a witty head for an editorial in 1956, whatever it may have been in

1916.) Politically, a conservative is someone like that admirable Republican, the late John Marshall Harlan, the "great dissenter" on the post-Civil War Supreme Court, whose respect for the Constitution was such that he insisted on interpreting the Fourteenth Amendment according to the clear intent of the Congress that passed it, as protecting persons (the newly freed slaves) rather than corporations from molestation by state laws; and such that, in his famous Plessy vs. Ferguson (1896) dissent, he gave the classic formulation to the doctrine that racial segregation in itself is discriminatory (because, although he himself was a pro-slavery man until after the Civil War and was never any special "friend of the Negro," in his old-fashioned simplicity he thought that Plessy, a Negro, had indeed been deprived of his rights under the Fourteenth Amendment when he was arrested for refusing to move from a "white" to a "colored" railway coach). In short, a true conservative, like a true liberal, sticks to his principles even when the result goes against his prejudices.

Not of such stuff are Buckley and his colleagues made. Indeed, they object to the Supreme Court's recent recognition, after half a century of shameful equivocation, of Harlan's Plessy doctrine. They don't meet the central issue, they don't quite dare to state that segregation is not in itself discrimination, because they generally don't meet awkward issues head-on (or perhaps just don't recognize them—one must allow for a general obtuseness), but they sneak in the back way with a pious declaration that segregation "is a problem that should be solved not by the central government, but locally—in the states—and in the hearts of men."

A true conservative appeals to the laws or, if desperate, to tradition, but certainly not to the "hearts of men." This is demagogy, or rather, since the *NR* is not very persuasive, attempted demagogy.

Again, an article in the *NR* objects to the Supreme Court's reversing Judge Medina's sentencing of Harry Sacher for contempt of court after the 1949 trial of the top Communist leaders, and also to the criticisms of Medina's judicial conduct which some of the justices made. The writer gives no reasons for objecting to the reversal and does not try to show that Medina's conduct was correct. He merely quotes from the Supreme Court's decision as if it were *ipso facto* scandalous—as, of course, it is to the hopped-up readers of *NR*—and then concludes: "The lesson which Communist lawyers will draw from the Supreme Court's decision—is: go and do likewise." Very likely, but hardly a conservative approach; bending the law to serve a Worthy Cause is more in the style of those terrible pragmatic Deweyan liberals. So, too, with the invasion of private rights by the state. Conservatives are concerned about this, and so is *NR*—except that *NR*'s concern is selective: it is sensitive about property rights but less so about civil liberties, unless someone it takes to be on its own side is involved, as in the firing of Professor Fuchs from George Washington University after he had been a cooperative witness (about his Communist past) before a Congressional committee. Mr. Bozell wrote a fine muckraking exposé about *that* scandal, but when liberal oxen are similarly gored, *NR* files the case under Saving the Republic. That the liberals have often behaved in the same way is interesting and, if one tends as I do to sympathize more with them than with the *NR* attitude, distressing, but really beside the point. To be simply anti-liberal is not to be a conservative—nor, of course, vice versa. It is to be, simply, anti-liberal—i.e., the opposite number of the liberals, and opposite numbers have a way of adding up to the same sum in the end. The true conservative, like the true liberal, is not simply anti-something; he is for a set of principles, and this is a much more painful business than just sticking with the gang.

JOURNALISTICALLY, the *National Review* actually manages to be duller than the liberal weeklies. It is even more predictable, much more long-winded, and a good deal less competent. Considering that its editors are by no means journalistic neophytes, it is a remarkably amateurish job. (I use the term in the bad sense: trying to do the same thing as the pros, but with inferior technique, as in amateur theatricals. There is also a good sense: trying to do something different from the pros, using a technique that is "unprofessional" only in that it is original, as in D. H. Lawrence's *Studies in Classic American Literature.*) Their idea of a hot series is four articles on "Presidential Inability" in which the Constitutional problems posed by Eisenhower's recent illness are explored with a grim thoroughness that includes the facsimile reproduction of two Congressional bills and one resolution. The cartoons are sometimes vapid (a seance of diplomats, with Stalin's specter hovering overhead; caption: "Spirit of Geneva, Are You There?"), sometimes primitive (Truman as a parrot on a perch saying "KWAK YAK YAK KWAK KWAK"), sometimes rather touchingly antique (a mousy, bespectacled figure leaps in the air as his backside is peppered with birdshot, his briefcase labeled, so help me, "John Q."), but always bad-amateurish. And the *longueurs!* I'm no devotee of the brief article, as reader or as writer, and one of the reasons for the dullness of the liberal weeklies has long seemed to me their habit of cutting every article down to a couple of thousand words; four 1,500 word articles can read much more monotously than one definitive job of 6,000. But an article can be long because the writer has a lot to say, or because he doesn't know how to say it. Almost everything seems long in the *NR*, even the short pieces.

Especially painful are the "light" efforts, like Mr. Schlamm's doggedly jocose "Arts and Manners" column ("My idea of a perfect evening has always been to listen to an old performance of *Don Giovanni,* my eyes closed so that they can see the perfection of the dear girl next to me"), or Morrie Ryskind's interminable "They'll Never Get Me on That Couch," a heavy-breathing onslaught on psychoanalysis which concludes: "Me—I've had enough. I've already served the trauma with eviction papers and I am sending him to military school. I'm making another three-year retreat to the w-mb. So long, folks; see you in 1958." The reader is served a number of these soufflés that collapse into soggy facetiousness. So many, in fact, that it seems likely the editors have made a deliberate effort to liven up the magazine, praiseworthy as against the pale earnestness of the liberal magazine—but, alas, it takes more than intention to be amusing.

Another trait of amateur (bad style) journalism is to use much space in the violent expression of one's opinions and very little in backing them up, or even defining them. Buckley rhetoricizes for two pages in support of the Eastland Committee's recent investigation of Communist sympathies among employees of the New York *Times*—opening, with customary elegance: "The other day the N. Y. *Times* demonstrated its mastery of the art of kicking a midget in the groin and then staging a parade in honor of itself"—but the only specific charge he makes is that the *Times* has "defended Owen Lattimore," and he gives no evidence to support it. The real question, of course, as in the case of the Hollywood Ten, is whether Communists have had any influence on the contents of the paper, but Buckley shows no interest in this, any more than Senator Eastland did, perhaps because the results would be disappointing. So, too, Willmoore Kendall, who produces a weekly column of abstruse indignation called "The Liberal Line," finds enough space to devote an entire column to reprinting quotations from an editorial in the *Progressive* giving Christmas greetings to various persons for services rendered to the liberal cause. But Professor Kendall—who in his unworldly enthusiasm for abstractions is the very type of "egghead" the rest of the magazine denounces—has never felt he had enough space to explain just what he means by "the liberal line." The closest he has come is in a five-point credo (Kendall is great on points, generally somewhat blunted) which merrily chases its tail:

1. That there *is* a Liberal point of view on national and world affairs, for which the word "Liberal" has been appropriated. [Fair enough.]

2. That the point of view consists, on the one hand, of a distinctively Liberal way of looking at and grasping political reality, and on the other hand of a distinctively

Liberal set of values and goals. [We're right back at Grand Central again.]

3. That the nation's leading opinion makers for the most part share the Liberal point of view. . . .

4. That we may properly speak of them as a huge *propaganda machine,* engaged in a major, sustained assault upon the sanity, and upon the prudence and the morality of the American people. . . .

5. That *National Review* must keep a watchful eye on . . . the Liberal propaganda machine . . . in a word, on the *Liberal Line.*

In short, there *is* a Liberal viewpoint that is called Liberal and that expresses Liberal "values and goals." It is a huge *propaganda machine* and must be kept an eye on. If italics were horses, intellectual beggars might ride.

Everything has a way of being converted to grist for the *NR's* political line—another bad-amateur trait, and one shared by the *Daily Worker.* A review of a book about the sinking of the *Titanic* turns into a parable about modern society, with the captains "in the chancelleries of London, Paris and Washington . . . smitten by the deadly sickness of mind and will that is called Liberalism," able only to "chatter incoherently on the bridges of their sinking ships." Reviewing a current play, Mr. Schlamm, who weirdly combines a rather sleazy *bon vivant* attitude with strait-laced vigilance against liberal sex, writes: "*Janus* is of course about adultery. Nobody would dare to produce a Broadway play that is not." The music critic tells Beethoven that he "may have thought he was expressing the misty complexities of the Rights of Man," but he was "in fact . . . transliterating for his age the spirit of Sophoclean tragedy," one of his roles being "Oedipus alone, his eyes' gore drenching his beard." One of Buckley's brothers writes a feature article warning sportsmen not to ask for Federal subsidies for game reservations because That Way Lies Statism. And so it goes. Never a bright moment.

The "Publisher's Statement" with which the first issue opens may fairly be taken as a sample of the *NR* prose style, since presumably it was written with special care. Four main qualities emerge, to wit:

Opacity: "*National Review* is out of place . . . because, in its maturity, literate America rejected conservatism in favor of radical social experimentation. Instead of covetously consolidating its premises, the United States seems tormented by its tradition of fixed postulates having to do with the meaning of existence, with the relationship of the state to the individual, of the individual to his neighbor, so clearly enunciated in the enabling documents of our Republic."

Brutality: "Drop a little itching powder in Jimmy Wechsler's bath and before he has scratched himself for the third time, Arthur Schlesinger [Schlesinger *junior* is clearly meant, not his father—but let's not quibble] will have denounced you in a dozen books and speeches."

Banality: "Let's face it," "when all is said and done," "after all, we crashed through," "a vigorous and incorruptible journal of conservative opinion" [they mean them], "we have nothing to offer but the best that is in us." (Compare a later editorial: "Our statesmen must be gluttons for punishment. One wink from a Soviet diplomat and they are ready to rush halfway across the world to get kicked in the teeth." [Twenty-nine words, two clichés, one kick in the teeth.])

Vulgarity: "And that, ladies and gentlemen, leaves us just about the hottest thing in town." On this note, the editor-in-chief concludes his *Apologia*, his *Areopagitica*, his call for a return to tradition. To borrow another snappy *NR* locution: "Well, brother, what do *you* think?"

THIS IS the voice of the *lumpen*-bourgeoisie. *NR*'s "Letters" department is revealing. There are almost no critical letters, not because the editors have suppressed them—or, at least, so I would guess—but because the magazine's level is not serious enough to stimulate them. Nor are there letters of correction or amplification; readers satisfied by so modestly endowed a journal are unlikely to have much to add. The whole atmosphere is that of the religious revival ("Amen, brother!") rather than of dialogue or communication. These are, essentially, love letters—brief, stammering protestations of affection. The writers are inarticulate, culturally underprivileged folk. The diction is either stiff, like a farmhand's Sunday suit —"Please permit me to wish the promoters every success in this worthwhile project"—or vulgar—"thanks for a home base." In both cases it is the language of people not accustomed to expressing themselves on paper. "I am crazy about it," a housewife writes from San Francisco. "Your wonderful weekly really fills a gap." A Lt. Col. pronounces it "a fine periodical," while a lady writes from Miami, "Your new magazine is magnificent. Every single word of the first three editions has been devoured by me." Another lady of Dallas confesses ". . . so satisfying. I myself find nothing to criticize." And a clergyman weighs in all the way from Huntsville, Utah: "Even for a first issue, it's a superlative job—honest, jam-packed factually, witty . . . something we have been waiting and praying for in America."

There is frequently a sort of pathos in this enthusiasm, like the joy of a long-beleaguered garrison when the U.S. Marines finally arrive: ". . . an oasis in the desert. The spring has been very dry since 1932. This is a second Valley Forge." "At last the faceless, voiceless, unorganized but patriotic genuine Americans . . . have a medium." "God knows it is high time." ". . . the long-needed house organ of the outnumbered but still dynamic American Underground that refuses to bend with the prevailing winds of Regimentation, Monopoly, Conformity and Ideological Sleepwalking."

This mood of helpless isolation is also present in the magazine itself. There are so many enemies; the liberal conspiracy is omnipresent; it includes not only Mrs. Roosevelt, Dean Acheson and Paul Hoffman, but also *Life,* the New York *Times,* nay, even Eisenhower himself, whose behavior is as constantly disappointing to the editors as that of F.D.R. was to the editors of the liberal weeklies in the thirties. Defectors are constantly cropping up, as David Lawrence (because of his "strange proposal" that both parties nominate Eisenhower in 1956), or the late Bernard DeVoto, whose obituary posed the usual problem for John Chamberlain: how could the man who had so valiantly battled for the Philistines against Van Wyck Brooks' egghead attack on Mark Twain in the twenties ("The stuff about Mark Twain being a displaced Russian novelist was strictly for the birds"), how could he have later fallen for all that liberal propaganda? (Bad company, concludes Mr. Chamberlain; Benny shouldn't have hung around the *Harper's* poolroom.)

In the dull lexicon of *NR* there is no such word as success. McCarthy was their one triumph, and where are the headlines of yesteryear? One of Buckley's sisters circulated a denunciation, among her fellow Smith alumnae, of certain professors as being tainted with Communism; the result was, as she reveals in an article in the first issue bitterly entitled "How to Raise Money in the Ivy League," that "in less than three months, the world's largest women's college received more money [from its alumnae] than had ever been collected in any full year in its history."

The most depressing article I found in *NR*—and that's saying a lot—was a lugubrious think-piece titled "The Atomic Disarmament Trap," which the editors summarized: "Our foreign policy, says an expert on atomic politics, is based on the premise that the USSR will continue to reject international control of atomic energy. But Moscow may disarm us by accepting—and keeping faith." The danger is clear, appalling, and up to now not noticed by anybody but *NR:* since we have more atom-hydrogen bombs than they do, we would be giving up a military advantage in exchange merely for avoiding the possible destruction of the world, including US, or us. It's no picnic, being an editor of *NR*—or even a reader.

Perhaps the most significant editorial *NR* has printed is "A Bow to the Left" in the January 18 issue, in which the editors confess a certain admiration for Paul Hoffman, Elmo Roper and the other directors of the Fund for the Republic.

> The point is that none of the directors has very much to gain, and all of them have considerable to lose, in the eyes of a public soberer than they, by their bizarre activities. But on they go. They are quite obviously prepared to lose not only a measure of personal esteem, but *also*, if necessary, tax exemption! . . . We think, by contrast, of the scores upon scores of timorous right-wingers we happen to know who will overwhelm you with dire talk about the engulfing age of socialism . . . and yet when the occasion presents itself to make a sacrifice in behalf of their convictions, the conversation quickly turns to the weather. . . . That is what sets them off from the directors of the Fund for the Republic. And that is why the Left marches on, while the Right retreats.

The editors don't try to explain this difference in left and right behavior. I suggest it is because the left—to use *NR*'s quaint terminology—has a set of ideas and ideals in which they can believe, which seem to them intellectually consistent and morally attractive, while the right does not. (For myself, I no longer find the left ideology either morally or intellectually satisfying, but that is another question; the point is that it is a far more plausible doctrine than the right's crude patchwork of special interests.) One of *NR*'s few literate letters-to-the-editor, from Frank S. Meyer of Woodstock, N.Y., comments on "the insistence [of other readers] that the magazine publish nothing that makes serious intellectual demands upon the reader," and continues: "But we are an opposition, and we have to fight conformity. . . . It is ideas they [the dominant liberal 'social engineers'] fear, for in the end it is ideas which are decisive. It was ideas developed in the *Nation* and the *New Republic* and the *Masses* thirty and forty years ago that seduced a generation and laid the foundations for the New Deal and what has followed. The circulations of these magazines were not large, but they spoke to the younger generation, in and out of the universities, and won them—with devastating effect." Ideas, however, or even sufficient journalistic skill to conceal their lack, are just what *NR* lacks. A more typical reader is a gentleman of Memphis, who writes: "I think you are going places. I have only one comment of criticism. Your writers are really too brilliant for the lay mind, if you know what I mean." I know what he means, and it isn't encouraging for the future of the *National Review.*

Commentary, April 1956

SAINTS

Gandhi

"A moment before he was shot, he said—some witnesses believed he was speaking to the assassin—'You are late.'"

—N. Y. *World-Telegram,* Jan. 30, 1948.

AND INDEED the man who killed Gandhi with three revolver shots *was* late—about two years late. The communal massacres showed that Gandhi's teaching of non-violence had not penetrated to the Indian masses. His life work had been in vain—or at least it now appeared that he had taught a "non-violence of the weak" which had been effective against the British but that the more difficult "non-violence of the strong" he had been unable to teach. He insisted on his failure constantly, and constantly thought of death. "I am in the midst of flames," he wrote last spring. "Is it the kindness of God or His irony that the flames do not consume me?" One imagines that he experienced a dreadful joy in the split-second he saw the gun aimed at him.

Three historical events have moved me deeply of recent years: the murder of Trotsky, the atomic bombing of Hiroshima, the murder of Gandhi. That all three should be simply catastrophes—hopeless, destructive, painful—is in the style of our period. The Spanish Civil War was the last of the 19th century type of political tragedies: the fight was lost, as in 1848 or the Paris Commune, but it had been a fight; there was hope while it was going on, and defeat might be due to some temporary relation of forces; there was a basis for a future effort.

But Trotsky and Gandhi were killed not during their great time of struggle to realize "Utopian" ideals, not while they were still fighting with a hope of success, but after their ideas—or at least their tactics—had been shown by the brutal logic of events to be inadequate. They were not shot in battle. They were executed. And their executioner was not the oppressive, conservative forces they had devoted their lives to fighting—the bourgeoisie and the British imperialists—but the scum that had frothed up from their own heroic struggle to liberate mankind: young fanatics representing a new order—of Stalinism and of Hindu nationalism—which is hopeless, deadening, corrupting, and monstrous, but which is also, alas, partly the product of their own revolutionary efforts. In the 19th century, czars and governors and secret-police chiefs were assassinated by radicals; today, it is revolutionaries (out of power) like Trotsky and Gandhi who are killed by our modern Nihilists, while Stalin and Hitler and Zhdanov and Himmler and Mussolini and Molotov escape (unless they lose a war). *Our* Nihilists have terribly perverted Liebknecht's slogan: "The main Enemy is at Home." Or perhaps they are just more prudent than their 19th century ancestors. Which would be in keeping, too.

Gandhi, like Trotsky, was killed after his most profound ideas and his lifelong political activity had been rebuffed by History. But, also like Trotsky, he was still alive and kicking, still throwing out imaginative concepts. The ideologue was baffled, but the human being—and by this sentimental phrase I mean the acute intelligence as much as the moralist—was not through: he had plenty of inspirations and surprises in store for us. Both men were still giving, by their personal example and still more by their unwearied experimenting with general principles, some kind of meaning, of *consciousness* to modern political life. Their assassins killed not only two men, but also two cultures. Which makes it all the more painful.

There was obvious irony in the great pacifist being killed by a gunman. But there was also an esthetic fitness. Gandhi was the last eminent personage who insisted on dealing directly with people, reasoning with them face to face as individuals, not as crowds roped off, watched by plain-clothes men, sealed safely behind bulletproof glass. It was a matter of principle with him not to deny anyone access to him, mentally or physically. He refused all police protection. I have heard people say he was a damn fool and got what he might expect to get. They are, of course, right. Our world is so structured that the "public man" can survive only by being private, and the most dangerous thing he can do is to meet his public face to face.

Gandhi was the last political leader in the world who was a person, not a mask or a radio voice or an institution. The last on a human scale. The last for whom I felt neither fear nor contempt nor indifference but interest and affection. He was dear to me—I realize it now better than I did when he was alive—for all kinds of reasons. He believed in love, gentleness, persuasion, simplicity of manners, and he came closer to "living up to" these beliefs than most people I know—let alone most Big Shots, on whom the pressures for the reverse must be very powerful. (To me, the wonder is not that Gandhi often resorted to sophistry or flatly went back on some of his ideas, but that he was able to put into practice as many of them as he did. I speak from personal experience.) He was dear to me because he had no respect for railroads, assembly-belt production, and other knick-knacks of liberalistic Progress, and insisted on examining their human (as against their metaphysical) value. Also because he was clever, humorous, lively, hard-headed, and never made speeches about Fascism, Democracy, the Common Man, or World Government. And because he had a keen nose for the concrete, homely "details" of living which make the real difference to people but which are usually ignored by everybody except poets. And finally because he was a good man, by which I mean not only "good" but also "man."

This leads into the next point. Many pacifists and others who have an ethical—and really admirable—attitude toward life are somewhat boring. Their point of view, their writing and conversation are wholly sympathetic but also a little on the dull side.

Intellectually, their ideas lack subtlety and logical structure. Ethically, they are *too* consistent; they don't sense the tragedy of life, the incredible difficulty of actually putting into practice an ethical concept. They have not succumbed to temptation because they have never been tempted; they are good simply because it has never occurred to them to be bad. They are, in a word, unworldly. Gandhi was not at all unworldly. He was full of humor, slyness, perversity, and—above all—practicality. Indeed, the very thing which leads people to think of him as unworldly—his ascetic ideas about diet, household economy, and sexual intercourse—seems to me to show his worldliness, or at least his imaginative grasp of The World: how could anyone be so concerned about such matters, even though in a negative sense, without a real feeling for their importance in human life, which in turn must come from a deep drive on his part *toward* gluttony, luxury, and sexual indulgence?

The Marxists, those monks of politics, were shocked by his intimacy with rich men like Birla and Tata, just as the Pharisees, the Trotskyists of their day, were shocked by Christ's sitting at table with bartenders. (The Marxist has a richer intellectual tradition than the pacifist, but his ethical sense is equally simplistic.) It is true that Gandhi "compromised" with the rich, those untouchables of the class struggle, living at their villas (though carrying on there his own ascetic regimen). But he also "compromised" with the poor, spending at least as much time in the "untouchable's" quarters (he constantly complains of the smells and lack of sanitation) as in the Birla Palace. In short, he practiced tolerance and love to such an extent that he seems to have regarded the capitalist as well as the garbage-man as his social equal.

Winter, 1948

Dorothy Day

MANY PEOPLE think that Dorothy Day is a saint and that she will someday be canonized. In 1933, with the late Peter Maurin, a French-born itinerant preacher, who has been affectionately described as "an apostle on the bum" and who advocated "a Utopian Christian communism," she founded the Catholic Worker movement, and, despite her best efforts to the contrary, she still dominates it. She is a rangy woman of fifty-five whose thick gray hair is braided tightly around her small, well-shaped head. High cheekbones and slanting eyes give her a Slavic look, although her ancestry is Scotch-Irish. Her face—patient, gentle and understanding—might suggest a passive temperament were it not for her wide, mobile mouth and the expression of her eyes, which is at times dreamily remote, at times as naïvely expectant as a young girl's, but always alive. Her own patron saint, after whom she named her only child, is the gay and impetuous Teresa of Ávila, who used to pray, "May God deliver me from surly saints." In her sensible shoes and drab, well-worn clothes, Miss Day looks like an elderly schoolteacher or librarian; she has the typical air of mild authority and of being no longer surprised at anything children or book-borrowers may do. She also looks like a grandmother, which she is, for her daughter now has five children. Upon first meeting her, most people who are familiar with her career are surprised to find that, far from being dynamic, she is quiet and almost diffident. Although she has been speaking in public for years, her platform manner is retiring and hesitant, and she makes not even a stab at rhetorical effect. She has no "presence" at all, but in spite of that, or perhaps because of it, she is impressive to meet or hear, communicating a moral force compounded of openness, sincerity, earnestness and deprecatory humor. She has lived with intellectuals all her adult life, from the time when, at the age of nineteen, she established herself in Greenwich Village society as a writer for radical publications, but she is not one herself. She is more a feeler and a doer than a thinker. Her mind works by free association rather than logic, and her writings and public talks—"speeches" would hardly be the right word—are as haphazardly put together as her clothes. Her temperament combines mystical feeling and practicality in a way not common in the everyday world but not uncommon in the annals of hagiography.

The physical manifestations of the movement that Miss Day and Maurin founded nineteen years ago consist of the *Catholic Worker*, a monthly paper with an anti-capitalist, anti-Communist viewpoint and a circulation of fifty-eight thousand, together with fifteen so-called Houses of Hospitality, in New York and other cities, here and abroad, and eight communal farms, scattered around the country—a total of twenty-three centers where the homeless are sheltered, the hungry are fed, and the ragged are clothed. New York is the headquarters of the movement, offering benign advice and encouragement to the centers elsewhere but, with the exception of two nearby farms, exercising no direct control over them. The whole organization is operated by perhaps a hundred men and women who give all or most of their time to it without pay, living cheerfully in voluntary poverty. All are lay Catholics, and almost all are under thirty and will presently leave, after a few years of the work, to go into the world again, usually to get married and raise a family, and their places will be filled by new young volunteers. The movement is thus a kind of university, constantly taking in freshmen and graduating seniors. It is also a large family, in which the voluntary and the involuntary poor, the helpers and the helped, live together in the houses and on the farms with no more distinction in the matter of dress, manners, bed and board than is to be found in any other family. Miss Day combines the functions of a headmistress—the cheerful gladhanding, the bringing out of shy individuals, the deft restraining of unruly ones and even the fund-raising—with those of a fond and watchful mother. She writes a lot and travels a lot, trying to persuade people that it is possible even today to live in peace and brotherhood, and recruiting new members for her staff. Wherever she is and whatever else she does during the day, she always spends from one to two hours in prayer and meditation; her religion is the center of her life, and it is significant that the one touch of luxury in dress she permits herself is a handsome black lace mantilla she sometimes wears to Mass.

The Catholic Workers are religious in a way that is hard for most people even to understand, let alone sympathize with. They practice their faith on Mondays, Tuesdays, Wednesdays, Thursdays, Fridays and Saturdays, as well as on Sundays. An eminent theologian has written that for the Anabaptists and Methodists, sects that the Catholic Workers in some ways resemble, religion ceases to be "a matter of outward forms and ordinances" and becomes "an affair of the heart." For them, too, religion is an affair of the heart, but, far from wanting to free themselves from outward forms and ordinances, they infuse their zeal into their reception of the sacraments and gladly accept the Pope's authority. As one of their admirers recently put it, "Their inner light is refracted through the hard, intricately cut prism of Catholic dogma."

"How do they stay in the Church?" is the question most often asked about the organization, the runner-up being, "What does Spellman think of them?" The latter question, at least, cannot be authoritatively answered, for the Cardinal has maintained a discreet silence on the subject. Like his predecessor, the late Cardinal Hayes, he has endorsed their works of mercy, but he will not be drawn further. Some time ago, at a reception, Miss Day tried. She asked him outright how he felt about the Workers. "You'll find that many of the bishops are on your side," the Cardinal answered, with a diplomatic smile. On most secular issues, from pacifism to psychoanalysis, the Cardinal and the Workers disagree. Perhaps one reason he doesn't "do something about it" is that his disciplinary and supervisory powers over laymen are more limited than many non-Catholics realize. Like the Pope's, they are confined to sitting in judgment on such "matters of faith and morals" as divorce and contraception and ruling on cases of error in connection with such theological dogmas as the Immaculate Conception and the recently proclaimed Assumption of the Virgin. It is true that, as Archbishop of New York, the Cardinal exercises much the same authority over his diocese as the Pope does over the whole Church (any layman has the right to appeal to Rome, but Rome almost always backs up its bishops); it is also true that by stretching a point, or several points, he might get the Workers on a faith-and-morals charge, since they not only advocate radical ideas—not in itself prohibited—but edge into theological territory by presenting these ideas as a logical development of Catholic doctrine. However, he has stayed his hand, whether from conscience or from expediency or because the Church is a house of more mansions than are dreamed of in Paul Blanshard's philosophy.

This is not to say that the Workers' relations with the Chancery—the administrative offices of the diocese, which occupy the old Whitelaw Reid house, across Madison Avenue from St. Patrick's—are always smooth. For a Catholic, a summons to the Chancery is a summons to the headmaster's study. Miss Day has received three such summonses. Once, it was because a priest who had conducted a retreat—that is, a gathering for the purpose of prayer, meditation, and instruction—at one of the organization's farms had fallen into the error of "too vigorous spirituality" through the vehemence with which he denounced liquor, lipsticks, and the movies. Once, it was because some influential laymen had complained about the Workers' anti-capitalist propaganda. In both these instances, Msgr. Edward R. Gaffney, one of the diocesan Vicars-General, simply notified her of the complaints and added his personal admonition. The third time was more serious. In 1948, the *Catholic Worker* advised young men not to register for the draft. Although this was clearly illegal, the editors didn't hear from the FBI, but they did hear from Msgr. Gaffney, who summoned Miss Day and "corrected" her —that is, ordered her to cease and desist, which she did.

For all her brushes with authority, however, Miss Day is a Catholic first and a radical second. "The hierarchy permits a priest to say Mass in our chapel," she remarked to a friend not long ago. "They have given us the most precious thing of all—the Blessed Sacrament. If the Chancery ordered me to stop publishing the *Catholic Worker* tomorrow, I would."

POLITICALLY, the Catholic Workers are hard to classify. They are for the poor and against the rich, so the capitalists call them Communists; they believe in private property and don't believe in class struggle, so the Communists call them capitalists; and they are hostile to war and to the State, so both capitalists and Communists consider them crackpots. They are often taken for some kind of Communist front inside the Catholic Church, but actually the *Catholic Worker* and the Communist *Worker* have little similarity beyond their names. Being as a general rule pacifists, most Catholic Workers refuse to serve in the army, to work in war industries and to pay federal income taxes (since most of the budget goes for war purposes) even on those rare occasions when they have enough income to pay taxes on. Despite the extreme position it takes on such issues, the organization has never had any trouble with the authorities, and Miss Day rather resents this tolerance, as a slur on its political effectiveness, just as she dislikes the protection its name gives them against local constabularies. During the strike of Ohrbach store employees in 1934, the police regularly hauled off to jail all the pickets except the Catholic Workers. "I'd as soon arrest the Holy Father himself!" exclaimed one uniformed co-religionist.

People who try to live their everyday lives according to an ideal are likely to make fools of themselves, which some critics think is just what the Catholic Workers have been doing for nearly twenty years. Others, more charitable, hold that there are two differences between their folly and plain foolishness. One is that theirs is premeditated; they are, so to speak, fools on principle. "Let us be fools for Christ," Miss Day says. "Let us recklessly act out our vision, even if we shall almost surely fail, for what the world calls failure is often, from a Christian viewpoint, success." She is also fond of quoting Saint Paul: "The foolish things of the world hath God chosen, that He may confound the wise." And she points to Christ's death on the cross, which Catholic theologians call "the Folly of the Cross," as the supreme example of successful failure. The other difference is that, unlike plain fools, the Catholic Workers, in spite of the most appalling miscalculations, cross-purposes, lack of planning and general confusion, have accomplished a lot even by worldly standards.

This second difference is not always obvious. Wherever two or three of the Workers are gathered together, chaos is almost sure also to be present. During Peter Maurin's last illness, a disciple had the happy thought of getting him to make a wire recording of some of his writings. After his death, someone who had not been alerted used the machine and innocently erased every word. The Workers' paper has a tradition of inaccuracy dating back to its founding, in 1933. Maurin's name appeared as "Maurain" throughout its first issue; its second issue was dated "June-July" and its third "July-August," an overlapping never explained and probably inexplicable; its chief artist sent in her first drawings signed "A. De Bethune," which is her name, but it came out "Ade Bethune," and has so remained to this day, Miss De Bethune apparently feeling this comes close enough. In recognition of the Workers' help to Catholics abroad after the war—among other things, *Catholic Worker* readers supplied five hundred packages of clothing and food to one Polish convent alone and completely equipped a hospital in Sicily—the Pope sent them his blessing on an ornately illuminated parchment scroll, but it is not to be seen anywhere around the *Worker* office; Miss Day thinks it got lost in moving. Several years ago, when the Workers wanted to sell one of their farms, they found they could not do so then—or, in fact, ever—because they had anchored the title firmly in midair; Miss Day holds the place in trust for the *Catholic Worker,* but the *Catholic Worker,* being unincorporated (on principle) and not a legal entity, cannot authorize her to sell its property. (The best the lawyers could suggest was that if every subscriber agreed in writing to the sale, the courts might take a lenient view of things—or, of course, might not.) There was also the woman Worker on a picket line who, asked by a passerby what it was all about, snapped, "None of your business!"

All this notwithstanding, the Catholic Workers are in general very practical fools. The *Catholic Worker* was started not on a shoestring but on the hope of one. When the first issue appeared, the editors had ninety-two cents between them. "This first number was planned, written, and edited in the kitchen of a tenement on Fifteenth Street, on subway platforms, on the 'El' and on the ferry," they wrote. "Next month someone may donate us an office. Who knows?" Miss Day had to sell her typewriter to help pay for the printing of the second issue. Then things improved. A sympathetic expressman gave them a desk and a filing cabinet. Visitors began to arrive in numbers, and they often helped out with work or cash. Circulation went up seven hundred percent in the first six months—from twenty-five hundred to twenty thousand. Even the paper's finances improved slightly. "During the month $201.55 came in (and went right out again)," the *Catholic Worker* reported in its third issue. "Every few weeks the editors were able to take to themselves five dollars' salary. We live in the daily hope that someone will come in and pay the printing bill or the rent." Down through the years, someone always has. Since 1933, the Workers in New York alone have put out their monthly paper, given coffee, bread and soup twice daily to from two hundred to eight hundred men, boarded between fifty and seventy-five people a day and handed out free shoes and clothes to indeterminable thousands. It costs about forty thousand dollars a year to do these things. There have also been such occasional special outlays as thirty thousand dollars to buy the Chrystie Street house, thirty-one thousand dollars to buy the two farms the Workers own in this part of the country—one up the Hudson, at Newburgh, and the other on Staten Island—and five thousand dollars to run a special soup kitchen during the 1936 seamen's strike, which lasted two months. Sums like these are not got by wishful thinking or, in the Workers' case, by business methods.

Under Miss Day's guidance, the Catholic Workers have devised an inexpensive and effective technique of fund-raising: they pray to Saint Joseph, their patron saint. "We appealed to him for help last month," the editors wrote in the second issue of the *Catholic Worker*, "and within two weeks not only our current printing bill was paid but money was there for the February bill, also." Their creditors pray, too. "The printer called us up this morning wanting to know, affably, when we were going to pay our bill," another editorial reads. "We told him he'd better get busy and pray for it hard." Later, the *Worker* reported, "Enough money has come in to pay $300 to our very forbearing printer, and he says he is still praying." Things get behind sometimes—their grocery bill for the Chrystie Street house has run as high as six thousand dollars, and last fall they discovered that they owed two thousand dollars for flour alone—but sooner or later Saint Joseph is always good for the money. Their credit is solid, and their business relations—with their printer (Rogowski, on Pearl Street), their butcher (Kantor Brothers, on Essex Street) and their grocer (Di Falco, at Mott and Hester)—are friendly to the point of sentimentality; the fact that the first two are Jewish firms doesn't seem to make any difference to Saint Joseph. At the very mention of money, Miss Day grows impatient. "That is all in the hands of Saint Joseph," she once wrote in the *Catholic Worker*, apropos of a particularly huge avalanche of debts that was threatening to engulf the organization. "He is our patron and it is up to him. I haven't any doubt about it. I've seen him perform daily miracles around here."

Some of the miracles are chronic. Twice a year, the Workers print an appeal in their paper, and twice a year they get enough donations, all in small sums, to cover their ordinary running expenses. Sometimes prayer doesn't get results, but then the remedy is clear. "When things go wrong, we know we are not praying enough," Miss Day says. And sometimes Heaven doesn't respond as expected, or, indeed, as wished—a common failing of supernatural agencies, as Macbeth, for one, discovered. Once, needing a thousand dollars in a hurry, Miss Day prayed for it, and got it when her Staten Island cottage, insured for precisely that amount, promptly burned down. Her gratitude was tempered by her affection for the place, and by the fact that it was worth a lot more than a thousand dollars. "Sometimes I wish God weren't quite so literal," she said later.

THE CATHOLIC WORKER movement began one evening in December, 1932, when Miss Day came home to the tenement on East Fifteenth Street where she was living with her five-year-old daughter, Teresa, and found a stocky, shabbily dressed elderly man, with a knobby, granitelike face and lively eyes, talking away to Teresa at the kitchen table. It was Maurin. The meeting was a case of ideological love at first sight. Miss Day's life up to the time she met Maurin had seemed to some of her friends to lack direction. Born on Brooklyn Heights, of Republican and Episcopalian parents, and brought up by them in Chicago, she attended the University of Illinois, and while there joined the Socialist Party. When she was nineteen and had just completed her second year at the University, she returned with her family to New

York. Once here, however, she broke with her parents and began to associate with the intellectual set in Greenwich Village. Supporting herself by working at a number of minor jobs and free-lance projects, mostly journalistic or literary, she fell in love after a few years with a biology instructor and entered into a common-law marriage with him that lasted until the birth of a daughter, in 1927—an event that, she has since said, caused her such an indescribable sense of joy and gratitude that she felt obliged to join the Catholic Church. This step meant either living in mortal sin or renouncing the child's father, who was an atheist and spurned the idea of marriage, and she reluctantly chose the latter. Then followed a period of five years during which Miss Day was at somewhat loose ends; she barely kept herself and her daughter alive by writing a novel, a play, and several short stories, none of which were very successful.

Miss Day's real career began when, at the end of those five years, she met Maurin. Their meeting was a turning point in his life, too. Maurin, a member of a huge peasant family in the south of France—he had twenty-three brothers and sisters—had studied in the Christian Brothers' school in Paris for five years, then taught for another five years, but for most of his life had bummed around Canada and the United States, working in lumber camps and steel mills, and on farms, roads and construction projects; his longest job—as janitor of a Chicago tenement—lasted a little less than two years. He lived in cheap hotels, ate in skid-row beaneries and owned only the clothes on his back. From his reading in public libraries, he acquired an extraordinary knowledge of political theory, Church history, economics and law, both canonical and secular. At some point in his wanderings (dates are hard to come by, for he was grandly uninterested in his personal life), he began to expound his ideas to all comers—in parks, flophouses and cafeterias. In the mid-twenties, he settled in Woodstock, New York, where, perhaps stimulated by the cultural atmosphere of the place, he worked out his own form of communication—the "Easy Essay." This consists of a theme with variations; it is a sort of verbal fugue, consisting of repetition and counterpoint, in short, stylized lines. The effect is soothing, hypnotic and droll, like that of a child talking to himself; it is often unexpected, too, for, like a child, Maurin took words and phrases literally and investigated them painstakingly, turning them around in different lights until fresh meanings flashed out. Following is a typical stanza:

The world would be better off
if people tried to become better.
And people would become better
if they stopped trying to become better off.

And another:

A bourgeois is a man
who tries to be somebody
by trying to be like everybody,
which makes him a nobody.

Before Maurin died, in 1949, at the age of seventy-two, he wrote a hundred and twenty Easy Essays, on such varied topics as war, capitalism, the Jews, the Irish, prostitution, higher education, banks, charity, Communism, Catholicism, the colonial question, birth control, industrialism and agriculture. He used to recite the essays, in a kind of slow chant, on all possible, and many impossible, occasions, the first of the latter variety arising in 1927, when he addressed the Rotary Club of Kingston, New York. The essays were also printed and reprinted in the *Catholic Worker*, and even now they appear there from time to time, giving many readers the impression that Maurin is still alive.

When Maurin met Miss Day, he was living at his favorite hotel—Uncle Sam's, on the Bowery, forty cents a night. After the movement got started, he lived in one or another of its various Houses of Hospitality and farms, but he never spruced up and to the end of his life continued to wear clothes that were shabby even by Catholic Worker standards. Once, he went up to New Rochelle to speak at a women's-club luncheon. At the hour set for his appearance, Miss Day received a frantic phone call from the club's secretary, asking, "Where's Peter?" (The secretary had never met Maurin, but everybody called him Peter, just as everybody calls her Dorothy.)

"He must be there," Miss Day replied. "I put him on the train myself."

"No," the secretary said. "There's no one at the station but an old tramp snoozing on a bench."

"That's Peter," said Miss Day confidently—and correctly.

"He was the most *detached* person I ever met," an acquaintance of Maurin's has recalled. "He seemed to have no material needs. He was not interested in people, or even in concrete problems, but only in abstract principles. He was a man drunk with ideas." When the first issue of the *Catholic Worker* appeared, Maurin was disappointed. "Everybody's paper is nobody's paper," he remarked, in his best Easy Essay fashion. Miss Day was puzzled by this at first; then she understood. "I realized that, in his simplicity, he wanted nothing but his own essays to be printed, over and over again," she says. It was not vanity, she is convinced, for he was as impersonal toward himself as toward others; it was just that he knew he had a message and that the essays precisely conveyed that message. It was all there, he felt, so why clutter up the paper with other material, which just blurred the essence? Maurin's thinking, like his life, was stripped of extraneous luxuries—nuances, subtleties, complexities. He was a simplifier, a sort of abstract artist of ideas whose specialty was eliminating the superfluous, a man whose speech was yea, yea and nay, nay, and who was so thoroughgoing an absolutist that Einstein's law of relativity made him uncomfortable.

"I am an agitator," Maurin used to say, and agitate he did—everywhere, all the time. In his old age, he traveled more than twenty thousand miles in one year, spreading his message. His groves of Academe were Union Square, Columbus Circle, and their equivalents in other cities, plus any public meetings that would invite him or, indeed, admit him.

In delivering his message, Maurin was as persistent as a process-server. When he got hold of the address of a likely prospect's home or office, he would go to see him all primed to talk as long as he was allowed to. Captive audiences especially attracted him, and he rarely wasted one. He would strike up a conversation in such stentorian tones with a fellow-passenger on a bus that all the other passengers had to hear, if not listen. Sometimes, he dropped in at amateur nights in neighborhood movie houses; when his turn came, he recited Easy Essays. He was perhaps at his best with one or two listeners, although, like most ideologists, he was deficient in small talk. On the other hand, Maurin often showed much ingenuity in adapting himself to his listeners' interests. One night, in a cheap hotel, a girl knocked on his door and asked, "Want to have a good time, honey?" "Come in, come in!" he cried, and when she did, he inquired of her, "Now, what would you say a good time *means*, exactly? Let's discuss it." What the girl learned is not known, but the incident got Maurin interested in the problem of prostitution. He thought a lot about it and finally proposed a double-barreled solution: Settle prostitutes and male alcoholics on Catholic Worker farms and let them marry and rehabilitate one another. Nothing much came of it, however.

IN MISS DAY, Maurin found his ideal auditor, one who already agreed with him on basic theories and who needed only his clear-cut formulations of them and his messianic energy to start on her life work.

Early in 1933, when this life work began, the Roman Catholic Church in this country was still deeply uninterested in liberal social causes. Abroad, especially in France, "social Catholicism" had already become strong, but in the United States the hierarchy felt it wiser not to meddle in such matters. Inspired by Maurin's idealism and Miss Day's intensity and drive, the Catholic Workers became agitators among the people; they foreshadowed that renaissance of the "lay apostolate" that has since arisen in the Church. A veteran of the early days recalls, "We just went out and *did* things. We didn't form a Committee to Promote Improved Interracial Relations. We took Negroes into our homes and lived with them. We didn't get up big-name letterheads to raise funds for strikers. We went out on the picket lines ourselves."

This direct-action approach, coupled with the fact that 1933 was the bottom year of the depression, gave the Workers a crusading appeal that struck fire among young priests, students in theological seminaries and some of the more enlightened members of the laity. Catholic Worker groups started up all over the place—often by spontaneous combustion, without any help from headquarters. A curious social paradox was involved. Theretofore, American Catholicism had been a lower-class affair, its followers consisting mostly of post-1840 immigrants from Catholic countries like Ireland, Poland, Italy and Austria-Hungary; the upper classes—rated as such simply by virtue of having got here earlier—were solidly Protestant. But by 1930 the immigrants had begun to rise socially and economically, their children and even their grandchildren were going to college, and Catholicism began to produce middle-class intellectuals as full of reforming zeal as their Protestant counterparts had been for a century or more. As long as the majority of Catholics were proletarians, the hierarchy could, if it liked, deal with them in an authoritarian way and dragoon them into a conservative social pattern, but as the laity became richer and better educated, there was an increasing ferment of liberalism in the old bottles of the Church. Today, the hierarchy is still largely conservative—Cardinal Spellman, of New York, being more typical than Bishop Sheil, of Chicago—but the lower clergy and the laity have produced such Catholic phenomena as the interracial Friendship Houses; the St. Francis Xavier Labor College, in New York; the Chicago Catholic pro-labor monthly, *Work;* and a whole crop of so-called "labor priests," like Father John M. Corridan, who played an important part in the 1951 insurgent longshoremen's strike.

Many of the individuals who are now working in such

strange Catholic vineyards were given their first impulse and their training by the Catholic Worker movement. As Father Dennis Geaney, a Catholic educator, wrote of Miss Day in *Work*, "It was a Christian revolution she was starting. She was opening the minds of bishops, priests, seminarians, and lay people to the fact that Christianity was not a stuffy sacristy affair. She was a trumpet calling for all of us to find Christ in the bread lines, the jails, as a tenant farmer, migratory worker or Negro. We think of Church history as being made by popes and bishops. Here is a woman who has placed her stamp on American Catholicism. The seed she sowed in the thirties is bearing fruit a hundred-fold in the fifties."

The *Catholic Worker* was started, as the name suggests, as a competitor of the Communist *Daily Worker*, and it was no accident that most of its first issue, in 1933, was distributed in Union Square on May Day. In their maiden editorial, which asked, in effect, "Why should the Devil have all the good tunes?" Maurin and Miss Day wrote. "It's time there was a Catholic paper printed for the unemployed. The fundamental aim of most radical sheets is conversion of its readers to radicalism and atheism. Is it not possible to be radical and not atheist?" The Church's social program is contained largely in two papal encyclical letters—the *Rerum novarum*, of Leo XIII (1891), and the *Quadragesimo anno*, of Pius XI (1931). These rebuke the greed of unrestrained capitalism, encourage labor unions and in general put the interests of the worker above the interests of private property. "Our job is to make the encyclicals click," Maurin once said.

In the thirties, the Catholic Workers were in the thick of events and Miss Day, despite a solid Republican and Episcopalian family background, was in the thickest of them. In a single year—1936—she traveled to Detroit to report on and help along the sitdown strikes out of which came the United Automobile Workers; to Lowell, Massachusetts, where there was a textile strike (the Catholic Workers fed the pickets and supported the strike so enthusiastically that the mayor of Lowell phoned the Chancery in Boston to check up on this crowd of Catholics who were making a noise like Communists; the Chancery reassured him—firmly, if with resignation—that they were Catholics, all right); to Pittsburgh, where the CIO was beginning to organize steel (she and Mary Heaton Vorse, the labor journalist, took a hotel room for a dollar and a half a day and visited every liberal priest in the district, including old Father Adalbert Kazincy, who had been almost alone among the Catholic clergy in backing the 1919 steel strike but now had many priests to keep him company); to Akron, where the rubber workers were striking; to Birmingham, where more steel workers were organizing; and to the Gulf Coast, where there was "trouble" in the shrimp fisheries. That year, the Catholic Workers in New York City spent thousands of dollars feeding and lodging pickets during the seamen's strike that led to the establishing of the National Maritime Union; the fact that Joseph Curran, who became the head of the union, and most of the other leaders were then enjoying active support from the Communists didn't bother them at all. In March, 1937, the Association of Catholic Trade Unionists was formed around a kitchen table in one of the Workers' early headquarters, a house on Mott Street.

Owing in part to the vast changes that have come over the social scene in the last few years, the Catholic Workers are no longer as active in public affairs as they once were, and the circulation of their paper has dropped from a high of one hundred and fifty thousand in the mid-thirties to fifty-eight thousand, which is about equal to the combined circulations of the *Nation* and the *New Republic*. It is true that the *Catholic Worker* costs only one cent a copy (and twenty-five cents a year, which gives it the perhaps unique distinction of costing twice as much to subscribe to as to buy each month on the newsstands), and it is also true that "bundle orders," which often end up as throwaways, account for many of the copies, and that the business department is dilatory about culling out lapsed subscriptions. But even if only half the copies get into the hands of interested readers, this is quite an achievement for an uncompromisingly high-brow and extremist paper.

THE *Catholic Worker* is an eight-page tabloid of approximately the same size as the *Daily News*, which it does not otherwise resemble. Typical front-page banner headlines have included "CHRIST THE KING CAN ALONE RECONSTRUCT THE WORLD," "THE PROBLEM OF WAR AND THE OLD TESTAMENT," "THE COMING COLLAPSE OF MODERN INDUSTRIALISM," "THE NATURE OF MAN," and (in an especially gnomic mood) "SEAMEN GO EVERYWHERE." In its coverage of world events, the paper's forte is clearly not spot news—except when it gets hold of a scoop like the Holy Father's Christmas Message.

The *Worker's* contents are schizoid, accurately reflecting the two aspects of the movement—works of mercy and a concern with ultimate philosophical questions. About half its densely printed columns are given over to reports of happenings in the Catholic Worker "family" and to columnists of the chatty, rather than the thoughtful, kind. The other half is devoted to philosophical discussions of such topics as original sin, the supernatural basis of values, the evolution of capitalism and the relevance of Freud, Marx and Kierkegaard to Catholic doctrine. The juxtapositions of these with the homey items are at times dramatic. In one issue, for instance, Miss Day wrote, "Downstairs the baby is crying while Rita gets her breakfast ready: mashed prunes, baby cereal, and milk, all mixed together deliciously," while in an adjoining column Robert Ludlow, one of her fellow-editors, was ruminating along these lines: "And so it is with war, which cannot be said to be *absolutely* opposed to natural morality during certain periods of history, but which of its nature is contrary to the full realization of a natural morality that is based upon the full potentialities of man's nature." Most readers prefer the prunes to the polemics, and Ludlow's cerebrations sometimes bother even Miss Day. "I stand personally behind everything Bob Ludlow writes, though his way of expressing himself is at times peculiar, to say the least," she told a friend. "I don't think the majority of our readers know what he is talking about when he says, 'The compulsion to revolt can be explained as a manifestation of the libido.' " This kind of frank criticism is frequent among the members of the *Catholic Worker* staff, and extends even to self-criticism. "I dislike writing, due to my lack of talent," wrote one of its columnists. "It kills you when you haven't got it. Right now, I feel cheated by having to meet a deadline with this tripe when I could be listening to the first game of the World Series."

One characteristic common to the two halves of the paper is length. Whether the contributors are writing about petunias or existentialism, they share a magnificent unconcern about space; it takes them a thousand words just to get warmed up. Another is Miss Day's column, called "On Pilgrimage," which is easily the paper's most popular feature—an odd composite of Pascal's "Pensées" and Eleanor Roosevelt's "My Day." A good hostess on the printed page as well as off, Miss Day in "On Pilgrimage" is constantly introducing the sublime if not to the ridiculous at least to the commonplace. In one installment, after quoting at length from Newman and Saint Teresa of Avila, she continued, "Every time I am making what I consider a thorough confession—that is, telling tendencies that I wish I could overcome, like eating between meals, indulging in the nibbling that women do around a kitchen—and mention it as a venial sin not only in regard to myself but also to my neighbor who is starving all over the world, the confessor makes no attempt to understand but speaks of scruples. . . . These are tendencies to gluttony, and gluttony is one of the seven deadly sins." Only a person who is deeply thoughtful about religion would be likely to see a connection between nibbling in the kitchen and the seven deadly sins, and it is one of Miss Day's outstanding achievements that she has revived the linking of the serious and the trivial that saints and prophets once did so effectively but that long ago went out of fashion. The union of the everyday and the ultimate is the essence of the Catholic Worker movement.

WHERE there is no love, put in love and you will take out love," wrote Saint John of the Cross. The Catholic Workers quote this and believe it. Usually it works, but when it doesn't, they are not resentful, since they consider love an end and not a means. Some years ago, they rented an apartment in Cleveland to shelter single women; a homeless married couple was temporarily admitted; once in, they wouldn't move out or let anyone else in. The Workers, although they had paid the rent in advance, sighed and looked for another apartment.

The Workers' abhorrence of coercion extends even to proselytizing. They never ask the religion of the people they help, and the men on the bread line don't have to pray or sing psalms to get fed, nor do their boarders (whose favorite paper is the *Daily News*, not the *Catholic Worker*) have to attend the two brief daily services held in the Chrystie Street house.

Some of the Workers have at times found freedom oppressive. One of the most energetic toilers on the Easton farm once went on strike because he didn't have a boss. Sitting down under a tree, he announced, "I won't work until someone asks me to and tells me what to do." No one did, and after a time he gave up and grumpily picked up his hoe again. Maurin used to do a lot of heavy work, like breaking rocks for making roads; sometimes he went so far as to leave mauls lying around in conspicuous places, but if no one took the hint, he just swung all the harder. More practical and less principled than Maurin, Miss Day admits that when she gets "really desperate," she actually asks members of her staff to do this or that. If they refuse, however, there is no penalty. "I could stay in my room all day reading or just sitting and no one would say anything," one of her present crop of Workers said not long ago. "After a month, they might act a little cold toward me, of course."

Miss Day does have a certain authority, but it is an authority that is yielded to her voluntarily, out of love and respect—all too voluntarily, from her point of view, for she is a leader whose chief worry is that her followers have too great a tendency to follow. "Low in mind all day, full of tears," she wrote one evening in 1936 in a journal she has kept since she was a girl. "What with Easton, New York, Boston, Ottawa, Toronto and Missouri groups all discouraged, all looking for organization instead of self-organization, all weary of the idea of freedom and personal responsibility—I feel bitterly oppressed. I am in the position of a dictator trying to legislate himself out of existence. They all complain that there is no boss. Today I happened to read Dostoievski's 'Grand Inquisitor,' most apropos. Freedom—how men hate it and chafe under it, how unhappy they are with it!"

In the old days, Miss Day used to look at Maurin in moments of discouragement and, with a groan, say, "Why did you have to start all this anyway?" In a gloomy passage in her journal, she remarks, "Sometimes you get discouraged, there's so little change in people. Those who drank go on drinking, those who were ornery go on being ornery." But faith and hope always rise again in her, no matter how great the despair of the moment, and a few pages farther on she is writing, "The goodness of people makes my heart expand in happiness."

The New Yorker, Oct. 4 and 11, 1952

BY THE WAY

The Question of God

[*Answer to a questionnaire on religion from* Partisan Review.]

I TAKE "religious belief" to mean a belief that God exists. And God? Not certainly the Old Testament Jahveh, with a beard and a human, all too human, personality. Nor, to me anyway, the other extreme: the Eddington-Jeans kind of God, whose presence manifests itself in the physical order of the universe. That the stars run in their courses, that the atoms split as per schedule—these regularities I can accept without calling in God to explain them. In such matters, I agree with the astronomer Laplace: "God? A hypothesis I have not found to be necessary." No, I take God to mean some kind of supernatural consciousness or order that is related, in a value sense (good, bad), to our life here on earth. This God I can neither accept nor reject. In fact, I cannot imagine him.

This insensibility, is not because I am unconcerned with

the moral problems that have driven men in the past to religious belief, and that today, in the age of Nazism, Stalinism and bombs from A to H, have understandably made many religious converts. On the contrary, since the thirties, when my mind was busy with all sorts of deep social, economic and historical problems (theories of capitalist crisis, historical materialism, unemployment, progressive v. imperialist wars, etc.) that now seem to me superficial, I have come to be interested in ethics to such an extent that I am constantly charged, by the people Philip Rahv has named the "secular radicals," with being religious myself. Yet such, unfortunately, is not the case. I say "unfortunately" because, from a purely intellectual point of view, God is a hypothesis I found to be, if not necessary, at least most convenient. For two reasons:

(1) I'm compelled to recognize the existence of two worlds which don't seem to connect: that of "science," where judgments can be established objectively, on the basis of quantitative criteria (measurements), and that of "values," where judgments are ultimately subjective and criteria are qualitative (one's own personal moral belief and esthetic taste—these may be communicated to others and may influence them, for men do have "something in common" in those fields, but they cannot be established with the precision and universality of scientific judgments, since the appeal is a subjective one, from "me" to "you," and "you" is always different from "me"). Despite John Dewey's technically impressive effort to bridge the gap, in his *A Theory of Valuation*, I see it as still gap-ing. For some reason, this dualism makes me uncomfortable, and I try instinctively to show that the good also "works," that honesty is the best policy and beauty is truth, truth beauty. The most satisfactory bridge between the two worlds is . . . God. But, for me, the bridge is out.

(2) An even more important intellectual function of God is to serve as an ultimate base for one's system of values. Discussing the basis of one's moral code is like taking apart one of those wooden Russian eggs, each of which encloses a still smaller one: "I believe it is wrong to kill people." "Why?" "Because I have respect for humanity." "Why?" "Because I

am human and recognize my brother's kinship." "Why?" etc., etc. If one believes in God, one finally gets down to an ultimate egg that is solid and so ends the taking-apart (analytical) process. God is simply and logically an absolute, an end and not a means, unique in our—that is, some of us—experience. But an unbeliever gets down to an egg that is hollow like the rest, but that contains no further egg. One's belief turns out to rest, ultimately, on air—"I just feel it to be so." This doesn't bother me too much emotionally, but it is undeniably awkward from a logical point of view.

Yet what can I do? I just don't seem to have the knack for religious experience. So many of my fellow men, past and present, have felt at home with the idea of God that I must admit it is a deep and apparently permanent human trait. Yet I'm sure that, if they had not, the idea would never have occurred to me at all. Not even in adolescence, when many Americans' personal experience seems to parallel the experience of the race (ontogeny recapitulates phylogeny) did I experience the slightest quiver of religious feeling. Nor do I now, although the brutal irrationality of the modern world has made me understand and sympathize with others' religious beliefs, and although in surprisingly many ways I find myself agreeing more with contemporary religious-minded people than with the "secular radicals." God, attractive though the idea is from an intellectual standpoint, simple does not engage my feelings or imagination.

This is all the more a pity since I have lost confidence in the dominant non-religious social tendency in this country today: the Marx-cum-Dewey approach represented by Sidney Hook (pure), the liberal weeklies (debased), the Reuther brothers and Senator Humphrey ("grass roots"), the Americans for Democratic Action (official) and *Partisan Review* (highbrow) This seems to me to have failed politically, culturally and even scientifically.

Politically: It has either failed or, where it has won power, has produced the horrors of Soviet Communism or the dull mediocrity of the Attlee and Truman governments. Lenin and Kautsky are the antithetical political types it has produced; both seem to me unsatisfactory.

Culturally: Its close connection with nineteenth-century Philistine progressivism, well-meaning but thoroughly bourgeois, has meant that the creators of living culture, from Stendhal to Eliot, have existed outside it and mostly opposed to it. As Leslie Fiedler has recently noted, this split affects *Partisan Review* itself: the editors have had to rely largely on writers whom they, as ideologues, consider "reactionary" and "obscurantist."

Scientifically: Confidence in scientific method, unchecked by an independent system of human values, has encouraged an indiscriminate development of technique which now gives us Ford's monstrous River Rouge plant, the H Bomb and the Nazi-Soviet organizations for controlling and conditioning human beings. This is a misuse of science, it is true, but one implicit in the ideology I am criticizing. For a more humane use of scientific method, grounded not on technique, know-how and "does it work?" but rather on a value judgment as to what life should be like, one must turn to thinkers quite out of the liberal-socialist mainstream: anarchists like Kropotkin, decentralists like Geddes, Borsodi and Gandhi, Utopians like Fourier.

The questions that now interest me are not the "big" ones: What To Do About Russia?, Is Planning Incompatible with Capitalism?, Will There Be a Depression?, Does America Need a Labor Party or a Revitalized Democratic Party—or just a Dozen More TVA's?, Is World Government the Answer to the H-Bomb? These seem to me either unimportant or unanswerable. So long as the dominant areas of the world are organized in vast super-states, whose economic base is large-scale industry and whose political base is tens of millions of helpless "citizens," I see no hope of significant improvement. Nor do I see any signs that any considerable number of my fellow men are now in a mood to break up such monstrosities into communities human in scale. So in terms of mass action (i.e., of politics as the word is now generally understood), our problems appear to be insoluble. They may yield, I be-

lieve, only to a more modest and, so-to-speak, intimate approach. Reform, reconstruction, even revolution must begin at a much more basic level than we imagined in the confident thirties.

It is the "small" questions that now seem to me significant. What is a good life? How do we know what's good and what's bad? How do people really live and feel and think in their everyday lives? What are the most important human needs—taking myself, as that part of the universe I know best, or at least have been most closely associated with, as a starting point? How can they be satisfied best, here and now? Who am I? How can I live lovingly, truthfully, pleasurably?

The thinkers I have found most helpful in answering, or at least talking about, these questions are: Christ, Socrates, Diderot, Jefferson, Thoreau, Herzen, Proudhon, Tolstoi, Gandhi, Simone Weil and Albert Schweitzer. Most of these are religious, which is natural enough, since the above questions are the kind that, in our age, are asked mostly by religious people. Yet, although when I read Tolstoi and Gandhi I see the logical convenience of the God-hypothesis, it does not move me emotionally; nor do I feel a spiritual need for it. I can believe that man is an end and not a means, and that to love one another is the greatest duty and pleasure, without giving this belief a religious basis. I suppose the period I feel closest to, in my values, is the Enlightenment, from which all that is most attractive in socialist as well as bourgeois-democratic doctrine derives.

Partisan Review, May-June, 1950

Too Big

THE TROUBLE is everything is too big. There are too many people, for example, in the city I live in. In walking along the street, one passes scores of other people every minute; any response to them as human beings is impossible; they must be passed by as indifferently as ants pass each other in the corridors of the anthill. A style of behavior which refuses to recognize the human existence of the others has grown up of necessity. Just the scale on which people congregate in such a city breaks down human solidarity, alienates people from each other. There are so many people that there aren't any people; 7,000,000 becomes 0; too big.

Some episodes:

(1) A friend was going home in the subway at about ten o'clock one night. About half the seats in his car were filled. Opposite him two men were sitting on either side of a third, who was very drunk. Without any attempt at concealment, they were going through the drunk's pockets and taking his watch, money, etc. A dozen people watched the performance from their seats, but no one, including my friend, did anything, and at the next station the two men let the drunk slide to the floor and got off the train.

(2) An elderly woman I know slipped going down the stairs in an "El" station and fell all the way to the bottom, where she lay stunned and gasping. A crowd of people—it was the rush hour—were waiting on the platform at the foot of the stairs. Some of them stared at her but no one moved to help her. She told me that she lay there several minutes, too shaken up even to speak; several people remarked "she must be drunk." Finally, a man did come forward and helped her to her feet. She was frightened by the incident. She had lived in New York all her life without realizing she was living among strangers.

(3) I was told a similar story about another person—the friend of a friend. He was knocked down on a mid-town street by a car late at night. The car didn't stop and no one saw the accident. He lay in the gutter, badly hurt and only half conscious, for five or six hours. There must have been scores, probably hundreds of people who passed by, saw him, thought "must be drunk" (the formula by which, in the city, one denies human recognition) and went on their way. Finally, the next morning, a policeman investigated and called an ambulance. (The policeman is the only person in a

big city who is professionally required to see people as people, to break the shell of apartness that encases each human being.)

(4) The wife of a friend of mine last year became psychotic and is now being treated in an institution. She had been acting "queerly" for some time, but the first big outburst came about ten o'clock one night as they were returning home after visiting friends in Brooklyn. The wife suddenly began to accuse her husband of attempting to poison her; she became increasingly violent and suddenly broke away and began running down the street screaming "Help! Help! He's trying to kill me!" She ran along thus for several blocks, shouting, before he could overtake her and try to calm her. Although most of the houses showed lighted windows, for it was still early, not a door opened, not a window went up, no one paid the slightest attention. When he finally got his wife back to their apartment building, she broke away again as he was unlocking the door, and rushed into the hallway screaming for help. This lasted at least ten minutes, he told me, and again not a door opened, no one appeared although her cries and screams echoed all through the building. Finally a youth came downstairs in his bathrobe and shouted: "Shut up! We're trying to sleep!" He disappeared again immediately. A half hour later, after my friend had persuaded his wife to go inside, he received the first help since the nightmare had begun: Again in the form of a policeman, who had been sent for by some of the neighbors. (When people are forced to see others as human beings, they make contact vicariously through the police. What a "style" of communal relations!)

But he, desiring to justify himself, said unto Jesus: "And who is my neighbor?" Jesus made answer and said: "A certain man was going down from Jerusalem to Jericho; and he fell among robbers, who stripped him and beat him, and departed, leaving him half dead. And by chance a certain priest was going down that way; and when he saw him, he passed by on the other side. And in like manner, a Levite also, when he came to the place and saw him, passed by on the other side. But a certain Samaritan, as he journeyed, came where he was; and when he saw him he was moved with compassion, and came to him, and bound up his wounds, pouring on them oil and wine; and he set him on his own beast and brought him to an inn and took care of him. And on the morrow he took out two shillings, and gave them to the host, and said: 'Take care of him, and whatsoever thou spendest more, I, when I come back again, will repay.' Which of these three, thinkest thou, proved neighbor to him that fell among the robbers?" And he said, "He that showed mercy on him." And Jesus said unto him, "Go, and do thou likewise."

December, 1946